CATHOLIC
AND
CURIOUS

Monsignor Charles Pope

Our Sunday Visitor
www.osv.com
Our Sunday Visitor Publishing Division
Our Sunday Visitor, Inc.
Huntington, Indiana 46750

Our Sunday Visitor Publishing Division
Our Sunday Visitor, Inc.
200 Noll Plaza
Huntington, IN 46750
1-800-348-2440

ISBN: 978-1-68192-158-7 (Inventory No. T1875)
eISBN: 978-1-68192-165-5
LCCN: 2018937018

Cover and interior design: Amanda Falk
Cover art: Shutterstock
Interior art: Shutterstock

PRINTED IN THE UNITED STATES OF AMERICA

About the Author

Monsignor Charles Pope was ordained in 1989 for the Archdiocese of Washington, D.C., after attending Mount St. Mary's Seminary in Emmitsburg, Maryland. There he received both a M.Div. and a Master's Degree in Moral Theology. Prior to entering the seminary, he received a Bachelor of Science degree from George Mason University in Virginia and worked briefly for the Army Corps of Engineers. During those years he was also a cantor, choir director, and organist in two Catholic parishes.

He has served in five different parishes in his twenty-nine years as a priest, eighteen of those as pastor in two different parishes. He is currently the pastor of Holy Comforter–Saint Cyprian Parish, and also a dean in the archdiocese. He has served on the priest personnel board, the Priest Council, and as one of the consultors for the archdiocese. Pastorally, he has served as the coordinator for the Legion of Mary and is currently the coordinator for the celebration of the Latin Extraordinary Form of the Mass. He has given numerous retreats and talks for laity and clergy around the archdiocese and elsewhere in the country.

He has authored the blog for the Archdiocese of Washington (http://blog.adw.org) for the past four years, which covers and discusses a wide range of topics. Of special focus at the blog is the intersection of faith and culture. As our culture continues to manifest some problematic trends, it is essential for us to understand how our faith and the teachings of the Church have wonderful and healing remedies for what ails us.

His writing and media work are linked at his website: msgrpope.com.

To all who have taught me.
And to God who taught them.

CONTENTS

ACKNOWLEDGMENTS

Our Sunday Visitor

Holy Comforter–St. Cyprian Parish

Mount St. Mary's Seminary

INTRODUCTION

Life is filled with questions. In a way, our faith begins with a question. On the day of your baptism you were asked a question: "What do you ask of God's Church?" And you (or your sponsor) answered, "Baptism." Adults who are baptized are asked further, "What does baptism offer you?" The answer: "Eternal life."

Life is filled with questions, from the very beginning. Question, from the Latin *quaero*, means to seek or search. Answers, when rooted in the truth, are very precious things — and difficult to come by. Fortunately, Our Sunday Visitor's *OSV Newsweekly* and its Questions and Answers column has long been a faithful guide for Catholics throughout the country. The volume of five hundred questions and answers you hold in your hands is compiled from that column.

These selected questions and answers cover many aspects of our life as Catholics, including our knowledge of and relationship with God, the Church's liturgy, the moral life, marriage and family issues, bioethics, culture and faith, Church history, apologetics, and much more.

Our Sunday Visitor has a long legacy in this country of informing and encouraging Catholics. I remember the OSV newspaper as a regular fixture of the periodical rack in vestibules of all my parishes going back to my youth. Even as a preteen I would often be asked by my mother to make a donation and pick up a copy to take home so we could read it during the week. Many fond memories!

It has been a great honor to be able to contribute to such a long-standing and informative Catholic newspaper. I hope these columns, collected and organized for ease of reference, will continue to be of use to Catholics seeking a deeper understanding of the faith we share.

PART I

GOD

Q.•Major religions address God by different names. Are •we all praying to the same God? — *Ed Eddy*

Whether we are praying to the same God is assessed on a case-by-case basis. A special understanding is given to the Jewish people. Of them, the *Catechism of the Catholic Church* (CCC) states: "The Jewish faith, unlike other non-Christian religions, is already a response to God's revelation in the Old Covenant. To the Jews 'belong the sonship, the glory, the covenants, the giving of the law, the worship, and the promises'" (839). They direct their prayers to God the Father as Christians do, but they do not understand God as Trinity or accept Jesus or the Holy Spirit as God. Yet it is fair to say they *do* direct their prayers to the same God, though imperfectly understood, to whom we direct our prayers.

The Muslims are monotheists, and, as the *Catechism* notes, "These profess to hold the faith of Abraham, and together with us they adore the one, merciful God, mankind's judge on the last day" (841).

The Church's relationship with other non-Christian religions is less certain and variable. Of these the *Catechism* says that God is clearly "the common origin and end of the human race" (842). In addition, the "Church recognizes in other religions that search, among shadows and images, for the God who is unknown yet near since he gives life and breath and all things and wants all men to be saved" (843).

As to what the majority of people can expect, especially those who do not know or obey Christ, the Church expresses hope for them, but also warns that though their salvation apart from Christ is possible, that does not mean it is probable. The *Catechism* also reminds us that sin requires the remedy of faith: "Very often, deceived by the Evil One, men have become vain in their reasonings, and have exchanged the truth of God for a lie, and served the creature rather than the Creator" (844). Thus unbelief or imperfect belief is a form of darkness that hinders salvation and needs the healing of true faith.

In the end, there is only one God, and all yearning for God is somehow directed to him. But there are often errors in the ways people of the world understand him. And thus it is essential for the Church to correct errors and draw everyone to the one, holy, Catholic, and apostolic faith in which there is the best hope for salvation.

THE HOLY TRINITY

Q. **Some people claim to have directly experienced the Blessed Trinity. And while all three Persons are experienced, it is usually the Holy Spirit who is out front. What does the Church teach about such experiences? Also, is this what the Protestants mean by being "born again"?** — *Bob Tisovich*

Since you do not cite a source, it is difficult to decipher some of what is stated in your question. However, to "directly" experience the Trinity, if that word is understood to mean the beatific vision, is not possible here on earth and on this side of the heavenly veil. If the experience of God being described is that of deeper or contemplative prayer, then such an experience is not only possible, but should be expected to some degree as our spiritual life matures.

Spiritual theologians generally distinguish two types or levels of prayer: discursive prayer (also called meditation) and contemplative prayer. Discursive prayer comes from the Latin word for "discourse." It thus implies a conversation with God using words and images. Since words and images mediate God's presence, this sort of prayer is also called "meditation."

As prayer deepens, however, words become fewer, less necessary, and one begins to experience God in a richer and deeper way, beyond words or images. Heart speaks to heart. Such prayer is called contemplative prayer and admits of deepening stages as the spiritual life matures.

In this context it is possible to say a person experiences the Trinity. And while one Person of the Trinity may be more experienced than another, since the prayer is without images it is more often a simple, deep, and loving experience of God as God: Father, Son, and Holy Spirit.

Protestants who speak of being "born again" may have aspects of this in mind, but what most of them mean is not nearly so deep and rich as what the Church means by contemplative prayer. The Protestant notion usually speaks to a powerful emotional experience wherein one acknowledges their sin and need for a savior and, repenting, calls on Jesus to be his or her savior. It is a strange substitution of sorts for traditional baptism. When Jesus spoke of being "born again," he clearly said it means being "born of water and the Spirit" (Jn 3:5). In this same scriptural sense, Saint Peter teaches baptism "now saves you" (1 Pt 3:2).

But being born again for many Protestants seems to take place apart from baptism and results from this powerful emotional experience and the recitation of some varying form of the "sinner's prayer" (found nowhere in Scripture). For most of them, the "water baptism" that usually takes place later is mere ceremony.

Thus being born again has little to do with the Catholic teaching on contemplative prayer. Though contemplative prayer speaks to a deep experience of God, it is not an event like certain Protestants say of being "born again." It is a deepening experience of God that is ongoing.

Q. The Church teaches ... that God is pure spirit. But do the members of the Trinity have souls? And how does a spirit differ from a soul? — *Name withheld*

Scripture often uses the words "soul" and "spirit" interchangeably. Thus it is difficult to give a definitive and indisputable answer to your question.

However, some Christian anthropologists have preferred to define the soul as the animating principle of a living thing. Therefore, human beings have souls, but so do animals and plants. In this anthropological tradition, it is really the spirit that distinguishes the human person from animals and plants. The spirit is the rational aspect of the soul that human beings and angels have. It is that part of us that gives us a capacity for God and enables us to think, to reason, and to engage beyond the physical to the metaphysical.

But again, Scripture does not maintain such a sharp distinction, and reasonable Christian theologians and anthropologists will differ. To address your question, therefore, requires that we use words which have debatable meanings.

With this caution in mind, I would say that, generally we do not speak of God as having a soul per se. Rather, as God, he is pure spirit, as are the angels. However, we do speak sometimes of the angelic soul.

But it is not traditional to speak of the divine soul. God is ultimately simple, admitting not of parts or distinctions as such. God is. God does not have a life-giving principle. He is existence itself. He is simple, undivided, and, though having soul-like qualities, is more than a soul and less than the soul. He is pure spirit, but in the sense of not having a body. The word spirit cannot describe him simply or fully.

Saint Augustine, when asked to explain the Trinity and to explain the essence of God, said simply, "If you ask me, I don't know; if you don't ask me, I know." He said regarding the Trinity that God is *Tres, nescio quid* (three, I know not what).

Therefore, though we can speak of God as being pure spirit and having soul-like qualities, we are really saying more what God is not than what he is. Saint Thomas Aquinas also said in his commentary on Boethius' *De Sancta Trinitate* that while we can know God through his creation, and in God's actions through history and revelation, what we know about God above is *Unknown* (*tantum tamquam Ignotum*).

So, pardon a sort of non-answer to your answer. God does not fit into our little categories. We can say what he is not, but we cannot fully say what he is. We do not speak of God as having a soul, for God does not have parts like we do, he simply "is."

God the Father

Q. **I find it helpful to envision God the Father as a wise old man with a beard. But does this detract from the honor due God?** — *Robert Bonsignore*

As pure spirit, God has no physical attributes. That said, Scripture does not hesitate to give him physical attributes by way of analogy and metaphor. For example, that God has "a mighty arm" (Ps 89:13) does not refer to a physical arm but speaks to God's strength and justice.

God makes use of these descriptions for our sake, speaking to us in terms we can understand more readily. It is in this light that it is permissible and understandable for us to imagine God in the humanlike terms you describe. He reveals himself to us as Father, and that evokes images for us. The *Catechism*, while acknowledging our need for images and analogies, also counsels:

> Admittedly, in speaking about God like this, our
> language is using human modes of expression;

nevertheless ... we must recall that "between Creator and creature no similitude can be expressed
without implying an even greater dissimilitude";
and that "concerning God, we cannot grasp what
he is, but only what he is not." (43)

God transcends all creatures.... Our human words
always fall short of the mystery of God. (42)

Q: On Trinity Sunday, our pastor started his homily, "God the Father, or if you think she is a woman, or however you want to worship." We were stunned. Questioning him later, he said God has no gender. Please comment. — *Marilyn Aron*

While it is true that God is pure spirit and therefore is not physically
male or female, it does not follow that we are free to call him "mother" or use female pronouns such as "she" or "her." The Scriptures are
not our words about God, they are his words to us. As such, we are
bound to speak of God in the ways he has revealed himself.

And indeed, nowhere does God's revelation use feminine
nouns or pronouns in reference to God. While it is true that in several places Scripture uses feminine imagery to speak to a quality of
God (see, for example, Is 66:13; Ps 131:2; Lk 13:34), the context of all
these passages is still that God the Father or God the Son is speaking, and the nearest pronouns are all male.

In revealing himself as Father, God sets forth a sacramental
truth about creation as well as human sexuality and sexual differen-
tiation. In the human sexual order, the husband acts upon the wife
and the woman receives from the husband. In the order of creation,
God acts upon creation and creation receives. God is Father and
uses male imagery — for example, the husband to his bride Israel
and the Church — because all of creation is feminine in relationship
to him. Creation receives from him.

Jesus in his incarnation is male, not merely by accident, but because he is revealed in Scripture as the Eternal Son of the Father, and because he is the groom to his bride the Church.

While some also wish to call the Holy Spirit "she," this too violates scriptural norms which always use male pronouns in reference to the Holy Spirit.

It is simply an overwhelming fact that God has revealed himself to us in male terms. While realizing that God is pure spirit and therefore neither male nor female per se, the language of faith accepts how God has revealed himself and limits itself to that expression. Thus we are not free to call God whatever we like or to speak to him "however we want to worship." No, we are bound to humbly refer to God in ways he has revealed.

God the Son

Q.We teach that God is changeless. But at some point the Second Person of the Trinity became man. How is this hypostatic union not a change in God? — *Tim Hart*

Among other things, the answer to your question is caught up in a very deep mystery of God's relationship to time. In fact, many of our questions about God, and our struggle to understand him, go back to this mystery.

The fact is, God does not dwell in time as you and I do. Rather, he dwells in the fullness of time, a mystery we call "eternity." The word eternity does not simply mean a long, long time. Rather, eternity means "the fullness of time": past, present, and future are all experienced at once.

To illustrate eternity, consider a clock. Let us say that the current time is noon. For us who live in serial time, that means that 3:00 p.m. is in the future, and 9:00 a.m. is in the past. But now move your eyes to the center dot of the round clock face. At that center point, all three times — noon, 9:00 a.m., and 3:00 p.m. — are equally present, and have the same relationship with that center dot.

This is an analogy of what we mean by eternity. Thus for God, who is eternal, the future is just as present to him as the past. God is not waiting for things to happen, neither is he reminiscing on things past. All is present to him in a comprehensive "now."

This is mysterious to us but helps illustrate why our questions about God are often wrong, even in the way we ask them. Your question about whether God "changed" when Jesus became Incarnate presupposes that God lives in time as we do. But he does not.

We are right to conclude, as you observe, that God does not change. And yet he is able to interact with us, who do change. But how exactly this is accomplished is caught up in our limited capacity to understand the mystery that we call time. In no sense is God waiting around to do things, like becoming man, nor is he changing as time goes along. All is present to him in a comprehensive now. God simply Is.

Q: What does it mean in the Creed when it says Jesus was "begotten, not made"? — *Name withheld*

This is the Creed's way of emphasizing that Jesus is not a creature, but rather is God, sharing fully in the one divine nature.

When humans make something, say a meal or a painting, we use created matter. And though the meal or painting says something about the person who made it, the meal or painting is not human, it does not share in our nature. But if a human father begets a son or daughter, that child *does* share in the same human nature as the parents.

In a similar way, to say that Jesus is "begotten" means he possesses the same divine nature as his Father and is not merely some thing or creature the Father made which is distinct from him, having something other than the divine nature. By distinction, you and

I are creatures of God since we do not have his divine nature. We are created by God, not begotten of him.

To emphasize the divinity of Jesus even further, the Creed adds that Jesus is "consubstantial with the Father" — that is, he shares fully in the one Divine Substance we call God. The Father and Son are distinct as persons, but one in nature and substance.

Q. We read in a recent Sunday Gospel that Jesus says the Father is greater than him (see Jn 14:28). Since we are all taught that each Divine Person of the Blessed Trinity fully possesses the nature of God, equally to be adored and glorified, what did Jesus mean by such a statement? — *Dick Smith*

The most common answer is that Jesus is speaking here of his human nature, not his divine nature. For as God he is equal to the Father, but in his human nature, the Father is greater.

However, even in terms of his divinity Jesus can speak of the Father as "greater" in one sense. Theologically, the Father is the eternal source in the Trinity. All three Persons of the Trinity are co-eternal, co-equal, and equally divine. But the Father is the *Principium Deitatis* (the Source in the Deity).

Hence, Jesus proceeds from the Father from all eternity. He is eternally begotten of the Father. In effect, Jesus is saying, "I delight that the Father is the eternal principle or source of my being, even though I have no origin in time."

Devotionally, Jesus is saying that he always does what pleases his Father. Jesus loves his Father; he's crazy about him. He is always talking about him and pointing to him. By calling the Father greater, Jesus says, in effect: "I look to my Father for everything. I do what I see him doing and what I know pleases him. His will and mine are one. What I will to do proceeds from him. I do what I know accords with his will." (See John 5:19 and 5:30 for similarities.)

So, though the members of the Trinity are all equal in dignity, there are processions in the Trinity such that the Father is the source, the Son eternally proceeds from him, and the Holy Spirit eternally proceeds from them both. Saint Thomas Aquinas speaks poetically of the Trinity as "*Genitori, Genitoque ... Procedenti ab utroque ... compar sit laudautio*" (To the One Who Begets ... and to the Begotton One ... and to the One who proceeds from them both, be equal praise.) So, though equal, processions do have an order, and the Father is greater as source, but equal in dignity to Son and Holy Spirit.

Q.•Why did Jesus say, "If you don't believe me, believe my Father?" — *Rita Schroder*

You likely refer to John 5, where Jesus presents four proofs of his status as Messiah and Lord: "You sent [testimony] to John, and he has born witness to the truth. But the testimony which I have is greater than that of John; for the works ... which I am doing, bear me witness that the Father has sent me. And the Father who sent me has himself borne witness to me. You search the Scriptures ... yet you refuse to come to me that you may have life" (Jn 5:32,36–37,39–40).

And thus the Lord points to his miracles, to the testimony of John the Baptist, to the witness of God the Father in their hearts, and to the Scriptures as witness that he is Lord and Messiah. As such, he effectively accuses them of stubborn disbelief and sends them away to reconsider. But the point in this text is that if they will not simply believe him, they have other evidence as well.

Q: Please explain how Jesus can be God as well as man at the same time. — *Anthony Retnam*

If I could explain it, I might be a heretic. There are mysteries here, which caused the ancient Church to fall to its knees when the words of the Creed in this matter were said. How can the infinite enter the finite? How can Mary's creator be born of her?

The mystery is described by the term "hypostatic union," which states that Jesus, though one person, has two natures, divine and human. These natures are united in his one person but are not mixed.

Your question of how this can be can only be answered by an appeal to God's omnipotence and will to save us. Jesus had to be God to save us, but also had to become man to represent us. Hence, it is fitting that Jesus be both, but how this is done is left to God.

Q: Did Satan know Jesus was the Messiah and God? — *Ann*

There seems to have been a growing awareness in Satan of the identity of Jesus. In the Nativity accounts, the devil seems to be aware and alarmed that some incursion into the world has occurred. Yet as demonstrated through his agent Herod, he is not sure exactly who or where Jesus is. He stabs wildly and in a rage, killing the innocent boys of Bethlehem under two years of age. Jesus then lives quietly and almost secretly for thirty years. Then, years later, in the desert, Satan tempts Jesus but also seeks to verify if he is Messiah and Lord. He begins the temptations with, "If you are the Son of God ... " (Mt 4:3).

By the time Jesus began his public ministry, it would seem that Satan and other evil spirits *did* conclude that Jesus was God, at least in some general way. Scripture reports, "Whenever the unclean spirits saw him, they fell down before him and cried out, 'You are the Son of God'" (Mk 3:11). Another time a demon cried out, "I know who you are, the Holy One of God!" (Mk 1:24). There are similar passages in Mark 1:34 and Luke 4:41.

That said, we ought not to conclude that Satan had a comprehensive or flawless knowledge of Jesus and the full plan of salvation. Had Satan possessed such a complete knowledge, he would not have inspired the crucifixion of Jesus, the very means by which he (Satan) was defeated.

Hence there is evidence that Satan had a basic understanding of Jesus' divinity and plan, but one that was limited and likely flawed due to his intellect being darkened by sin and rage.

Q: **The Bible says that Jesus was like us in all things but sin. I was also taught in Sunday School that Jesus was fully human. But how can we say that he is fully human if he never sinned? To err is human. It just seems to me that his lack of sin puts him into a category other than fully human.**
— *Nelson Ridlick*

Your question shows you may be considering things backward. It is Jesus who is fully and perfectly human. It is we who are less than perfectly human. This is due to the wounded nature we have as a result of original sin. Jesus is the model; we are not, and we must resist any tendency to seek to refashion him in our likeness. Rather, he shows us what it means to be fully complete and lacking in nothing as a human being. We are summoned to his likeness. Scripture says, "It does not appear what we shall be, but we know that when he appears we shall be like him, for we shall see him as he is" (1 Jn 3:2).

Even now, if we are faithful, our human nature, though currently wounded (especially in terms of a darkened intellect and a weakened will), will experience increased healing as we make our journey with God in grace. And in heaven all the wounds to our soul and body (at the resurrection of the dead) will be fully healed.

The expression "to err is human" is neither biblical nor theological. Further, it does not speak to our nature per se, but simply records our tendency, in our currently fallen or wounded state, to easily sin and be mistaken.

Q. Is there an appropriate name for our Savior in the context of certain situations? Should we refer to him as Jesus, Christ, Jesus Christ, Christ Jesus, etc.? — *Name withheld*

As your question suggests, exactly how we address Jesus will vary in certain contexts. Perhaps it is most important to distinguish at the outset that "Christ" is not part of Jesus' proper name; rather, it is his title. In this sense, it sometimes helps to put the definite article the in front of Christ, saying, "Jesus the Christ," to remind us that Christ is not his surname. Jesus is "the Christ," which means "the anointed one" and translates the Hebrew word "Messiah," meaning the same thing.

His proper name, Jesus, means in Hebrew, "God saves." Thus the name and title of Christ Jesus means, "Anointed Savior."

While it is certainly fine for us to call him simply by his proper name, Jesus, in the formal liturgy of the Church, we often speak of him more fully, such as Christ our Lord, or Our Lord Jesus Christ, and so forth.

All this said, it must be added that there are more than one hundred titles and many ways of referring to him in the Scriptures, which can also be appropriate ways of referring to him in certain circumstances. For example, he is called Alpha and Omega; Author and Finisher of Our Faith; Son of David; Son of Man; Good Shepherd; Emmanuel; I AM; King of Israel; the Way, the Truth, and the Life; Light of the World; Redeemer; Teacher; Rabbi; Son of God; Son of Mary; True Vine; and so forth.

Thus we do well to remember that the magnificent truth of Jesus Christ, Our Lord, often requires us to speak of him in many ways, pondering his glory from many different perspectives through these titles.

Q. Why is Jesus called "Son of man" in the Gospels? What does Son of man mean, and why is it used so often in the Gospels? — *Arlene Farrell*

In the Scriptures, the title "Son of God" is used in many different senses and is, paradoxically, more vague than the title "Son of man." Son of God can be a title of Israel itself (see Ex 4:22; Hos 11:1), of the Davidic king (Ps 2:7), and of the angels (Gn 6:2). All humankind, all the just, and peacemakers are also called sons of God (Mt 5:9).

In view of the ambiguity of the title, Jesus did not simply say, "I am the Son of God." Rather, he spoke more clearly, saying for example, "I and the Father are one" (Mt 10:30). Indeed, the anger and charges of blasphemy by many of the Jews at Jesus' time show that his claim to divinity was far better accomplished this way than it would have been by using the more ambiguous title Son of God.

Paradoxically, Son of man is a clearer profession of divine transcendence that can be traced to Daniel 7:13, which Christ appropriated to himself. That prophecy speaks of "one like a son of man" coming on the clouds to judge the earth, who has a kingdom that shall never end.

Jesus' preference for the term is shown when Caiaphas the High Priest said: "I adjure you by the living God, tell us if you are the Christ, the Son of God" (Mt 26:63). Jesus answered: "You have said so. But I tell you, hereafter you will see the Son of man seated at the right hand of Power, and coming on the clouds of heaven" (Mt 26:64).

Thus Son of man is a more clear and lofty title, which Christ prefers for himself.

Q. Since every human child receives half of his chromosomes from his father and half from his mother, where does the Church teach Jesus got the other half of his chromosomes, since he had no earthly father? — *Peter Stein*

I am unaware of any official Church teaching in this regard. Knowledge of DNA, etc., is very recent and still deepening. Hence one would not expect a thorough theological treatise on a matter of this sort now.

However, one principle must surely apply — namely, the teaching from both Scripture and Tradition that Jesus as a divine person also had a complete, intact human nature and was like us in this regard in all things but sin. Hence he had the complete and proper number of chromosomes. How exactly God supplied the part usually supplied by a human father is not revealed.

Speculation, though always a human tendency, would remain only speculation. We are dealing with miracle and mystery. But this truth remains clear: Jesus, though one Person, is fully divine and fully human.

Q. I never understood the baptism of Christ, since he is sinless and born of a sinless mother. Please explain. — *Lydia Volpe*

It is clear, that Jesus was without sin (see, for example, Heb 4:15). Even as Jesus approaches John for baptism, John instinctively protests. However, the Lord explains, saying, "Let it be so now; for thus it is fitting for us to fulfil all righteousness" (Mt 3:15).

Jesus is referring to the righteousness (justice) of God. God's justice is his fidelity to his promises. And God had promised to send us a Messiah to go ahead of us and lead us out of sin and into righteousness.

At the River Jordan, Jesus is like Moses, who did not just tell the people to cross the Red Sea. He went ahead of them, courageously leading through the stormy waters. Jesus does no less. And he does not tell us merely to go to the waters of baptism; he leads us through baptism, out of slavery, into freedom.

The liturgy of the Church speaks of Jesus not being made holy by the waters, but making the waters holy to bless us.

Jesus also does this with the "baptism" of the whole Paschal Mystery. He does not merely tell us to take up a cross; he takes up his cross and bids us follow him. He does not merely point to the hill of Calvary; he leads us up over that hill and unto glory.

This is God's righteousness, his justice, his fidelity to his promises.

Another aspect of Jesus' baptism is the remarkable fact that he identifies with sinners, though he himself is not a sinner. "He is not ashamed to call [us] brethren" (Heb 2:11). He who was sinless was seen as a great sinner and crucified publicly. Such love, such emptying, such humility. For the Lord conquers Satan's pride, and ours, by astonishing humility. And in this, too, Jesus fulfills all righteousness by being baptized, going into the waters ahead of us.

Q. **I don't understand why Judas's betrayal of Jesus is so important. Surely the chief priests and others who wanted him dead knew who he was and could have found him without Judas. And didn't Peter also betray Jesus by denying him three times? Was his betrayal less harmful than Judas's?** — *Name withheld*

Practically, the Temple leaders could have found and arrested Jesus when he was out in public, but, as Scripture says, they feared the crowds who might riot upon such an act (see Mt 21:46). To find Jesus at a more private moment would surely have required more "inside knowledge," which Judas could provide.

Theologically, no one could lay a hand on Jesus until his "hour" had come. He was always able, until he freely chose to lay down his life, to evade their attempts at arrest (see Jn 8:20). This may also have caused the Temple leaders to conclude they needed inside information.

And while God could have allowed another way for Jesus to be turned over, Judas fulfills Scripture, which says: "Even my bosom friend in whom I trusted, / who ate of my bread, has lifted his heel against me" (Ps 41:9).

Betrayal and denial are fundamentally different. Through betrayal Judas handed Jesus over. Denial, while surely sinful, is to deny association with Jesus, and does not amount to handing him over. Thus Peter's actions are less harmful to Jesus than Judas's.

Q: When the crowds hailed Jesus as "Son of David" and "King of the Jews," wasn't that enough for Pontius Pilate to crucify him? — *Robert Bonsignore*

No. Pilate was aware of these attestations, but he was not particularly impressed by them. He did interrogate Jesus about this matter, and Jesus said, "My kingship is not of this world" (Jn 18:36). Even if Jesus had claimed to be a king in a rival sense (which he did not), Pilate had him under arrest and Jesus appeared quite powerless. Pilate might have been more alarmed if it seemed Jesus wielded political power and influence, but his "own people" had handed him over, and the religious leaders and the crowd were saying, "We have no king but Caesar" (Jn 19:15).

With all this in mind, Pilate wanted to release Jesus after some sort of punishment.

What Pilate *did* fear was the crowds and a riot if he did not accede to their demands to crucify Jesus. This demand appalled his sense of justice (see Lk 23:16) and carrying it out went against a warning he had received from his wife who told him of a dream she had that Jesus was innocent (Mt 27:19).

Pilate thus violated his own conscience out of fear, and this weakness is more the cause of his actions.

Q. Are there any teachings about what Jesus did when he went to hell, as described in the Apostles' Creed?
— *Robert Lusby*

It is important to distinguish the hell of the damned from the place of the dead, which the ancients termed variously "Sheol," "Hades," or "Hell." Since the *Catechism* answers your question quite thoroughly. Here are some excerpts:

> Jesus did not descend into hell to deliver the damned, nor to destroy the hell of damnation, but to free the just who had gone before him.

> "[So] the gospel was preached even to the dead." The descent into hell brings the Gospel message of salvation to complete fulfillment. This is the last phase of Jesus' messianic mission, a phase which is condensed in time but vast in its real significance: the spread of Christ's redemptive work to all men of all times and all places, for all who are saved have been made sharers in the redemption.

> Christ went down into the depths of death so that "the dead will hear the voice of the Son of God, and those who hear will live." (633–35)

And an ancient sermon says, "Greatly desiring to visit those who live in darkness and in the shadow of death, [Jesus] has gone to free from sorrow Adam ... and Eve, captive with him. [And finding them he says,] "I am your God, who for your sake have become your son.... Awake O Sleeper, I did not create you to be a prisoner in hell.

Rise from the dead, for I am the life of the dead" (excerpt, Ancient Holy Saturday Homily, c. second century).

Q.I was told Jesus is without sin. But on Easter, at Mass, I heard a reading that said, "Jesus died to sin." Which is true? — *Alan Smith*

You are quoting Romans 6:10, which says, "The death he died he died to sin, once for all." In saying that Christ "died to sin," Saint Paul is not saying he died on account of his own personal sins. The Greek word *hamartia* (sin) is often used by Paul to refer to our own personal sins. But it is also used to refer, in a more collective sense, to the sin of the world. This fallen world of ours is immersed in sin, in an attitude of rebellion, pride, greed, lust, and so forth. And this climate of sin is like a force, a mindset, initiated by Satan and connived in by human beings. It is to this world of sin that Christ died. He broke its back by dying to it and rising victorious over it. And he defeated it in the most paradoxical way: he conquered pride by humility, disobedience by obedience, and death by dying and rising.

It is to this regime of sin that Christ died, not his own personal sins, of which Scripture is clear he had none (see 1 Pt 2:22).

In the Letter to the Romans, we are also taught to realize that we, too, have died to sin, and that this world of sin is to have no more power over us (see 6:2,11). We must come to experience increasing power, authority, and victory over the influence of this world of sin. We are to lay hold of the life Christ offers us, wherein this world of sin has no more power over us.

Q.•In John 20, we read that when Jesus appears to Mary Magdalene on Easter morning, he told her not to touch him. We then read later that he asks Thomas, in the Upper Room, not only to touch him but also to put his hands into the very wounds of Our Lord. How is this discrepancy explained? — *Erin*

Some older Bibles rendered Jesus' words to Mary Magdalene as "Do not touch me." But this rendering is not a particularly accurate representation of the Greek. The Greek verb is *haptou*, a present imperative verb in the middle voice, and means more accurately, "Do not cling to me." The likely reason is that at this moment Jesus wants her to be a messenger to the apostles. He has something for her to do. It is not that he is averse to being touched at all.

Hence the discrepancy related to Thomas being told to touch him falls away. It is not the touch that is a problem. Further, the context of the two stories is different. Mary most certainly did believe in Jesus' resurrection. But Thomas' need to see and touch in order to believe on his own terms is being rebuked, not encouraged. Though in mercy the Lord permits him to do so, he warns that faith is not about seeing, it is about hearing. "You have believed because you have seen. Blessed are those who have not seen and yet believe" (Jn 20:29).

Thus, in a way, the terms of your question are actually reversed. Mary is not rebuked at all for touching per se, but rather is encouraged to run and share her faith with others. Thomas is rebuked for his need to touch on account of his lack of faith and refusal to listen to those sent to preach the Good News to him.

Q. Jesus tells Mary Magdalene in one of the Resurrection appearances, "I am ascending ... to my God and your God" (Jn 20:17). This has always confused me since I thought Jesus is God. — *Mary Taylor*

Yes, Jesus is God. But Jesus is also one Person with two natures, divine and human. When he speaks of ascending "to my God," he does so in terms of his human nature. As God, he cannot ascend to God, there is nowhere for him to go. But in terms of his humanity he can use expressions such as "my God," and he has the capacity to ascend.

It is important to realize that the Resurrection accounts place heavy emphasis on Jesus' human nature. For it does not pertain to Jesus' divine nature to rise from the dead, since God cannot die. Only as man can he rise from the dead.

Not only is his human nature raised up, but it is transformed. We speak of his resurrected humanity as a glorified humanity. And in this sense he is ascending — that is, he is taking up his glorified human nature to dwell forever at the Father's right hand.

God the Holy Spirit

Q. To me, the Holy Spirit is an enigma. Please teach me how better to understand the Holy Spirit. — *James*

When Saint Paul went to Ephesus, he inquired if the disciples there had received the Holy Spirit. They replied, "We have never even heard that there is a Holy Spirit" (Acts 19:2). You, of course, have heard, but like many are not sure of his role in your life and wonder how better to experience him.

Within the Blessed Trinity the Father beholds the Son, and the Son beholds the Father. And there flows from them both, and between them, a divine love that is so perfect, and of such infinite ardor, as to be a living Love and a divine Person (for it is the very nature of God to exist). We call this Love the Holy Spirit.

To have the Holy Spirit living in us, received at baptism, is to be caught up into the very love and life of God. The work of the Holy Spirit is, first, to sanctify us, to make us holy and pleasing to God. The Holy Spirit also bestows on us countless graces and charisms to transform us and make us a blessing to others.

It is no surprise that one image of the Holy Spirit is that of fire. For as tongues of fire came to rest upon the first disciples, so, too, the Holy Spirit lights the fire of God's love in us, purifying and refining away impurities and instilling in us, with increasing perfection, the life, love, and glory of God.

Another image of the Holy Spirit is that of the rushing wind that came upon the disciples at Pentecost. The word "Spirit" means "breath." Yes, God the Holy Spirit breathes new life into us. By his power we become more and more alive in the new life Christ purchased for us. We receive a new mind by the Spirit's inspiration, a new heart by his love, and a growing transformation and a share in every good and perfect gift by his grace.

What does the Holy Spirit do for us? Consider the transformation of the first disciples at Pentecost. Anxious individuals gathered in the Upper Room were suddenly transformed and, throwing open the door, went forth with love and confidence to boldly proclaim Christ. This the Holy Spirit offers us as well.

PART II

THE BIBLE

THE OLD TESTAMENT

Q: Original sin is based on the belief that Adam and Eve are the parents of all mankind. Where and when did they live? — *Rex Gogerty*

The nature of your question asks the Genesis account to be what it really is not — namely, a scientific and strictly historical account of creation. It proposes to be neither of these. Rather it is more of a poetic account of God's creative act. Hence the chronological dating of Adam and Eve to, say, 6,000 B.C. based on Genesis is not possible.

The account *does* seem to locate the Garden in Mesopotamia, but here, too, we need not presume this is meant as a precise map but could be more allegorical. What we must hold is that God created everything out of nothing and guided all the stages of creation, even to this day. Catholic teaching does prefer to see Adam and Eve as directly created by God and as actual, historical persons.

Q: In the garden of Eden, God said to the serpent, "I will put enmity between you and the woman, / and between your seed and her seed; / he shall bruise your head / and you shall bruise his heel" (Gn 3:15). There are many details here that puzzle me. Could you explain this? — *Helen Schulte*

Genesis 3:15, the text you cite, is often called by theologians the "*protoevangelion*" (meaning "the first good news"). For, after all the harm caused by original sin, God announces the good news that he will send a savior to rescue us through the woman — that is, through a descendant of hers. And that is what the word "seed" means here.

The "enmity" spoken of here is an older English word meaning hostility, adversity, or even hatred. In effect, God indicates that Satan and "the woman" would be particular enemies, or by extension that she would be his greatest enemy.

The Genesis text would seem to indicate that Eve was the woman. Yet she died, and none of her direct children rescued us from Satan. Thus "the woman" came to be regarded as a symbol of a woman who would one day come. In John's Gospel, Jesus indicates that his mother Mary is in fact that woman, for Jesus calls his mother "Woman." John also looks at her in this way in the Book of Revelation when he speaks of the "woman clothed with the sun" (12:1) and goes on to describe a woman who is historically Mary, for this woman gives birth to a Son (Jesus) who is destined to rule the nations.

The image of striking at the heel and being crushed is drawn from the image of what snakes and humans will often do. A snake will strike at the heel of a person since that is the part closest to the ground. A human being will often seek to defend himself by trying to crush the head of the snake. And all of this is used as an allegory of the spiritual battle which takes place between the seed (son) of the woman and Satan.

An interesting sidebar in this discussion was the practice of older Catholic translations that rendered the pronoun as "she." Hence the text would read, "She will crush your head while you strike at her heel." Many older statues of Mary show her standing on a snake for this reason. The Hebrew pronoun *hu* is ambiguous and can be rendered he, she, or it. Saint Jerome, in the Latin Vulgate, rendered it she (*ipsa*), and this influenced later translations.

However, theologically it is more apt to render the text, "He shall crush," since it is Jesus, who is the seed and the Savior, who crushes Satan. Thus most modern translations render the pronoun as he. So, while Satan has a special hostility for Mary and she has a special power over him, her power is derived from the fact that it is her Son, Jesus, who conquers Satan.

Q •Adam and Eve sewed fig leaves together to cov-
•er their nakedness. But God then changes that by
clothing them in animal skins. Is there some significance
to this? — *Jason Corby*

Yes. One might immediately (and humorously) perceive that fig
leaves make lousy clothes and would tend to cause itching. Adam
and Eve likely used them because they were at hand as they sought
whatever was available to quickly resolve the shame of their nakedness.

However, that God took animal skins and clothed them (see
Gn 3:21) has the significance of being the first shedding of blood.
Death enters the world through sin. And though one could argue
that the cycle of life and death was already operative in the world
before man, the Scriptures connect the killing of these animals
with what sin has done. Now animals must die to provide food and
clothing to man — something not necessary in the garden of paradise, which provided ample food from the trees, and where nakedness did not need covering. The Genesis text thus hints at what
Saint Paul said: "The wages of sin is death" (Rom 6:23).

Q •In Genesis, there is the whole story about Cain and
•Abel. Why did God not approve of Cain's offerings?
What did he do that was so disappointing to God? I get
that Cain murdered his brother, but before that? — *Carl*

While it is true that there is no obvious explanation given for the
rejection of Cain's offering in this text, there are differences in the
details of the two offerings that provide some clues.

First, Abel gives of the firstlings (first fruits) of his flock.
There is no mention that Cain gave of the first fruits of his crop. In
biblical legislation, God commanded that the tithe be given. But it
was not any tenth that was to be given, rather it was the first tenth
that was to be given (see Ex 23:16,19; 34:26; Lv 23:10, to name just a

few). Thus Cain erred by not presenting first fruits, and God did not regard his offering. We are not to give God leftovers.

A second, though less certain, problem may be that Cain offered a cereal offering, not a blood offering. Scripture attests that it was necessary to shed the blood of animals for the remission of sin. Hebrews 9:22 says, "Indeed, under the law almost everything is purified with blood, and without the shedding of blood there is no forgiveness of sins." This is confirmed throughout the Old Testament, wherein God specifies the sacrifice of certain animals for temple worship. This theory is not without a problem, however, since cereal offerings and other offerings from the harvest are elsewhere commanded and acceptable to God (see Lv 2:14 as one example).

Most likely, then, Cain's offering was less acceptable since it was not from the first fruits of his increase, and possibly because it was not a blood sacrifice. Whatever the full reason, the Letter to the Hebrews attests, "By faith Abel offered to God a more acceptable sacrifice than Cain, through which he received approval as righteous, God bearing witness by accepting his gifts" (11:4).

Cain's reaction to God's response goes further to indicate a third area of concern, not for Cain's offering, but for his disposition. The First Letter of John says that Cain's offering was not just lacking, it was evil (see 3:12). And this indicates not merely an external problem with Cain's offering, but an internal disposition of sin that rendered his offering displeasing to God. Thus one can offer a technically perfect sacrifice to God, but if we offer it in unrepented and serious sin, God is displeased, and we can even bring condemnation on ourselves (1 Cor 11:29).

Here, too, the Genesis text hints at the "heart problem" Cain brought to the moment. Scripture says: "Cain was very angry [that God did not regard his sacrifice], and his countenance fell. The Lord said to Cain, 'Why are you angry, and why has your countenance fallen? If you do well, will you not be accepted? And if you do not do well, sin is lurking at the door; its desire is for you, but you must master it'" (Gn 4:5–7).

The image of sin lurking at the door is a powerful one. In permitting his anger and envy to grow toward his brother, Cain is moving toward darkness and sin. He must learn to master his anger, and all his passions, or sin, like a lurking shadow or crouching predator, is near the door of his heart.

Sadly, as you already note, Cain gives way to sin and murders his brother. Thus the First Letter of John tersely notes: "Cain ... was of the Evil One and murdered his brother. And why did he murder him? Because his own deeds were evil and his brother's righteous" (1 Jn 3:12).

Q.In Genesis 25:23, Rebecca is pregnant with twins, Esau and Jacob, and they struggle within her womb. She is distressed and asks the Lord why. "And the Lord said to her, / 'Two nations are in your womb, / and two peoples, born of you, shall be divided; / the one shall be stronger than the other, / the elder shall serve the younger.'" My questions: What are the two nations, and does this text mean that God cursed Esau from the beginning? — *Frank Donall*

The two nations are Israel and Edom. Jacob was the patriarch of the twelve tribes of Israel. His name was changed to Israel by God, and his twelve sons headed the twelve tribes of what would become the nation, the people of Israel. Esau became the patriarch of what would become the Edomites and the nation of Edom, who were known for their reddish and hairy skin, which Esau possessed.

In many ways the story of Jacob and Esau is a dark tale, full of treachery. Jacob acted manipulatively and deceitfully against his brother, and also his father, Isaac, to obtain the birthright. Rebecca participated in this. Esau, though a physically strong man and a good hunter, was somewhat weak-willed, going so far as to sell his birthright to Isaac for a bowl of soup (for he was very hungry). Jacob was something of a "mama's boy" and stayed close to home, but he was shrewd and conniving and secured his father's blessing by deception, with his mother's help. Esau, realizing he had been tricked, sought his brother's life, and Rebecca arranged for Jacob to flee to the north and live with her brother, Laban. And while there is a touching reconciliation between Jacob and Esau later, the nations and peoples they founded had tense relations down through the centuries.

To say that God "cursed" Esau from the beginning may be too strong. God is Lord of history and he mysteriously permits many human struggles to unfold on their own but uses them for his designs. The ancient Jews were more prone to attribute the flow of history to God's direct will more than his permissive will. They were more comfortable in emphasizing that God was the primary cause of all that happens since he holds everything in existence. God the Holy Spirit also spoke to them in this way. In modern times, we tend to emphasize secondary causality, which looks to the cause of things in the created order and the decisions of human beings.

Both insights are important. God is sovereign, but man has freedom, and there is a mysterious interaction between both truths. Jacob, though quite sinful at times, was someone God chose to work with and establish as the patriarch of his Chosen People. Esau's descendants were less favored in this sense (see Rom 9:13). But in Christ, all are now called to be God's people.

Q: I heard recently at Mass, "Now Moses was by far the meekest man on the face of the earth." Not to sound impious but it made me laugh. Moses in the Scriptures was often stern, temperamental, and spoke so rashly once that God said, in effect, "No Promised Land for you." What can this text possibly mean? — *John*

Part of the answer to your concern may lie in reading univocally — namely, in a very literalist, straightforward way — what is meant more as hyperbole. The mention of Moses' meekness is set in contrast to the bold denigration of his authority by his brother Aaron and his sister Miriam. In their anger at him for marrying a Cushite woman, they declare with great boldness: "Has the LORD indeed spoken only through Moses? Has he not spoken through us also?" (Nm 12:2). This remark provokes God's anger, and they are punished.

It is in contrast to this boldness of theirs that Moses is called "the meekest" (some translations say "humblest") man on the face of the earth." Given the context, it is possible to assign to a text like this a genre of comparative hyperbole. Thus the text essentially means, "Compared to them Moses was the meekest man you'd ever meet."

The text is indicating that Moses wasn't the sort to take offense at personal disrespect. He wasn't stuffy and didn't expect to be shown all sorts of deference, nor did he try to lay hold of certain offices and charisms all for himself. In fact, Moses had said elsewhere: "Would that all the LORD's people were prophets, that the LORD would put his spirit upon them!" (Nm 11:29).

So, the text in Numbers is not an indication that Moses was perfect, nor that there was literally no one else on the whole face of the earth who was more meek and humble and controlling of anger than Moses. Rather, the text sets the stage for Moses' intercession to God on behalf of his brother and sister, even though they had rebuked his authority and tried to undermine it. And God heard Moses' prayers and healed them.

As for foibles, he surely had them. But here, too, is a picture of the need for grace. For if even the likes of Moses, who had so many graces under the Old Law, could not make it in, all the more do we see how necessary the grace of God is for us to enter heaven. Jesus would later say of another great hero of the Old Covenant: "Truly, I say to you, among those born of women there has arisen no one greater than John the Baptist; yet he who is least in the kingdom of heaven is greater than he" (Mt 11:11).

Q. In the Psalms and Canticles of the Liturgy of the Hours there are frequent calls for plants and animals, and even concepts like light and darkness to praise the Lord. But how can animals and plants, rocks and hills, or darkness praise the Lord? Most of these have no will or minds. — *Sharon Kurchiwinski*

Language is not always used in a technical sense. Language also has creative and allegorical (figurative) senses.

The Scriptures are, as you note, filled with references to creation. Creation, of course, does not praise God consciously or by an act of will as angels and human beings do. Rather, creation praises God by its very existence and by revealing some particular aspect of God's glory, who made it. In calling on all creation to "praise" or "bless" the Lord, we are recognizing this and joining our conscious and intellectual voices to the allegorical "voice" of all creation, which "shouts" to us in our intellect the glory of our common Creator.

Q. I have always found comfort in Ezekiel 37 because it seemed to describe what we might expect during our own bodily resurrection. Then I read in a biblical commentary that "it has been thought, wrongly, to foretell the resurrection of the body," but rather refers to the future restoration of Israel. Have I been wrong all these years? — *Gene Walker*

The passage to which you refer is the familiar passage where Ezekiel is shown a field of dry human bones and told to prophesy over them. As he does, the flesh forms on them and they eventually arise, alive.

It is true that the historical context of this vision of Ezekiel was not one which envisioned the resurrection of the body, but rather the raising up of Israel as a nation. Both Israel, and later Judah, suf-

fered terrible destruction at the hands of the Assyrians and Bab-
ylonians. Ezekiel foresaw a time when they would rise from their
ruins and be reunited. The key to interpreting the passage begins:

> Then he said to me, "Son of man, these bones
> are the whole house of Israel. Behold, they say,
> 'Our bones are dried up, and our hope is lost; we
> are clean cut off.' Therefore prophesy, and say to
> them, Thus says the LORD GOD: Behold, I will
> open your graves, and raise you from your graves,
> O my people; and I will bring you home into the
> land of Israel. And you shall know that I am the
> LORD, when I open your graves, and raise you
> from your graves, O my people. And I will put my
> Spirit within you, and you shall live, and I will
> place you in your own land." (Ezekiel 37:11–14)

It would be a mistake, however, to identify this passage merely with a political or national resurgence and lock it away in a brief
historical moment. The Jewish people did not so easily divide the
spiritual from the world as we do. They often spoke of spiritual
blessings in worldly ways. Further, God's word speaks to all times,
beyond the merely historical context in which it was given.

Thus it is not inauthentic to see this passage spiritually and
allegorically as a word of encouragement to all of God's people of
all times, that he will raise them up to better things and restore
them. Even more, that he will raise them from the final blow that
this world inflicts, which is death.

DIFFICULT PASSAGES IN SCRIPTURE

Q.**I was speaking to a friend about the angel of death in Exodus, and she responded that she couldn't believe in a "killing" God, only a loving God. How do I explain passages like this?** — *James Cayea*

Pope Benedict XVI, in his post-synodal exhortation *Verbum Domini*, referred to events like this as the "dark passages" of the Bible. And while they are difficult for many modern people to digest, they do speak to times where modern forms of conflict resolution were little known. God had not yet led these ancient cultures to a clearer grasp of justice and the dignity of the human person. That would take centuries of sending the Law, prophets, and, finally, his Son to teach us in these ways and deepen our grasp of justice and mercy.

As such, warlike solutions were rather common in the ancient world, and conflicts were often "resolved" with one side winning.

As for Pharaoh, it took the death of the firstborn to finally secure the release of the Jews from slavery. One can argue that God acted in a way that was necessary in those conditions to secure the common good. Your friend may wish to ponder if she has the scales to measure what is worse: the tragic death of a certain number of firstborn Egyptian children, or the cruel enslavement of the entire Jewish nation for 400 years. How does one weigh the common good of action by God or continued inaction? Remember, too, that none of the previous plagues were enough to secure the release of the slaves.

In addition, your friend might wish to recall that God, who gives life, has the right to take it when and how he sees fit. God numbers all of our days. Some of us will live long lives, others not. Some of us will die in bed, others by violence. Only God knows what is best for us and for the common good.

Q. •I remember the Bible describing the Holy Land as •flowing with milk and honey. When I visited there recently, I found it dry and more desertlike. Was the Bible exaggerating? — *Richard Evans*

Probably not. There is good evidence that the Holy Land as we know it today is somewhat warmer and drier than in biblical times.

For example, in the Book of Genesis, the region of Sodom and Gomorrah is described as being well-watered and like a rich garden. But the text makes it clear that this was its appearance "before the LORD destroyed Sodom and Gomorrah" (13:10). Today that region, likely the area around the Dead Sea, is deep desert.

Other areas of the Holy Land seemed to have featured more trees and agriculture in biblical times than they do today. For example, Solomon (around 1000 BC) is described as being able to harvest prodigious amounts of trees for his building projects. Land-use studies and archaeology also provide evidence of the prevalence of crops and forests suited to cooler, wetter climates. In Jesus' time, too, there is evidence of a bit more rainfall than today, given in descriptions by Josephus and others who lived at the time.

Over time, however, due to many wars and poor land management, the area has been gradually deforested. This, plus other climatological factors over two millennia, has contributed to a process of moderate desertification. The result is that the region today is likely somewhat warmer and drier than in biblical times.

Israel currently has a program attempting to reverse the desertification by planting trees, a program that has received large financial support, in an attempt to partially reforest Israel. Your visit may also have been affected by topography and season. Israel has a wet season from October to April, and a dry season from June to September, which influences the greenery a great deal. Further, the region up north around the Sea of Galilee is far more green and lush than the areas in the south near Bethlehem and Jerusalem. To the east, the elevation drops and the Dead Sea and Jericho are dry and deep deserts.

Therefore, the Promised Land in biblical times likely did flow with "milk and honey." This expression speaks to abundant livestock and the rich crop life of an area more green and lush than today.

Q. The Old Testament mentions that many of the patriarchs, like David, had numerous wives. The Lord even says to David through Nathan: "I gave your master's house, and your master's wives into your bosom" (2 Sm 12:8). How are we to understand this permission of polygamy, and when did God forbid it? — *Teresa Thompson*

When God first established marriage, it is clear that his vision was that "a man leaves his father and his mother and clings to his wife, and they become one flesh" (Gn 2:24). Hence, there is one man, with one wife, and the two are stably united by clinging to one another as the text says. So, divorce and multiple wives were not part of God's design for marriage.

However, on account of human sinfulness, and out of fear that men would kill their wives to be free to marry another, Moses allowed divorce. It is also clear that the customs of the ancient Near East also infected Israel's notion of marriage and that many, at least wealthier men and patriarchs, did often take more than one wife. Thus we see that sin corrupted what God intended, and that, for a time, God overlooked this sinful behavior.

Nevertheless, we ought not equate the mere reporting of sinful behavior with approval of it. For, while the polygamy of the patriarchs is reported, so is all the trouble it caused when brothers of different mothers challenged, and even killed, one another. For example, there are terrible stories told of the sons of Gideon, and also the sons of Jacob, to mention but two. The well-known story of Joseph being sold into slavery by his brothers emerges from the internecine conflicts of brothers of different mothers. Hence while reporting polygamy the Bible also teaches of the evil it brings forth.

Gradually, God led the ancient Jews away from approving of polygamy such that, by the time of Jesus, it was rare. As for divorce, Jesus sets it aside by teaching the people at that time that although Moses allowed divorce due to their hardness of heart, it was not this way at the beginning, and it was now time to return to God's original plan (see Mt 19:4,8): We should not separate what God has joined.

As for Nathan saying that God gave David his many wives, this can be understood as the ancient tendency to stress God as the primary cause of all things. It does not necessarily mean that God actively wanted and approved of polygamy, only that he is the first cause of everything that exists and happens.

Q.: **A friend of mine, referencing some sort of "black studies" program she attended, says that the opening lines of the Song of Songs (also known as the Song of Solomon) are racist. It says, "I am black but beautiful, O Daughters of Jerusalem" in some translations. She tends to be radical, but I must admit I couldn't really give her an answer. Can you help?** — *Name withheld*

The reference to the woman's color in the text is more likely a reference to her economic class than to race. She is a Jewish woman (not African), from the region of Shulem, speaking to other unspecified Jewish women about how she found love. She speaks to her complexion but goes on to explain it: "Do not gaze at me because I am swarthy, / because the sun has scorched me. / My mother's sons were angry with me, / they made me keeper of the vineyards; / but, my own vineyard I have not kept!" (Song 1:6).

Hence her skin was darker because she was consigned by her noble family to work outdoors in the vineyards. Spending extensive time outdoors has scorched and darkened her skin.

It was the lot of the economically poorer classes to work outdoors, while richer Jews could stay indoors or under cover and be protected from the sun. In today's culture, we speak of white-collar and blue-collar jobs in this context. Thus she is explaining how she, though from a wealthy family (for they seemingly owned vineyards) has the sun-scorched look of one from a poorer family. She references some undisclosed sins from her past that angered her family, which caused her consignment to the lowly work of the vineyards. It might be like a son from a wealthy family explaining why he was working in the mailroom even though his father owned the company.

But despite all this, her beloved (perhaps King Solomon) loves her, and she loves him. The Song of Songs is about love, not race or even economic class. To reduce it to race says more about us and our modern preoccupations than it does about 900 BC.

This mention of her physical appearance is one of the rare occurrences of such descriptions in the Bible. Skin color, height, weight, etc., are seldom supplied by the text. The tendency should also encourage us to be less preoccupied with such physical descriptions and listen to what the text is really focusing on.

Q: **I was recently reading the passage from the New Testament at Luke 14:25–33, where Jesus says, "If anyone comes to me and does not hate his own father and mother and wife and children and brothers and sisters … he cannot be my disciple." I am shocked by this wording, especially since the Spanish Bible renders it, "*Si alguno viene a mí y no sacrifica el amor*" ("if anyone comes to me and doesn't sacrifice the love" — instead of "hate"). How could Jesus ask us to hate anyone?** — *Peter Kinghorn*

In this case the English renders the Greek word *miseó* (hate) more accurately. Jesus is using a Jewish manner of speaking in which hyperbole (exaggeration) is used to emphasize the point being made. Jesus is teaching that we are to prefer no one to him and what he commands.

However, simply to render it as "prefer" in English would not deliver the full impact of what Jesus says. Thus the English translators properly retain the literal meaning: "hate." For Jesus is not merely asking for some preferred place in the world of loyalties and ideas, he is asking for a radical preference. Jesus is not just part of our life, he IS our life. The impact of what he is saying is that we must so strongly love and prefer him that others might think at times that we hate them by comparison.

Thus hate here does not mean to despise, condemn, or harbor grudges. But it is a call for a radical preference that the use of the simple word prefer does not capture. Jesus uses hyperbole as a way of emphasis. We do this a lot in English as well when, for example, we say things like, "There must have been a million people there." There may not even have been a thousand, but our emphasis is a hyperbole that means there were a lot of people there.

Q: I was telling my daughter that the Bible teaches against homosexual acts and thus same-sex marriage. She dismissed the Bible and said it once approved slavery and thus carried no moral authority for her. What can I say? — *Name withheld*

There are several problems in both the logic and the understanding of Scripture involved in this objection.

The first problem involves equating what is a definitive precept with what is at best a tacit tolerance. Homosexual acts (as well as all heterosexual acts outside of marriage) are explicitly condemned throughout the whole of Scripture, from the early pages of the Old Testament through the closing pages of the New Testament. We are commanded to refrain from any such acts. But nowhere are we commanded to own slaves.

The Scriptures treat slavery as part of the existing social structure of the ancient world and set norms so as to avoid the excesses that sometimes accompanied it. But the mere tolerance of a questionable practice should not be equated with supporting it, let alone prescribing it as something good. An argument from silence does not connote approval.

The second problem is the term slavery itself. While the same word is used for the ancient reality and the practice of the colonial period, there are important differences that made the condemnation all the more necessary and ultimately required. In the ancient biblical world slavery resulted from essentially three sources: one owed debt they could not repay, one had been a solider in a defeated army, or one may have committed certain crimes. As such, slavery was an alternative to death or imprisonment. It was not without its questionable dimensions, but neither was it intrinsically evil. Even today we often seek alternatives to imprisonment (such as probation and house arrest) wherein one forfeits some of their rights, is forbidden certain freedoms, and must report to a state official.

But the slavery of the later colonial period (of the sixteenth to nineteenth centuries) exploited and enslaved people who had no debt, had committed no crimes, and had not waged war. This is a very different situation, morally speaking, from the slavery of biblical times. It required the condemnation and rejection it received.

Finally, even if one were to insist that Scripture once approved slavery (a point not conceded here), and therefore it discredits the Bible as a source for moral teaching, then we ought to ask what would happen if this same standard were applied, for example, to the U.S. Constitution. Is the Constitution fully discredited since it once remained silent or gave tacit approval to slavery? Is your daughter's right to free speech discredited because the U.S. Constitution was once imperfect or even wrong on another topic? Most would find this notion too extreme. And neither does Scripture lose its value even if it was once less severe on slavery than we would wish today.

Q: I hear a lot about the love of God, but then I also see a lot in the Bible about his wrath and anger. I don't know which view of God to believe in. — *James Westenholmer*

The biblical concept of the wrath of God must be understood with a good degree of sophistication. It does not simply mean that God is angry. We do not have a God who is moody, grouchy, or prone to fits of temper. God's anger, or wrath, must be understood in the light of his love. From this perspective, one good definition of God's wrath is his decisive work to set things right. God, out of love for us, must level the mountains of our pride and fill in the valleys of our despair and neglect. In his bold action it may at times seem to us that he is angry, but it is truer to say that he loves us, as well as truth and justice, and is seeking, for our benefit, to establish them more firmly.

In another sense, it is proper to say that the wrath of God is an experience that is more in us than in God. From this perspective, the wrath of God is our experience of the complete incompatibility of our sinful state before the holiness of God. That which is unholy simply cannot endure the presence of God who is utterly holy. It is like wax before fire.

Consider, too, the image of fire and water. They do not mix or coexist in the same spot. One hears the conflict between them as a kind of sizzling and popping. One element will win; the other must depart. Unrepentant sinners before God also experience this conflict within themselves. Though they may attribute the problem to God, calling him wrathful, the problem is really in us, not in God. Think of how at night we will often have lights on in our room. But then the lights are put out and we sleep. Early the next morning the lights are put back on, but now the light seems obnoxious. Yet the light has not changed at all, it is the same wattage light bulb it was the night before. But notice how we say the light is "harsh." Yet the light is not harsh; it is what it always is. It is we who changed.

It is like this with God, who does not change — in whom the Letter of James says, "there is no variation or shadow due to change" (1:17). Therefore, as you can see, wrath is a notion that must be balanced with other truths about God: that he is love and that he does not change. Neither is he given to irritableness or arbitrary outbursts of anger.

Q. Why does the Lord's Prayer ask God not to lead us into temptation? Why would God do that? I have also read texts in the Bible about God hardening people's hearts. Again, why would God do that? — *Gerald Phillips*

Part of the problem in understanding biblical texts like these comes down to the philosophical distinction between primary and secondary causality. Primary causality refers to God's action in creating, sustaining, and setting into motion all things. From this perspective, God is the first (or primary) cause of all things — even things contrary to his stated and revealed will.

Thus if I hit you over the head with a bat, I am actually the secondary cause of this painful experience. God is the primary cause because he has made and sustains all things in the process, such as me, the wood of the bat, and the firm resistance of your skull. As such, God is the first or underlying cause, without which nothing at all would be happening or existing. God is surely opposed to my action and even has commandments against it. However, given his establishment of physical laws and respect for human freedom, he seldom intervenes by suspending these.

So, to be clear, in my horrific little example, God is the primary cause, since he is the cause of me and the bat, but I am the secondary cause of my shameful act of violence.

The biblical world was more conversant with and accepting of primary causality. Biblical texts often more freely associate things with God because he is the first cause of all things without excluding the human agency that is the secondary cause. However, with the rise of the empirical sciences and secularism, in modern days we are far less comfortable in speaking to primary causality (God's world) and focus more on secondary causes (our world).

When the Lord's Prayer says "lead us not into temptation," it is not asserting that God would directly and intentionally lead us into temptation; rather it is averting the fact that God is the first cause of all things. We are thus asking that God's providence will allow fewer opportunities for us to be led into temptation by the world, the flesh, and the devil.

Likewise, texts that refer to God hardening hearts employ similar thinking. God hardens hearts only insofar as he is the first cause of all things. But it is usually we who harden our own heart. God only permits the conditions and sustains our existence (primary causality), but it is we as secondary causes who directly will the sins that harden our hearts.

Q. **At a recent Bible study, the deacon said that Satan is the prince of this world, so he's in charge down here. That didn't really sit right with me. Is this really what the Bible teaches?** — *Name withheld*

As your question implies, we need to be careful. It is true that in the Gospel of John Jesus, describing his passion, death, and resurrection to his disciples, concludes by saying: "I have told you before it takes place, so that when it does take place, you may believe. I will no longer talk much with you, for the ruler [prince in some translations] of this world is coming. He has no power over me" (14:30–31).

Thus Jesus does refer to the prince of this world, thereby indicating that Satan has some power and influence here. However, whatever influence he may have, Jesus remains the king of the universe and thereby limits Satan's power and overrules it. Jesus says elsewhere that he will be driven out and condemned (see Jn 12:31; 16:11).

All these texts must be carefully balanced. The title "prince of this world" is fundamentally limited to the hearts of those who have refused the kingship of God and accepted the practical authority of the evil one. Sadly, through them, Satan exerts influence in this world. And though Jesus has cast him out and made clear his condemnation, the Lord mysteriously allows Satan to wander through the ruins of the world he once had greater authority over. But Jesus, who is king, limits Satan's power and influence.

Though Satan's activity at times seems intense, it always remains under God's power, who permits his influence only to obtain greater good from it in the end. We should not so exaggerate Satan's power that we forget God's grace, which is greater. Scripture elsewhere says that, for now, Satan's power is limited (see Rv 20:1–3), and that at the end of time he will be released for a brief period, and then utterly cast into the lake of burning fire forever (Rv 20:7–10).

Be assured of this: Satan, whatever power he may seem to have right now, is the loser. His plans are going nowhere. Christ has already conquered, and we ought to be clear of the final victory for the Lord and all who choose and trust in him.

JESUS IN SCRIPTURE

Q: I love the Faith and the Scriptures. But I wonder and sometimes get asked how accurate the accounts of Jesus' life are considering they were written, often, thirty years after his death. — *Robert McBride*

From the standpoint of faith, Jesus himself says to the apostles: "But the Counselor, the Holy Spirit, whom the Father will send in my name, he will teach you all things, and bring to your remembrance all that I have said to you" (Jn 14:26). Thus we trust in the guidance and inspiration of the Holy Spirit, who has a very good memory.

From the human standpoint, we should recall that Luke, for example (who was not an eyewitness), says, "Many have undertaken to compile a narrative of the things which have been accomplished among us, just as they were delivered to us by those who from the beginning were eyewitnesses" (Lk 1:1–2). Thus the Gospel writers were in communion with and careful collectors of the remembrances of the other eyewitness to the events they describe and teachings they report. Prior to widespread literacy, people were more careful than we are in modern times at preserving and handing on teachings and stories.

Last, it is debatable that more than thirty years elapsed before written accounts appeared. A good amount of evidence says that written accounts of the Lord's teaching and ministry existed early on. These accounts circulated and influenced others, even if they were not yet the complete and fully edited Gospels we have today.

Q: •Why does Matthew's Gospel claim to list the ancestors of Jesus when they are really those of his stepfather, Joseph, with whom he shares no genes? — *Salvatore Leone*

The purpose of a genealogy for ancient Jews was more complex and rich than to simply demonstrate physical descent. The modern science of genetics, chromosomes, and the genetic code were unknown in the ancient world. But even today, relationships are set up both by blood *and* by marriage — that is to say, two people can be related either by direct, physical descent, or legally through marriage. While Joseph and Jesus shared no physical genes, Joseph's family and Jesus are one through Joseph's marriage to Mary. So, Joseph's family tree matters to us and to those in ancient Israel because, through Joseph and his marriage to Mary, Jesus relates to many others in Israel.

In ancient Israel, genealogies existed to show that one was in fact a member of the nation of Israel, which located them in a particular tribe and showed their relationships with others. These are Matthew's main purposes — namely, that Jesus belongs to the family of Israel both as a son of Mary and through his relationship to Joseph, the husband of the Virgin Mary.

Matthew also has other complex purposes in mind in the names he highlights and the way he groups them in patterns of fourteen, all laid out according to different periods of salvation history. There are also other numerological details too complex to lay out here. So, as you can see, there is more than a question of physical descent involved in the recitation of ancient genealogies. Human beings relate in more than physical ways, but also through a complex network of relationships we call families, tribes, and nations.

Q. The Old Testament said that the Messiah would be called Emmanuel, but the angel told Joseph and Mary to call him Jesus. Is this a problem? — *John Carter*

No. The name Emmanuel means "God with us," which is not so different from Jesus, which means "God saves." Thus the key concept of God being with us to save us is maintained and fulfilled despite the names being different in a literal sense. Prophecies usually have a general character that do not require the exact precision that many of us in modern literary times demand. Therefore, Matthew has no problem in connecting the names Jesus and Emmanuel when reporting the words of the angel to Joseph: "'She will bear a son, and you shall call his name Jesus, for he will save his people from their sins.' All this took place to fulfil what the Lord had spoken by the prophet: / *'Behold, a virgin shall conceive and bear a son, / and his name shall be called Emmanuel,* / (which means, God with us)'" (Mt 1:21–23).

Q. If they were only betrothed, why did Joseph contemplate a divorce when he discovered Mary was with child? — *Robert Bonsignore*

You seem to be equating betrothal with the modern concept of engagement. The two are not the same. Jewish custom at the time considered a couple to be married once the general agreement for the marriage had been obtained. The couple did not live together or consummate the marriage, however, for about a year while the families worked out the details (dowry, etc.). If for some reason the arrangement fell through, a divorce was required since they were considered to be married even before the final ceremonies and consummation.

While all this may sound complex or fussy, it was really to protect the woman. Virginity was prized in Jewish culture for a bride and, without this, she was considered less marriageable. Thus she would not surrender her virginity until all the final details were made and the couple was found compatible. Joseph was striving to follow the Law as he understood it at the time. But God instructed Joseph to proceed differently.

Q. I recently heard an author interviewed who denies that Jesus was born in Bethlehem, and even seems to wonder if he existed at all. What are we to make of this? — *Arthur Johns*

A lot of modern skepticism regarding Jesus and details of Scripture center around a rather stubborn refusal to regard the Gospels as a historical source. This a priori assumption about the historical reliability of the Scriptures is a kind of skepticism that surrounds almost no other historical documents.

More has been recorded about Jesus than almost any other person in history. There are four rich essays depicting his life, which we call the Gospels, and more than a dozen epistles. These combine both eyewitness and credibly collected accounts by others who lived at or very near the time of Jesus.

Some modern scholars like to dismiss these accounts because they are written from the perspective of faith. But all history is written from some perspective. Simply excluding Scripture as a historical source, therefore, is not reasonable, nor does it comport with approaches we use in studying other historical figures and events.

Q. I was reading an article that says the Magi didn't actually visit Jesus in Bethlehem as Nativity sets depict. Is this true, or just more modern skepticism? — *Brian MacArthur*

While there is plenty of modern skepticism and a tendency to be hypercritical of even small biblical differences, the article you refer to is probably making a valid point.

The biblical references to the visit of the Magi are vague as to time frame. Further, the text that describes their visit says, "And going into the house they saw the child with Mary his mother" (Mt 2:11). As we can see, the Gospel speaks of them finding Jesus in a house (*oikia*), not a cave apart from an inn or other proper dwelling. So, there would seem to be some undetermined period of time from Christmas night when the shepherds found Christ and when the Magi found him.

Some scholars think this could be as long as two years later, since Herod called for the death of boys two years old and younger. However, it does not seem likely that Joseph and Mary would stay two years in Bethlehem, since they went there originally to register for a census. Therefore, it may have been much sooner after Jesus' birth that the Magi came. But the location does seem to have been different than the actual place of birth.

Nativity sets and many stories and songs of the Nativity weave together many details from the Gospels of Matthew and Luke and, as such, tend to simplify what is more complex. Clearly the Scriptures must be a more fundamental source for us than carols or other cultural traditions.

Q **.** **I was reading a Catholic commentary on Scripture by a priest (I don't recall his name) who maintains that the star that guided the Magi was not a star at all but some sort of moving ball of gas in the atmosphere. Is this Catholic teaching? I have never heard this.** — *Brad Coughlin*

You were probably reading the commentary by Father Cornelius A' Lapide who speculates the star was not really a star but was formed of condensed air and dust, with brightness infused into it and moved by the angels as a guide for the Magi. This is not official Catholic teaching, just the opinion and speculation of an exegete.

My own thought of this view is that it reads too much into the text. It is true that the star is said to move, but there is no mention of its makeup at all. It is called a star and therefore no reason to doubt this.

Scripture seems more interested in mentioning the star as the fulfillment of prophecy (see Nm 24:17) than describing it in detail. The fact is the star seen by the Magi is mysterious. It was something they clearly saw and which guided them. Beyond this it is shrouded in mystery, and there is a place to simply accept that mystery and admire it, rather than try to "solve" it with theories.

Q. •Scripture says that Joseph had no relations with Mary until she bore a son and named him Jesus (see Mt 1:25). Does this imply that they had relations afterward?
— *Rosemary Easley*

The word "until" can be ambiguous without a wider context of time. It is true that in English the usual sense of until is that I am doing or not doing something now, "until" something changes, and then I start doing or not doing it. However, this is not always the case, even in Scripture.

If I were to say to you, "God be with you until we meet again," I do not mean by this that after we meet again God's blessing will cease or turn to curses. In this case until is merely being used to refer to an indefinite period of time which may or may not ever occur. Surely, I hope we meet again, but it is possible we will not, so go with God's blessings, whatever the case.

In Scripture, too, we encounter until being used merely to indicate an indefinite period whose conditions may or may not be met. Thus we read, "And Michal the daughter of Saul had no child [until] the day of her death" (2 Sm 6:23). Of course, this should not be taken to mean that she started having children after she died. Likewise, Paul says to Timothy, "[Until] I come, attend to the public reading of Scripture, to preaching, to teaching" (1 Tm 4:13). But this does not likely mean that Timothy should stop doing these things when and if Saint Paul arrives.

Thus, while it often suggests a future change of state, until does not necessarily mean that the change happens, or even *can* happen. Context is important. It is the same in the Greek language where *heos* or *heos hou* (the terms are used interchangeably and translated "until") require context to more fully understand what is being affirmed.

The teaching of the perpetual virginity of Mary does not rise or fall on one word. Rather, there is a body of evidence: Mary's question to the angel about how a betrothed virgin would conceive; Jesus entrusting Mary to the care of a non-blood relative at his death; and the long witness of ancient Tradition are some other sources.

Q. The Bible says in the Gospel of Luke that Jesus was presented in the Temple after forty days. But Matthew's account says they fled to Egypt. How can these incidents happen at the same time? — *Francis Talbot*

There is no indication that they did happen at the same time. Matthew is unclear as to the timing of the visit of the Magi. In the popular imagination, many think of the Magi visiting the same night as the shepherds, but this is unlikely. Matthew says the Magi found Jesus and Mary in a "house," not in a stable or cave. Hence some time had elapsed since the birth. It could have been days, months, or even up to two years (since Herod ordered the death of boys two years old and younger).

It is likely that the Holy Family stayed in Bethlehem after the birth of Jesus, eventually found lodging, and after forty days made the short journey to Jerusalem to present Jesus in the Temple. Returning to Bethlehem, the Magi visited sometime afterward, and the flight to Egypt took place shortly after that.

Q. In the finding of the child Jesus in the Temple, I have always had trouble with two things. First, that Joseph and Mary would not have kept watch over him and went a whole day before they knew he was missing. Second, that Jesus seemed to care little for their feelings at having lost him. Please explain. — *Rich Willems*

Two factors need to be kept in mind to understand the loss of Jesus. At age twelve, Jesus would have been considered almost an adult in the culture of the time, perhaps similar to a seventeen-year-old in our culture. It does not pertain to parents to keep as close a watch on a much older child as with a very young child.

Second, pilgrims making the journey from Galilee to Jerusalem and back (a walk of over seventy miles) often walked in fairly large groups. It was common for people to divide out, women walking with women, men with men. Older children might also walk together; the younger children would stay with their mothers.

As an older child, nearing adulthood, it is easy to understand how Jesus might have walked with a group apart from his parents. And this would go unnoticed until the evening when families would reunite. Immediately upon noticing Jesus' absence and inquiring among other relatives, they rushed back to Jerusalem to find him.

So, they were not negligent. The temporary separation from him was understandable, and immediately upon noticing it they sought him out.

As for Jesus' reaction, it is mysterious. But we need to remember that we cannot hear his tone of voice. Further, it could simply be that he was surprised, in terms of his human knowledge, at their wonderment in a genuine way, figuring they knew where he was.

Q. I heard a Protestant minister say that when Jesus drove demons out of the young boy near Mount Tabor, the boy wasn't really possessed, but just had epilepsy. Is this true? — *Mel Johnson*

Well, Jesus, who was on the scene (and rather smart), seems to have concluded differently than the preacher you mention. That said, we do not usually bring people with seizures to an exorcist, but seek always to rule out natural causes first. In rare cases, what manifests as seizures may have demonic causes, but not usually.

So, rather than second-guess Jesus, or consign biblical insights to "primitive" thinking, we do better to assess what is before us, humbly realizing that there are often many levels to human struggles. While some ailments are simply physical in origin, some may include demonic dimensions as well.

Q: **Jesus' relatives are identified as brothers and sisters due to language variables. In Luke 1:36 the word relative is used in regard to Elizabeth: "And behold, your kinswoman [relative] Elizabeth in her old age has also conceived a son." Did the original word in the Greek use "sister" for Elizabeth? If there was a word for relatives, why did the Gospels use brother and sister and not relatives when speaking of Jesus' "brothers and sisters"?** — *Leonard Loftus*

The Greek word used in Luke 1:36 is *suggenes* and does mean "relative" or "kinsman." It is from the Greek roots *syn* (with) plus *genos* (seed or offspring). Thus the word refers here to Elizabeth as being related to Mary in some physical but unspecified way. The Greek word for sisters (*adelphai*) is not used in Luke 1:36.

Why certain words are used or not is a complex question. Modern-day listeners tend to crave a kind of specificity in written texts that they do not always provide. This is likely because they did not begin as written texts, but as oral stories.

Even today we are often flexible in our use of terms such as relative, brothers and sisters, etc., when speaking. For example, when it comes to the word "brother" in its most technical sense, there are only two men on this planet who are my brothers, in that we physically share the exact same father and mother. However, on any given Sunday, I stand before hundreds of people and call them "my brothers and sisters." But here I am using the terms in a broader sense of our shared humanity, and in the spiritual sense of our shared Father in heaven.

In Jesus' day things were similar. People used terms in both the strict sense and the wider sense, freely interchanging terms like brother, cousin, relative, etc. Many Protestants today, seeing references to Jesus' brothers and sisters, simply presume these terms were meant in a very strict sense, and that such references therefore disprove that Mary was ever-virgin.

But in this matter the Church would argue that they have fallen into a linguistic fallacy by insisting that the terms can only be interpreted in the strictest sense. The early Church was not unaware of these references, nor troubled by them as she handed on the sacred Tradition of Mary's perpetual virginity. Rather, the terms brothers and sisters were understood by the Church more broadly to mean cousins, and this is the ancient sense of those texts.

Q. **Please explain why Nathanael is not considered to be the first disciple to recognize Jesus as Messiah and Son of God when Scripture has him say, "Rabbi, you are the Son of God, you are the King of Israel" (Jn 1:49). We seem to discount his statement and accept Peter's statement in Matthew 16:16: "You are the Christ, the Son of the living God." — *Name withheld***

When you ask why we do this, it is important to note it is actually Jesus who does this. We will have to wait and ask Jesus why he responded with great solemnity to Saint Peter yet seems little more than amused with what Saint Bartholomew (Nathanael) says. That said, permit the following provisional answer to your question.

At one level, the two responses do seem similar. But in analyzing the texts we must first notice some linguistic differences. Nathanael refers to Jesus as the "King of Israel," whereas Peter calls him "the Christ." And though some Scripture scholars think that first-century Jews would have used these terms interchangeably, they are nevertheless not identical. The term Christ (Greek for Messiah) is more theologically precise.

Second, we must remember that context is important. Nathanael makes his comment as an early and almost ecstatic claim. Peter, however, makes his declaration after Jesus has spent time teaching and leading the apostles. Although the Father inspires his utterance, it is also rooted in the formation he has received from Jesus.

There may be many other factors that are unknown to us simply in reading a written text. For example, there may have been significance in the tone of voice, or the look on the face of Peter or Nathanael, that add shades of meaning. There may also have been discussions or events prior to the utterances that influence the moments.

We can only trust that the Lord Jesus not only experienced all of these contextual things, but also knew the mind and heart of those who spoke. And thus he reacts one way to Nathanael and in a more solemn way to Peter. At times, this is the best that we can do. Biblical texts supply us with what we need to know, not necessarily everything we want to know.

Q. **I am eighty-seven years old and have prayed the Lord's Prayer all my life. I was surprised to notice in certain forms among non-Catholics they say "forgive us our debts," where we say "forgive us our trespasses." What does it mean to have debts forgiven and for us to forgive our debtors?** — *Carmine Alfano*

There is no essential difference at work. "Debts" is an older English translation that has fallen away in favor of "trespasses." Both are references to sin.

The Greek word in question is *opheilemata*, which most literally refers to having debts. But debts are not understood as financial in this case. Rather, we have incurred a debt of sin. Saint Jerome, who translated the most widely used Latin translation (the Vulgate), used the Latin word *debitoribus*, which most naturally came into English as debts. Later, because of the tendency of debt to refer more exclusively to financial matters, the term trespasses became a more common translation in English. However, trespasses has its problems, too, since it tends in current English to mean that I am illegally on someone else's property.

Currently, there are those who want to simply say "forgive us our sins as we forgive those who sin against us." But this loses some of what the original Greek, and likely the Lord, conveyed. For what is said here is not merely that we sinned (in some abstract sense), but that we have incurred an enormous debt, and that we have strayed into places we have no business being. Indeed, our debt is huge. The Lord, in summoning us to forgive one another as we have been forgiven, speaks of a man who owed ten thousand talents (an almost unimaginable amount). But that man is us.

So, sin is not an abstraction, it is a very heavy debt we cannot pay on our own. This is what the Greek word *opheilemata* (debts) is conveying.

Q. **Jesus drove out some demons into a herd of swine, which ran down a bluff, into the water, and drowned. Could not such an action be construed as cruelty to animals?** — *Peter Tate*

Well, the pigs are not really the point of the story, and we ought not to get too focused on them. More to the point of the story is the authority of Jesus Christ to cast out demons.

One might respond to the cruelty charge that the Lord has the capacity and authority to do this to the pigs, just as you and I might go to our garden, uproot withered tomatoes, and replace them with corn. Further, having authority over animals, we also lead pigs to slaughterhouses.

One might still argue that driving the demons into the pigs was an arbitrary and unnecessary act by Jesus. But perhaps the Lord had reasons. For example, he may have wished to inspire a holy fear in those who saw the action. It was surely a memorable action, and while the townsfolk initially reacted with fear, it would seem they later welcomed Jesus back with faith (see Mk 5:17–20; 7:31). Hence Jesus made use of the animals to bring blessings to human beings, which is fitting.

Culturally, pigs were considered by the Jewish people to be unclean animals. Thus the pigs also help to fittingly illustrate the uncleanness of demons, and the fate of those who persist in uncleanness.

Q. **A priest told us recently at Mass that Jesus did not actually multiply the loaves and fishes; he just got people to share; that this is the real miracle. Is this so?** — *Name withheld*

No, it is not so. Jesus actually multiplied the loaves and fishes. The spin given in these words is a rather tired and dated notion that developed in the 1970s. It has a seemingly clever insight with a moral imperative, that if we learn to share, there will always be enough.

Denying that a true and plainly described miracle took place is not respectful of the text. Jesus says plainly, they have no food (see Mt 15:32). The apostles observe the same and offer as evidence a mere five loaves and two fish. Further, the texts are clear that it is from *these* five loaves and two fishes that Jesus feeds the multitude miraculously. The apostles take and distribute the food from these very sources. There is no indication whatsoever that people started taking out other food that they had been hiding and learned to share.

Q. In one of the Gospels, Jesus talks about leaving nine-ty-nine sheep to go in search of one stray sheep, and he says the ninety-nine have no need to repent. But I thought we were all sinners. What does Jesus mean that the ninety-nine don't need to repent? — *Ben Johnson*

According to a well-established tradition among the Greek Fathers of the Church, such as Irenaeus, Gregory of Nyssa, Gregory Nazianzus, Cyril of Jerusalem, and others, the ninety-nine who have no need to repent are the angels. The straying or lost sheep is wayward humanity.

The verse you reference is Luke 15:7: "Just so, I tell you, there will be more joy in heaven over one sinner who repents than over ninety-nine righteous persons who need no repentance." Note that the verse refers to the rejoicing "in heaven." And this would seem to strengthen the notion that the ninety-nine are the angels, who at that time would have been the sole occupants of heaven other than God. And so, too, on this account, it can be said that Jesus "leaves" them and goes in search of the one straying sheep (us). And this refers to his Incarnation and to his saving work among us.

Finally, angels have no need to repent, since their "yes" to God is once and for all. They do not sin or need to repent.

Q. You stated in a previous column the ninety-nine sheep who need no repentance are the angels, who at that time would have been the sole occupants of heaven other than God. What about the Transfiguration, which describes Jesus speaking with Moses and Elijah? Where did they come from? — *Richard Juetten*

The tradition about the ninety-nine sheep being angels is the common explanation of the early Fathers of the Church. As for Moses and Elijah (and we might add Enoch, who Scripture says was taken to God without dying [see Gn 5:24; Heb 11:5]), where exactly they were prior to Christ reopening the gates of heaven is not clear.

Scripture uses the word "heaven" in different senses. Sometimes it means areas above the earth, where the clouds and the rain are. Sometimes a higher or second heaven is referred to where the stars and planets are. At other times it refers to the abode of God, sometimes called the third heaven. When Saint Paul speaks of being caught up into the "third heaven" (2 Cor 12:2), he is most surely speaking of the very abode of God, and he speaks of such glory as cannot be described.

When Moses, Elijah, and Enoch are taken up to heaven, we cannot be certain exactly where they abided. However, it seems very unlikely that they were taken to the third heaven and beheld the very face of God. That surely had to wait for Christ and his ascension with all the members of his Body, the Church, to take his seat at the Father's right hand. But there is no other way to the Father except through Christ. Thus it is more likely that Moses, Elijah, and Enoch were taken to some heavenly realm instead of Sheol (the usual abode of the dead that was shadowy and generally described in unpleasant terms). But they were not likely taken into the very presence of the Father.

Q.I was taught that wisdom and prudence were good. But why then does Jesus praise his Father for hiding things from the wise and prudent (see Mt 11:25)? — *William Lewis*

Strictly speaking, in Catholic theology we limit the term "wisdom" to refer to a gift of the Holy Spirit by which we lay hold of sacred truths pertaining to God and the things of heaven. And we use the term "knowledge" to refer to the gift of the Spirit whereby we lay hold of the things of this world and see how they relate to our last end, our goal of holiness and heaven. Prudence, strictly defined, is an infused virtue which enables us to see the best way or means to attain our goals of holiness and heaven. It is distinct from the acquired and natural virtue of prudence.

However, the strict sense of these terms as used in theology and in certain catechetical settings is not always used in other settings. Many Bible texts, such as the one you cite, use these terms in a wider sense, and distinctions are important to understand what is being praised or condemned.

Thus Scripture does speak to a "wisdom" of this world which is folly to God (1 Cor 3:19). The same text says that God catches the wise in their craftiness. But here wisdom is not being used in the strict theological sense of an infused virtue in which one grasps the things of God. Rather, it is being used in a wider (and negative) sense to refer to the "ways of this world" — in other words, to the tactics and knowledge of those who know how to navigate this world in an astute, clever, or even cunning way to achieve worldly ends. As such, prudence is also understood more as a slyness or cunning. It is not understood in such passages as the virtue whereby one avoids rash decisions or hasty judgments; instead, it gives careful consideration to the way forward given one's goals of holiness and heaven.

Q. Why did Jesus tell a man whose father had just died to let the dead bury their dead and that he should follow him immediately? This seems very harsh. — *Mary Ludwig*

The context of Matthew 8:22, which you cite, is not necessarily that the man's father has just died. It could be that the man is saying he will follow more intensely in the years to come after his father has died.

Jesus therefore rebukes the notion common to many of us that we can always find some good reason not to follow him today, but wait until I am retired or healthier, etc. Thus Jesus' teaching is, essentially, "No more excuses, follow me wholeheartedly now or be consigned to the ranks of those whose faith is dead."

The context and focus of this section of the Gospel of Matthew is on the urgency of discipleship and how many allow worldly demands and preoccupations to eclipse the priority of faith and discipleship they should have.

Q. In Luke's Gospel, Jesus said, "Leave the dead to bury their own dead; but as for you, go and proclaim the kingdom of God" (9:60). What did that mean? Sounds a bit harsh. — *Name withheld*

The context of this passage is important. Here is the fuller text: "To another he said, 'Follow me.' But he said, 'Lord, let me first go and bury my father.' But he said to him, "Leave the dead to bury their own dead; but as for you, go and proclaim the kingdom of God'" (Lk 9:59–60).

To be sure, the text is blunt, but we want to set aside at least one aspect of its harshness. The Greek text does not necessarily mean that the man's father has just died. It is an active, aorist participle in the dative case. Another interpretation is that the man is saying in effect, "My father is getting up in years, and when he does eventually die and I have buried him, then I can commit myself to following you." Thus it need not be seen that Jesus is rebuking a man who has just experienced a loss.

That said, there *is* an impatience that Jesus expresses for this man and, by extension, for many of us. For indeed, too easily do we set aside the demands of discipleship and try to postpone them until something in our life is a little better. Perhaps when we have retired, or met some other set of obligations, *then* we will more wholeheartedly be a disciple of Jesus! Jesus is dismissive of this notion. He does not want a place on our list; he is our list. The works of this world are ultimately the works of death. This world has one thing finally to offer us: a stone-cold tomb. We are summoned to radically reconsider our priorities, but many of us resist this.

All of us are called to examine our priorities and see if they are focused on the works of Christ, not the works of death.

Q•**The Gospel records Jesus as saying the following: "If you then, who are evil, know how to give good gifts to your children, how much more will your Father who is in heaven give good things to those who ask him!" (Mt 7:11). It seems a bit harsh for Jesus to refer to mankind as "evil." Can you explain?** — *Gerry Reeding*

The Greek text underlying the translation "evil" is rather intensive and clear: *poneroi hyparchontes. Poneroi* means "bad, of a bad nature or condition." *Hyparchontes* is translated as "from the very beginning" or "being inherently so."

Thus the translation focusing on "you ... who are evil" is accurate, but more precisely translated as, "If you then, being evil from the beginning." So, it seems the bottom-line analysis of the text in Greek is that we're stuck with the fact that the Lord is calling us "evil."

Venerable Bede, a seventh-century monk, interprets the phrase to refer to "the human mortal, weak and still burdened with sinful flesh ... earthly and weak, [but] children whom he loves" (*Homilies on the Gospel*, 2.14).

Hence we need not interpret the Lord's words as merely harsh. Jesus, it would seem, is speaking by comparison or degree here. He does not likely mean that we are evil in an absolute sense, rather, that we are evil in comparison to God, who is absolute good. The Hebrew and Aramaic languages have fewer comparative words, and ancient Jews would often use absolute categories to set forth comparison or degree. Hence Jesus is setting forth a comparison in a Jewish sort of way. In modern English we might say, "If you then, who are not nearly as holy as God and are prone to sin, know how to give good gifts to your children, how much more will God, who is absolutely good and not prone to sin, give good things to those who ask him?"

However, the point of the hyperbole should not be missed or set aside. Created things may share in God's goodness, but God *alone* is absolutely good. So good is God that everything else is nearly evil in comparison to him. The hyperbole places the emphasis on God's absolute goodness. We have no goodness apart from God's goodness. Thus, Bede says in the same place, "the apostles even, who by the merit of their election had exceeded the goodness of mankind in general, are said to be evil in comparison with Divine goodness, since nothing is of itself good but God alone."

Q: As I understand it, Jesus came as Savior for all. Yet Jesus spoke in parables, and when asked why, he says that knowledge of the mysteries of heaven has not been granted to everyone (see Mt 13:10–17). I am puzzled. It seems as if Jesus is speaking in code and purposely excluding many, especially those in most need of his mercy. Would you please help me understand? — *Robert McBride*

It may seem in this passage that God (somewhat arbitrarily) grants knowledge of the Kingdom to some, but not others. Yet we ought to note that the Lord explains himself and that his explanation discloses the part we play in the reception of the gift of the Kingdom.

Regarding those to whom the knowledge of the mysteries of the Kingdom is not given, the Lord says: "For this people's heart has grown dull, / and their ears are heavy of hearing, / and their eyes they have closed, / lest they should perceive with their eyes, / and hear with their ears, / and understand with their heart, / and turn for me to heal them" (Mt 13:15).

So, the Lord wants to heal them, but their hardened hearts and resistant minds mean that they just won't listen or be converted. To them the Lord speaks in parables, most of which are in the form of a riddle. But riddles have the capacity to both disclose and hide. As such, they incite curiosity, and curiosity is actually a good way to engage people who are otherwise disinterested in what is being said. In effect, people are left asking questions and may be drawn to seek answers.

Ideally our hearts are open to hearing the truth. And in this context, a more thorough and lengthy teaching disclosing more of the mysteries of the kingdom is suitable. And to such as these the Lord says, "Blessed are your eyes, for they see, and your ears, for they hear" (Mt 13:16). In other words, you receive blessings because you are willing to listen and have not hardened your hearts. Therefore, "To you it has been given to the know the secrets of the kingdom of heaven" (Mt 13:11).

In the end, the teaching for us is that we should not, through hardened hearts, force God to speak to us in riddles. Rather, through open and tender hearts, we should permit him to speak to us at length and usher us into the mysteries of the Kingdom.

Q: **I heard a preacher on the radio say recently that when Jesus said it was easier for a camel to go through the eye of needle than for a rich man to saved, he was actually referring to a short, narrow gate in Jerusalem called the "eye of the needle." Is this so?** — *Lawrence Elliot*

No, not likely. There is a tendency at times to over-explain certain texts of the Bible. This is especially the case with odd or idiomatic expressions that come down to us from biblical times. Such expressions are seldom to be taken literally.

Consider that in English we have usual and idiomatic expressions such as, "It was raining cats and dogs," "The world is upside down," or "I'm living in a lunatic asylum!" Thousands of years from now it would be fruitless for linguists to look for literal or physical explanations for these phrases, and we'd probably have a good laugh if we could overhear them doing it.

Expressions we use like these are odd, but they surely do not mean that actual dogs and cats are falling from the sky, or that the planet has reversed its axis, or that a given speaker actually spent time in a mental institution. These are examples of hyperbole. Hyperbole is a form of exaggeration used to emphasize the point being made. Thus the hyperbole of these expressions is meant to emphasize that the rain was very heavy, that the world is dramatically changed, and that there is a lot of "crazy" stuff going on. Looking for explanations other than "this is hyperbole" is to over-explain them and thus miss the point.

In Jesus' image of a camel going through the eye of a needle (see Mt 19:24), the simplest explanation for Jesus' expression, based on the overall context, is that he is using hyperbole. He is saying that it is very difficult for us in our richness to enter the kingdom of God. Indeed, it is so astonishingly difficult to save us in our stubbornness, pride, resistance, and obtuseness that only God can do it. Our only hope is to surrender to God's grace and mercy by recognizing our utter poverty of the holiness needed to find heaven.

Looking for some sort of low gate in the ancient walls of Jerusalem misses the radicalism of the point Jesus is making and seems an attempt to soften a teaching that ought not be softened: We are in absolute need of God's grace to be saved. Further, there is no evidence of this so-called explanation from the ancient world that small or narrow gates were often called "the eye of the needle." This explanation appears to have emerged less than 100 years ago.

Q: In Saint John's Gospel, Chapter 8 describes the woman caught in adultery. Wasn't the man with whom she was committing adultery subject to the same consequences? Why is he not also brought before Jesus? — *B. Quinn*

Yes, he should have been subject to the same penalty. Scripture says, "If a man is found lying with the wife of another man, both of them shall die, the man who lay with the woman, and the woman; so you shall purge the evil from Israel" (Dt 22:22). And again, "If a man commits adultery with the wife of his neighbor, both the adulterer and the adulteress shall be put to death" (Lv 20:10).

That only the woman is brought shows the hypocrisy and duplicity of those who report this woman to Jesus. The text of John 8 says the woman was caught in the very act of committing adultery, so they know very well who the man was. It is difficult to say if this example of accusing the woman and not the man was widespread in Israel at the time of Jesus. Many today assume a kind of duplicity in the ancient world regarding these matters, but again we are not sure.

What is clear here is that only the woman is reported. Jesus does not point to this fact, but more personally appeals to each accuser by his action of tracing on the ground, and thus some sort of record of sin exists for those who accuse her as well. One by one they leave. Perhaps among the things the Lord records there is something of their duplicity in not reporting the man as well.

Q. Jesus says, "I have not come to call the righteous, but sinners to repentance" (Lk 5:32). But I thought the Scriptures said that no one is righteous and that to say we are without sin made God a liar. Why does Jesus imply that there are some who are righteous? — *Steven Manning*

Jesus may be using the expression ironically, as if to say, "Well, since God is in the business of saving sinners, maybe you'd better get into the category 'sinner,' if you seek his graces." Jesus is not affirming necessarily that there is a category of human beings who are righteous in an absolute or unqualified sense. As you point out, that would be contrary to the Word of God and common sense.

However, culturally speaking, the term "righteous" at the time of Jesus also had another sense. The righteous were a category of pious Jews who carefully followed a body of law, some 613 precepts, which regulated not only the moral life, but also a great deal of daily life. It emphasized many external behaviors, mandating washings and other purifications, the manner in which one dressed, days of fasting, etc. The observers of this rather strict code, because of these externalities, often stood out, even as Hassidic Jews do today. They went by various descriptions: the Righteous (ones), the Just, Observers of the Law. The Pharisees were certainly the most numerous of those identified in this manner.

The term righteous did not necessarily mean sinless in an absolute sense. But, when you start to call yourself righteous and those who do not follow your way — that is, sinners — something happens in your soul. A superiority begins to manifest and matters that are not essential (such as certain ritual purifications or types of clothing) come to be seen as essential. Thus the Pharisees by Jesus' time were often depicted in a cartoonish way as prideful, aware of everyone's sins but their own, and legalistic. It is a sad display of the sins of the pious. There is beauty in their conformity to God's law, and an orderliness to their life that is appealing. But there is also a great ugliness to the pride that so easily grows and mars what is good.

Jesus uses the terms righteous and sinner in the verse you cite in both senses. It is a sociological category (strict observers of the law versus those who were less strict). But the terms are also used in a more ironic sense where Jesus, in effect, pokes fun at the Pharisees' objection that he cares for sinners.

Q. •Regarding Matthew 24, it would seem Jesus' predictions on Jerusalem's ruin were fulfilled. However, what of his descriptions of alterations in the sun, moon, and stars? Were these fulfilled? — *Paul Forester*

Biblical scholars have differing opinions on what elements of the Mount of Olives discourse relate to the destruction of Jerusalem in AD 70, and what might refer to the end of the world. Some of the details quite clearly relate to the events of AD 70, such as wars, Jerusalem becoming surrounded by armies, etc. Even some other details, such as earthquakes and famines, occurred around that time.

Other details may be references to the end of the world — for example, the sun and moon darkened, signs in the heavens, and the Son of Man coming on the clouds — or they may also have occurred in AD 70. Josephus, a historian at that time, describes clouds of smoke as Jerusalem burned, which dimmed the sun, the moon, and stars. He also describes strange wonders in the heavens, possibly a comet, and strange lights near and above the Temple at night.

A balanced approach would be to acknowledge that all the signs had a historical reference, rooted in AD 70, but also symbolically point to the end of the world, of which Jerusalem is a sign. As for Christ coming, this is prophetic language and an image of judgment on ancient Israel for lack of faith. It is also clear that Jesus will come in judgment on this world as well.

Q. Matthew 25:31–46 describes that the Lord will judge fiercely those who did not give food to the hungry, drink to the thirsty, etc. But what about those who take advantage of the charity of others and are either lazy or break immigration laws and so forth? — *Albert Dee*

They, like any of us, will have to answer to God for what they did or failed to do. But our summons to what is just and charitable does not cease because some take advantage or are not sinless in their need. It is a general norm to care for the poor, and it is required of us. There may be individual cases where we discover that we are not helping an individual but only facilitating their sin, and we can adapt the general norm to the specific case.

At a larger level, too, the obligation to care for the poor can have undesirable effects such as creating welfare dependence, etc. But the solution to this must seek to fix the problem, not wholly cast aside our general obligation to care for others.

We fix what we can, but some things have to be left to God and to the Day of Judgment. Meanwhile, we err on the side of care.

Q. I was talking with a Protestant friend who scoffed at the literal interpretation of "This is my body" by saying, Jesus also said, "I am the door." How should I answer this objection? — *Emma Simthson*

As with any written text, some sophistication is necessary when reading the Scriptures. All-or-nothing approaches which hold that the Bible is to be read in an entirely literalist way, or that it is all merely symbolic, must be avoided. The more authentic question is, Which texts are to be read and understood literally, and which texts employ metaphor, simile, hyperbole, or other literary techniques?

To cite your friend's example, it would be strange to read Jesus literally when he says, "I am the door" (Jn 10:9). This would require us to think of Jesus as a large wooden plank, with a doorknob. It is reasonable to conclude that Jesus is speaking metaphorically when he says this, since the specific context of the saying, and the wider context of the overall Scriptures, in no way encourage us to think that Jesus spoke in a literalistic manner here.

When it comes to the Eucharist, however, there is a very different conclusion to be reasonably reached. When Jesus says over the bread, "This is my body," and over the wine, "This is my blood," we are on good ground to conclude that he is not speaking metaphorically, but literally. This is because the wider context of Scripture supplies and insists upon a literal interpretation.

In particular, Jesus insists in John 6 that the bread he gives is his true flesh for the life of the world. The Jewish people listening to him that day understood him to be speaking literally, and most of them scoffed and murmured in protest. Though Jesus could have corrected their interpretation and insisted he was only speaking metaphorically, he did nothing of the sort. Rather, he intensified a literalist interpretation by insisting that they must eat his flesh and drink his blood. Many, horrified at this, left him and would no longer walk in his company.

Thus Jesus pays a rather high price for a literal (not a metaphorical) understanding of the fact that holy Communion is in fact a receiving of his true body and true blood. Saint Paul also teaches that holy Communion is a partaking of the Body and Blood of Christ, and he insists that those who receive it unworthily sin against the body of the Lord.

A final bit of contextual evidence in this case is supplied by the fact that the early Church, as witnessed in the writings of the Fathers, universally understood these words in a literal way.

Hence we are on good ground in insisting that the utterances of Jesus, "This is my body" and "This is my blood" are to be interpreted literally. This also illustrates the kind of sophistication necessary when approaching sacred Scripture.

Q. •I read in a certain spiritual work that at the Last Supper the holy Eucharist returned to being bread only when received by the traitor Judas Iscariot. Is this true? — *W. B. Flores*

No, when the bread and wine are consecrated and become the body, blood, soul, and divinity of Jesus Christ, this effects a permanent and substantial change, such that the Body and Blood of Christ will not go back to being something else. Further, there is no reason biblically or theologically to hold that the case of Judas would be any different.

Q. •Why did Judas betray Jesus? — *Robert Bonsignore*

When we consider this, we must first recall that we are dealing with what Saint Paul referred to as the mystery of iniquity or lawlessness (see 2 Thes 2:7). This mystery is bigger than why Judas specifically sinned. Why did Lucifer and the other angels, who did not have the weakness of concupiscence, rebel? Why did Adam and Eve, who were sinless and knew God and walked with him in the garden, rebel? It is a deep and shocking mystery. For that matter, why do *we* sin? It is true we possess the weakness of a fallen nature, but we know better and experience the harm that our sins cause us and others, and still we do it. This is the mystery of iniquity, a sort of "dark side" to the radical freedom that human and angelic persons were given. At its heart, it is deeply mysterious.

That said, Scripture speaks to Judas's betrayal as rooted in his yielding to Satan: "Satan entered into Judas called Iscariot, who was of the number of the Twelve; he went away and conferred with the chief priests and captains how he might betray him to them" (Lk 22:3–4).

There were storm clouds gathering for Judas by which he may have opened the door to Satan. Scripture reveals that he was a thief, stealing from the common moneybag (see Jn 12:6). Jesus also hints that Judas was grieved by the Bread of Life discourse where many left Jesus when he insisted that they must eat his flesh and drink his blood. Jesus said: "'Did I not choose you, the Twelve, and one of you is a devil.' He spoke of Judas the son of Simon Iscariot" (Jn 6:70–71).

Psychologically, we can only guess as to Judas's motivation. The most likely explanation is that he was disillusioned and impatient when Jesus did not measure up to the common Jewish notion of the Messiah as a warrior and revolutionary, overthrowing Roman power and reestablishing the kingdom of David. Judas may have been a member of the Zealots or influenced by them. Zealots were seldom interested in hearing of their need for personal healing and repentance, let alone the call to love their enemies. But this is only speculative in regard to Judas. His personal motivations remain to a large degree shrouded in the mystery of iniquity.

Q. •Somewhere in Scripture it is written that a naked **man was seen running from the scene of Jesus' arrest. Where is this, and what does it mean?** — *Joan Beaulieu*

It is in the Gospel of Mark: "A young man followed him, with nothing but a linen cloth about his body; and they seized him, he left the linen cloth and ran away naked" (14:51–52).

Who this young man is, and the exact meaning of this passage, is rather debated and uncertain. Most modern scholars think the young man is Mark himself, who is describing a humorous story of when his faith was not strong. Note, he is described as a young man, meaning possibly younger than twelve, which may explain why he was lightly clothed. Just like today, youngsters are often permitted to wear fewer clothes. Some also see the image of youthful virility in this description of his being clothed lightly, since the description of the clothing points also to gym clothing.

However, we should recall that naked in the Jewish use of the term rarely meant complete nakedness. The Greek word here is *gymnos*, which referred to one who was wearing only his inner tunic, not an outer tunic. In our culture it would be akin to a person wearing underwear. So, the image of the man running off stark naked is not likely what the text asserts here; only that his outer tunic was torn away and he ran off wearing only his inner tunic.

The meaning of the text is much debated. However, two explanations seem most likely. First, there is the link to Genesis 39:12 described by several Fathers of the Church. In that passage Joseph, seeking to escape the seduction of the wife of Potiphar, flees naked. Thus the Christian must be prepared to leave everything behind to avoid the snares of the sinful.

A second explanation focuses on the youthful strength of the young man as inadequate and ties the event to a prophecy of Amos: "'And he who is stout of heart among the mighty shall / flee away naked in that day,' says the LORD" (2:16). The text indicates the weakness of even strong men and the need for God to save us.

Q: In Luke 23:44, the writer states that an eclipse of the sun took place at the time of Christ's crucifixion. Is there a basis of fact as to its occurrence? And, if so, was this solar eclipse coincidental and in accord with the laws of science? — *Chick P.*

It isn't biblically accurate to insist it was an eclipse (at least as we use the term today) that caused the darkness. The Gospels of Matthew, Mark, and Luke speak to the darkness using the Greek term *skotos*, meaning, simply, "darkness." Only Luke goes on to state the reason for the darkness: "the sun's light failed" (23:45), and even he uses the Greek word *eklipontos*, from which we get the English word eclipse. But in Greek the word simply means darkened, while for us it refers to a particular kind of darkening due to the moon blocking the light of the sun and casting a shadow. That is not necessarily or even likely what Luke means here.

As a general rule we should avoid applying scientific or other meanings to texts that are more specific than the author intends. That there was darkness over the land from noon till 3:00 p.m. is certainly attested in the sacred texts. But the cause of that darkness is asserted to be an eclipse as we scientifically use the term today. Perhaps God made use of other natural causes, such as very heavy clouds, to cause the light of the sun to dim. But it is also possible that the darkness was of purely supernatural origin and was experienced only by some.

Hence trying to explain the darkness simply in terms of "the laws of science" risks doing disservice to the text by missing its deeper meaning — namely, that the darkness of sin has reached its height. Whatever the mechanism of the darkness, its deepest cause is sin and evil.

Jesus says elsewhere, "This is the judgment, that the light has come into the world, and men loved darkness rather than light, because their deeds were evil" (Jn 3:19). He also says, referring to his passion, "Night comes, when no one can work" (Jn 9:4). And when Judas leaves the Last Supper to betray Jesus, John observes simply and profoundly, "And it was night" (Jn 13:30). Yes, deep darkness had come upon the world.

You ask if there is a "basis of fact" that this darkness actually occurred. Though a few modern scholars consider it a mere literary device, there seems little reason to doubt that it actually occurred. While some refer to a purported letter of Pontius Pilate to Tiberius that verifies it, the historical value of the document is highly disputed. Yet three of the Gospels record it, and most of the Fathers of the Church treat the darkness as historical.

That said, how widely experienced, and how deep the dark, is not specified. We should balance accepting its historicity with an appreciation that the texts are restrained in terms of precise details.

Q .In Luke's Gospel, there is mention of the good thief
• on the cross near Jesus who repents. No name is giv-
en him, but most say his name is Dismas. Is this true? — *B.*
Quinn

We don't know. The story itself is quite moving and there is naturally a human tendency to want to know more. Thus traditions
and legends often set up in cases like these. But the historical ac-
curacy of such things is often difficult to assess. Saint Dismas is a
name that tradition supplies us in the Western Church. However,
other names have also accrued to him in the East and in other eras
such as Titus, Zoatham, Demas, and Rach.

As interesting as these traditions may be, we sometimes miss
the main point when biblical figures are not named. Here, if you
are prepared to accept it, *you* are a good thief who "steals heaven";
if you are willing to repent, take up your cross, be crucified with
Jesus, and persevere to the end, asking God's mercy and admission
to his kingdom.

The good thief was not so much good as he was smart. He
knew that he was a sinner, justly condemned, and that his only
hope was grace and mercy. Having repented, he turns (which is
what conversion means) to Jesus and, in faith, seeks his salvation.
Jesus says, "Him who comes to me I will not cast out" (Jn 6:37). And
thus he is saved. Smart!

Q .I heard a Protestant use the story of the good thief
• on the cross to say that instant salvation at an "altar
call" is possible. What are your thoughts? — *Paul VanHoudt*

Part of that claim hinges on an interpretation of Jesus' words that
are not consistent with the context of Jesus' words. If "today" is
interpreted literally, then the words were not fulfilled for the good
thief. Jesus himself did not go to paradise that very day. Rather, he
descended to Sheol, to the place of the dead. So Jesus, by using the

word today, does not necessarily mean, "this very day, before sundown." Further, the Greek text can also be read to say, "And so today I tell you, you will be with me in paradise."

Yet even in the Catholic understanding, instant (or quick) salvation is possible if one is baptized and dies shortly thereafter without sin. But baptism followed by quick death is rare. The Catholic understanding of salvation is not a mere change in legal status (as many Protestants understand it). Salvation means being in heaven. More commonly the Catholic Church uses this passage of the good thief to illustrate baptism of desire.

Q. **Matthew says that both thieves on the crosses next to Jesus derided him. But Luke says only one did and the other honored him. Which is true, and why this difference?**
— *Paul Bonaserra*

The most common and likely answer is that not every Gospel records every detail of each event described. Thus it would seem that Matthew (see 27:44) and Mark (15:32) speak in a general way of the robbers on either side deriding Jesus. But Luke (23:39–43) supplies the detail that one of them, at some point, repented of this.

This should not surprise or trouble us. We often recount events — for example, a recent trip somewhere — with a different level of detail based on our purpose and our audience, the amount of time we have to speak, etc. We may leave whole details out and elaborate others. We do not thereby deny the events we do not recount. We simply focus on the details that seem most opportune to share. The main point is that there is no essential or absolute conflict in the texts of Matthew, Mark, and Luke.

Q. In Bible study we recently discussed Jesus saying from the cross, "My God, my God, why have you forsaken me?" (Mt 27:46). Was Jesus merely reciting Psalm 22, or was he crying out in pain and giving voice to a kind of despair? — *Paul Hummel*

With sacred Scripture, there are many levels of meaning at work. You are correct in observing that Jesus is quoting from Psalm 22. And many argue, with good merit, that by quoting the first line of Psalm 22 Jesus intends the whole of that psalm for himself and us.

In Psalm 22, we are alerted to the many ways in which prophecies are being fulfilled. It speaks of an afflicted man who feels downcast, but also mentions others who divide his garments among them and cast lots for his vesture; who pierce his hands and feet; and who ridicule him in his suffering. And all these prophecies are being fulfilled as Jesus is on the cross.

Psalm 22 is also an important catechism for us about suffering because, considered as a whole, it is not a psalm of despair and grief, but one of trust and hope in God's deliverance. It recalls how God has delivered devout men and women in the past and asserts that God never spurns those who cry out to him in their misery. The psalmist confidently expects God's help and to be able, one day, to tell his descendants of the glorious things the Lord has done. While Psalm 22 surely gives voice to the pain and grief that we experience in our suffering, it also reminds us to call on the Lord and trust that he will deliver us.

So we see, first of all, that Jesus, in quoting Psalm 22, is a great teacher, even from the pulpit of the cross. We are taught to revere prophecy, and also to trust God in our afflictions.

And yet we ought not to wholly exclude that Jesus is also quoting the psalm for his own sake as well. Surely, as man, he suffered great anguish, physical and mental, emotional and spiritual, on the cross. He, for his own sake, has recourse to Psalm 22. Indeed, how often have many of us in our sufferings found in Scripture great consolation and vindication. Perhaps we will say, "This

Scripture text expresses exactly how I'm feeling!" In this there is a kind of consolation that God knows what I am experiencing and that others have endured similar trials. We also experience consolation as Scripture teaches us how God has delivered others and will in due time deliver us, too. Surely, at the human level, Psalm 22 consoled Jesus in these and other ways.

Q. **I am aware that when we say in the Creed that Jesus descended into hell, we do not mean the hell of the damned, but merely the place of the dead. But do we have any idea what that place was like? Also, were the justified and the condemned in that place together?** — *Leonard Loftus*

You are correct in your distinction between the hell of the damned, and the hell that refers to the place where all the dead were until the Messiah came. It is an unfortunate fact that in English, hell is used to refer to both places. But the Jewish people clearly distinguished between Sheol, where all who had died were detained, and the hell of the damned, which Jesus often called Gehenna.

As for what Sheol was like, we are, unfortunately, left to a great deal of conjecture. Generally, Scripture describes it as a place of darkness, as the pit (see Job 17:13–16). The state of the deceased there is described as a place of utter inactivity. The souls there would seem to be in a sleeplike, semi-comatose state. No one there is able to thank the Lord, or praise him (Is 38:18). It is a place from which no one emerges and is sometimes conceived as a kind of fortress with gates and bars (Is 38:10). It would seem that both the just and the wicked went there prior to the coming of Christ, though some are said to go down there "in peace" (1 Kgs 2:6), and some go down there in sorrow or mourning (Gn 37:35).

Further, in this sort of suspended state, there does not seem to be any mention of punishment of the wicked or reward for the just. Rather, it would seem that all waited until the Lord, who alone can deliver them from Sheol, would come (see 1 Sm 2:6; Ps 16:10). Mysteriously, God is present to those there (Ps 139:8), but how the dead might experience that presence is not described.

It is to this place that the Lord descended. As Scripture implies, he awoke the dead (see Eph 5:14) and preached to these "spirits in prison" (1 Pt 3:19). And while we have no complete biblical description of what took place, we can reasonably speculate that some among them, in particular the just, rejoiced in him and accepted him, while others, the wicked and the self-absorbed, rejected him even in death, and from there descended to the hell of the damned.

Q. **Matthew 12:40 says that Jesus was in the tomb three days and three nights. Matthew 8:31 says the Lord would rise after three days. These texts seem either erroneous or point to the fact that Jesus was crucified before Good Friday.** — *Reynaldo Yana*

In terms of the reckoning of days, your implicit premise is too strict by biblical standards. The text, in saying "days" does not necessarily mean seventy-two hours exactly. The Lord was in the tomb for one whole day, and parts of two others. The ancient Jews were comfortable in reckoning partial days as a whole day. Thus the concern for three days is addressed by understanding that day does not necessarily mean three whole days, as the ancient Jews (or Gentiles for that matter) would not have had the concern you express here. "Day" was reckoned more broadly.

The concern about three nights is a bit more complex, but has a similar solution. Part of the difficulty of the texts you refer to as indicating three nights is linguistic. The Scriptures were written in Greek, but the words of Jesus were more likely spoken in Aramaic. The Jews, like most ancients, would speak of three days and three nights as three "night-days." Therefore, the text may be trying to express in a Greek way a more complex Jewish reality which, as noted, reckons partial days as whole days but also includes the night along with the day. Today, we divide out night and day in a way the ancient Jews (and to some extent the Greeks and Romans) usually did not. Also, for us a new day begins at sunrise; for the ancient Jews the new day began at sundown. Hence the concept of "night-days."

The solution to your concerns involves three premises regarding time, which we should bring to the text. First, we ought to avoid insisting on a precision about time that the ancients did not and could not have (clocks and precise calendars are modern inventions). Second, they more comfortably reckoned partial days as whole days than we do. Third, they thought more in terms of "night-days" since the new day began at sundown.

With these premises in mind, Jesus *was* in the tomb three days and nights, since: Friday is "night-day one"; Saturday is "night-day two"; Sunday is "night-day three." As with all biblical scholarship, there are other aspects that could be explored (such as how biblical prophecies are used and understood), and not every exegete approaches the problem in the same way. But in a brief answer such as this, allow an essentially linguistic and cultural explanation to suffice.

Q. In John's Gospel, why is the head cloth of Jesus found folded separately from the rest of the burial cloths?
— *Henry*

There are different views as to what this means. The most common explanation is that John's focus on the grave linens serves to emphasize that Jesus' body was not stolen. Normally, if grave robbers stole a body, they would not expend any effort to remove the linens in which the body was tightly wrapped. Indeed, it was not usually the body they were after. Rather, it was the fine linens in which many bodies were wrapped. This is especially true of the face cloth, also called the *sudarium.*

In addition, there is a subtlety in the Greek text that seldom reaches English translations. The usual English rendering of John 20:9 is, "[Peter] saw the linen cloths lying [there]." But the Greek word *keimai* means more literally, "to lie outstretched." And thus the impression is given by John and the Greek text that the cloths are lying outstretched as if a body had been there, then disappeared, and the cloths just fell in place. There was no unwinding evident, no signs of a quick, chaotic robbery.

As for the face cloth, it was usually the most valuable linen of all. But instead of being taken as a thief would likely do, it was carefully folded. Saint John Chrysostom says of this careful folding, "For a thief would not have been so foolish as to expend so much effort on a trifling detail" (*Homilies on John*, 85.4).

Q. •Why do some of the Gospel accounts of the Resur-•rection say three women went to the tomb and others say only one? There also seem to be other differences that I can't recall. If these contradictions are real, how can I deal with them? — *Ben Acton*

The Resurrection accounts in the Gospels do have some differences in detail. How many women went out to the tomb that morning, one (see Jn 20:2), two (Mt 28:1), or three (Mk 16:1)? How many angels did they see that morning, one (Mt 28:2; Mk 16:5) or two (Lk 24:4; Jn 20:12)? Did the women run to the disciples and tell what they had seen (Mt 28:8; Lk 24:9), or did they say nothing out of fear (Mk 16:8)? Did Jesus see them first in Galilee (Mk 16:7; Mt 28:7–9) or in Jerusalem (Lk 24:33–36)? Among the apostles, did he appear to Peter first (Lk 24:34), all eleven at once (Mt. 28:16), or the eleven minus Thomas (Jn 20:24)? Did Jesus appear to them in a room (Jn 20:19) or a mountaintop (Mt 28:16)? Last, did Jesus ascend on Easter Sunday (Lk 24:50–53; Mk 16:19) or forty days later (Acts 1:3–9)?

Most of these apparent discrepancies are not actual conflicts. Upon closer examination, they are easily explained. We cannot look at them all in a short column. But as to your specific question, it would seem most likely that several women went out that morning. That John only focuses on Mary Magdalene is not a denial that others were there. Matthew and Mark, in saying two or three, may not be engaging in a headcount per se, but perhaps are engaging in generalization, such as when we say words like "couple" or "several."

We should not be surprised that there are some differences in the accounts. Even today, eyewitnesses of an event often emphasize certain details and have different recollections as to the particulars. People often summarize longer stories as well and speak only of essentials. This does not mean that the event did not happen or that unmentioned details by one person are in conflict with details mentioned by another. Given the numerous times Jesus appeared and the many people who saw him, we should not be surprised to find certain differences in the accounts.

In this light, the differences actually lend credibility to the Gospel accounts, which do not try to paper over them, but realistically report them (see CCC 642–43).

Q.**In Bible study I learned that the Gospels of Matthew and Mark do not even mention Jesus appearing in Jerusalem (as John and Luke do), and that they have the angels tell the brethren to go to Galilee where they will see Jesus. This seems like a major discrepancy. Did Jesus appear in Jerusalem or not?** — *Name withheld*

Yes, he did. To not mention something is not to deny that it happened. Consider, for example, if someone would ask you to recount your summer vacation. You might not include every single detail in your reply. Perhaps for the sake of brevity you omit some aspects of the vacation. Further, you might choose to include or exclude certain details based on the audience or person you are addressing. Perhaps to one group you would include certain aspects and to another you describe very different aspects. This is the nature of human interaction, and there is nothing necessarily dishonest or problematic about it.

Thus, for theological and pastoral reasons of their own, Matthew, Mark, Luke, and John treat different aspects of the Resurrection stories. Luke and John speak of the Jerusalem appearances as well as others, while Matthew and Mark skip right to the Galilean appearances. Perhaps they do this to keep things brief, or perhaps they know that most readers have already heard recountings from other sources. Perhaps Matthew and Mark use the Galilean appearances in order to use Galilee as a symbol of heaven, or as a return to where the disciples were first called.

As for the instruction of the angel to the women that the brethren should go to Galilee where they will see him, here, too, Matthew and Mark are likely truncating longer instructions by the angel. And they do this, likely, for the sake of brevity, and to draw our attention immediately to Galilee where they choose to focus the recollections.

Rather than destroying the credibility of the Resurrection accounts, such differences actually serve to underscore the credibility. It is clear through the variations and selection of material there were no attempts to control the message. Rather, the ordinary human modes of communication are retained as people joyfully recount the events. It makes a lot of sense that people, in recalling such stunning events, would report differences in details, or talk about only selected aspects, lest they overwhelm the listener.

Q: **During the forty days between the Resurrection and the Ascension, did Jesus stay consistently with the disciples the whole time? Or did he appear and disappear?**
— *Marty Spaulding*

It seems he did not abide consistently with them as he did before the Resurrection. Scripture says, "Eight days later, his disciples were again in the house ... Jesus came and stood among them" (Jn

20:26). This implies he did not appear to them between those eight days.

It is true that we do not have a precise chronology of the forty days after Easter. Thus we cannot say definitely how much of that time Jesus spent directly with the disciples. But it seems clear it was not every day. We may wonder why this is so.

Saint Thomas Aquinas says it was to better manifest his glory that he did not abide them simply and consistently in the familiar way he had done before. Rather, by his own authority he appeared and disappeared at will. As such he helped the disciples better grasp that he is Lord.

It is also likely he was helping accustom them to the fact that, after the Ascension, they would no longer see him as before, but instead they would encounter him mystically in the sacraments and the liturgy.

SAINT JOHN THE BAPTIST

Q: Two things about Saint John the Baptist puzzle me. He denied he was Elijah, though Jesus said he was. He also later asked Jesus whether he was the Messiah. How can we understand these things? — *Cheryl Bunch*

Regarding Saint John the Baptist's denial that he was Elijah, there are two common explanations. The Fathers and Doctors of the Church argue that John was only denying that he was Elijah reincarnate, which he presumed the questioners to be asking. He is not specifically denying that he goes about in the spirit and power or office of Elijah.

A second, more psychological explanation is simply to point to the humanness of John. It does not pertain to the human person to have plenary knowledge of things, even of the things pertaining to our own stance before God. Part of our journey in this life is to come to understand the man or woman God has created us to be. What the Lord knows of us is surely greater than what we know of ourselves. Thus Jesus knows that Saint John is the Elijah figure prophesied in Malachi 4, but John does not yet appreciate this about himself. As a prophet, Saint John accurately points to Christ, but it does not follow that he is infallible in his knowledge of other things, including himself. Hence, if his self-knowledge is flawed or not yet fully understood, it need not trouble us, for he was still inspired by God to recognize the Christ, point to him, and prepare others for his coming.

Regarding Saint John's later question to Jesus from jail, "Are you he who is to come, or shall we look for another?" (Mt 11:3), the solutions are similar. The Fathers and Doctors of the early Church surmise that Saint John is asking this question on behalf of his disciples to reassure them, but also that Saint John himself had no doubts at all.

Another explanation is more willing to posit that perhaps Saint John is, to some degree, discouraged. He had presented a picture of the Messiah as ushering in the Kingdom in a rather fiery and sudden way, bringing justice for the oppressed (see Mt 3:11–12). But instead of this, John is oppressed in jail and Jesus is more gently calling disciples, healing the sick, and patiently summoning people to repentance. So perhaps John's question is authentically his, not just asked on behalf of others.

The approach in this understanding is less to lionize the biblical saints and more to emphasize that even great saints have their struggles and difficulties in understanding God's ways. Some today are appreciative of these sorts of insights, others are alarmed and even scandalized by them. As a preacher and disciple, I do not share the alarm that humanized explanations of biblical figures may cause; it makes their witness more credible and courageous. Whatever John's inner struggles (if they existed at all), he fulfilled the task of preparing God's people and pointing to Jesus. He died courageously as a martyr for the truth.

Q. In Matthew 11:11, Jesus says that John the Baptist is the greatest among those born of women. Aren't both Mary and Jesus greater than John, and weren't they both born of women? — *Paul VanHoudt*

But Jesus adds, "Yet he who is least in the kingdom of heaven is greater than he" (Mt 11:11). And in this way Jesus indicates the power of grace to sanctify more than any natural virtue. Privileged though the Jewish people of the Old Covenant were (and John was the greatest among them), God's grace in the New Covenant offers true forgiveness of sin and the power to become a new creation in Christ (see 2 Cor 5:17).

Jesus and Mary, while unique on their own and possessed of special qualities, are also of the New Covenant. As such, they are "greater" than John the Baptist in many ways.

Q. Some say the last prophet was Saint John the Baptist. But how can this be? Are we without prophets today? — *David O'Flaherty*

As always with questions like these, it is going to depend on whether the word prophet is being used in a strict sense or a wider sense. In the strictest sense, prophet refers only to a group of seventeen men in ancient Israel whose writings and prophecies are contained in books bearing their names, and to others attested as prophets in the Old Testament such as Samuel, Elijah, and others.

Tradition varies about whether John the Baptist is added to this number, since he does not have a book bearing his name, though he is referred in all four Gospels. The *Catechism* says: "John the Baptist is 'more than a prophet.' In him, the Holy Spirit concludes his speaking through the prophets. John completes the cycle of prophets begun by Elijah" (719).

So, in the strict sense, the period of the prophets is closed and no new prophets can join this group. Scripture confirms the close of the age of the prophets. For example, Jesus says, "The Law and the Prophets were until John" (Lk 16:16). The Letter to the Hebrews says, "In many and various ways, God spoke of old to our fathers by the prophets; but in these last days he has spoken to us by a Son" (Heb 1:1–2).

Yet, though the age of the prophets is closed, permitting no new enrollees, as even these texts indicate, this does not mean that all prophecy itself is at an end. Indeed, the Church's baptismal theology indicates that every baptized Christian shares in the prophetic office of Christ. As Christ is priest, prophet, and king, so do we, as members of his body, share in his prophetic office in a subordinate sense.

In this wider sense of the word prophet, the world is teeming with them. But note this difference. We prophets of the New Testament have our office subordinated to Christ. Our prophecies do not independently carry an infallible and canonical status as do the words of the biblical prophets. We do not produce new revelation. Rather, we announce the Gospel that is given, and we can never add to or subtract from that which is given by the Lord Jesus.

The New Testament does refer to prophets in this wider sense of the word. Acts 13:1 mentions certain prophets at Antioch; Acts 15:32 speaks of two prophets named Judas and Silas; and Acts 11:28 and 21:10 mention a prophet named Agabus. Ephesians 2:20 says that the Church rests upon the foundation of the apostles and the prophets; Ephesians 3:5 says that the mystery of the Church has been revealed by the Holy Spirit to the apostles and prophets. Finally, Ephesians 4:11 says that prophets, along with others holding various offices, have been given to the Church for the equipping of the saints.

SAINT PAUL

Q: Why does it say in Acts 9:7 that when Paul was struck down on the Damascus road, his companions heard the voice of Jesus. Yet, in Acts 22:9, when Paul recounts the event, his companions do not hear the voice of Jesus? — *Paul Vanhoudt*

The answer is rooted in the subtleties of the Greek language. In both passages the Greek verb is *akouo*, which means "to hear." We get the English word acoustics from this. However, in Greek, when the verb "to hear" is paired with the accusative case, there is a hearing of the voice with understanding. But when it is paired with the genitive case, one may hear a sound but not understand what they have heard. And in this second sense, they do not really hear since they do not hear with the intellectual perception we attribute to true hearing.

This is akin to the subtle distinction in English we can make between hearing and listening. We can hear innumerable sounds and either screen them out or just wonder, "What was that?" But when we listen, we are hearing with focus and understanding.

So, in Acts 9:7, Saul's companions heard a voice speak, but they did not understand what was said. Acts 22:9, which is usually rendered in English, "they heard not the voice," is pairing the verb hear with the genitive case. And therefore Acts 22:9 does not contradict Acts 9:7. Rather, it clarifies it by indicating that the sound heard in 9:7 was a hearing without understanding.

Q.•Saint Paul calls James the "brother of the Lord." But
•we Catholics say Jesus had no brothers or sisters,
calling them "cousins" instead. Is there no word in Hebrew
for cousin? I do see a reference to Uzziel as "uncle of Aaron" (Lv 10:4). — *Robert Tisovich*

There are a number of places in the New Testament (see Mk 3:31–
34; 6:3; Mt 12:46; 13:55; Lk 8:19–20; Jn 2:12; 7:3,5,10; Acts 1:14; 1
Cor 9:5) where Jesus' kinfolk are mentioned using terms such as
"brother" (*adelphos*), "sister" (*adelphe*) or "brethren" (*adelphoi*).
But the term brother has a wider meaning in the Scriptures, and at
that time in general. It is not restricted to our literal meaning of a
full brother or half-brother.

Even in the Old Testament, "brother" had a wide range of
meanings. Lot, for example, is called Abraham's brother (see Gn
14:14), but his father was Haran, Abraham's brother (Gn 11:26–28).
So, Lot was actually a nephew. Jacob is called the brother of Laban
who was actually his uncle (Gn 29:15). The term brother could also
refer widely to friends or mere political allies (2 Sm 1:26; Am 1:9).
Thus, in family relationships, brother could refer to any male relative from whom you are not descended. We use words like kins-
men and cousins today, but the ancient Jews did not.

In fact, neither Hebrew nor Aramaic had a word meaning
cousin. They used terms such as brother, sister, or, more rarely, kin
or kinsfolk (*syngenis*), sometimes translated as relative in English.
The passage you cite from Leviticus uses the Hebrew word *dod*,
which more strictly means "loved one."

James, whom Saint Paul called "the Lord's brother" (Gal 1:19),
is identified by Paul as an apostle and is usually understood to be
James the Younger. But James the Younger is elsewhere identified
as the son of Alphaeus (also called Clopas) (see Mt 10:3) and his
wife Mary Clopas. Mary, the wife of Clopas, was one of the women
who stood with Jesus' mother Mary at the foot of the cross, along
with yet another Mary, Mary Magdalene (Jn 19:25).

Even if James the Greater were meant by Saint Paul, it is clear that he is from the Zebedee family, and is not a son of Mary or a brother of Jesus (in the strict modern sense) at all.

The ancient Church was well aware of the references to Jesus' brethren, but was not troubled by them, still teaching and handing on the doctrine of Mary's perpetual virginity. This is because the terms referring to Jesus' brethren were understood in the wider, more ancient sense. Widespread confusion about this occurred after the sixteenth century with the rise of Protestantism and the loss of understanding the semantic nuances of ancient family terminology.

READING SCRIPTURE

Q. I have heard that chapters and verses were not part of the Bible until much later. Who added these? — *Addy Thomas*

You are correct. Modern, and helpful, devices such as the enumeration of chapters and verses are not part of the original biblical text. These conventions were added much later.

The setting of the biblical text into chapters occurred in the thirteenth century when the Catholic archbishop of Canterbury, Stephen Langton, assigned chapter numbers in order to make the reading of the Bible easier. The enumeration of the text into verses did not happen until 1551 when Robert Stephanus (also known as Robert Estienne), a Protestant and former Catholic, a classical scholar, and also a printer, published the first such Bible in Paris.

Q: Why does the Catholic Church and Catholic Bibles fail to use the uppercase — that is, capitalize — for pronouns referring to the persons of the Trinity? Does not the Lord's Prayer say, "hallowed be Thy name?" — *Joseph Krueger*

Capitalizing pronouns — for example, he, him, his, you, your, etc. — referring to the Blessed Trinity has not been a widespread practice in Christian tradition. In fact, these pronouns are never capitalized in the source documents. They are not capitalized in the Greek text of the Scriptures. Neither did Saint Jerome capitalize them when he translated these texts into the Latin Vulgate.

Even as the biblical texts were translated into English, the pronouns remained in the lowercase. This is true of both Catholic and Protestant translations of the Bible. The Douay-Rheims Bible did not use them, nor did the King James. Neither do more than thirty current or old translations that I consulted online.

Outside the Scriptures, official English translations of Church documents and texts do not use the uppercase for the pronouns either. For example, the English translation of the *Catechism of the Council of Trent* used lowercase, as does the current *Catechism of the Catholic Church*. Thus we see that the use of the lowercase for pronouns, even pronouns referring to the Divine Persons, are always in the lowercase, beginning with the very biblical text.

Some years ago, at least in English-speaking countries, there was a pious practice that began using the uppercase for pronouns referring to members of the Trinity. However, this practice was neither widespread nor ancient.

As for God's name being holy, this is absolutely true. When referring to God by name, or proper title, we should capitalize these proper nouns. Thus Father, Son, and Holy Spirit are capitalized, as is the name of Jesus. But pronouns are not proper names, they are by definition words that stand for, or point back to, proper nouns.

One may well argue that such pronouns *should* be capitalized, but given the widespread and ancient practice to the contrary, one ought to be careful not to impugn motives of impiety for those who do not do so.

Q. You wrote recently about the dates in the Genesis text and said it is not a requirement of a Catholic to accept a very literal reading of the Bible. I have always understood that it is a requirement that we accept the Bible pretty much as written — that is, a literal interpretation. — *John S.*

The principle stated applies to the early Genesis texts (and the references to "days" and other time indicators). It is not to be understood as a sweeping principle for all of the Scriptures. Certain biblical texts describe people and events in very literal ways. Other texts use parables, poetic images, allegory, metaphor, hyperbole, and other genres and modes of speech.

Thus we must rightly attend to the nature of a text by determining the genre and mode of speech used, view it in context and relation to the whole of Scripture and sacred Tradition, and defer to the judgment of the Church, which exercises the divinely conferred commission of watching over and interpreting the Word of God (see CCC 108–19).

Some texts are understood literally, others metaphorically, but they always confer divine Truth.

Q.**I get a little frustrated when the Church is so quick to dismiss the Genesis texts as mere stories and yet still claim that the Bible is inerrant. I don't get the logic. It seems to me if the Church says creation may not have occurred in six actual days, then it is saying the Bible is wrong.** — *Name withheld*

The Church has always upheld the inerrancy of Scripture. But we must be careful to distinguish what a biblical text asserts from the way in which it says it, for it is what the text asserts that is inerrant.

We can note this distinction in the following example. If I say, "It is raining cats and dogs!", what I assert may be true, though what I say is not literally true. My assertion is true and without error if it is raining heavily. But though my assertion is true, I am using a figure of speech which is not literally true, because small and mid-sized mammals are not actually falling from the sky. Yet most understand I am using an artful way of speaking which, while not literally true, is true in what I am actually asserting.

So, when we come to texts like the Genesis account, the Church *does* insist that what the text asserts is inerrant and true — namely, that God created everything out of nothing and that he did so in stages guided by him directly, purposefully, carefully designing and creating everything according to its kind. But this does not mean that the text's manner of saying this must all be understood as literally true. Whether a day is understood as a literal assertion or a figurative way of describing a stage is a matter of debate. The Church does not insist that Catholics or others hold to a literal or figurative meaning of the word "day." The consensus in the Church today is that the days of creation are figurative, not a literal twenty-four hours.

The Church need not insist that every detail of Scripture be read literally, and it is unwise to do so. Context, genera, and literary modes or techniques such as hyperbole, simile, metaphor, allegory, etc., are frequently employed in all human communication, including the Scriptures. The task is to discover what the scriptural text is asserting. It is this that is inerrant, not per se what the mode of speech may artfully proclaim rather than literally.

The Scriptures inerrantly set forth actual historical events and immutable truths of what God has said and done. But some sophistication is required to distinguish what is said from how it is said.

Q. My older Bible has a Book of Ecclesiastes and a Book of Ecclesiasticus. I am confused. — *Janet Jones*

The Book of Ecclesiasticus is more commonly called today the Book of Sirach. Historically it had the name "Ecclesiasticus" ("Church Book") since, among other things, it was used by the ancient Church as the basis for the first instruction of catechumens. Since they were coming from a world tainted by teachings, values, and priorities at odds with the Church, it was deemed by many in the early Church as a good way to help catechumens purify their minds. As such it was an influential book in the early Church and commonly read at meetings. It is therefore interesting that such an influential book was discarded by Martin Luther in his purging of certain Old Testament books.

In recent times the title "Sirach" (since it was compiled by Jesus Ben Sira) is used to avoid the confusion you point out.

Q. The Song of Songs, a book of the Bible, seems very strange. I am very surprised God would allow such lurid poetry in the Bible. Can you explain? — *Name withheld*

The Song of Songs (the Song of Solomon in some translations) does celebrate romantic love. But the Church sees the book as an allegory of God's love for his people and our love for God. The Lord is the Groom and we are the Bride. The content of marriage and chastity in the book are safeguarded by no less than five warnings that this love must not be stirred until the proper time. To consider the book

lurid says more about the loss of innocence in our hypersexual-
ized culture than about the book itself which, while vivid, is not
improper.

Q. The Catholic Bible contains the books of Macca-bees, the King James version does not. Why? — *Robert Bonsignore*

Interestingly enough, the original 1611 version of the King James
Bible did have these, plus other disputed Old Testament books, in
it. Later, they were removed.

In addition to the issue related to the books of Maccabees,
there are a number of other omissions that make Protestant Bibles
shorter. The following Old Testament books were deleted from
Protestant Bibles: Tobit, Judith, Baruch, Wisdom, Sirach, First
Maccabees, and Second Maccabees. There are also sections of Es-
ther and Daniel that are omitted. Why these differences exist is
complex, but the central facts focus on ancient Christian tradition,
and the departure from this by Martin Luther.

The most widely used version of the Old Testament at the
time of Jesus was a Greek translation of the Old Testament called
the Septuagint. This remained the case with the emergence of the
Church in the apostolic age and going forward. The earliest Church
documents and the Church Fathers all make widest use of this version, which included the books that Protestants later rejected.

The Fathers of the Church often referred to disputed books,
and the Book of Sirach was widely used in the early Church as a
first book of instruction for catechumens and converts to the faith.
By the mid-fourth century, the Church settled on the definitive
list of sacred Scripture, which now included the New Testament
books. Three synods (or councils) of bishops, at Carthage, Hippo, and Rome, largely settled debates about the New Testament
books, and also included the Old Testament list from the Septuagint, which contained the disputed books and passages the Prot-

estant Bibles later removed. Therefore, we see that the Bible emerging from antiquity is the Bible that Catholics still have today.

In the sixteenth century, Martin Luther removed a number of books from the Bible. Originally, he also wanted to remove New Testament books such as James and the two books of Timothy. However, friends prevailed on him to leave the New Testament list untouched. But he *did* remove the books listed above largely because they supported a number of Catholic teachings that he rejected, such as praying for the dead, etc. He claimed that the Jewish Bibles of his day did not contain most of these passages. And that is largely true. However, it is a serious matter to set aside 1,500 years of Christian tradition, rooted in apostolic authority, in favor of the opinions of the Jewish rabbis of his time.

From this perspective, therefore, Protestant Bibles are deficient by failing to include significant sections of the Old Testament that nourished the Jewish people of Jesus' time and have been part of the Christian Bible for 2,000 years.

Q.It seems logical that many other individuals than Matthew, Mark, Luke, and John wrote the life of Jesus. Why then were these four Gospels chosen to be the accepted ones, especially since Mark and Luke where not apostles? When and how was this determination made? — *Robert McBride*

While there certainly are other reputed accounts of Jesus' life, and some of these have the names of apostles attached to them — for example, Thomas and James — the evidence seems pretty clear that these Gospels were written long after the deaths of these apostles.

As for Mark and Luke not being apostles yet having Gospels, Saint Mark was likely the assistant to Saint Peter, so his Gospel is largely held to be Saint Peter's account. As for Saint Luke, he states clearly that he carefully analyzed eyewitness account in preparing his Gospel.

Which books ended up in the canon (a word which means list) of sacred Scripture was a complex process that developed in the early years of the Church under the guidance of the Holy Spirit. Even through the late fourth century there were some disagreements among believers as to which books belonged to the canon. The Book of Revelation and some of the epistles were disputed. Likewise, some proposed other edifying writings from the early years, such as the Epistle of Pope St. Clement and the *Didache*, for inclusion in the canon.

The resolution of the final list, or canon, of sacred Scripture, was largely resolved in a series of councils in the late fourth century: the Synod of Rome in 382, the Council of Hippo in 393, and the Council of Carthage in 397. These councils, in consultation with popes, gave us the list of books in the canon of sacred Scripture that we have today in the Catholic Church. This canon was largely undisputed until the sixteenth century, when Martin Luther removed a number of Old Testament books and certain other Protestant denominations followed his unfortunate and unauthorized move.

The primary standards used by the council fathers and popes were liturgy and doctrine. Did a particular book have widespread use and acceptance in the liturgy of the Church? Did a particular book comport well with the Faith and received doctrine of the Church? These standards, along with some particulars too numerous to mention here, produced the list that we have today of sacred Scripture. Surely, by faith, we know the Holy Spirit inspired this process as well.

Q. One of my great frustrations with Scripture as a historical source is that it leaves so much out. Almost thirty years of Jesus' life receives no mention at all. How can this be that the life of the most pivotal figure of history receives such vague biographical treatment? — *Name withheld*

Part of the answer to this is to understand that the Gospels do not propose to be chronological histories of the Lord's life. The Gospels record the things that Jesus actually said and did, but do so in a selective way. Saint John says why near the end of his Gospel: "Now Jesus did many other signs in the presence of the disciples, which are not written in this book; but these are written so that you may believe that Jesus is the Christ, the Son of God, and that believing you may have life in his name" (Jn 20:30–31).

The material selected focuses on those things most necessary for us to understand that Jesus is the longed-for Messiah and the true Son of God. As such the Gospel writers selected a lot of their material based on its indication of the fulfillment of Old Testament prophecies and on events that show forth the divinity of Christ.

Another reason the Gospels do not seek to cover every aspect of Jesus' life may be more practical. Modern methods of setting forth history comprehensively presuppose the possibility of lengthy books that can be cheaply reproduced. But in the centuries prior to the invention of the printing press, books were copied by hand. In addition, papers and parchments were expensive; brevity therefore was far more necessary. And since books and scrolls were expensive and hard to come by, most early preachers had to rely more on memory than today. Therefore, short, memorable stories focused on the essentials of Christ's life and message were of greater use. Preaching to crowds without amplification also favored brevity with a focus on essentials.

As to the hidden years of Christ, there is great mystery to be sure. But the silence, while explained above as theological and practical, does have a possible advantage. Truth be told, most of us live lives that are hidden, and it is quite possible that history will barely note our existence, let alone the daily details of our life.

But this hiddenness of our lives to the sweep of history does not diminish our dignity. That Jesus lived in obscurity for thirty years, laboring quietly and likely dwelling in small villages among humble and ordinary people, is testimony to the dignity of every human person, even the most hidden and forgotten. The Lord of all creation himself chose to spend the majority of his walk among us in a hidden, humble, and ordinary life. It is a silent testimony to the dignity of the ordinary.

Q.Our parish priest asked us at Mass which book of the New Testament was the oldest. Most of us said Matthew. He said we were wrong, and that First Thessalonians was the oldest. This doesn't seem right, does it? — *Donald Wilde*

When we speak of the age of a particular book in the Bible we can speak about its age in terms of the events it describes, or of the likely date it was put into the written form we have today. Usually when scholars speak of the age of a book, they refer to the time of its appearance in final written form. And in this sense it is largely accepted that the First Letter to the Thessalonians is probably the oldest book, the first of Saint Paul's letters, and written AD 51–52.

The writing of the letters in the New Testament was a fairly straightforward process and, while Saint Paul and others may have had made some final edits, or even a second draft, it is likely he dictated to a scribe, who wrote it and then had it sent within a matter of days. Other copies may also have been made and circulated.

The emergence of the Gospels in written form was a much more complicated process. While the events they detail are older (from the early 30s), the writing out of these events went through several stages.

Obviously, the first stage of the Gospels was the actual events themselves, the words and deeds of Jesus. But it will be noted that Jesus did not write a book, or even say to the apostles, "Go write a book." Rather, he sent them to preach, teach, and baptize disciples into the life of his body, the Church. Thus the second stage was the oral stage, wherein the apostles went forth proclaiming what Jesus taught and did, and who Jesus was. During this time, the teachings began to be written by scribes, collected, and circulated.

Then we begin to see the written stage. The idea that either Matthew or John just sat down and wrote the Gospel attributed to each one is probably inaccurate. Recall that most people could not write in the ancient world. Scribes and others acted as secretaries for the author, who helped refine and edit the final product. Some think that Mark was Peter's assistant and scribe.

Gradually the Gospels were collected and edited in what came to be their final form as we know them. The exact dates and order of their final form are hotly debated among scholars. However, it is safe to say that the four Gospels took their final form between AD 60 and 90, some time after Saint Paul had sent forth his letters.

Q. **You Catholics pray to saints, but the Bible says there is only one mediator, Jesus. How can you justify this?**
— *Jason, via email*

Jesus, of course, mediates a relationship with the Father in a way no one else can. No one comes to the Father except through him. However, in terms of our relationship with him, Jesus has established things and people which help mediate our relationship with him: apostles, evangelists, teachers, and roles of service to build up the Body of Christ. Faith comes by hearing the Word of God. Therefore, our relationship with Jesus is mediated by both Scripture and those whom the Lord sends to evangelize us.

You seem to understand "one mediator" in a completely uni-vocal and absolute sense. If so, then you should never ask anyone to pray for you. Neither should you listen to a sermon or even read Scripture. For these are things and people which mediate Christ to us in some sense.

Catholics do not hold that the prayers of saints substitute for Christ's mediation. Rather, we believe their prayers are subordinate to Christ's mediation and facilitated by him. For, as Head of the Body, the Church, he creates a communion of all the members, allowing and expecting that all the members of the Body assist and support one another. This does not substitute for Christ's mediation, but presupposes it.

Q. **My husband, who is not Catholic, tells me the Church used to discourage reading the Bible. Is this true and why?** — *Name withheld*

Reading the Bible is, of course, to be encouraged. The problem is not reading, it is interpreting. If in the past priests once encouraged the faithful to be cautious in reading the Bible, it was only to protect them from the Protestant tendency of private interpretation, which leads to a lot of divisions. If priests ever did discourage the faithful from reading the Bible, it is exaggerated by our detractors in terms of its extent and severity.

However, any such warnings ought to be seen in the light of what private interpretation has wrought — namely, some 30,000 different denominations of Protestants all claiming biblical authority for their differing views. Today, Catholics are strongly encouraged to read and pray with their Bible, but also to strive to conform their understanding of the text to Church teaching and norms of Catholic biblical interpretation articulated in the *Catechism*.

Q. My brother-in-law is Protestant and often says the Church forbade the reading of the Bible and only grudgingly permits it now. How should I answer? — *Name withheld*

It is good to recall that the Catholic Church extends to a time when literacy was rare among the populace. This was because books and written material were rare and costly, not because people were un-intelligent. Prior to the printing press, books had to be copied by hand, and for this reason were very precious — costing thousands of dollars. Therefore, telling people to read their Bibles in a parish church in AD 950 would have been met with puzzled looks.

For this reason, the Catholic Church used many other methods to acquaint people with the Scriptures: sermons, art, hymns, stained glass, sculptures — for example, Nativity sets — plays, feast days, etc. This also explains the often-elaborate design and beauty of older churches.

As inexpensive Bibles became available, it became more obligatory to recommend reading it. However, it does not follow that we must abandon the previous methods. We should also recall that the Catholic Church is worldwide and, even today, literacy is uneven throughout the world.

Finally, we do well to recall the danger of private interpretation of the Bible. The Church does encourage the reading of the Bible today, but it cautions against a Protestant approach of becoming one's own magisterium. Divisions among Protestants illustrate the danger of private interpretation with no reference to sacred Tradition.

Q.•My wife, who is not Catholic, says that in her Prot-
•estant denomination they count the Ten Commandments differently because we Catholics eliminated the
Second Commandment forbidding graven images, so we
could worship statues. I know she is wrong but am not
sure how to answer. — *Name withheld*

It is true that there are two different numerations for the commandments, but it is not as simple as saying Catholics and Protestants have different ones, since both Catholics and Lutherans
follow the same numerations (based on the Jewish Talmud and
Saint Augustine). Baptists, Presbyterians, and evangelicals follow
a different numbering system based largely in the classifications of
the Jewish philosopher Philo.

The difference is based in the fact that the original biblical
text does not assign numbers to the commandments, and some
go on for several verses, especially the commandments against
worshiping other gods and keeping holy the Sabbath. There is a
further difficulty, since the text concerning the commandments
is given twice (in Exodus 20:1–17 and Deuteronomy 5:4–21), and
the wordings are close but not exactly alike. Thus how to divide
the seventeen verses into Ten Commandments is a matter that has
two traditions.

The Calvinist/Baptist/evangelical tradition takes the First
Commandment in our traditional First Commandment and breaks
it into two: one forbidding the worship of other gods, and a second
about not carving images and worshiping them. But the Catho-
lic/Lutheran numerations see the worshiping of graven images as
part of the First Commandment forbidding worship of other gods.
We do not worship statues, which would be a grave violation of the
First Commandment. It is also silly to worship statues or trust in
them since they cannot see or hear us and have no power. Perhaps
your wife mistakes us for fools. We are not.

At the end of the commandments, the Calvinist/Baptist/
evangelical tradition brings our final two commandments about

coveting into one commandment against coveting. The Catholic/ Lutheran numbering, however, sees these as different commandments since the English word "covet" is actually translating two different Hebrew words. The text (especially from Deuteronomy) most literally says that we ought not "desire" our neighbor's wife, neither shall we "covet" his goods. And this permits us to distinguish the coveting (desire) rooted in lust from the coveting rooted in greed.

Either numeration is fine at the end of the day, so long as we remember that our division of the seventeen verses in the Ten Commandments is not part of the original biblical text but is merely a traditional break out of them.

LIVING SCRIPTURE

Q. Matthew 5:48 says, "You, therefore, must be perfect, as your heavenly Father is perfect." It seems to me that, knowing man's fallibility and knowing the impossibility of man being perfect, perhaps Jesus was not saying "perfect" as we understand the word. Could it mean "strive to be complete" or some such thing? — *Michael Peerless*

It is true, the Greek word here is *teleioi*, which speaks more of perfection in the sense of completion. Therefore, we are to attain to a state of being complete, fully grown, or of full age. It also has the sense of "reaching the goal." So, we are not dealing with a merely moral perfection, but a completeness of character that is not merely absent of sin but is possessed of all the virtues. Clearly, this is more than a moral injunction for the moment, but rather something attained by God's grace in stages and accomplished fully only after a journey with the Lord. Saint Paul speaks to this when he says, "And [the Lord's] gifts were that some would be apostles, some prophets, some evangelists, some pastors and teachers, to equip the saints for the work of ministry, for building up the Body of Christ, until we all attain to the unity of the faith and of the knowledge of the Son of God, to mature manhood to the measure of the stature of the fullness of Christ" (Eph 4:11–13).

But we ought not consign the Lord's words to a sort of flourish or exaggeration and see our perfection as impossible. No, this is our dignity and our future if we persevere to the end. The saints in heaven have attained to this by the Lord's grace, which has been accomplished in them already.

To the degree that this seems impossible, it only seems so from the standpoint of human achievement unaided by grace. In the Sermon on the Mount, the Lord is setting forth a moral vision. He is describing the transformed human person. He is doing more than uttering moralisms or new duties, he is painting a picture of what happens to us when he lives his life in us through his indwelling Holy Spirit. You might say he is describing the normal Christian life, which is to be in a life-changing, transformative relationship with God. It is in this way that we attain, in stages, to being perfect as the heavenly Father is perfect.

Being perfect isn't just something we start doing today. It is something we grow into, until it is complete, until it is perfected in us.

Q. Scripture says: "Do not love the world or the things in the world. If any one loves the world, love for the Father is not in him" (1 Jn 2:15). Does this mean we cannot love the beauty of the natural world and find the presence of the Lord in its beauty? To me the natural world lifts my heart and mind to the Lord, and I feel wonder at what he has made. — *Jini Druliner*

Scripture uses the word "world" in three different senses. One is that it is what God has made — namely, the physical world. In that sense it is good, though marred by Adam's sin and disfigured by death and natural upheavals. Still, as you point out, it is good and beautiful. In a second sense the world is the theater of redemption — namely, it is where we live. And, in this sense, it is also good.

But in the third sense, as used most commonly in the New Testament texts, world is a term that refers to that set of powers, opinions, priorities, philosophies, etc., that are arrayed against God and his kingdom. And in this sense the world is something evil. It is this world that we are not to love or in any way be mesmerized or impressed by; it tempts us and torments. Ultimately, it turns on us and consigns us to a grave. It promises to be the answer to what our heart seeks. However, this world is a sinking ship. And whether you are in first class or in steerage, it is going down. The real goal is to get on Noah's Ark (an image for the Church and the Lord). The present accommodations may be less appealing, but at least the Ark will get us safely home.

Q. I recently heard you on the radio give a good explanation on turning the other cheek. Could you summarize that here? — *Margaret Meyer*

I was summarizing the teaching of Bishop Robert Barron, who explains that Jesus' solution to withstanding the scorn or attacks of others involves a kind of third way. One reaction is to strike back and thereby become like the one who attacks. Another reaction is to flee or acquiesce to the unjust incursion of another.

But as the good bishop teaches, neither solution is suitable or what Jesus teaches. Rather, to "turn the other cheek" is to stand your ground, look your opponent in the eye, and say, in effect: "I will not become like you and enter your world of scorn. Neither will I flee from you and supply you that victory. I will stay here, as I am, and make you confront the injustice of your own stance — that you cannot ultimately prevail over me by making me like you or making me flee."

This is fundamentally the stance employed by the civil rights movement and other nonviolent resistance to injustice.

Q.In Matthew 6 the Lord says not to worry about what we will eat, drink, or wear. But how do we explain all the people who are suffering want of these things? — *Kay Hall*

It is possible with a biblical passage that we can miss its central point and focus on secondary issues. The point in this passage is to address the human problem of worry or anxiety, not to deny that hunger or nakedness will ever exist. Jesus elsewhere acknowledges the realities of destitution (see Mt 25:41–45 and Mt 26:11 as just two examples) and summons us to care for those who suffer in this way.

The overall context of the verse from Matthew 6 is the call to be increasingly free from anxiety by developing a deep relationship with the heavenly Father. And this relationship with him will increasingly do a number of things. It will put an end to the hypocrisy and posturing that reveals our obsession with the praise of others, rather than God. Knowing God as our Father means it will be enough to know that he is pleased with what we do (see Mt 6:1–18). And the more we love God and seek him, the more our treasure will be with him rather than with the uncertain and decaying trinkets of this world (Mt 6:19–21). This in turn will make us generous with others instead of fearfully clinging to money and things. We will look to the poor man who begs from us and not avoid eye contact because we are prepared to be generous. Our fear abates since we realize God provides and know we no longer need to hoard. Our generosity flows from our freedom from fear (Mt 6:22–23).

Further, knowing God as our Father and seeking only to please him heals our divided heart, wherein we seek to please both God and man. And this frustrating division is the source of many anxieties and fears (see Mt 6:24). The remedy for all the anxious maladies listed is to know and have a tender relationship of trust with the heavenly Father, which can even alleviate fears about losing our life, or of being bereft of needed food or clothing.

The point is to be free of our obsession and fear with these things. Famines do occur, but worry about these things should not preoccupy us. Life is not fundamentally about this world at all, but about God and the good things waiting for us in heaven.

The text ends with an admonition (put God first), a general norm (God provides what is necessary for us to be holy and inherit the Kingdom), and a call (thus don't worry): "But seek first his kingdom and his righteousness, and all these things shall be yours as well. Therefore do not be anxious about tomorrow, for tomorrow will be anxious for itself. Let the day's own trouble be sufficient for the day" (Mt 6:33–34).

So, our goal in this life is the kingdom of heaven. The worst thing this world can do to us is kill us. But when it does (and it will), then we get to go home to God who is our heart's truest desire. And in this way we are less anxious for the things of this world, realizing that even tragic things can work for our good if we love and trust God (see Rom 8:28). God will provide us with the things we most need (not necessarily all the things we want) until he chooses to call us home.

PART III

LITURGY AND SACRAMENTS

THE SACRAMENTS

Q:Where are the sacraments found in the Scriptures? I know there are seven of them, but how can I show Protestant friends that they were in the Bible? — *Peter*

The seven sacraments have their roots in the New Testament, not the Old Testament. However, one can find shadows or types of the sacraments there also. Let's cite both Testaments, where possible.

Baptism is rooted in the Great Commission: "Go therefore and make disciples of all nations, baptizing them in the name of the Father and of the Son and of the Holy Spirit, teaching them to observe all that I have commanded you" (Mt 28:19–20). It is necessary for salvation that we not reject baptism. Jesus says, "Unless one is born of water and the Spirit, he cannot enter the kingdom of God" (Jn 3:5). And Saint Peter says, when asked what we must do to be saved, "Repent, and be baptized every one of you in the name of Jesus Christ for the forgiveness of your sins" (Acts 2:38).

In the Old Testament, there are roots of baptism to be found in the flood, the crossing of the Red Sea, and the many ceremonial washings.

Confirmation is found in the Pentecost event (see Acts 2:1–36), where the frightened and confused disciples were filled with the Holy Spirit and found courage and clarity. It is clear that they understood that this experience was to be extended to all subsequent believers, for when Phillip the deacon went to Samaria and baptized new believers, he sent for Peter and John: "Who came down and prayed for them that they might receive the Holy Spirit; for the Spirit had not yet fallen on any of them, but they had only been baptized in the name of the Lord Jesus. Then they laid their hands on them and they received the Holy Spirit" (Acts 8:15–17).

In the Old Testament, there are many references to the Holy Spirit coming upon God's people in fullness one day. One example is in the Book of Joel: "And it shall come to pass afterward, / that

I will pour out my spirit on all flesh; / your sons and your daughters shall prophesy, / your old men shall dream dreams, / and your young men shall see visions. / Even upon the menservants and maidservants / in those days, I will pour out my spirit" (2:28–29).

The **Eucharist** is widely attested in the New Testament in all the accounts of the Last Supper, where Jesus tells us to "take and eat, for this is my Body ... take and drink, this is the chalice of my Blood." The Lord also gives an extended treatise on the Eucharist in John 6 and links it especially to the manna in the wilderness (see Exodus and Numbers).

Confession is found in John 20, when Jesus "breathed on [the Apostles], and said to them, 'Receive the Holy Spirit. If you forgive the sins of any, they are forgiven; if you retain the sins of any, they are retained'" (Jn 20:22–23). The many atonement rituals, washings, and sprinkling with blood instances prefigure this.

Anointing of the Sick finds its biblical roots in Jesus' sending forth the apostles to prepare towns for his arrival. The text says: "They went out and preached that men should repent. And they cast out many demons, and anointed with oil many that were sick and healed them" (Mk 6:12–13). The epistle of James also says: "Is anyone among you sick? Let him call for the elders of the Church, and let them pray over him, anointing him with oil in the name of the Lord; and the prayer of faith will save the sick man, and the Lord will raise him up; and if he has committed sins, he will be forgiven" (Jas 5:14–15).

In the Old Testament, the Archangel Raphael anointed Tobit's eyes, and he recovered his sight.

Holy **Matrimony** as a sacrament comes from the fact that Jesus calls it a work of God: "What therefore God has joined together" (Mt 19:6). Saint Paul also calls it a mystery (in Latin, a *sacramentum*) in Ephesians 5:32.

The Old Testament root, referenced by Jesus himself, is, "A man leaves his father and his mother and clings to his wife, and they become one flesh" (Gn 2:24).

Holy Orders is found in the Gospel: "And when it was day, he called his disciples, and chose from them twelve, whom he named apostles" (Lk 6:13). To these twelve alone Jesus gave certain powers and mandates: to baptize, teach, govern, sanctify, celebrate the Eucharist, forgive sins, and confirm.

The Old Testament roots are many, and rooted in the Old Testament priesthood, but not directly synonymous with it, for the Letter to the Hebrews clearly distinguishes the Levitical priesthood from the priesthood of Jesus in the order of Melchizedek.

Baptism

Q. **It is a very common practice for parishes to refuse baptism during Lent, and I am wondering what recourse parents can take. Is there anywhere in the Church's teaching that supports this practice? Is there anything that explicitly condemns it?** — *Name withheld*

Parents have the right and obligation under law to have their infants baptized shortly after they are born. Canon law states this clearly: "Parents are obliged to see that their infants are baptized within the first few weeks. As soon as possible after the birth, indeed even before it, they are to approach the parish priest to ask for the sacrament for their child, and to be themselves duly prepared for it. If the infant is in danger of death, it is to be baptized without any delay" (Canon 867).

Further, since there is certainly no requirement or even a provision in the law for pastors to deny (or for parents to refrain from) the baptism of infants during the entire season of Lent, there is no basis to introduce or maintain such a practice in a parish.

If the birth occurs very late in the Lenten season, one might envision a pastor suggesting that the baptism be delayed until Easter. In this regard, Holy Week is not usually a fit time to celebrate a baptism (except in danger of death), though even here it is not strictly forbidden on Monday through Thursday of Holy Week.

Therefore, I would say you are on good ground to appeal your pastor's stance if he is unmoved by your request for reconsideration. I suppose if a dialogue with the pastor is not fruitful, the bishop, the dean, or the priest personnel director could be consulted and asked to direct the pastor in this regard.

Q. **In John 3:5, Jesus says that no one can enter the kingdom of God except by water and the Spirit. So it seems that unbaptized children, Muslims, Jews, et al., cannot go to heaven. I am personally worried about my five unbaptized grandchildren.** — *John Rebar*

The Church teaches the necessity of baptism for salvation in accordance with the holy Scriptures. Thus a person who willfully refuses to be baptized, knowing the requirements for faith in Jesus and the reception of baptism, cannot be saved.

However, not everyone fully knows or understands the necessity of baptism and faith in Jesus. Some, as you note, are young children who cannot reasonably know, and whose parents have failed in their duties. Others may be raised in largely non-Catholic settings or even in settings that are hostile to the Christian faith. God does not absolutely require of people what they cannot have reasonably known. Therefore, we presume that, since God is just, he can and does deal with those sorts of situations in ways known only to him, and that people will be judged on what they could have reasonably known. Though we cannot know absolutely the fate of unbaptized children (since God has not revealed it) or even adults, we can be confident that God, who wants to save all, will deal with them justly and reasonably.

Jesus' clear teaching, however, on the necessity of baptism must not be lightly cast aside, simply based on reasonable speculation by us. You as a grandfather should firmly admonish your own children of the need to have their children baptized at once and warn them that their own salvation may be at stake if they fail to do so. Mere encouragement, if it is not enough, may need to give way to insistence and vigorous warning. You may do well to consult with your parish priest and other family members to turn this rather unfortunate state of affairs into an evangelical and teaching moment.

Q.•My son refuses to have his young children baptized. He says the priest who celebrated his wedding indicated that infant baptism is only a tradition, not a mandate. Is this so? — *Name withheld*

If the priest said this, he was wrong. Canon law states: "Parents are obliged to see that their infants are baptized within the first few weeks. As soon as possible after the birth, indeed even before it, they are to approach the parish priest to ask for the sacrament for their child, and to be themselves duly prepared for it" (Canon 867). This is a mandate, not a mere cultural tradition.

The mandate is rooted in the child's need and in the teaching of the Scriptures, which say: "Now they were bringing even infants to him that he might touch them; and when the disciples saw it, they rebuked them. But Jesus called them to him, saying, 'Let the children come to me, and do not hinder them; for to such belongs the kingdom of God'" (Lk 18:15–16). The children referred to here are little children or infants, since the Greek word in verse 15 (*brephe*) clearly means infants. And Jesus calls them *paidia*, a diminutive form of *pais*, which means children in Greek. Hence we are not to hinder the little children from access to the Kingdom and to Jesus. Elsewhere, Jesus adds, "Unless one is born of water and the Spirit, he cannot enter the kingdom of God" (Jn 3:5). So, the way even little children gain access to the Kingdom is through baptism.

That children are in urgent need of baptism is rooted in the reality that each of us is born with original sin (see Rom 5:12), which is a grave spiritual wound. Healing from this condition should not be delayed but should be offered as soon as reasonably possible.

For these reasons, and others, the Church has always baptized infants. Early documents both affirm and witness to this. Saint Irenaeus, writing in AD 189, says of Jesus, "He came to save all ... infants ... and youths, and old men" (*Against Heresies*, 2:22:4). Hippolytus, writing in 215, taught: "Let the children be baptized first. All those children who can answer for themselves do so, and to those children not yet able to speak, their parents shall answer for them" (*Apostolic Tradition* 21:16).

Q. My non-Catholic wife sees my baptism as unacceptable since I was not immersed in water. How can I answer her? — *Name withheld*

While the words to be used for baptism are given us by the Lord (see Mt 28:19), the exact method — immersion or infusion (pouring) — is not mentioned.

Historically in the Church, immersion was used more widely than today. The first generations of the Church included a much higher percentage of adult converts. But as infant baptisms became more numerous, immersion was difficult and even dangerous. Hence the pouring of water over the head became more common.

Today the Church permits and encourages immersion for adult baptisms, but pastoral and practical matters often make this more difficult to do.

It would seem that your wife is dogmatizing what is merely her preference. This is a common human tendency, wherein we see only our experience and preference as authentic or allowable. This is not always so. Scriptural images of baptisms in the Jordan River are beautiful. But it does not follow that only rivers and creeks are valid locations. Perhaps, given your wife's background, you might humbly ask her to show where in Scripture baptism by full immersion is always required and where other forms such as pouring are explicitly disallowed.

Q. **A friend wants a grandmother and aunt to be the godparents for her daughter. But the pastor says this is not possible, that one must be male, the other female. I know other pastors permit this practice. What is correct?** — *Sharon Malay*

The first pastor in your question is correct. The Code of Canon Law says, in regarding sponsors for baptism, "One sponsor, male or female, is sufficient; but there may be two, one of each sex" (Canon 873).

Catechesis is necessary today regarding the role of sponsors. Too frequently the role is seen as merely ceremonial and is often misconstrued as a way of bestowing honors on certain adults. The role of a sponsor in infant baptism is to ensure the Catholic formation of the child if the parents are unable to do so. In this regard, only one sponsor is needed. If two are chosen, however, they are usually called "godparents" and ought to be in the model of parents: male and female. However, as canon law says, one suffices.

Q. **Some people refer to baptism as "christening." Is this term correct or allowed?** — *P. Smith*

The word "christen" is an inaccurate term for baptism. In the literal sense, to be christened is to be anointed with oil. But the key sign in baptism is the washing with water. Even though there are anointings in the baptismal rite, they are not the essential sign. Thus the term "baptism" (rooted in the Greek term for washing) is the correct one for this sacrament in the Latin rite.

As for the term being allowed or not, some use the term christening and merely mean it as a synonym for baptism. It can be good to charitably and privately correct them and supply the proper term of baptism, But to say that christen (used and intended as a synonym) is disallowed is too strong.

Penance

Q. **Does confession remove all sin? If so, why purgatory, especially if one has received the last rites when dying?** — *Robert Lusby*

Confession absolves all sin, but not necessarily all effects of sin. For example, consider a man who, in an angry outburst, broke and damaged several things in his home and broke his hand as well. He also upset his wife and children, who are now fearful of future outbursts. If he goes to confession (as he should), he is absolved from the guilt of what he did before God. However, his broken hand does not suddenly heal, neither do the broken items in his house suddenly repair, and his wife and children do not instantly recover their confidence and good will toward him. This will require some sort of restitution by him and a commitment to restore trust with his family.

There are also likely personal issues that need healing. Perhaps he has personality traits that cause him to be easily angered. Perhaps he must learn to master his emotions. Maybe there were issues of drinking or stress management.

So, confession absolves us from the guilt of our sins, but not necessarily all their causes or effects. Over time, through grace, the sacraments, growth in faith, and holy fellowship we can grow in holiness which includes self-mastery. If this process is not complete when we die, ongoing and final purgation is necessary in purgatory so that God, who has begun a good work in us, might bring it to completion (see Phil 1:6) and that we may be perfect, even as the Father is perfect (Mt 5:48).

Q. If we go to confession regularly and are trying to live a good life, why must we be reminded that we are sinners every time we go to Mass? — *David O'Flaherty*

The invitation at Mass is: "Let us acknowledge our sins and so prepare ourselves to celebrate the sacred mysteries." The invitation is meant communally and should not be taken as a personal accusation. In any communal gathering, people are at many different stages and in different conditions. Some are frequent with confession, others not. Some are in a state of grace, others are not. Some are struggling habitually with serious sins, others are not, but likely have venial sins. Some make light of sins, others have greater compunction. Thus the admonition to acknowledge our sins makes sense in a communal gathering.

But even individually we all have some degree of sin, and acknowledging this is an invitation to the truth about our self and our need for God's ongoing grace to preserve us from serious sin. We come to Mass because we need the medicine of God's word and grace, and even the just man sins seven times a day (see Prv 24:16).

Q•When I learned the second precept of the Church as
a child it was: "To go to confession once a year if you
have mortal sin." The current *Catechism* states on the second precept: "You shall confess your sins at least once a
year" (2042). Have the bishops changed the second precept
on their authority? — *Ed Smetana*

The *Catechism*, while less than exact in the quote you supply, does
footnote Canon 989 for greater precision, which says, "All the faithful who have reached the age of discretion are bound faithfully to
confess their grave sins at least once a year."

The *Catechism* states elsewhere: "According to the Church's
command, 'after having attained the age of discretion, each of the
faithful is bound by an obligation faithfully to confess serious sins
at least once a year.' Anyone who is aware of having committed a
mortal sin must not receive Holy Communion, even if he experiences deep contrition, without having first received sacramental absolution, unless he has a grave reason for receiving Communion and
there is no possibility of going to confession" (1457).

Therefore, there is no change in the precept, though one may
admit the *Catechism* could have been more precise in the text you
cite.

That said, it may be of some pastoral advantage to remember that there is a tendency today to minimize the possibility and
frequency of mortal sin. It is not hard to understand that most of
the adult faithful ought to be getting to confession more than once
a year. It is quite likely that most adults, even if not guilty of sins
against life and sexual purity, are often guilty of rather serious sins
against charity. It is quite possible to cause serious harm and emotional or spiritual distress to people by harsh things we say. Further,
lies can cause more than minimal harm, reputations can be tainted,
people misled, and error flourish. Sins of omission through greed,
neglect, or laziness can also cause grave harm. Missing Mass is a
mortal sin, and being significantly neglectful in handing on or de-
fending the Faith can also become quite serious.

More could be said here, but one ought not to causally dismiss that they should get to confession even more than once a year. The Church encourages the faithful to confess frequently even if they are not aware of mortal sin since the Sacrament of Penance not only confers the grace of absolution, but also the grace to avoid sin in the future.

Q: **At confession in the church recently, the priest interrupted me and asked me to wait, he stepped out of the confessional due to a noise and seemed to hold a short conversation with a repairman. I was annoyed. Can a priest leave in the middle of a confession?** — *Name withheld*

As a general rule, no. If an urgent situation arises however, there is no absolute forbiddance of this as long as he returns to finish the confession. Perhaps the repairman had come to fix an urgent problem? Without more information, I cannot say. Only rarely should a priest step aside from the celebration of any liturgy or sacrament. But some provision must be made for serious reasons.

Q: **If I'm aware of a sin, either mortal or venial, may I receive the Eucharist at Mass? Or would I have to go to confession first?** — *Rachael*

As the *Catechism* notes, only mortal sins would exclude one from receiving Communion. If one is aware of mortal sin(s), one should refrain from going forward to receive if they have not first gone to sacramental confession.

The *Catechism* further notes, however, there are rare exceptions to this rule. Canonists define "grave reason to receive Communion" in different ways, but most concur that the reason must be more serious than ordinary embarrassment at not going forward. Most restrict it to danger of death. Even in such cases the communicant is required to make an act of contrition that includes the intent to confess the sin later, if a priest can reasonably be found.

There are some who struggle with habitual mortal sin — for example, masturbation — and in such cases they should work closely with a confessor so as be able to stay faithful to Communion.

Q. Can someone who is not in the state of grace pray and have their prayers heard? Does God listen to the prayers of someone still with mortal sins on their soul? — *Doris DeHay*

It depends a bit on what is meant by the word "heard." It can never be argued in a literal sense that God cannot hear something. For nothing escapes God's notice, and in no sense could he be said to be incapable of hearing a prayer. However, if heard means that a prayer would be favorably received by God, that is another matter. And that is what the second sentence of your question seems to focus on.

Generally, it would seem that God pays little heed to the prayers of unrepentant mortal sinners, though there are surely some exceptions. For example, in the Scriptures we read: "Behold, the LORD's hand is not shortened, that it cannot save, / or his ear dull, that it cannot hear; / but your iniquities have made a separation / between you and your God, / and your sins have hidden his face from you / so that he does not hear" (Is 59:1–2). Or, again, "He who closes his ear to the cry of the poor / will himself cry out and not be heard" (Prv 21:13).

So, it would seem that there is a good basis for concluding that unrepentant mortal sinners are going to have a difficult time getting their prayers answered as they would like. However, experience teaches that even mortal sinners do partake of many of God's blessings. And this, too, Jesus affirms: "For [the Lord] makes his sun rise on the evil and on the good, and sends rain on the just and on the unjust" (Mt 5:45).

How God chooses to bless or withhold blessings from the unjust is therefore not an all-or-nothing proposition but is caught up in the mystery of his providence. Perhaps he knows a person will one day repent; perhaps he knows that an answered prayer now will help lead to repentance later. Perhaps, too, he knows that to withhold a blessing is the better course. Thus God remains sovereign in applying wisdom to each situation.

That said, we ought to remain sober about the need to pray in righteousness. For if God cannot trust us with the blessings we already have, why should he trust us with further blessings?

The First Letter of John has some advice about praying with and for those in serious sin: "If any one sees his brother committing what is not a deadly sin, he will ask, and God will give him life for those whose sin is not deadly. There is sin which is deadly; I do not say that one is to pray for that. All wrongdoing is sin, but there is sin which is not deadly" (1 Jn 5:16–17). While the instruction of John here is complex, he is saying in effect that, if we are reasonably sure that someone is in serious sin, we ought skip over praying for lesser things like a new job for them, etc. Rather, the essential and only really efficacious prayer for them is to pray for their repentance. For to be dead in sins is to rather powerfully block any other blessings.

While God can bless even serious sinners, we ought not presuppose that he will do so and should make it our priority to pray for life-saving repentance.

Q.:Our CCD students never received a penance at recent confessions. The priest involved did not deny this but offered no explanation. Is the giving of a penance by the priest required, and is the performance of it necessary for the sacrament to be valid? — *Name withheld*

The priest is required to impose a penance, or satisfaction, on the penitent. It should be helpful, prudent, just, and suitable based on the kind and number of sins, and on the character and the condition of the penitent. The priest is only excused from imposing a penance when there is some physical or moral inability on the part of the penitent to perform it — for example, if the penitent is near death or too weak.

The penitent has a serious obligation to accept and fulfill a reasonable penance imposed by the confessor. If a penitent considers a penance unreasonable, he is free to ask for another penance from the same or a different confessor.

The giving and fulfilling of the penance does not affect the validity of the absolution that is given, unless perchance the penitent approaches confession with such a determined will to refuse any penance that it affects the necessary contrition he must bring.

More often, the failure to give or fulfill a penance is due to forgetfulness, and in such cases the validity of the absolution is not affected. If, however, a priest intentionally fails to give a penance, he sins by disobedience. Likewise, a penitent who intentionally refuses to do a penance commits sin. The gravity of that sin is weightier if the material of the confession was grave, or serious.

Q. When I was young I was taught to conclude my confession by saying, "For these and all the sins of my past life, I ask pardon and absolution." This is a strange expression and almost seems to imply a kind of reincarnation, as if I've had other lives in the past, does it not? — *John R.*

No, it does not. This is a mode of speaking, an expression, and should not be understood in a strictly literal manner. There are all sorts of expressions and manners of speaking which, if read in a literalist manner, make little sense, but everyone knows what they mean euphemistically.

For example, a mother may say to her child, "Put on your shoes and socks." Literally, this would be difficult and clumsy, since it seems to say that I should put on my shoes, and then my socks on top of the shoes. But, of course, it means no such thing. And while it is truer to say one ought to put on his socks and shoes, everybody knows what the first phrase means. Another example is the expression "coming and going." But, of course, one cannot really come until they first go. So, the expression more accurately should be "going and coming." But despite poor word order, everybody knows what coming and going means and adjusts.

In the same way, when we ask forgiveness for the sins of our "past life," it is clear we are referring merely to the sins we have committed in the past. If this saying is bothersome to you, then you may amend it, for it is not a formal or prescribed way of ending a confession; it is simply a common sentence many use to tell the priest they are done mentioning their sins.

Theologically, one is not required to ask forgiveness for sins of the past which have already been forgiven in the sacrament. Another way a penitent can end his confession is to say something like, "For these, and other sins I cannot recall, I ask for pardon and absolution."

Q. May Catholics confess their sins directly to God, as do non-Catholics, to have their sins forgiven — even though it is not as efficacious as the sacrament? — *A. F. Koselke*

When it comes to venial sins, Catholics are able to confess their sins directly to God. Mortal sins, however, require the sacrament. While it suffices to confess venial sins privately to God, Catholics are still encouraged to get to confession with some frequency, even if they are not aware of mortal sins. There are many salutary reasons for this. On the one hand, it instills a reflective discipline regarding sin. Being accountable to another person is also helpful. Alone we are often too easy or too hard on ourselves. Ideally, most priests have training and experience that can help them guide people in their moral reflection. Also, when we sin, we harm not only ourselves, but also the community. The priest represents not only God, but also the community of the Church.

As you point out, the celebration of the sacraments is always more efficacious. The Sacrament of Penance grants absolution and the grace to avoid sin in the future, along with sanctifying grace.

Q. How specific does one have to be when confessing sexual sins? And does one have to mention how many times a certain sin is committed? — *Armel Audet*

Serious or mortal sins need to be confessed in kind and number. Sexual sins are considered, objectively speaking, to be serious sins and thus it is important to say how many times a certain sin was committed since one's last confession. This helps the priest gauge whether a mortal sin is a frequent problem or rare.

Likewise, any mortal sins need to be specified to some degree: missing Mass, telling a serious lie, committing a certain sexual sin, being violently angry, and so forth. Since sexual sins come in various types, it is important to distinguish what sort of sexual sin is meant: entertaining lustful thoughts, looking at pornography, looking with lust, masturbation, inappropriate touching, fornication, contraceptive sex, adultery, homosexual acts, etc. Simply to say, "I sinned against the Sixth Commandment" or "I was impure" is not usually enough. Thus sins of this sort should be confessed in kind and number. If the number is not exactly known, an estimate is fine.

In a way, it is similar to going to the doctor and saying, "I have had serious headaches." The next thing the doctor needs to know is how frequently, and to some degree the nature of the headache: throbbing or dull, is one's eyesight affected, does it hurt more in the back or front of the head, etc. Then the doctor can provide better assistance and know whether it is a serious matter.

It should also be said that, regarding sexual sins, one should avoid giving too much information. The list above should usually be sufficient for the priest to understand. Too much information can unsettle the priest and cause temptation. If a priest is confused or needs some clarity, he can discretely ask, but should himself avoid asking in ways that humiliate or in any way seem to pry. The goal is to have the necessary information, no more and no less.

Q. **In my last confession, the priest used words of absolution that were not what I'm used to hearing. I can't remember what they were, but they weren't even close, and I did not hear the word "absolve." Was the sacrament valid?** — *Name withheld*

It is doubtful. Matter (in this case, the imposition of hands) and form (in this case, proper words of absolution) make the sacrament. It is not possible to affirm that a sacrament took place when one or both of these is significantly violated. It is, of course, hard to imagine God holding you responsible for the sinful or inept actions of a priest, since you approached the sacrament in good faith. Hence you need not fear the judgment of God regarding any serious sins you might have confessed in the botched confession.

However, it is advisable for you to consult another priest for your next confession and review with him any serious sins since the last good (valid) confession you had. You might also seek his advice on reporting the incident to local Church authorities. I am sorry this happened.

Q. Suppose for some reason that a priest refuses to grant absolution. What is a person supposed to do? Can you go back to confession immediately? I would be grateful for your insights. — *Name withheld*

In the rare cases when a priest refuses absolution, he needs to state why and offer the penitent a way forward. The most common reason that absolution is denied is that the penitent does not manifest a firm purpose of amendment so as to make reasonable efforts to avoid the sin in the future. This is often because they are living in an irregular situation such as an invalid marriage, or perhaps they are cohabiting and engaging in illicit sexual union. If they indicate no willingness to try and cease committing the sin, the priest must withhold or delay absolution. He will usually explain why and offer to speak to the person more substantially on the matter at another time. He may be able to indicate options, such as an annulment, or indicate a willingness to offer absolution if the cohabiting couple can agree to cease illicit sexual union. In other types of cases, such as a manifest refusal of the penitent to cease vengeance unjustly or to stop stealing, etc., the priest can offer counsel and ask the person to reconsider their stance and return later.

Any penitent who has been refused absolution is free to approach the priest again, or to go to another confessor or seek counsel with other confessors as to how to resolve the ongoing issue that prevents absolution being extended.

The denial of absolution is relatively rare, but every priest has a duty to ensure that the Sacrament of Penance be celebrated integrally. That means grave sins since the last confession are to be confessed in kind and number, and the penitent needs to manifest a firm purpose of amendment. A firm purpose of amendment does not mean you need to supply guarantees that something will never happen again. Rather, a firm purpose indicates a willingness to make efforts to overcome sinful habits and avoid occasions of sin insofar as reasonably possible.

The priest is called to gently ensure that what makes for the sacrament is present, and to help the penitent supply contrition and amendment. Any refusal to grant absolution ought to be accompanied by a pastoral solicitude that teaches and advises the penitent of a way forward to God's mercy.

Q: Are communal penances allowed? — *John Meniman*

If by "communal penances" you mean communal penance services, they are allowed. Such services include a brief Liturgy of the Word and (often) a communal examination of conscience, followed by individual confessions.

If by "communal penances" you mean general absolution, that is not allowed except in the rarest of circumstances, circumstances which are difficult to imagine existing regularly in the United States. General absolution involves the priest absolving a large number of people without hearing their individual confessions.

The use of a general absolution may only occur if legitimate, grave circumstances arise which may impede private confession. Such circumstances could arise in a time of crisis involving significant danger or imminent death, and if a sufficient number of confessors is not available to hear individual confessions in a reasonable period of time. If so, this might deprive many of the sacramental grace of confession or holy Communion for a long period of time. Except in urgent and grave circumstances — for example, a plane going down — the bishop alone may grant permission for general absolution.

Holy Eucharist

Q. **When holy Communion is distributed, why is "The Body of Christ" said? Why not say, "The Body and Blood of Christ." Or better yet, "This is Jesus"?** — *Name withheld*

We use the word "body" for several reasons. First of all, Jesus himself used the word body (*soma* in Greek) when giving the Eucharist for the first time: "Take and eat, this is my body." Hence we, in conformity to Christ, use this way of speaking of the Eucharist.

Second, both the English word body and the Greek word *soma* can refer strictly to the physical dimension of a person or, more broadly, to the whole person. In English, I can say, "I am somebody," which refers not only to my physicality but to my whole self. We can also do this in the plural, such as when we speak of the "body of believers" or the "body politic." In these cases we do not refer to a physical body, but rather to the sum total or the majority of some group.

Therefore, we do not exclude any dimension of Christ by referring to his body, as if we were only referring to his flesh. Rather, body here refers to the whole Christ. Surely it pertains to a living human body (and Jesus is quite alive) to have not only flesh but also blood and soul together. We also receive with his body his divine nature, since it is united to him hypostatically.

And while we do speak of what is in the chalice more specifically as the Blood of Christ, this is only to distinguish its species —

that is, what we perceive — from the host. But once again Jesus is alive and glorified, and his Body, Blood, Soul, and Divinity are all together. Even in the smallest drop of Precious Blood, the whole Christ is received.

Q. **I have been wondering about the bread that Jesus used at the Last Supper. Would it have been unleavened, and if so what did it look like and how was it made? What is the theological significance of unleavened bread?**
— *Gordon*

Historically, it seems clear that Jesus would have used unleavened bread at the Last Supper. The ancient Jews were instructed to use unleavened bread during the feast of Passover. This is scripturally and historically linked to the fact that, in their hasty exodus from Egypt, there was no time to fully knead the dough and allow the bread to rise before baking it (see Dt 16:3). Thus they baked it quickly without yeast. The Passover meal that commemorated the Exodus was therefore to be eaten with unleavened bread (Ex 29:2; Nm 9:11).

Theologically and spiritually, in the New Testament yeast (or leaven) is often equated with sin, impurity, and hypocrisy (see, for example, Mt 16:6; Lk 12:1; 1 Cor 5:8); unleavened bread comes to symbolize sincerity, purity, and integrity.

Regarding what the bread was like, we must keep in mind that the highly refined and whitened flour of today was unknown in the ancient world. Further, bread can be baked in such a way that it has a dryer, crackerlike quality. Or, bread can be baked in such a way that it has a doughy, more pitalike quality. And this is so for both leavened and unleavened bread. Thus, other than affirming that the bread at the Last Supper was unleavened, we cannot be utterly certain of its other qualities.

Q.•Since the Eucharist is the Body of Christ, when we eat •it, are its elements still existing as our Savior, or are they digested and become part of our own body? Or do we become part of Jesus' body? And would those receiving the Eucharist become part of one another's bodies in Christ? — *Vernon Edwards*

In John 6, Jesus teaches a kind of mutual indwelling, for he says, "He who eats my flesh and drinks my blood abides in me, and I in him" (Jn 6:56). While this process is mysterious and not easily reduced to mere human language, the mutual indwelling is very real, such that we are in Christ, and he is in us.

At one level, the Eucharist — the Body, Blood, Soul, and Divinity of Christ — is food. As Jesus says, "For my flesh is food indeed, and my blood is drink indeed" (Jn 6:55). As human beings, the food we receive is wonderfully assimilated into us, and it becomes the very stuff of which we are made — that is, our food becomes the building blocks of the cells in our body. In the same way, the food of Jesus' own Body, Blood, Soul, and Divinity becomes part of our very substance. In this sense, Saint Augustine says, "Christian, become what you are" (see Sermon 272).

But as all the Fathers of the Church note, unlike every other food we receive, the fruit of Christ is both living and greater than we are. All other foods we eat are dead. But since Christ is alive, it is not merely that we take him into ourselves; even more, he takes us into him, making us members of his own Body. And this assimilation of us into him is far greater than our assimilation of him into us. So, we most properly speak of becoming a member of his body, for that is the greater effect of holy Communion. But it is true that he also becomes one with us.

Ultimately, our oneness with one another is in Christ. And, while avoiding overly physicalist notions, we can say that we have communion in and with one another in Christ, for we are all members of the one Body, and when we receive Christ, we receive the whole Christ, which includes all his members. This is why faith and orthodoxy are also essential for Communion. For one to be truly a member of the Body of Christ requires that one live in union with all the members, and with its head. Ultimately, the Church is *unus Christus, amans seipsum* ("one Christ, loving himself") (Saint Augustine, *Homilies on 1 John*, 10,3).

So, properly understood, and with necessary distinctions, your insights are correct.

Q. **The biblical accounts of the Last Supper show Our Lord offering his body and blood to the apostles. There is no mention of his partaking of either species. Why then does a priest, who acts in the person of Christ, consume the precious body and blood?** — *David*

Well, to some degree, your premise is based on an argument from silence. That the Scriptures do not mention Jesus partaking does not necessarily mean he did not. However, if we accept the premise that Jesus did not himself partake of the Eucharist he offered, then your question still stands, and some further distinctions are needed.

Although it is true to say that the priest, when celebrating Mass, acts *in persona Christi*, that is not all he is or does. The priest does not cease to be himself. It is not as if he were merely an actor taking up a role, or, like a robot, one who the Lord is acting through. And, as a man, the priest remains a disciple, a sinner in need of grace and mercy.

For example, prior to the Eucharistic prayer, the priest asks the Lord to wash away his iniquities as he washes his hands. The priest also says other penitential prayers such as the *Confiteor* ("I confess"), the "Lord I am not worthy," etc. Such prayers he utters on his own behalf and as one of God's people. It would not be appropriate for him to utter these words if he were *only* in the person of Christ.

In other ways the priest does manifest his role as acting in the person of Christ, particularly at the moment of consecration. He is also a sign of the presence of Christ in the liturgical assembly. Thus the people stand as he enters, he is given a seat of some prominence, etc.

So, while the Lord does act through the priest, the priest does not thereby cease to be a human being in need of the sacraments. He needs holy Communion just like everyone else.

Q. **Why can we not receive the Eucharist by intinction? At one time it was permitted. Why has it been stopped, especially in this age of communicable diseases?**
— *Donald Pellegrino*

Communion by intinction (where the Host is dipped in the Precious Blood by the priest or minster and then given to the communicant) is still permitted. Therefore, it would seem that the decision to end the practice is a decision rooted in your own parish.

Though permitted, intinction is not a widespread practice in parishes in America. There are likely several reasons for this.

First, the practice introduces a complexity into the distribution of Communion. For example, when intinction is used, Communion cannot be received in the hand, which is an option many prefer, indicating that only some distribution stations could have intinction. This creates further complexities about who lines up where and how various options are explained to the faithful at each Mass.

Further, the practice requires either special equipment (such as a paten with a small cup for the Precious Blood) or someone standing nearby with a chalice of Precious Blood. The norms also require the use of a chin paten when intinction is used. None of these complexities are impossible to overcome, and intinction can be, and still is, practiced in some places, but these complexities help to explain the rarity of the practice.

As for wanting to receive the Precious Blood in a way other than a shared cup, please note that in fact you do receive the Precious Blood. For in the Host alone, even in a small fragment, there is contained the whole Christ: Body, Blood, Soul, and Divinity.

The use of the common cup(s) has reference to the fact that Christ shared his Precious Blood from a common cup. The concern for communicable disease is understandable, but not a definitive concern for most healthy people. The option always remains to refrain from partaking under that sign, and the Precious Blood is still received in the Host alone.

Q. **At several recent family funerals, a number of my family members who are not Catholic insisted on receiving Communion despite my explaining they should not and the priest inviting only practicing Catholics to come forward. How can I better explain our practice of limiting Communion, and are there dangers with them receiving?** — *Thomas O'Neil*

The Catholic practice of reserving Communion to fellow Catholics is fundamentally rooted in two things. First, there is a norm of Scripture: "Let a man examine himself, and so eat of the bread and drink of the cup. For any one who eats and drinks without discerning the body eats and drinks judgment upon himself" (1 Cor 11:28–29).

For Saint Paul, the issue is not only sin (which might exclude some Catholics as well), but also the need to recognize the body. A great majority of Protestants do not believe holy Communion to be the Body of Christ, but only a symbol. Hence they cannot truly say the "Amen" that is required to the acclamation "The Body of Christ." Thus, out of respect for both them and the sacrament, we do not ask them to assent in faith to something which they regretfully do not believe.

A second reason for not sharing Communion is rooted in the fuller meaning of the sacrament. In receiving holy Communion, we do not merely speak of a personal communion of the believer with Jesus, but also of communion with one another in the Church. But sadly, there are many things that divide Catholics and non-Catholics. In coming forward, one attests union with Jesus Christ, but also union with his Church and all she teaches. Since this is also what communion means, it is inappropriate for those who do not share this communion with us to come forward and signify what is not fully true, nor should we ask them to pronounce the "Amen" that affirms this community. Rudeness is not intended by this practice. Rather, there is a respectful, but regretful, acceptance that others do not share our beliefs in certain significant matters.

As to dangers, note that Saint Paul warns of incurring condemnation if we receive Communion either in serious sin or without discerning the body. When we consider the meaning of our "Amen" at Communion, it is also sinful to solemnly affirm what may not, in fact, be believed.

Q. **I'm having a bit of a debate with a fellow. Is it possible to receive Communion if a person does not believe Mary was conceived without sin, that the pope is the Vicar of Christ, and believes justification is by faith alone?** — *Oliver*

If a person dissents as you describe, he or she probably should not receive holy Communion since there is dissent on such significant doctrines. Holy Communion is more than a confession of the True Presence. Our "Amen" at the moment of Communion indicates that we are in communion with the whole Christ, Head and members together. Our Amen means that we believe all that the holy Catholic Church believes, teaches, and professes to be revealed by God. If one cannot mean this, then their Amen is false, or at least incomplete.

Of course, such a matter should be discerned with a parish priest. Perhaps he can help guide them in understanding the disputed teachings or at least help them to realize that faith is about more than membership or historical connections. Communion speaks to a deep unity of faith and practice.

Confirmation

Q: Where is the Sacrament of Confirmation in the Bible? — *Mary Tempi*

On Pentecost Sunday, the apostles and disciples experienced a powerful outpouring of the Holy Spirit that they continued to share with later converts by the laying on of hands. The Scriptures describe this as distinct from baptism.

Thus Phillip (a deacon) went to Samaria and baptized many there. Hearing of the conversions and baptisms, Peter and John then came and laid hands on them, and they received the Holy Spirit (see Acts 8:14–17). This was done as the text says, "for the Spirit had not yet fallen on any of them, but they had only been baptized in the name of the Lord Jesus" (v. 16). This shows some separation in the celebration of these sacraments and a reserving of confirmation to bishops.

However, later in Acts we see Saint Paul (who was a bishop) first baptizing a group and then imposing hands on them so they would receive the Holy Spirit (see Acts 19:5–6). This shows the sacraments, though distinct, being celebrated together.

Q: We renew our baptismal vows each year, why don't we renew our confirmation? — *Dianne Spotts*

In effect, we do renew our confirmation when we renew our baptismal promises. In the Rite of Confirmation itself we begin by the renewal of those very vows and take them up into our intention as we approach the bishop to be confirmed.

To be confirmed means to be strengthened to give witness to the very faith our baptismal vows announce. As such the two sacraments, while distinct, go hand in hand. To affirm the one is to affirm the other.

Matrimony

Q: I cannot escape the conclusion that the Bible downplays marriage. We are told by Paul that we should live as though we had no spouse (see 1 Cor 7:29), and Jesus says that in heaven there will be no marriage or giving in marriage. The Church also calls priesthood and religious life "higher callings." What am I to make of all this negativity toward marriage? — *Joseph Harris*

The solution is to understand the statements you reference in their wider context. The statements by Saint Paul and Jesus, rather than denigrating marriage, actually use marriage as an image of high glory and joy. In effect, they say, as good as this is, heaven and life in Christ is even greater.

Saint Paul notes that marriage can have its hardships and that, in the natural sense, one is focused on pleasing his or her spouse (see 1 Cor 7:32–34). But, supernaturally, even the most intimate and precious relationship of marriage cannot take precedence over our relationship to Christ. And Saint Paul specifies his statement about living as though having no spouse in the following way: "I say this for your own benefit, not to lay any restraint upon you, but to promote good order and to secure your undivided devotion to the Lord" (1 Cor 7:35). In other words, Christ must be first in your life, even if you are married, and pleasing God takes precedence over pleasing your spouse. If your spouse should ask something of you not in keeping with the faith, the response has to be, "Sorry dear, I love God more." Hopefully such conflicts are rare, but if they exist, God is obeyed. And in this sense we live "as having no spouse" to please.

Jesus' remarks about heaven also take up the theme of heaven far exceeding even the greatest earthly comparisons. The Sadducees challenge him with a complex marriage question (see Mt 22:23–28), asking how it will be resolved in heaven. Jesus dismisses their legalism by saying, in effect, that heavenly realities cannot be understood in even the most beautiful and intimate earthly terms. Marriage here implies a deep intimacy and oneness, which points to the intimacy in heaven among all the saints. Here it is expressed and experienced sexually, but there even more deeply, richly, and widely among all the saints. This does not mean that one's spouse in heaven will merely be a face in the crowd, but that what marriage signifies here on earth is a sign of even greater things to come: a nonsexual but more profound communion and intimacy with God and all the members of Christ's body.

And this is why the Church calls celibate vocations a "higher calling." Not that they are simply better in human terms, but that they point higher to what will one day be for all: a deep intimacy which marriage signifies, but wherein we live like the angels (see Mt 22:30) and experience this union nonsexually.

Q. My best friend is renewing her marriage vows. I stood up for her when she was married in the Church ten years ago, and she's asked me to do the same this time around — except that she has since left the Catholic Church and this ceremony is taking place in a Methodist church. Am I permitted to witness the renewal of her vows? — *Name withheld*

There are cases when a Catholic ought to not be present at a wedding or wedding-related ceremony. For example, when a Catholic is marrying outside the Church without permission, or when one of the parties is unqualified to enter the marriage — for example, when one or both have been married before and there are no annulments. In such cases, Catholics, even family members, ought not attend such ceremonies.

However, in the case you describe, there are no canonical issues involved, because this is not actually a wedding or the celebration of a sacrament per se, rather a renewal of vows for an anniversary. Thus we are left with a prudential judgment on your part. Usually in such cases we ought to do what will best keep the relationship strong and the lines of communication open. This will likely help a possible return to the Church. Not to attend might cause hurt or alienation and make your friend's return to the Church even less likely.

Your attendance at this renewal of vows, even standing for her as one of the wedding party, does not of itself affirm her decision to leave the Church. Rather, it would seem, it is an affirmation of ten years of marriage, which is certainly something worth celebrating.

Q:When a Catholic has been married by a justice of the peace and approaches the Church to have the marriage blessed, what does the ceremony consist of? — *Pat Burke*

The process is called "convalidation" ("to make valid"), since a Catholic married outside the Church without permission of the bishop marries invalidly. The convalidation ceremony is usually quite brief and private. There may be short scriptural readings and then the priest or deacon has the couple exchange their vows in his presence with two witnesses.

Prior to such a ceremony, however, there should be marital instruction and a determination that the couple is free to enter into marriage. The ceremony also enables the Church to confer the nuptial blessing on the couple.

Q:I recently received an annulment from the Church and had my current marriage validated by the priest. And yet, in Matthew 19, Jesus says to divorce and marry another is to commit adultery. What am I to do? — *Name withheld*

Trust the Church in this, to which Christ gave the power to bind and loose.

In the passage you reference, Jesus says, "What therefore God has joined together, let no man put asunder" (Mt 19:6). But not every exchange of marriage vows is *ipso facto* a work of God. Vows must be properly exchanged by people of requisite maturity, etc. The annulment process seeks to investigate if God had, in fact, joined the couple or not, based on evidence supplied. If you received a decree of nullity, it means the Church determined your first marriage was, for whatever reason, not valid in the eyes of God. This means you are free to marry, for you were not truly married the first time.

Q:With all the talk about annulments and marriage issues lately, I have heard of something called the Pauline privilege. Someone on the radio was saying how this is just another example of how the Church plays loose with Jesus' teaching, and therefore should further loosen her rules. — *Ed Jensen*

The Pauline privilege is the dissolution of a natural (not sacramental) marriage which was contracted between two non-Christians, one of whom has since become a Christian. It is called the Pauline privilege because it is based upon Saint Paul's words in 1 Corinthians: "If any brother has a wife who is an unbeliever, and she consents to live with him, he should not divorce her. If any woman has a husband who is an unbeliever, and he consents to live with her, she should not divorce him. But if the unbelieving partner desires to separate, let it be so; in such a case the brother or sister is not bound. For God has called us to peace" (7:12–13,15).

Such marriages begin when neither party is a Christian or a Catholic, but at a later time one partner converts and is baptized. The Pauline privilege is not really an annulment because it dissolves a real but natural marriage, whereas an annulment is a declaration that there never was a valid marriage to begin with. But it is possible to see at least some "natural marriages" as meeting Jesus' own exception to forbidden divorce and remarriage. For Jesus only forbade the dissolution of what God has joined together.

But note, as Saint Paul says, if the nonbelieving party agrees to live with the believer in peace, then they should remain married. Only if the nonbelieving party does not agree to live in peace — for example, by abusing the Christian religion, tempting the Christian to infidelity, or preventing the children from being raised in the Christian faith — can the believing party be released from the bond of the nonsacramental marriage and be free to remarry.

It is difficult to argue that the Church is "playing loose" with Jesus' teaching when the Pauline privilege is drawn right from the same inspired Scripture and from the writings of one of the apostles whom Jesus commissioned to teach in his name. In hearing Saint Paul, we hear Jesus (see Lk 10:16).

Q.•**Although the Church insists on the biblical teaching of marriage, in the current marriage debates many of our critics like to point out that the Bible reports polygamy as a widespread practice that is not condemned by God or the prophets, and thus even the Bible sets aside what we call God's plan for marriage. How should I answer this?** — *Mary Carter*

That something is reported in the Scriptures should not necessarily be seen as approval. Murder, incest, and theft are reported, but this should not be seen to condone what God elsewhere condemns.

It is clear that many of the patriarchs, including those highly favored and praised by God, did practice polygamy. David and Moses were among them, along with Jacob and others. How widespread the practice of polygamy was in ancient Israel is unclear, but it seems unlikely that most Jewish men would have had enough money to support more than one wife.

It is notable and mysterious that there are not strong denunciations of polygamy from God and his prophets. Though reporting the fact of polygamy rather neutrally, the Scriptures also do not neglect to report the many problems that emerge from the practice. The problems occurred not so much among the wives, but between the different sons of the different wives. At stake were inheritance rights and other significant blessings that accrued to favored sons.

The memorable story of Joseph and the way his brothers conspired first to kill him and then later to sell him into slavery emerges from the jealousies of brothers by Jacob's different wives and the perception that Jacob favored Joseph. King David's house was also wracked by internecine conflicts related especially to a rivalry between Absalom and Solomon — who had different mothers. Horrifying bloodshed also occurred in the household of Gideon.

By the time of Jesus, the practice seems to have all but disappeared. Jesus also makes it clear that whatever provisions Moses and the patriarchs may have allowed in the reign of sin, God's original plan was going to be observed in the reign of the kingdom of God. That plan was announced in Genesis 2 and clearly states that God's vision for marriage is one man for one woman in a stable, lifelong relationship bearing the fruit of children.

This has been and remains the Church's constant teaching.

Q. During the past few years, I have attended three weddings of Catholic couples. But there was no Mass, and Communion was not offered. After the vows and some prayers, the couple was sent down the aisle and everyone left. What is going on here? Why no Mass? — *George Reiss*

The full nuptial Mass is certainly encouraged when two Catholics marry, but it is not required. The exchange of matrimonial vows outside of Mass takes place in what amounts to a Liturgy of the Word. Following the bridal procession there is an opening prayer, followed by the readings from Scripture, which usually includes an Old Testament reading, a psalm, a New Testament epistle, and the Gospel. A homily follows, and then the couple exchange their vows. The rings are blessed and given, the nuptial blessing is conferred, and the newly married couple is announced and sent forth.

Weddings *outside* of Mass are required when one of the couple is unbaptized. Though a nuptial Mass is permitted when one of the couple is Protestant, it is not usually done due to family sensibilities and the fact that only one from the couple can received holy Communion.

As stated, a full nuptial Mass is encouraged when two Catholics marry. However, even in this case there may be pastoral reasons to celebrate the Sacrament of Matrimony apart from a full Mass.

Sometimes, one or both individuals have recently converted to Catholicism and most of their family are non-Catholics. Sometimes there are tensions in families about this. Further, having a full Mass where most of the attendees cannot receive Communion is deemed problematic.

There are rarer circumstances during which the relative brevity of a wedding outside of Mass is necessary. This might be due to other weddings scheduled that day at a parish, or to health concerns in or among the immediate families of the couple, etc.

Surely the ideal is for two Catholics to be wed in the context of holy Mass. But charity and prudence may indicate that even this supreme preference should be adjusted for some of the reasons stated.

Q. If a Catholic member of my family gets married outside the Church, are there any rules about attending the wedding, bestowing gifts, and so forth? — *Name withheld*

As a general rule, one ought not attend weddings ceremonies where the couple invalidly marries. The word "ceremony" generally indicates that something is being celebrated. But we should not celebrate what is invalid and therefore untrue. Further, it is sinful for a Catholic to enter into a marriage invalidly, and sin should not be celebrated. Attendance at such ceremonies usually indicates support for what is taking place and bestows a kind of honor upon the proceedings. Therefore, we should not attend such ceremonies in most cases.

There may be, however, prudential judgment necessary in some cases. If the failure to attend might so poison family relationships as to cut off the likely possibility of future conversion, one might decide to attend, while expressing concern and a hope that things are rectified very soon.

On the other hand, too many Catholics are forever compromising the truth or remaining silent to "keep the peace." At some point, mere silence becomes tacit approval. It would seem that, if one makes a judgment to attend an invalid marriage, there ought to be some purpose at work where the truth of the Gospel can eventually be proclaimed in a clear and helpful way. If one attends, the goal should be to stay in relationships so that one can draw others to conversion and holiness, not merely so that everyone is pleased and happy.

Q. **My sister is being married outside the Church to a man who is divorced. She wants me to attend. Am I permitted to attend?** — *Name withheld*

There is no absolute rule of the Church in these matters since there are prudential matters to consider. For example, to refuse to attend a wedding of a close relative may so poison the family relationships that one may on rare occasions decide to attend for the sake of maintaining a relationship. It may be that very relationship that will later allow for the counseling and help to get the marriage validated.

However, if you are seeking advice, as I presume you are, it is generally not a good idea to go to weddings that are illicit, since attendance at such celebrations implies a joyful approval of what is taking place. Except in the rare situation described above of serious family conflict, you ought not to go, though it is good to be gracious as you decline, explaining your concern.

Your sister is entering into a union that is illicit and which the Lord describes as adultery (see Mt 5 and 19). This should not be celebrated or given even tacit approval by you. The same goes for other illicit unions such as same-sex unions.

Q. My nephew and his fiancée, both Catholic, and despite being warned, are planning to be married outside the Church. Can I and other family members attend the wedding? — *Art Osten*

You ought not attend. Both of them are bound to have their marriage witnessed by a priest or deacon in the sacred setting of the Church. In celebrating the marriage outside the Church without permission, they are entering into an invalid marriage. To attend and to celebrate with them signals support of this sinful action.

While these sorts of situations are awkward, you are not the source of the awkwardness, they are. A firm line is appropriate in such serious matters to underscore the sinfulness of the situation. Your explanation to them of your incapacity to attend should be done charitably, leaving the door open for further discussions leading to convalidation in the near future, should they still go forward with their plans.

Finally, avoid harsh debates with other family members who may still go. While attendance at such weddings is strongly discouraged, Church law does not absolutely forbid it given the human complexities involved in such situations. Some respect for prudential judgments that differ is appropriate.

Q. I was delighted to see three million people at Mass on the beach in Rio de Janeiro with the pope at World Youth Day 2013. However, this stands in contrast to the Church's stricter rules that a marriage must be celebrated inside a church building. I wonder what to tell my nieces who are upset they cannot have weddings outside. — *Karen Nelson*

All the sacraments, as a general rule, should be celebrated in a sacred space. Therefore, a dedicated parish church or oratory is almost always the proper place for the celebration of any sacrament.

But, as is almost always the case with general norms, there are exceptions. For example, in danger of death, baptisms are sometimes celebrated in the hospital. On account of urgency, or as the result of a pastoral moment, confessions are sometimes celebrated in settings other than a church.

In the example you cite, no Church building exists to accommodate the three million who assembled in Rio. The use of the beach was actually a backup plan that had to be implemented when the large open field that had been designated was rendered soggy by pouring rains. Hence, for urgent pastoral reasons, many general norms can be adapted where necessary.

Regarding weddings, certain permissions can be obtained for weddings to be celebrated outside of a sacred space. However, the reasons ought to be serious, not just because it would be more convenient or pleasing to someone in the wedding party.

While permissions are sometimes granted, most dioceses resist granting these permissions too easily. Of all the sacraments, the celebration of holy matrimony tends to be most influenced by secular trends. And many of these trends take the focus away from Christ and the sacrament being conferred. The emphasis too easily falls on dresses, flowers, food, and other social aspects. Moving weddings to beaches, backyards, reception halls, and other such places shifts the focus even further away from the sacrament itself. It also tends to open the doors even further to certain passing trends, many of which are questionable, even frivolous or scandalous.

The celebration of the sacraments ought generally to take place in the parish church. For serious pastoral reasons, such as stated above, exceptions can be made. But weddings seldom present pastoral conundrums significant enough to warrant the movement of the sacrament outside the church.

Q.If a priest who has had five years to discern his vo-
Q.cation can be laicized, why does a couple, who may
court only six months to a year, need a Church annulment,
especially if it was due to abuse or alcoholism and the like?
Doesn't a person who wishes to remarry deserve happiness without having to go through a long emotional process? — *Jeannine*

Your question seems to imply that laicization is a simple process.
It is not, and often takes investigation, the preparing of a petition,
and sometimes the gathering of testimony. This may take years to
complete. Annulments, while not easy, can often be accomplished
in six months to a year, depending on the diocese and complexity
of the case. But the fact is, neither is easy.

That said, there is an important difference. Laicization does
not generally seek to prove an ordination never took place or was
invalid. It presumes the man was validly ordained and only re-
leases him of his ecclesial obligations to live all the disciplines of
priestly life, such as perpetual celibacy and the duties of saying the
Liturgy of the Hours and celebrating Mass, etc.

Annulment, on the other hand, is the recognition by the
Church, based on evidence given, that a valid Catholic marriage
never occurred, since something essential was lacking. This, of
course, requires proof that must be presented and then considered. That, like the process of laicization, takes some time.

Both processes ultimately involve matters of great sadness
and have significant pastoral implications. For while recognizing
human struggles, the Church must also seek to uphold the gravity
of vows that are made. Showing compassion to individuals who
seek annulments or laicization must be balanced with the common good, the reality of the sacraments, and what the Scriptures
teach. The happiness of certain individuals cannot be the Church's
only concern. Hence the pastoral process involved must necessarily be thorough and careful.

Q•We hear of priests leaving the priesthood and then subsequently getting married. Is sacramental marriage possible for a man who has received holy orders? I thought once a priest always a priest? — *Kathy Cain*

Your insight "once a priest always a priest" is a correct one. A man who leaves the priesthood is not leaving the priesthood per se, but is setting aside the practice and discipline of the priestly ministry.

For a priest to validly and licitly marry in the Church, he must first be "laicized." That means that, while his priestly character remains, he is permitted and then required to live as a layman in the Church. And so, except in very rare danger-of-death situations, he cannot hear confessions or give anointing of the sick, and nowise celebrate the Sacred Liturgy or exercise other offices related to the priestly ministry.

When laicized, he is usually dismissed from the discipline of celibacy and free to marry. Note that celibacy is a discipline; and while a common and expected discipline of most priests, it is not utterly intrinsic to the priesthood. There are married priests, most of them in the Eastern rites of the Catholic Church. But even in the Western (Latin) rite there are some married priests. Most of these have converted and come over from Anglican or Lutheran ministry and were then ordained Catholic priests. Therefore, when a man leaves the active priesthood and is laicized, he can also have the discipline of celibacy relaxed for him by the Church, such that he can marry.

It is certainly lamentable that some men do leave the priesthood, a ministry they agreed to accept for life. Yet the Church, as a loving mother, does make a pastoral provision for men who regrettably have need of leaving the active priestly ministry for grave reasons. These provisions are in place so as not to utterly lose them to the practice of the Faith, and to hold them as close to Christ and the Church as possible.

Q •Since the Church says that having children is intrin-
•sic to sex and marriage, should we just forbid those
who are sterile and older people to marry? — *Name withheld*

The *Catechism* says that sex must be "ordered *per se* to the procreation of human life" (2366). "Per se" does not mean every act can
be fertile, but only that "by itself" — that is, per se — the act is
not intentionally hindered from its natural ends. This is what contraception, homosexual acts, and certain heterosexual practices
that do not complete or naturally render the marital act do. But
it is clear to any biology novice that not every sexual act results in
conception.

Consider by analogy that I call a friend, and this might result
in speaking with her or perhaps being sent to a voice mail. Whatever the final result, my reason and purpose for calling was to try
to reach my friend. One would likely consider me a madman if, in
dialing the numbers, I had no intent of reaching my friend and was
angry if she did pick up the phone and begin to speak. Whatever
the final result, the calling of my friend is per se related to speaking
with her.

And this is what it means that marriage and sexual activity
must be per se related to the procreation of children, even if the
results of that activity do not always attain the full purpose of that
action. Older and/or sterile people do not intentionally exclude
one of the two fundamental reasons for marriage and sexual activity. It is simply the result of natural barriers. All the Church asks is
that couples not intentionally exclude procreation.

Q:•With premarital sex and cohabitation so common, what is a priest to do when preparing these couples for matrimony? It seems most clergy just look the other way. Is that right? — *Name withheld*

As you rightly point out, fornication (premarital sex) is a serious sin, which has sadly received widespread acceptance in our culture. The related sin and trend of cohabitation makes matters even worse because of its public nature and capacity to give scandal. Scripture in many places describes the sin of fornication as a mortal sin, declaring that it excludes one from the kingdom of heaven (see, for example, Eph 5:5; 1 Cor 6:9; Gal 5:21; among others).

God consistently condemns fornication because of the harm it does the human person, the Sacrament of Matrimony, and children. Children conceived of fornication are at higher risk for abortion since 85 percent of abortions are performed on single women. If they survive this risk, the children are still likely to be raised in irregular situations that are not best for them. This in turn leads to many other social ills. Consequently, fornicators not only sin against God's gifts of marriage and sexuality, but also against justice by engaging in behaviors that harm society and children.

What then is a priest to do when he prepares couples for marriage who are cohabiting? Of course, there are many prudential factors involved. At least the couple is trying to set things right. Having them seek separate domiciles is best, but not always feasible. Every priest ought to teach such couples of the seriousness of their sin and insist they live chastely and sleep in separate rooms. While he cannot enforce this, he ought to instill in them a holy reverence for God who sees all things.

In order to avoid scandal that is easily given by cohabiters who cannot separate, many priests make some mention at the wedding of the fact that he instructed the couple to live chastely and was glad that they were willing to give heed to the holy instruction of God. He can be discrete but clear, and even use a little humor. But simply ignoring the issue altogether when a couple has publicly cohabited offends against the common good by giving the impression that such behavior is good or no big deal. Silent pulpits are a sadly common source of scandal.

Holy Orders

Q: **I know women cannot be priests because Jesus chose only men to be apostles. A priest recently said another reason is because of the nuptial meaning of the body. What does this mean?** — *Alfred Corigan*

To speak of the nuptial meaning of the body means that the very design of our body orients us toward a marital relationship. The man is meant for the woman, the woman for the man. And in this complementary relationship we call marriage there is the fruitfulness of children. In effect, our body says to us, "You were made for another who will complement and complete you, making your love fruitful."

This is also an image for the spiritual life, wherein God speaks of his relationship to his people using marital imagery. Israel was frequently described as God's bride. In the New Testament, Jesus is the groom and his Church is his bride. The Church and her members are called to relate to the Lord, to be completed by him and complemented by him such that their love bears fruit. The Sacrament of Matrimony is also a sign of God's relationship to his people — he the groom, we the bride. Even celibates manifest the nuptial meaning of the human person. As a priest, I am not a bachelor. I have a bride, the Church. Religious sisters also manifest a marital relationship, where Jesus is the groom.

To speak, therefore, of the nuptial meaning of the body is to insist that the sexual distinctions of male and female are not merely arbitrary physical aspects. Rather, they bespeak deeper spiritual realities that we must learn to appreciate and respect. Men and women are different and manifest different aspects of God's relationship. Women manifest the glory of the Church as bride. Men manifest the glory of Christ as groom.

In terms of the priesthood, this is important because Christ in his humanity is not simply male, he is groom, and the Sacred Liturgy is a wedding feast; Christ the groom unites intimately with his bride the Church. Thus your pastor is invoking rich theological teaching, which helps to explain one reason why Christ chose only men for the priesthood.

Q. If a permanent deacon gets divorced and remarried, would he still be a permanent deacon? — *Allen Eberle*

No. A man in the situation you describe could not continue to function as a permanent deacon. However, some distinctions are necessary so as to clarify the answer.

While celibacy is not required of a married man who becomes a permanent deacon, celibacy does apply to some permanent deacons. And this can happen in a couple of different situations. First of all, if an unmarried man becomes a permanent deacon, he is required to promise celibacy at his ordination and to remain celibate for the rest of his life. Second, if the spouse of a permanent deacon dies, he is expected to live celibately from that point forward. He is not to date or seek a new spouse.

In the unfortunate situation you describe of a deacon who is divorced, he also would be expected to live celibately from that point forward. This would be true even if his marriage received a declaration of nullity from the Church.

In the thankfully rare situation where permanent deacons become divorced, the local bishop usually permits such a deacon to continue ministering as a deacon. But the bishop also needs to ensure that the deacon did all he could to reasonably save his marriage and did not casually cast aside his marital vows, which would be a scandal. Presuming this can be assured and that scandal can be avoided, the bishop can permit a divorced permanent deacon to continue ministering. But, as already stated, he must live celibately from that point forward.

What if the deacon were to refuse to follow Church law, either by flagrantly divorcing and remarrying, or by remarrying after the death of a spouse? In such cases, he would be suspended from practicing his ministry as a deacon and likely be laicized. Since ordination confers a character, he would still "be" a deacon, but could not in any way perform the ministry of the diaconate.

Q: Please explain the difference between a priest who is suspended and one who is defrocked. — *Barry Quinn*

The term "defrocked" is not used in the Church's canon law, and even its secular use varies. Church law speaks of priests who might be suspended and those who are laicized.

A priest who is suspended has his faculties to publicly preach and celebrate the sacraments removed. In certain cases, he may be permitted to say Mass privately and may still retain some obligations to say the Divine Office. He still lives celibately. If the troubles that led to his suspension can be resolved, he can be restored to public ministry.

A priest who is laicized, however, is legally regarded as a layman. He cannot say Mass at all, even privately; he is no longer obliged to say the Divine Office; he may get married. Some priests are punitively laicized because they committed serious sins as a priest. Other priests are laicized at their own request because they sadly are no longer willing to live the life to which they were ordained.

Q: When Christ died on the cross, the heavy curtain that separated the Holy of Holies was torn from top to bottom. What does this mean? Someone told me that this means we no longer need priests to intercede for us to the Father. — *Name withheld*

We most certainly do need, and have, a priest to intercede for us. Jesus is the Great High Priest. Scripture says of him: "When Christ appeared as a high priest of the good things that have come, [and entered] through the greater and more perfect tent (not made with hands, that is, not of this creation) he entered once for all into the Holy Place ... [by means of] his own blood, thus securing an eternal redemption" (Heb 9:11–12).

Christ, as our Great High Priest, entered not merely into a figurative holy of holies in a stone temple on earth, but into the actual Holy of Holies in heaven to which the Temple pointed. He goes there as High Priest to intercede with the Father on our behalf.

Catholic priests do not have a priesthood apart from or different from that of Christ. There is only one High Priest, and Catholic priests are configured to Christ the High Priest by the grace of God. Christ ministers his priesthood through them by his ministry of word and sacrament.

The tearing of the veil indicates that Christ Jesus has restored access to the Father by his blood. By the blood of Jesus Christ (and only by his blood) we have a restored right to come before the Father and praise him. Christ who is High Priest and head of the body, the Church, has entered into the Holy of Holies in heaven. But where the head of the body goes, so also the whole body goes. And in this sense, by the blood of Jesus and by being made members of his body, we also go with him into the holy place in heaven. The ancient veil that denied access has now been parted by Jesus.

Anointing of the Sick

Q.•There is a long-standing practice in our diocese
•where the members of the charismatic movement
anoint one another, and especially the sick, with something called "St. Joseph's Oil." Some others call this the "Oil
of Gladness." Does the Church permit this practice of laypeople anointing the sick with oil? — *Name withheld*

Strictly speaking, it is not permitted. In a letter dated September
1, 2008, the Congregation for Divine Worship and the Discipline
of the Sacraments issued the following directive: "This Dicastery
observes that Canon 1003.1 expressly forbids anyone, other than
a priest, to administer the Sacrament of the Anointing of the Sick.
Furthermore ... no other person than a priest may act as ordinary
or extraordinary minister of the Sacrament of Anointing since such
constitutes simulation of the sacrament. This Congregation also
observes that there are only three blessed oils used in the Roman
Ritual, namely, the Oil of Catechumens, the Oil of the Sick, and the
Sacred Chrism. The use of any other oil or any other 'anointing'
than those found in the approved liturgical books must be considered proscribed and subject to ecclesiastical penalties. (cf. Can.
1379 and 1384) (Prot. 824/08/L)"

The letter goes on to direct that the bishops of South Africa,
who had requested the ruling, should restore proper sacramental
discipline where it is lacking and provide catechesis.

Hence it would seem that such anointings as you describe in
public charismatic prayer services should cease. Even if well-intentioned, such anointings cause confusion and are difficult to
distinguish between the similar-looking Sacrament of the Anointing of the Sick. One might certainly pray for the sick, and even lay
hands on them, but anointing them with oil is going too far, for the
reasons stated.

It would therefore be proper for pastors to end such practices that might be occurring in their parish. Clearly, such a move should be accompanied by a charitable catechesis and the presumption of goodwill.

Finally, there are some provisions for the use of exorcized, blessed olive oil in exorcisms. One might also use such oil privately, or in a very small group. But in large public church services, it seems the Church frowns on the use of blessed oil because of the confusion that is caused.

THE CHURCH'S LITURGY

The Mass

Q. If everybody only understood what Mass was really about there would not be a dry eye in the house. Is there a plan in the Church to incorporate this kind of reeducation in the homilies, etc.? — *Josie Rodriguez*

Education is only part of the solution. In the modern world we tend to think that education is the main answer to most things. To be sure, education is essential and of great value. One cannot love someone or something they know nothing about. But the biblical world speaks to an aspect of the problem we often overlook today: the will. Plainly stated, people do not know much of the Mass or the things of God because they don't want to.

Jesus spoke to this problem when he said: "For this people's heart has gown dull, / and their ears are heavy of hearing, / and their eyes they have closed, / lest they perceive with their eyes, /

and hear with their ears, / and understand with their heart, / and turn for me to heal them" (Mt 13:15). The the Letter to the Hebrews rebukes certain believers, saying, "About [Jesus] we have much to say which is hard to explain, since you have become dull of hearing" (5:11).

In other words, it is not that people simply have a lack of information. Information abounds in our world today as never before. It is not that people aren't smart. There is great skill evident in worldly matters such as careers, sports, and hobbies. Rather, the problem stems more from hardened, sinful, and unrepentant hearts of many who are not interested and are resistant to the things of God.

What, then, is the solution? Education, to be sure. But to this we must add prayers for conversion and the call to repentance. Saint John Vianney surely taught his congregation, but above all he prayed and fasted for them and exemplified a ministry of repentance thorough hours in the confessional. Such a ministry of prayer should not be limited to priests. Parents should not cease praying and fasting for their children to stay faithful to Mass and/ or return to the Faith. Parishioners should pray and fast for the return of many to the Church in their territory or region.

So, education is essential, but so is prayer with fasting (or abstinence). Education will generally be ineffective for those with hardened hearts and closed minds. For them, the logjam must be broken through the grace of repentance, a grace we must be more intentional about seeking and pleading for.

Q. Our pastor talks of the Mass as a sacrifice, but the deacon always calls it a meal. What is the Mass, meal or sacrifice? — *Name withheld*

Perhaps we should first remember that the Mass is not simply one thing or another. At its heart the Mass is the once-for-all sacrifice of Jesus made present to us. But the Mass is contextualized by

Christ in the heart of the Passover meal, where he links the bread and wine to his body and blood that are given over for us in the sacrifice of the Cross. There has been a modern tendency to over-emphasize the meal aspect and even set aside the sacrifice. But for the Church and for Christ, these aspects are joined. In a hymn he wrote, Saint Thomas Aquinas describes the Mass as: "O Sacred banquet, in which Christ is received, and the memory of his passion is renewed."

Q. **Does the Church have a position on saying Mass in a private home? A retired priest lives near our parish and says Mass in his home. A few people who do not seem to like our liturgies attend it, and this causes tension. —** *Name withheld*

There is not a juridical problem here, given the situation you describe. However, "home Masses" ought not be conducted without the approval of the territorial pastor. These days many dioceses have limited the celebration of home Masses, which used to be very popular. Masses are best celebrated in a church or oratory, at a dedicated altar. Home Masses should only be celebrated for serious pastoral needs (see the Vatican instruction *Redemptionis Sacramentum*, 108).

However, the norm can allow for a retired priest to celebrate in his home (especially if he has mobility issues), and a few of the faithful may attend. So, if the local pastor and diocesan norms permit, what you describe is allowable as a pastoral provision for a retired priest.

As for the tensions you describe, it is unfortunate, but allow the priests involved to work that out. Pastors sometimes choose to leave certain things unresolved, since resolving them might cause more problems.

Q. In one parish in our area, the altar has six candles; at another parish there are only two. Is there a proper number? Also, one parish places flowers ringing the whole altar, while another says flowers cannot be placed on the altar. — *Agatha Morris*

As for the number of candles, there are different options and traditions. The General Instruction of the Roman Missal (GIRM) says: "The altar is to be covered with at least one white cloth. In addition, on or next to the altar are to be placed candlesticks with lighted candles: at least two in any celebration, or even four or six, especially for a Sunday Mass or a Holyday of Obligation, or if the Diocesan Bishop celebrates, then seven candlesticks with lighted candles" (117). Since many altars nowadays face the people, fewer candles have been preferred. However, following the lead of Pope Benedict XVI, some took to placing six candles and a cross on the altar again, as was common before 1970.

As for flowers, instructions in the GIRM state, "Floral decoration should always show moderation and be arranged around the altar rather than on the altar table" (305).

Q. I was told that if a latecomer to Mass gets there by the homily the obligation to attend Mass is fulfilled. Is this so? — *Name withheld*

The Church does not teach these sorts of pastoral guidelines officially. Such exacting distinctions may be helpful but can also tend to a legalism or minimalism that is unbecoming for one called to love. A young man does not negotiate with his beloved as to the least amount of money he can spend on a date. This is not the language of love. In a similar way, one who loves God is eager to get to Mass and is seldom late. If something rarely comes up, he can repent for whatever part he played in the delay, trust and seek God's mercy, rather than insist on exacting delineations.

That said, pastors of souls, to assist troubled consciences and provide some parameters, have often set the demarcation you reference, but there is no official teaching regarding this.

Q.**As an older Catholic, a number of things bother me about Mass today. First, so few come. When I was young, we were taught that missing Mass was a mortal sin, period. Second, almost everyone goes up for Communion, and I doubt all of them are free from serious sin. Third, I come to hear Mass, not to sing Mass. We are so pressured to sing. I look forward to thoughts about these things. —** *Joanne DiOrio*

The Church still teaches that it is a mortal sin to miss Mass without a serious reason. The *Catechism* says: "The faithful are obliged to participate in the Eucharist on days of obligation, unless excused for a serious reason (for example, illness, the care of infants) or dispensed by their own pastor. Those who deliberately fail in this obligation commit a grave sin" (2181).

While the teaching has not changed, the preaching and understanding of this teaching has waned. In the period of the 1970s, notions that religious observance should be "authentic" (and therefore not compelled under pain of sin) led many preachers and catechists to tell young people merely to follow their hearts and feelings in such matters as this and other aspects of the moral law. The poor pedagogy of such an approach cannot be underestimated.

The *Catechism of the Catholic Church* sought to correct such a misguided approach. However, poor preaching and teaching has lasting effects that include not only mistaken ideas, but a kind of reticence to confront prevailing practices. Few clergy today teach the necessity of attending Mass or the reason why and the benefits received. This is gradually being corrected, and younger clergy are more prone to preach on such subjects.

It is much the same with holy Communion. There was a well-intentioned desire to get people back to receiving Communion more frequently beginning in the early twentieth century. Many had been taught, with a heavy emphasis, on our unworthiness to receive, so they only rarely received, usually once a year. Yet, what we have now is something of an overcorrection that downplays sin and overlooks the clear warning of the Scriptures that those who receive Communion unworthily bring condemnation on themselves, not blessing (see 1 Cor 11:27–32). Here, too, this is not preached regularly for likely the same reasons as stated above. It should be more widely taught, nationally by bishops and locally by priests.

As for music, you are entitled to your preference, but liturgically the Sunday Mass should ideally feature some degree of singing. This is not a new idea. The Solemn Mass and High Mass of the Latin Mass featured a lot of singing, though more "low" Masses were available then. Today, most parishes have at least one recited Mass on Sundays; it may be possible for you to attend that Mass given your preference.

Q: Why is there no dress code in the Church? There is immodesty and a lot of overly casual dressing for the miracle that takes place. — *Lois Doelz*

There is an understandable concern today about the way many people dress for Mass. There are issues of modesty and of people attending in clothes that seem far too casual for the holiness of the Mass and of God's house. The problem begins as a cultural one. The fact is Americans seldom dress up anymore for anything. Even many workplaces that once featured uniforms or suits and dresses have become very casual. Modesty, too, is a cultural problem that includes clothes that are often too tight or too revealing.

Culture is very influential for most — often, sadly, more influential than faith. Deep faith would seem to inspire devotion and a sense of the sacred. But due to poor formation in many, the influence of culture prevails, and most think little of how they dress when going to Mass. Frankly, most do not intend any irreverence but simply dress without a lot of thought.

A problem in issuing a dress code is that there is a range of acceptable views on clothing. In fact, the word "modesty" comes from the word "mode," referring to the middle of some range of views. And, frankly, standards vary across time and cultures, and especially regarding age. I have often found that many younger people are surprised (and a little irritated) to hear that what they wear might be considered irreverent. Older folks (such as me) remember times when standards were different.

That said, a general norm for men might be trousers, not jeans, a button-down shirt, or at least a T-shirt with a collar, no crazy slogans. For women, a skirt and blouse, or a dress with a hemline at knee level or lower. Women should avoid low-cut blouses. Sleeveless blouses are debatable.

Perhaps the best we can do is gently remind all people of the sacredness of the holy Mass and seek to grow their faith regarding how special the Mass is.

As for modesty, more significant moral issues are involved, but so are greater sensitivities. It is a delicate matter for a priest to speak in great detail about women's fashions. Frankly, we wish older women would take the lead here and speak to younger women. Priests and men can speak to younger men, but here, too, laymen ought to lead in this manner.

Q: There has been an attempt in my parish to end the talking before Mass by having the Rosary recited. However, it starts to drone and sound like a race to finish the decades. Others say it makes it difficult for them to pray quietly. Any thoughts on this practice? — *Art Osten*

Most medicines have some undesirable side effects. Similarly, the recitation of the Rosary before Mass can help to create a framework of some prayer, but it is not a quiet prayer, one of the unwanted side effects for those who like quiet time before Mass.

To those who like the church to be very quiet before Mass, I would offer one gentle correction: Though there is a legitimate need for some private preparation for Mass, the church is not, first of all, a private oratory. It is a place of public, communal prayer. Thus the recitation of the Rosary is not out of place in a space designed for public, communal prayer at a public time. Other things being equal, some preference should be given to the communal prayers over mere silence.

I would agree and add to the concerns you list that in some parishes where the Rosary has been tried to quiet the talkers, the talkers don't quite get the message. They just talk louder, usually in the back of church. And this results in the Rosary getting louder, and the cycle continues to amplify. Further, the Rosary may take on an almost angry tone, as those who seek compliance in praying the prayer grow frustrated (even if unconsciously) at the noncompliant talkers.

The problem of talking in church remains an annoyance for some but is also rooted in the trend in our culture toward extreme informality. In the "old days," people dressed for church and saw the parish church as a formal place where respect was due. In our current setting, people almost never dress up anymore, for anything. Formal behaviors are also all but gone. Post-1970 church design also encouraged informality. In such a context, thinking that things will improve "if only Father would say something" is somewhat wishful. I have tried this, only to find that people return to talking within a week or two.

This sense of futility, combined with the fact that greeting one's neighbor is not intrinsically evil, makes many pastors reticent to engage in a great battle for silence. In diverse Catholic parishes, it will be difficult (though not impossible) to regain a more formal stance and a quieter tone. The Rosary can help, but at day's end, it is going to be a long journey back to the kind of hushed formality many of us fondly remember.

Q. **Our priest uses large quantities of incense at Mass, creating difficulties even in being able to see with so much cloud. Also, people with respiratory issues are struggling. When we speak to him, he is dismissive and goes on about history and liturgy. Any thoughts?** — *John McElroy*

As with most things, moderation is proper when it comes to the use of incense. It would seem, as you describe it, too much incense is being burned at one time. While certain factors such as the size of the church, the height of the ceiling, and the ventilation may affect how much can be used, the goal in the modern use of incense is not to overwhelm or to make it difficult to see.

Your pastor's reference to history may indicate that he has something of the Old Testament concept in mind. When the high priest went into the Holy of Holies of the ancient Temple, ample amounts of incense were used, lest he catch sight of God and be struck dead. But given Jesus' ministry to us of sanctifying grace, this sort of concern is not a preoccupation today. Indeed, we are instructed in the liturgy to "behold the Lamb of God." So, the use of incense to create a kind of impenetrable cloud is something of a misapplication of an Old Testament concept, and also an excess to be avoided.

However, also to be avoided is the complete rejection of the use of incense in the liturgy. The use of incense is permitted, even encouraged, by the Church for feasts of greater solemnity. It is a beautiful image of prayer and worship ascending to God, as Psalms 141:2 says, "Let my prayer be counted as incense before you, / and the lifting up of my hands as an evening sacrifice." Incense symbolizes our prayers and praises going up to God, and its fragrant aroma is a sign of his blessings descending gently upon us.

Incense is not to be equated with cigarette smoke. It is not a known carcinogen, and it is not a pollutant when used moderately. In fact, incense, like holy water, is often blessed by the priest and therefore brings blessings. That said, there are some who suffer from various forms of respiratory distress who may suffer with excessive incense, at least physically. One compromise in these sorts of situations is to follow the older norms of the traditional Latin Mass. According to those norms, incense was not carried in the aisle, or the opening and closing processions, but was only imposed and used in the sanctuary area around the altar. This way, at least in larger churches, its effect on the whole congregation can be moderated.

Q. **I recently saw a picture of Pope Francis seated near the back of the chapel instead of up front in the special chair for the celebrant. I am moved by this humility and wonder why the priest sits up front during Mass.** — *Name withheld*

To clarify, Pope Francis was seated in the back of the chapel prior to the Sacred Liturgy. Once the liturgy began he vested and moved forward to the celebrant's chair. The celebrant of the Mass sits up front in virtue of the fact that he acts *in persona Christi*. The priest being seated in a prominent, visible place in the sanctuary is not honoring the man, but honoring Jesus Christ who acts in and through the priest, who is configured to Jesus by holy orders.

In this sense, through the Sacrament of Holy Orders, the priest in the liturgy is a kind of sacrament of the presence of Christ.

It is Christ who is honored and has a prominent seat. Jesus Christ is the true celebrant and high priest of every liturgy.

Q. Throughout the prayers of the liturgy, such as the *Kyrie*, we often speak of and to "the Lord." Are we referring here to Jesus or the Father? — *Helen Streeter*

In the *Kyrie* we are referring to Jesus. This is made fairly clear in the verses, such as, "You are the Son of God and the Son of Mary, *Kyrie Eleison.*"

However, more frequently Lord refers to the Father. Most of the prayers of the Mass, and especially the Eucharistic prayer, are directed to the Father through Christ. There are certain exceptions to this in the opening and closing prayers, but, in those cases, that we are referring to Jesus rather than the Father is made clear from the wording and context of the prayer.

Generally, the Mass is understood as a prayer of Christ the High Priest, directed to his Father, and it is in Christ's own prayer that we join. Thus, with certain clear exceptions, Lord almost always refers to the Father.

Q. The new *Gloria* says, "on earth peace to people of good will." The old *Gloria* said, "and peace to his people on earth." Are we only praying for non-evildoers? What is the emphasis of this change? — *Kevin Hansen*

The phrase you cite from the *Gloria* (itself a quote from Luke 2:14), is not about who or what we are praying for. Rather, it is about how God's peace comes to rest upon us and upon this world.

God's peace is not just a human wish that we have for others; it is the result of being in conformity to his will and about being reconciled to him. There can be no true peace where there is a refusal to live according to the vision of his kingdom. The biblical concept of peace (*shalom*) does not simply mean an absence of conflict, it means that there is present in the relationship everything that ought to be there — for example, justice, love, reciprocity, and truth.

God's peace can only rest on those who are of good will. The Greek word from Luke's Gospel, translated here as "good will," is *eudokia*, a word which describes one who manifests a desire and delight, who is disposed and open to the kingdom of God.

Therefore, the new translation is both more accurate in terms of the biblical text and more theologically accurate. Peace does not just drop out of heaven on all people. Rather, it results for those who, by God's grace, are open and disposed to what he is offering. Peace is the result that accrues to those who, by their good will and openness, accept what God offers.

Q.In my parish, at daily Mass, the Alleluia and verse before the Gospel are omitted. Is this permitted? — *Roseanna Miller*

Yes. The General Instruction of the Roman Missal indicates that the Gospel acclamation, if not sung, may be omitted (see 63). And while this does not seem to forbid reciting it, the acclamation is generally envisioned as a sung text. Hence if no one can reasonably lead the singing, omitting it is allowed. Another possibility is to sing the Alleluia without the verse. Generally, most congregations are able to sing a well-known melody of the Alleluia without a cantor. But here, too, situations vary, and the celebrant remains free to omit the Gospel acclamation.

Q•I write about a serious problem that is getting worse: priests telling jokes in church during sermons. Should this be allowed? People are coming to church to hear about God, but this makes light of it all? — *David O'Flaherty*

Humor or the telling of jokes is not intrinsically wrong. One might offend by excess of jokes or unsuitable content, but humor is widely regarded as a memorable way to teach. Jesus used humor, though at times that humor is less obvious to us. For example, he gave a parable about a man with a two-by-four in his eye who was anxious about a speck in his brother's eye. It's a funny picture. On another occasion, he told a parable about a persistent widow who wore out a judge with her complaints. The judge says to himself that he had better take care of her quickly before she gives him a black eye. Funny!

So, other things being equal, humor has its place and need not be construed as "making light" of the faith per se. As you illustrate, people have varying degrees of appreciation for humor. Its use should be balanced, but forbidding it is neither possible nor reasonable.

Q•Our new assistant pastor sometimes uses his iPad on the altar instead of the book. This seems strange to me. Is it allowed? — *Jeff*

You are not alone in thinking it strange. It is one of those newer things on the scene that seem odd in the context of an ancient liturgy. To most I have discussed this with, the iPad and other tablets are not ready for prime time, in its current form, for liturgical use.

Indeed, the bishops of New Zealand recently clarified for the priests that while the iPad may have many good uses, for the liturgy, the priest should stick with liturgical books. They wrote on April 30, 2012: "All faiths have sacred books which are reserved for those rituals and activities which are at the heart of the faith. The Catholic

Church is no different, and the Roman Missal is one of our sacred books, and its physical form is an indicator of its special role in our worship." Based on this, they go on to say that electronic devices may not be used by the priest at the liturgy in place of the sacred books. Exceptions can be made if a book cannot conveniently be located, or if the celebrant has difficulty seeing and the electronic device can help.

One can envision a time in the future when sacred books may take on electronic form, just as current printed books replaced ancient handwritten scrolls and paper replaced parchment and lambskins. But now is not that time.

Q. Since the pulpit is no longer used to inform Catholics what the Church teaches (the sermons I hear only reflect on the Gospel of that day), how are Catholics to know Church teaching? — *Name withheld*

It is true that many Catholics today are poorly formed in the Faith. Yet there are many reasons for this, not just silent pulpits. Neither is it necessarily fair to describe pulpits as silent. I know my own isn't, and I know many brother priests who carefully teach the Faith from their pulpits. This is certainly an ongoing process. I would say it takes at least five years in a parish before I can say, with Saint Paul, that I have proclaimed "the whole counsel of God" (Acts 20:27).

All that said, it is problematic to place exclusive focus on the pulpit. For there are many ways the Catholic faith must be taught. This is especially the case since most Catholics Masses have sermons lasting little more than twelve minutes. Thus other things must be added beyond the sermon in order to teach the Faith.

At the heart of handing on the Faith is the family. Therefore, catechesis should focus on renewing and equipping the family to better teach the Faith. In my own parish, while the children are in Sunday-school classes, I, as pastor, teach the parents what their children are learning. I also model for them how to teach. For example, we read Bible stories together, and then I show them how to teach using those stories. We also learn how to use the *Catechism* to find answers.

Beyond the parish, there are many wonderful resources for Catholics to learn of their faith. There are also many publications, blogs, websites, and various forms of Catholic media, including movies and lecture series. We are very blessed today with many resources that help to teach the Faith.

Q. The Nicene Creed says, "he suffered death and was buried and rose again on the third day." Why the word "again"? Did Jesus rise more than once? — *Name withheld*

Christ rose from the dead only once. The Latin text of the Creed merely says, *resurrexit tertia die* (he rose on the third day).

The use of the word again is merely an English mode of speech. While not strictly required, we tend in English to use again to indicate a restoration of a previous state. Thus I might say, "Joe went to the store and came back again." I clearly don't mean he came back more than once. In a general sense, again is emphasizing his return, that he is here now, that his status of being away is no longer the case. But more basically, it's just the way we talk. The translation of the Creed is simply using this common mode of speaking.

Q. At our parish the priest says a shortened Creed. Some Sundays he omits it altogether. When I talk to him about it, he gets angry. Should I go to the bishop? — *Name withheld*

The Creed is to be said each Sunday. It is possible that the shortened version you mention is the Apostles' Creed, which is a permitted option. Complete omission of the Creed is wrong, and if your request that the priest follow the requirement continues to be ignored, you should inform the diocesan bishop and ask for a written reply from his office as to how your concerns will be addressed.

Many have died for what the Creed announces. It is no mere ritual recitation.

Q. • The *Catechism of the Catholic Church* makes a rather heavy distinction between the "We believe" of the Nicene Creed, and the "I believe" of the Apostles' Creed (see 167). In effect, it teaches that the Nicene Creed emphasizes the communal nature of faith, and the Apostles' Creed emphasizes the faith professed personally by each believer. If the original Nicene Creed had "We believe," and the *Catechism* teaches on this so clearly, why then did the new English translation of the Mass render it "I believe"? This seems to be erroneous both in the light of the Greek text, of the Creed, and also the teaching of the *Catechism*.
— *Deacon Lawrence Gallagher*

The new English translation of the Creed to "I believe" is to bring the text in conformity with the authorized Latin text, which has "*Credo*" — namely, "I believe" — for the opening word of the Creed.

You are correct in noting that the text of the Creed coming forth from the Council of Nicaea used the Greek word *pisteuomen*, a first-person plural meaning "we believe." It was worded in this way because it came forth as a statement of all the bishops, speaking as a body, or college of bishops. Thus they rightfully said, "We believe."

However, in the years that followed, when the Creed was brought into the liturgy, the form was switched to the first-person singular, *pisteuo*, "I believe." This change was made because the Creed was now said by the individual believer in the context of the liturgy. This liturgical adaptation of the text is quite ancient and has been respected by the Church ever since. As the Greek liturgy moved to Latin in the West, the first-person singular, *Credo*, was thus used.

Your frustration related to harmonizing the new translation with the *Catechism* is understandable. However, it is possible to expect too much of liturgical texts, which have a particular context and are of their nature briefer when it comes to expressing the Faith. The *Catechism*, however, is able to develop richer aspects of the teachings of the Faith and to explore historical and/or biblical roots. Rather than see the *Catechism* and the Mass in competition or conflict, one can see them as complementary. In this case, the *Catechism* helps to further articulate what the liturgy announces.

Q. **In my new parish, the prayers of the faithful go on for a long time, including the reading of long lists of the names of the sick and selections from a prayer-request book in the vestibule. Is this proper?** — *Name withheld*

The prayers of the faithful are general in nature and should thus avoid overly specific prayer requests. For example, we pray for all the sick, not just some of the sick mentioned by name. "The intentions announced should be sober, be composed with a wise liberty and in few words, and they should be expressive of the prayer of the entire community" (GIRM, 71). When intentions become overly specific, they stray from the needs of the whole community and become too individualistic.

Q. I have heard that some prefer priests to face east more often. What does this mean inside a building? Also, I doubt the Last Supper was done this way. — *Name withheld*

To speak of facing east during the Eucharistic prayer is not simply equated with facing "compass east." Given street grids of cities and the layout of buildings, churches cannot always be situated facing east. Facing east (*ad orientem*) refers to a stance of the priest and the people during the Eucharistic prayer, where both priest and congregation face toward the crucifix. As such they are looking through Christ to the Father. Christ is our *oriens*, our "east," and he orients us to his Father.

This stance emphasizes that the priest, acting in the person of Christ, the head, is speaking to the heavenly Father on our behalf. Consider that one who represents a group before an official usually stands facing that individual with the people behind or beside him as he speaks. So, too, here.

As for how the Last Supper was celebrated, the Mass is not per se a reenactment of the Last Supper. It is the making present of the once-for-all perfect sacrifice of Jesus on the cross and his glorious resurrection. Christ himself pointed beyond the moment of the Last Supper to the cross: "This is my body which is given for you" (Lk 22:19).

Q. Our young priest faces the altar rather than the people for Mass. Is this allowed? — *Name withheld*

Technically, yes, and there are good liturgical and theological roots for the practice. Pastorally, however, as your puzzlement shows, a lot of teaching is necessary to explain the practice. Further, one might also argue that an individual priest ought not make a large change like this at a Sunday Mass without consulting his bishop. Careful teaching and organic change is the better way to reintroduce the ancient and, many would say, correct stance for the Eucharistic prayer. This can help avoid misunderstandings and backlash, as well as local and regional divisions that become a countersign of the charity and unity that should pervade the Sacred Liturgy.

Q. In my town there are parishes that vary tremendously in liturgical styles. I remember a day when the Mass was the same everywhere. How can we end this division? — *Name withheld*

There is a balance to be had between legitimate diversity and avoiding merely ideological divisions in liturgy. Truth be told, there has always been diversity, especially when one considers how different the Eastern rites of the Church are from the Western (Latin) rite. Current norms in the Latin rite allow for wider diversity, but there are set norms that must be followed. We must remain united in essentials and charitably allow for legitimate diversity that may not always appeal to our sensibilities. Our real unity is in charity and the essential truth of the Mass, not in merely external similarities.

Q. Why does the priest put water in the wine at Mass? — *Name withheld*

The practice of mixing water and wine was common in the ancient world. Wines were usually heavier than most modern vintages, and to dilute them a bit made them more palatable and less inebriating. People also drank more wine then since water in the ancient world could not be purified easily as is done today. Thus the wine used at Mass was mixed with water before the consecration in the usual manner of all wine.

Mystically it came to represent our inclusion into Christ's body by our baptism. The priest says: "By the mystery of this water and wine, may we come to share in the divinity of Christ who humbled himself to share in our humanity." Though the practical reason to mix water and wine is no longer needed, it still remains a powerful symbol, so its practice remains.

Q. Our new priest does not wash his hands at the offertory during daily Mass. He says that without a server it is difficult and the rite no longer has practical use. Is this correct? — *Bill Eitenauer*

The priest celebrant should wash his hands, even if there is no server. Though it is a bit awkward to pour water over one's hands from a cruet, finger bowls can perhaps be used for the purpose.

The explanation that there is no practical necessity to wash his hands does not hold. It is true that hand-washing in ancient times had more practical purposes due to the reception of many and varied gifts during the offertory procession. Handling these things often soiled the priest's hands. But liturgical rites don't have a merely practical point. The washing of the priest's hands has an important spiritual dimension as well, indicating his desire to be free of sin before offering the Holy Sacrifice and handling the Body and Blood of Christ. Omitting this rite is not permitted.

Q. I noticed while he was in Washington, D.C., in 2015 that Pope Francis went on with the celebration of the Mass while the choir was still singing at the offertory. Is this permissible today for priests? — *Name withheld*

Current liturgical principles counsel against proceeding with the Eucharistic prayer as you describe while other actions — for example, singing — are taking place. However, I would not make too much of what you saw. Outdoor Masses sometimes make hearing difficult, and the pope was not in his usual setting. It also appeared that he was in significant pain (from sciatica) that day. Norms, by definition, are oriented to normal settings. Large outdoor Masses are seldom able to observe every usual norm.

Q. I was visiting a parish out of my area and was surprised to see that the altar was bare until the offertory when, along with bread and wine, altar cloths and candles were brought in procession. The altar was then clothed and candles placed and lit, along with the bread and wine. Is this something new? — *Janet Murphy*

This is an innovation not allowed except in the rare circumstance of an altar being consecrated, or on Good Friday when the altar remains bare until the distribution of holy Communion. But in no case should altar cloths be brought up during the offertory procession.

The General Instruction of the Roman Missal directs and presumes that the altar is prepared before the Mass begins. It says: "The altar is to be covered with at least one white cloth. In addition, on or next to the altar are to be placed candlesticks with lighted candles: at least two in any celebration" (117). Thus the instructions direct that the altar should be prepared in this way prior to Mass.

Q. In Eucharistic Prayer 1, there is a phrase that implies the laity can make their own offering: "or they offer it for themselves." What does that mean? — *Peter*

The line you reference says, "For them, we offer you this sacrifice of praise or they offer it for themselves and all who are dear to them: for the redemption of their souls, in hope of health and well-being, and paying their homage to you, the eternal God, living and true."

While only the ordained priest can act in the person of Christ, all the baptized share in the royal priesthood of Jesus since they are members of his body. Priests are to offer sacrifices to the Lord. Thus each member of the faithful is called to bring to the Sacred Liturgy a sacrifice of praise or prayer and of our very selves. No one should come to the Lord empty-handed. We join our praise and sacrifices to the perfect offering of Jesus.

So, place your very self on the paten with the bread that the ordained priest offers. While the offering of money is also a sign of our sacrifice to the Lord, it is really our own self that we offer. This is in imitation of Jesus who offered himself. In the Old Covenant, the priest offered something distinct from himself — for example, an animal or a libation. In the New Covenant, priest and victim are one and the same. Therefore, we should offer our very self to the Lord in each Mass.

Q. **Why was the acclamation "Christ has died, Christ is risen, Christ will come again" eliminated from the new Roman Missal? It went from being the most popular of the memorial acclamations to becoming nonexistent.**
— *Jason Jackson*

The acclamation you cite was a loose translation of the first acclamation, "*Mortem tuam annuntiamus Domine ...* " That acclamation is now rendered more faithfully as, "We proclaim your death, O Lord, and profess your resurrection, until you come again."

There were some requests to retain the "Christ has died" version since it was so familiar, but those requests were not heeded. The essential problem with this rendering of the acclamation is that it spoke of Christ in the third person, speaking about him as if he were not present. All the memorial acclamations speak directly to Christ in the grammatical second person: "you." For he is present on the altar after the consecration. Hence in the new translation the acclamations speak directly to Jesus, not about him.

The old acclamation "Christ has died ... " could not withstand this critique and was dropped. Of itself it is a valid acclamation, and it can be used in songs or other settings, but it is not suited to the moment immediately following the consecration when the faithful are invited to speak to Christ in the grammatical second person — you — for he is present.

Q. **This past Sunday our priest had us sing a Protestant version of the Our Father. The congregation really enjoyed it, but I wonder if it is approved for use in a Catholic Mass.** — *Carolyn Pohlen*

Presumably, you refer to the well-known musical version of the Our Father by Albert Hay Malotte, which has the soaring doxology at the end: "For thine is the kingdom and the power and glory for ever and ever. Amen."

Liturgically, this presents two problems. One is the translation of the doxology, which, though the difference is minor, is at variance with the approved Catholic translation.

The second problem is that the musical arrangement does not reasonably allow the celebrant to proclaim or sing what is known as the "embolism," the prayer that begins, "Deliver us, Lord, we pray, from every evil, graciously grant peace in our days ... " This is because the musical arrangement of Malotte's Our Father is reaching a climax and moves right into the doxology. To stop the song at that moment and have the celebrant recite the embolism is clumsy, at best, and does dishonor to the musical setting as well. It is almost like stopping the national anthem at its musical climax and inserting a verbal interjection. It just doesn't work well.

When Malotte's Our Father is proposed for use in a Catholic Mass, it is usually sung straight through. But this is improper liturgically and cannot reasonably be used during Mass. It would seem that it can, however, be used in other liturgical settings with minor adaptations, since in those liturgies the embolism is not required.

Q.:In my parish, during the latest flu season, the staff was pressured by some to eliminate handshakes at the sign of peace. There were also suggestions to remove the holy water from the fonts. Are there any norms here? — *Name withheld*

No norms exist on this. These are prudential matters best left to personal discretion rather than parish policy. If one is concerned about germs and thinks his immune system is low, it is best to avoid shaking hands. We should, however, resist sweeping policies that could cause the liturgy to suffer harm, except in grave need (such as a plague). The sign of peace is optional and can be reasonably eliminated for pastoral reasons, but removing holy water is going too far.

Q.:Is it permitted for the cantor to add tropes or phrases such as "King of kings" to the Lamb of God? Also, should it be sung during the sign of peace? — *Bill Manners*

No. The U.S. Conference of Catholic Bishops clarified in September 2012 that is it is no longer permissible to alter the text of the Lamb of God. The number of times it is sung may be lengthened, however, to cover the action.

The *Agnus Dei* is meant to be sung during the breaking of the Host. The sign of peace, which should be brief, ends, and then the *Agnus Dei* is sung. It remains problematic that the sign of peace is often difficult to end, since many treat it as a kind of meet-and-greet rather than a quick sign of charity to those immediately nearby. Catechesis is necessary to keep the sign of peace brief.

Q. The new priest in our parish just stands at the altar when we sing the acclamations such as the mystery of faith, the great Amen, Lamb of God, etc. The previous pastor sang loudly with us. Should the priest not participate more fervently in these acclamations? — *Name withheld*

Actually, his stance is the correct one. The liturgical directives indicate that the people proclaim the mystery of faith, the great Amen, the conclusion to the Our Father ("for the kingdom the power and glory ... "), and the Lamb of God. Those are acclamations that belong to the congregation, not the priest. The priest is directed to say or sing the *Sanctus* and the "Lord I am not worthy" with the people. Since there are responses and acclamations that belong to the people, for the priest to say or sing them does harm to the dialogue and shared responsibility that is intended by the liturgy.

The priest should not look bored as the people respond. Rather, he should reverently and prayerfully attend to the response of the people.

Q. Our deacon told us that the small particle of the Host dropped into the chalice symbolizes the Resurrection. Is this so? — *Mary Tucker*

That answer is spiritualizing a practice that has a more complex history. Previously, bishops broke the Host and the small parts of it were taken to local parishes and dropped into the chalice as a sign of communion. Later, when that practice of the bishop fell into disuse, the priests continued this practice with the Host at Mass. It is not wrong to see it spiritually as the deacons says, but it is a somewhat contrived meaning.

Q. •During the consecration and before the distribu-
•tion of Communion, I see the priest break off a small
piece of the Host and drop it into the chalice with the Precious Blood. Why does he do that, and what does it signify?
If he fails to do it, does it invalidate the Mass? — *Dana*

The priest breaks off a small part of the consecrated Host during
the *Agnus Dei*. The rubrics in the *Roman Missal* specify: "Then he
takes the Host, breaks it over the paten, and places a small piece
in the chalice, saying quietly: 'May this mingling of the Body and
Blood of our Lord Jesus Christ bring eternal life to us who receive
it.'" The celebrant breaks the bread because that is what Jesus did
at the Last Supper, and on that very night Jesus said, "Do this in
memory of me."

Furthermore, the priest drops that little piece of the consecrated Host into the chalice with the Precious Blood to signify
the unity of the Church. As the General Instruction of the Roman
Missal explains: "The gesture of breaking bread done by Christ at
the Last Supper, which in apostolic times gave the entire Eucharistic Action its name, signifies that the many faithful are made one
body (1 Cor 10:17) by receiving Communion from the one Bread of
Life, which is Christ, who for the salvation of the world died and
rose again" (83).

If the priest, for whatever reason, fails to do it, that does not
invalidate the Mass.

Q. •A friend says that Martin Luther was the first to use
•wine at Mass. I think it was used from the beginning.
Which is correct? — *Orlando Santangelo*

Wine has always been used in the liturgy. At every Mass bread is
consecrated to become the Body of Christ, and wine to become
the Blood of Christ. What has changed is the degree to which the
chalice is commonly offered to all the faithful. Spillage and other

practical problems limited this over the centuries. The Church has also insisted that the whole Christ is received in the Host alone, and to offer the chalice to the faithful, while good and a fuller sign, is not strictly necessary. Only the priest is required to receive from the chalice.

Q. **I was taught to abstain from food or drink at least one hour before receiving holy Communion. Lately, I've been seeing people at Mass drinking bottled water before Communion. This includes a deacon sitting with the priest at the altar. I don't understand this. Has there been a change in the rules for fasting, etc.?** — *Joe Sikora*

Drinking water does not break the fast before Communion. The current rule, in place since 1964, says, "Whoever is to receive the blessed Eucharist is to abstain for at least one hour before holy communion from all food and drink, with the sole exception of water and medicine" (Canon 919).

It is a bit odd for a liturgical minister to be drinking bottled water in the sanctuary. Perhaps the deacon has a health issue. But, precluding that, one would think it is usually possible to go without water for an hour or two. Water bottles are a kind of modern fad. We previously managed quite well without them.

Q. **Our parish posted the availability of "gluten-free hosts." Is this not another diminishment of the True Presence? How could the Body of Christ make anyone sick?** — *Susana Gilardi*

So-called gluten-free hosts are not utterly free of all gluten. There are still some trace amounts. The U.S. bishops conference allows the use of very low-gluten hosts and urges additional caution by listing three reputable suppliers of them on the USCCB website.

As for the Blessed Sacrament making someone sick, it is not the sacrament that does so, but the "accidents." While your acknowledgment of the True Presence is laudable, it is important to remember that Catholic teaching states that, though the bread is transubstantiated, the accidents remain. The accidents are the physical attributes of the bread and wine — that is, what can be seen, touched, tasted, or measured. These remain, though the substance of bread and wine change to become the Body, Blood, Soul, and Divinity of Jesus. Hence it does not follow that one could not be affected by gluten in a consecrated Host, or by alcohol in the consecrated wine, for these attributes remain to our senses.

Q. **Our archdiocese has decided that those receiving Communion should remain standing until all have completed receiving. The rationale is a sign of unity. However, this does not seem very worshipful, and though we are permitted to be seated after the celebrant is seated, very little time is given for prayer. I've chosen not to remain standing, but rather to observe the traditional practice of returning to my pew and kneeling in prayer. Am I being disobedient?** — *Name withheld*

The instructions in the Roman Missal are silent regarding the posture of the faithful during the Communion Rite, though after the rite they may sit or kneel during the silence (see GIRM, 43). A bishop does have some authority to establish norms that do not violate universal norms. Other things being equal, it would seem the faithful should give due consideration and strive to follow these norms.

However, the norm you have articulated does present a few practical issues. Most notably, it would seem that the elderly and others with issues of physical stamina might find it difficult to stand for so long. Also, as you point out, it does make prayer difficult at a time that is often very precious to people seeking a quiet moment with the Lord. Given the rather hurried nature of most

American liturgies, it seems unlikely that significant time will be reserved after all are seated for quiet prayer.

Given that the local bishop does have the authority to request certain norms be observed, I encourage you to strive to listen to what he is teaching. Perhaps there is an issue in the local church that he is trying to address. While prayer certainly pleases the Lord, obedience pleases him even more. Scripture says, "Sacrifice and offering you do not desire; / but you have given me an open ear" (Ps 40:6).

In terms of answering your question in an absolutely legal sense, while not a canonist, I suspect that this norm should be interpreted in the same way that the norm for receiving Communion standing in this country is interpreted. While the norm requests, for the sake of unity, that the faithful receive Communion standing, an exception is to be made for those who strongly prefer to receive kneeling (see GIRM, 160). So, it seems allowance needs to be made for the faithful who strongly prefer kneeling in silent prayer.

As in all things, balance is required in understanding the nature of holy Mass. Mass is essentially the communal act of Christ with all his people; it is not essentially a private devotion. However, times of silent prayer and reflection are often mentioned in the general norms. But frankly, with the rather hurried Masses of modern times, periods of silent reflection are often nonexistent. In this sense, your concerns are understandable.

I surely encourage you to stay in communion with your bishop, and to continue to raise your concerns.

Q. •Do you know of a document that gives norms of what •extraordinary Eucharistic ministers can and can't do? Also, are they able to expose and repose the Blessed Sacrament for adoration? — *Name withheld*

Yes, there are norms. The most authoritative norms come from the U.S. Conference of Catholic Bishops, which takes the universal norms of the Church and applies them to the American setting. The title of the document is "Extraordinary Ministers of Holy Communion at Mass."

Among many other requirements, this document stipulates the following: Extraordinary ministers of holy Communion should be theologically and spiritually trained for this ministry. They should exhibit the greatest reverence for the holy Eucharist by their demeanor, their attire, and the manner in which they handle the consecrated species. They should only be used if ordinary ministers of holy Communion (bishops, priests, deacons) are not present. They should not approach the altar until after the celebrant has himself received Communion. If patens or ciboria are brought from the tabernacle, this should be done by the priest or deacon. Extraordinary ministers must receive Communion before distributing it to others. They should not take patens or chalices from the altar themselves; they should receive them from the priest or deacon.

In distributing holy Communion, they must use this wording: "the Body of Christ" or "the Blood of Christ." No words or names should be added.

Only a priest, deacon, or instituted acolyte may purify the vessels after Communion. If there is an extra amount of the Precious Blood that remains, extraordinary ministers may assist in consuming it.

In the absence of a priest or deacon, an extraordinary minister may expose and repose the Blessed Sacrament for adoration. But this may be done only simply. Extraordinary ministers do not confer blessings or wear the cope or veil, and they do not incense or say prayers. They simply place the Blessed Sacrament out for adoration or return it to the tabernacle.

Q.**Are there theological reasons that only the priest or deacon can purify the sacred vessels at Mass?** — *Chris Cunningham*

I am not aware of theological reasons for this norm. More likely, it is a prudential pastoral stance to encourage the priest to be more vigilant that vessels are properly purified.

Over the past decades there have been problems associated with the proper purification of vessels, which led to small fragments of the Host and drops of the Precious Blood being dropped or scattered. There were also problems associated with the Precious Blood being poured down sinks, etc. Priests are expected to be guardians of the sacred Eucharist. The requirement that the priest now personally attend to purifications seems more a disciplinary norm than a strictly theological matter.

Liturgical Seasons and Feasts

Q.**Why is the *Gloria* dropped in Advent, but not the Alleluia? In Lent, both are set aside.** — *Jermaine Lewis*

There is a tendency in the Church to "fast" from something to highlight and enjoy it more later. In Advent, we fast from the *Gloria* a bit so that when this song of the angels rings out at Christmas it will be more noticeable and festive.

Q.•I don't like the Advent wreath for two reasons. First, it is a modern innovation, not proper to the Roman (Latin) rite. Second, it had its origins in the Lutheran Church. Are not Advent wreaths really an illicit intrusion into the Roman Catholic liturgy? — *Name withheld*

I don't suppose it's an unwarranted intrusion any more than poinsettias are during Christmas, or any other extraneous decoration. Decorations are not intrinsic to the liturgy and are not really referenced in liturgical books.

Perhaps there is some violation of liturgical norms in some parishes where a kind of para-liturgical service is conducted for the lighting of the Advent candles. I have observed where families are invited to come up to light the candle while some verse of Scripture is read, etc. These sorts of things might be considered an intrusion. But if the Advent wreath is simply there, and the candles lit before Mass, there seems to be little harm in it.

As for Lutheran roots, most historical researchers would probably confirm this. Catholic parishes have adapted the Advent wreath by the use of purple rather than red candles.

You are certainly free to like or dislike the tradition of the Advent wreath. Most Catholics I speak with find it meaningful. But some caution is in order regarding your rejection of something simply because it is either modern or comes from outside Catholic sources. In the first place, your concern is somewhat at odds with the Catholic instinct, which down the centuries has often taken up things from the secular world or other religious traditions, even non-Christian ones. It is part of the genius of Catholicism to take up whatever is good, true, or beautiful in the cultures where she interacts and give them a distinctively Catholic meaning and flavor.

I would also offer caution based on the words of Jesus, who counsels a kind of prudential wisdom about things like these when he says: "Therefore every scribe who has been trained for the kingdom of heaven is like a householder who brings out of his treasure what is new and what is old" (Mt 13:52).

Therefore, categorically excluding something because it is modern or outside explicit Catholic origins is not the instinct either of the Church or the Scriptures.

Q. **I was told that the animals in the Christmas Nativity set have a symbolic meaning. Is this so, and if so what?** — *Jennifer Ladd*

Yes, the traditional animals of the Nativity set are chosen for a reason. The ox and the donkey are a reference to Isaiah 1:3, which says, "The ox knows its owner, / and the donkey its master's crib; / but Israel does not know, / my people does not understand."

This biblical verse is actually rather an unflattering self-accusation of our own human family, in effect declaring the animals are sometimes smarter than we are. And sure enough, there was no room at the inn of our human city, so the animals welcomed Christ. There is an antiphon from Christmas that says, "O great mystery and wondrous sacrament that animals would witness the birth of Christ and see him lying in a feed box [manger]." So, the question for you and me is: Are we smarter than oxen or donkeys, and can we understand the sacramental sign of Jesus the living bread come down from heaven lying in a feeding trough in a town called Bethlehem (which means "House of Bread")?

As for the sheep who arrive with the shepherds, they surely point to Jesus, whom John called the "Lamb of God, who takes away the sins of the world" (Jn 1:29). And this clearly points to Passover, wherein the blood of a lamb on the doorposts caused the angel of death to pass over, to spare the Jewish families the death of the firstborn males. It also points to the Temple sacrifices that sought atonement for our sins. Jesus is now this for us, who by his blood saves us from eternal death, and whose death atones for our sins.

Q.I regularly attend daily Mass, and I must admit I get • a bit confused at Christmastime. The very day after Christmas we are celebrating the feast of Saint Stephen, the first martyr, and later in the week we celebrate the feast of Saint John the Apostle. Why do we jump around so much at Christmas? It feels like we lose the focus on Jesus' birth. — *James*

Yes, and to add to your reflection, we also seem to move forward and backward in time during the Christmas cycle. The feast of the Holy Family, celebrated on the Sunday between Christmas and New Year's, features a Gospel of Jesus at twelve years of age. And then at Epiphany, celebrated a week later, Jesus is back to being an infant. Further, we observe the feast of the Holy Innocents on December 28, a terrible slaughter that took place after the visit of the Magi, and then we move backward in time to celebrate the feast of the Epiphany on the Sunday nearest January 6.

Some of these anomalies are explained by the fact that the liturgical year did not develop evenly over the centuries. The feasts of Saint Stephen and Saint John are ancient feasts on the Church's calendar. The celebration of Christmas, and the feasts related to Christmas, developed in later centuries.

It surprises many of us in modern times that the ancient Church did not focus a great deal on the birth of Christ. We are sentimental about Christmas and the baby Jesus, but the early Church focused primarily on the Paschal Mystery of Jesus' passion, death, and resurrection.

In later centuries, the Christmas feast became more elevated, but the focus was still more theological than sentimental. Thus it did not seem so alarming that the day after Christmas we were back to celebrating other saints such as Stephen and John.

Later, as the celebration of Christ's Incarnation deepened theologically and culturally, the octave of Christmas was developed. But the Church did not feel free simply to move aside the ancient feasts of Stephen and John.

As for the chronological whiplash of moving back and forth in time within the Christmas feasts, we should recall that in the celebration of the Sacred Liturgy we access eternity, rather than merely chronological time. For God, all times and events are equally present, and we meet him there, rather than simply on our schedule.

Q. A friend of mine in another diocese of the United States told me that her pastor said January 1 is not a holy day of obligation. Is this correct? — *Name withheld*

January 1, the solemnity of Mary, Mother of God, is a holy day of obligation, unless it occurs on a Saturday or a Monday. When that is the case the obligation to attend Mass does not bind in the United States.

The statement of the U.S. Bishops on holy days of obligation (in a 1991 decree) goes as follows:

> In addition to Sunday, the days to be observed as holy days of obligation in the Latin Rite dioceses of the United States of America, in conformity with canon 1246, are as follows: January 1, the solemnity of Mary, Mother of God; Thursday of the Sixth Week of Easter, the solemnity of the Ascension; August 15, the solemnity of the Assumption of the Blessed Virgin Mary; November 1, the solemnity of All Saints; December 8, the solemnity of the Immaculate Conception; December 25, the solemnity of the Nativity of Our Lord Jesus Christ.
>
> Whenever January 1, the solemnity of Mary, Mother of God, or August 15, the solemnity of the Assumption, or November 1, the solemnity of All

Saints, falls on a Saturday or on a Monday, the
precept to attend Mass is abrogated.

Also, in some dioceses the solemnity of the Ascension is
moved to Sunday, which results in one less holy day of obligation.
December 8 (because it is the patronal feast of the United States)
always binds, as do Christmas and the Ascension (where it is celebrated on Thursday).

To many, this system seems confusing, where some holy days
bind in some years and not others. It was a kind of compromise
the bishops made between two viewpoints. One view said that
holy days were important and should be observed. The other view
emphasized a pastoral solicitude wherein Catholics ought not be
required to come to Mass two days in a row.

As you can see, even experienced priests and parish staffs
struggle to remember all this. The old system, though more de-
manding, was easy to understand and remember. As you might
suspect, attendance at holy days has plummeted in recent years.
This is due as much to confusion as to a perception that most holy
days are only relatively important (when they don't inconvenience
too much), not intrinsically important.

One may wish for a simpler rule in the future, but it seems
unlikely we will ever again have "high holy days" in the Church like
we once did.

Q. Why do we celebrate the visit of the Magi on a day
   different from Christmas? Also, someone told me
there we more than three Wise Men who visited. — *Gene
Smith*

There are details of the Christmas story in the modern imagination that come to us from sources other than Scripture. These details may or may not be accurate.

So, it is true we do not know the exact number of the Magi who visited Jesus. Many presume the number three, since three gifts are mentioned: gold, frankincense, and myrrh. But there may have been two, four, or more; we just don't know for sure.

Likewise, the modern imagination tends to bring the Magi to the crèche the very night of Jesus' birth. Yet Scripture implies that their visit took place, likely, at a later time. This is because the text speaks of them finding Mary and the child in a house (see Mt 2:11), not at the crèche.

Liturgically, we distinguish the two events, emphasizing in Epiphany the "manifestation" (which is what "Epiphany" means) of Christ to the Gentiles and the call of the nations to faith and worship of Christ.

Q. Where does the word "Lent" come from? In my native Spanish we just call the season "*cuaresma*," which seems more descriptive. — *Anna Gonzalez*

You are right. The Latin title for this period is *Quadragesima* and is best translated "fortieth day (before Easter)," or more loosely "the forty days." Most of the Romance languages keep this root in their words for the season — for example, *cuaresma, quaresma, carême, quaresima* — and these are, as you say, more descriptive and less abstract.

The word Lent seems to have Germanic roots, wherein the words *lenz* and *lente* refer to the spring season, when days "lengthen." Thus the word Lent describes less the liturgical time frame and more a seasonal one. So, as the days lengthen our thoughts move to Easter and, beginning forty days before, we spend time spiritually preparing for that greatest feast of the Church's year.

The notion of forty days, of course, reminds us of the forty days Christ spent in the desert fasting and praying in preparation for his public ministry. We are encouraged to go into the desert with him spiritually and be strengthened through the spiritual exercises of resisting temptation, praying, and fasting.

"Giving up something" for Lent is not merely for its own sake, but rather to make room for other things. Thus if we forgo some lawful pleasure we can perhaps be freer to pray. And whatever money we may save by simplifying can be given to the poor.

Q. Someone said that Lent is not exactly forty days. If this is true, then why do we call it the forty days? — *Melissa Romano*

The General Norms for the Liturgical Year and the Calendar, published by the Vatican, says, "Lent runs from Ash Wednesday until the Mass of the Lord's Supper exclusive" (28). This is forty-four days. Omitting Sundays (which are part of Lent) from the count does not help, since that yields thirty-nine days. Saying Lent doesn't really begin until the first Sunday of Lent yields forty but defies the definition given in the General Norms and by tradition.

Therefore, in saying "forty days of Lent" we speak generally, not in a literalistic way. The period is approximately forty days, so we call it the forty days. This troubles some, but really it shouldn't. Exactitude and specificity have their place, but we often speak inexactly and generally. For example, we may say something "lasted a month," but that could mean twenty-eight days, thirty days, or thirty-one days — and even occasionally twenty-nine days! But the word month still applies, and we adjust.

Q. Many years ago, in my youth, I recall that Passion Sunday and Palm Sunday were different Sundays. Is this so, and why then is the Passion read on Palm Sunday? — *Leo Renne*

Yes, prior to 1970 the Fifth Sunday of Lent was called "Passion Sunday," and statues and crosses were traditionally veiled beginning that Sunday until Easter. The reason for this title was that the Church was setting her sights on the Passion. The following Sunday was called Palm Sunday and opened Holy Week. After 1970, the two Sundays were combined on Palm Sunday and became "Passion (or Palm) Sunday."

The reading of the Passion on Palm Sunday, however, is a very old tradition, since it was accepted that many would not or could not attend on Good Friday. Given the importance of the Passion being heard in its entirety by the faithful, the Church assigned the reading to Palm Sunday, the Sunday closest to Easter.

Q. On this most recent Good Friday, at my parish, Communion was offered at the evening service under both forms — that is, the Host and Precious Blood. When I asked the pastor, he said it was a long tradition at the parish to save the Precious Blood from the night before and receive it on Good Friday. He told me of all days, Good Friday, when Christ shed his blood, was the most fitting day to receive the Precious Blood. Is this practice allowed? — *Name withheld*

No, it is completely irregular.

Not only is the practice itself wrong, but the sacramental theology to justify it is erroneous. The doctrine of the Church teaches that under either species alone, the whole and complete Christ is received. To suggest, therefore, as it seems the pastor does, that the Precious Blood is somehow not received when only the Host is consumed, is a flawed notion.

Further, since no Mass is celebrated on Good Friday, the practice you describe requires that the Precious Blood be reserved overnight. But the norms currently in force forbid the reservation of the Precious Blood after the celebration of Mass: "The consecrated wine, on the contrary, should be consumed immediately after communion and may not licitly be reserved" (*Inaestimabile donum*, 14; see GIRM, 163, 182, 247, 249; *Redemptionis Sacramentum*, 107).

Canon 925 does state that, in the case of necessity, it is permitted to give Communion under the species of wine alone to a sick person. In this case, the Precious Blood may be reserved briefly in a properly sealed vessel in the tabernacle after Mass. However, it should not be considered an ordinary occurrence.

Q. •Our pastor uses a single crucifix for the veneration •of the cross on Good Friday. He explains that this is the Church norm (which I don't doubt). However, with the large crowd, it took fifty minutes this past Good Friday to complete the adoration. Other parishes I know use multiple crosses when there are large numbers. Your thoughts please. — *John Downs*

As you have noted, the norms do specify that only one cross should be used for adoration at the Good Friday service. The norm states: "Only one cross should be used for adoration. If, because of the large number of people, it is not possible for all to approach individually, the priest, after some of the clergy and faithful have adored, takes the cross and, standing in the middle before the altar, invites the people to adore ... and holds the cross elevated higher for a brief time, for the faithful to adore in silence" (*Missale Romanum*, "Rubrics for Good Friday," 19).

The adoration of only one cross, though time-consuming, makes sense. Only one cross is solemnly brought into the church and unveiled. It is the real focus of the Good Friday service.

A pastor and congregation have a decision to make when large numbers are present. Either they are going to extend time for adoration and make it a time of meditation while all adore, or the adoration will be shortened in the way the missal describes. Adoration is accomplished in other ways than a kiss.

Further, the full singing of the reproaches and other chants, and meditating on them, is one way the Church seeks to draw us into prayer rather than merely waiting for the adoration to be completed.

The fifty minutes you describe is surely long and probably required abbreviation. In less extreme cases, we ought not be in a hurry during the Triduum services, which are, of their nature, extended and meant to provoke deeper meditation on the sacred mysteries.

Q. Why is Easter a floating holy day? Why can't the Church celebrate Easter on the same Sunday each year? The bishops have moved other holy days for convenience. Why not Easter? — *Bill Bartkus*

The date of Easter varies each year because it is linked to the cycle of the moon relative to the cycle of the sun. In order to set the date of Easter one must first look for the vernal (spring) equinox, which is generally March 20. The word "equinox" refers to that time when the lengths of day and night are equal. It is also the date we set for the official beginning of spring.

Having set our sights on March 20, we next look for the first full moon following March 20. Some years, the first full moon occurs quickly, within days of the equinox. Other years it occurs weeks later.

For the Jewish people, this first full moon after the equinox also signaled Passover. And since it was at the Passover feast that our Lord Jesus suffered, died, and rose, we Christians always fix Easter to coincide with Passover.

So then, Easter (which is always on a Sunday since Christ rose on the first day of the week) is celebrated on the Sunday following the full moon after the vernal equinox.

Historically, there have been great debates within the Church in the East and West about setting the date of Easter. The system described above was finally settled upon. But today, we still find that the exact date for Easter varies a bit in the Western and Eastern parts of the Church, since many of the Eastern rites still use the more ancient Julian calendar, rather than the Gregorian calendar used by the Church in the West.

Your wish for a fixed day for Easter, as is the case with Christmas and other feasts, is understandable. But as you can see, the relationship of the moon relative to the sun doesn't fit perfectly into our modern systems of timekeeping, and to fix the date as you suggest would probably open old debates that caused great harm in the early Church.

Q. **Several years ago, a priest said in a sermon that Easter is a more important holy day than Christmas. This rather upset my young daughter, eight at the time, who said that Jesus could not rise unless he had been born. Even several years later she will mention this and express irritation at the priest's claim. Is there something I should say to her, or just leave this matter to the realm of opinion?** — *Name withheld*

The first and foundational dogma of the Christian faith is that Jesus is risen from the dead. Saint Paul says: "If Christ has not been raised, then our preaching is in vain and your faith is in vain. We are even found to be misrepresenting God, because we testified of God that he raised Christ. If Christ has not been raised, your faith is futile and you are still in your sins. Then those also who have fallen asleep in Christ have perished. If for this life only we have hoped in Christ, we are of all men most to be pitied. But in fact Christ has been raised from the dead" (1 Cor 15:14–15,17–20).

Easter proclaims and celebrates this fact, which make it the most important feast of the Church's year. While it is true that Christmas celebrates Christ's birth, without which there would be no resurrection, it does not follow that the day of one's birth is the most significant thing about him or her. For example, few people know or remember the birthday of Thomas Edison. What they remember is that he invented things, such as the light bulb. Birth is common to all people, and to the degree that we remember or know their birthday, it is because they did something memorable.

Jesus rose from the dead, fulfilling his many promises to do so. By this act his authority and identity as Lord and God is confirmed, and every other truth taught by him is thereby confirmed. His human birth confirms his identity as a man, something common to prophets, rabbis, leaders, and all others. His resurrection confirms that he is Lord.

You might also explain to your daughter that Christmas is actually a "late" feast on the Church's calendar. There is little evidence that Christmas was widely celebrated in the Church before the fifth century. Epiphany is older and was the first feast of the Christmas cycle to be observed. Further, two of the Gospels contain no narrative of the birth of Christ.

Last, and to be clear, the Incarnation is certainly an essential doctrine. But if that be the case, the feast of the Incarnation (March 25, the Annunciation) should really be your daughter's focus. For, based on her logic that nothing else happens if we don't exist, the beginning of Christ's human nature is celebrated on March 25, not December 25.

Q: Is there a difference in meaning between the words Hallelujah and Alleluia? If not, why are they spelled differently? — *Donella Matthews*

No, both words are the same. Hallelujah is a Hebrew word (*Hallal* [Praise] plus *Yah* [The LORD]). But the exact way the Hebrew letters are transliterated into English and other languages has varied a bit over time. Perhaps most influential is the fact that the Greek New Testament rendered the Hebrew word as *allelouia*. Since Greek is generally more influential in English spellings than Hebrew, many English translations render the word as Alleluia.

However, not an insubstantial number of English translators have preferred over the centuries, especially when translating the Old Testament Hebrew, to render the term Hallelujah. Some translators will use Hallelujah for the Old Testament and Alleluia for the New Testament.

Music has also influenced the decision over which spelling to use, since some of the famous compositions from the Baroque period, such as Handel's *Messiah*, used the spelling Hallelujah that was more common in earlier English translations of the Bible.

At the end of the day, it is the same word, just with different spellings.

Q: Shouldn't we be celebrating Pentecost for more than one day? Given the amount of time we celebrate Christmas and Easter, it seems appropriate that Pentecost be given at least a short season. — *Dianne Spotts*

Prior to 1970, the Church emphasized Pentecost in two ways. The first was the celebration of an octave. The octave was a stretch of eight days that included and followed the actual feast of Pentecost Sunday.

It is one of the quirks of the post-conciliar liturgy of 1970 that the octave of Pentecost was dropped. Generally, the post-conciliar age has tried to emphasize the gifts and works of the Holy Spirit. But, paradoxically, the octave was eliminated. (The feast, as you note, ranks right up there with Easter, which has an octave, and the Nativity, which has an octave.) Therefore, suddenly, on the Monday after Pentecost, we are back to Ordinary Time and using green vestments.

Priests, however, have the option of celebrating votive Masses of the Holy Spirit for the days that follow Pentecost (unless there is an obligatory memorial or feast). Perhaps you might encourage your priests to consider celebrating a sort of unofficial octave of Pentecost through the use of votive Masses.

A second way that Pentecost was emphasized prior to 1970 was that the Sundays and weeks of the year were counted in relation to the feast of Pentecost. Thus a certain Sunday would be called the "Fourth Sunday after Pentecost" or the "Fifth Sunday of Pentecost." In 1970, that was dropped, and a practice of numbering the weeks independently of Pentecost was adopted. Now we hear of the "Third Sunday of Ordinary Time" and so forth.

The reasons for such changes are obscure, and some wish for a return to the previous enumerations and restoration of the octave of Pentecost as an official observance. I would support such a move, but liturgical changes generally move slowly.

It should be noted that currently, with the wider use of the Extraordinary Form of the Mass and its calendar, there does still exist in the Latin rite the octave of Pentecost. Hence it is still officially celebrated and enumerated in that form of the rite.

Inside the Church

Q. **I am a veteran and currently debating with my pastor who refuses to allow the American flag to be displayed in the front of the church. It is back in the vestibule. Are there rules about this?** — *Joseph*

There are no specific rules about flags in either the liturgical books or the Code of Canon Law. However, some time ago the U.S. bishops' Committee on the Liturgy encouraged pastors not to place the flag within the sanctuary itself, which is for the altar, the ambo, the presidential chair, and the tabernacle. They recommended an area be found outside the sanctuary or in the vestibule of the church. But these are recommendations only, and it remains for the diocesan bishop to determine regulations in this matter.

So, your pastor is on fairly good ground. Patriotism remains an important virtue for Christians, but how that patriotism is expressed in the location of the flag can admit of some local differences and should conform well to liturgical norms as well as pastoral solicitude.

In my own parish, by tradition, the flags are in the sanctuary off to each side. But they do not usurp the prominence of the altar or ambo.

Q. **Our new pastor says the altar in our church is too far away from the pews, so for daily Mass he uses a table outside the sanctuary. Is this proper?** — *Name withheld*

Generally, the norms of the Church indicate that the altar should be fixed — that is, immovable — made of stone, and located in the sanctuary of the church — that is, in an area of the church distinguished from where the people gather and are seated (see "Built of Living Stones: Art, Architecture, and Worship," by the U.S. bishops).

At first glance, it would seem that your pastor is operating outside these norms and that the appropriate place for him to celebrate Mass is at the main altar of the church. Sometimes, however, in older or larger churches, the pastoral challenge you described is present. In such cases the use of a smaller altar, closer to the people (as is done in some larger basilicas), is employed.

The movable altar should be truly noble, not a simple folding table, and should be dedicated to no other purpose than the celebration of the Sacred Liturgy. While this is not ideal, in some instances it may be pastorally allowable, especially if recourse to a chapel for daily Mass is not possible.

Q. **I attend a parish named Immaculate Conception. Recently installed was a large painting of Mary on the back wall behind the altar, and I was upset since I think the altar area should remain wholly dedicated to Christ and not give the impression we are directing worship to Mary. I am so upset that I may leave this parish.** — *Susan*

Your concerns are not without merit. While there are no rules absolutely forbidding images of the saints in the sanctuary, current norms and customs speak of the sanctuary area of the Church as emphasizing the altar, the ambo (pulpit), and the chair. There should also be, on or near the altar, a crucifix. Further, the tabernacle, in most parish settings, is usually in a prominent place, either within or very near the sanctuary (see "Built of Living Stones").

That said, while images of Mary and the saints in the central axis of the sanctuary are not common in modern church design, it is not absolutely forbidden, either. There may be some merit to have the patron of the parish church, in your case Mary, prominently displayed (as many older churches do) somewhere near the front, presuming it does not overly dominate the sanctuary.

Perhaps there may be some merit in placing a crucifix on the altar, but only if any other crucifixes in the area are well out of sight, since more than one crucifix in the sanctuary is discouraged (see, again, "Built of Living Stones").

It is regrettable that this has caused you such grief as to consider leaving the parish. Perhaps a spiritual way to accept what you consider less than ideal is to remember that we *do* gather with the saints at Mass. According to the Letter to the Hebrews, "We are surrounded by so great a cloud of witnesses" (12:1). There may also be benefit in recalling the description of the early Church at prayer: "All these with one accord devoted themselves to prayer, together with the women and Mary the mother of Jesus" (Acts 1:14).

As you rightly express, we pray *with* the saints, and they with us, we do not worship them.

Q. Our new parish priests forbids the ringing of the tower bell before Mass. This is a rural area and we have done it for years. He gets quite angry about it and has made many of us angry, too. Is there anything wrong with ringing a bell? — *Theresa Lichty*

No, there is no prohibition on ringing the bell. It is difficult to say why your priest would find this practice problematic. But the ringing of the bell to call people to Mass is traditional, especially in rural areas. In my city parish, the tower bell rings fifteen minutes before each Mass and also rings for the noon and 6:00 p.m. Angelus.

It is true that this practice comes from times when watches and clocks were rare among ordinary people. The church bells actually helped people tell the time of day and know when services were to begin. Today, they are not often necessary for that reason. However, they do serve as a sacred reminder and a call to prayer, even for those who know the time of day.

The same holds true for the ringing of the small bells inside a church at special times of the liturgy, such as the elevation of the Host and chalice. Some argue this practice comes from a time when the priest, facing the altar, celebrated the Mass quietly and the bells were necessary to get the attention of the people, who may have been saying personal prayers during the Eucharistic prayer. This may have some truth to it, but things in the liturgy seldom have a merely practical purpose, or only one meaning. When most Catholics are asked what the ringing of the bells means to them, they say it conveys a sense of the sacred, or a call to prayer.

Your question does not indicate if you spoke to the priest and asked his reasons. Of course, this is always the best option when wondering why people do things. Perhaps asking him at a time remote from the anger or conflict will help.

Sacred Music

Q. **As a music minister, I read with great interest a question posed to you regarding the exclusion of some hymns by a parish priest on grounds of doctrinal error. The hymnal we use at my [parish] does not have a "*nihil obstat*" or *imprimatur*. However, it does indicate it is published with the approval of the Committee on Divine Worship, United States Conference of Catholic Bishops. Therefore, all the hymns contained in the hymnal are accepted for liturgical performance by the USCCB. So, who has ultimate authority over the published liturgical music — the parish priest or the USCCB?** — *Richard Derry*

There is some oversight by a committee of bishops on the publication of hymnals, but that should not be taken to remove any authority of the pastor whatsoever. He has a duty to oversee the liturgy in his parish.

There are, at times, issues in local communities that might mean a hymn which is otherwise acceptable could create problems locally. Perhaps the pastor is seeking to overcome a misunderstanding that is prevalent in his parish and a certain hymn would not help. Some parishes (say, in the deep South) have been more influenced by Protestant notions than others. A pastor needs the capability to recognize this and act accordingly. Committees of bishops cannot know the situation in every local parish or locality.

While a pastor should not reject certain music or hymns merely as a result of his own preferences or taste, he may have good reasons, and the divine worship committee of bishops at the USCCB does not intend to take authority away from him. Their declaration simply states that there are no doctrinal errors per se. That a given text or song is not erroneous does not mean that it is expedient or helpful.

Even as an individual bishop is the chief liturgist of his diocese, in a subordinate sense the pastor is the chief liturgist of his parish. As long as he follows required norms, he is within his rights to make judgments about the appropriateness of hymns both textually and stylistically for the parish he is obliged to oversee.

Q.**Our parish priest won't allow two songs to be sung in church anymore: "Amazing Grace" and "How Great Thou Art." They're beautiful and well loved by the parishioners! What's going on?** — *Sandy Vignali*

Since I cannot speak directly to the priest involved, I am going to presume he has some doctrinal concerns with the words of these songs rather than a mere dislike of them.

Certain songs in the Catholic hymnal, some from Protestant tradition and others newly composed in Catholic circles, have doctrinal imprecision that seems to persist even when critiqued. For example, songs of certain Catholic composers from recent decades exhort: "Let us build the city of God," or they bid us to "Sing a new church into being" and "create ourselves anew." We do no such things. God builds his city, there is no "new" Church, and the act of creating pertains to God alone. In modern Eucharistic hymns there is also a lot of imprecision, such as Jesus being "in" the bread and wine, and suddenly we sound like Lutherans, not Catholics.

Protestant hymns, even when edited by certain Catholic hymnals, also may contain imprecisions that can mislead. Thus in "Amazing Grace" we refer to ourselves as a "wretch." This is a classically Protestant view, which sees man as totally depraved. But Catholicism does not use such language and teaches that, even in our fallen state, we retain dignity and the image of God. We are wounded, but not totally depraved.

Another line in the hymn speaks of grace coming "the hour I first believed." But here, too, there is imprecision since grace comes not from the act of believing per se, but solely from Christ. It is really at baptism, the act whereby Christ sanctifies us and makes us members of his body, that grace "appears." Further, grace does not simply appear, it actually changes us.

I am unaware of any doctrinal problems with the hymn "How Great Thou Art," so I cannot speak directly to your pastor's objection there.

In all these matters a balance must be found. At times the imprecisions of hymns (which speak poetically more than academically) can be understood in a Catholic, orthodox way. While not being wretches in the absolute sense that Luther and Calvin taught, our state is wretched apart from Christ, in the qualified sense of being deeply wounded and needy. Singing a "new church" into being can be understood as renewal and our cooperation with God's work of constantly renewing his Church, etc.

Prudentially however, priests and liturgists differ on what to do. Some tolerate the imprecisions; others use them as a preaching opportunity to clarify. Still others seek to remove the songs altogether. Your pastor seems to have chosen the third approach. Talk with him and find out more; ask him to teach and clarify.

Q. •I was told that we can't sing the song "Yahweh, the •Faithful One" anymore. I haven't heard anything from the Church magisterium about this issue. — *Craig Kappel*

In 2008, the U.S. bishops' conference sent word that the Tetragrammaton YHWH (what most of us know as Yahweh) should not be said or spoken aloud in Catholic liturgy. In Jewish tradition, it was held to be unpronounceable and hence was replaced by an alternate name *Adonai* ("Lord"). Similarly, Greek translations of the Bible have used the word *Kyrios* and the Latin *Dominus*, both of which also mean Lord. This request to avoid speaking this particular form of the divine name is a way of remaining faithful to the Church's tradition, stretching back to those earlier days.

The original Roman directive was given in *Liturgiam Authenticam*, the 2001 document on liturgical translations. Hence it seems clear that songs and biblical translations that use Yahweh should be adapted so that this form of the divine name is not said or sung aloud.

Q. •In our hymnal there are many lines which concern •me. One hymn says, "I myself am the bread of life ... you and I are the bread of life." Another says, "We become for each other the bread, the cup." — *Name withheld*

Such lines ought to cause concern. Interpreted in a rather literalistic way, they seem to declare equivalence between the sacrament of the holy Eucharist and of our communion with one another.

It is true that the concepts are related, but they are not equivalent or substitutable. One, in fact, causes the other: our communion with Christ in holy Communion effects our communion with one another. I suspect that is what these hymns are trying to get at, but they do so in a clumsy way, as if the two were simply and merely the same. They are not. For Christ is not simply reducible or equivalent to the sum total of his members. He, as God, is greater than and is the cause of the communion we enjoy with one another.

That said, we must accept the limits of what art and poetry do. Hymns are a form of poetry and cannot always have the doctrinal precision that we might expect of a theological treatise. Context is important, and hymns use a poetic genre. Nevertheless, some of the older Eucharistic hymns were able to speak poetically and yet not sacrifice doctrinal precision. Perhaps we could hope for more than we often find in many modern compositions.

Q.At our parish, when the psalm is sung, the text used routinely varies from my new and authorized prayer book. Is it acceptable for the musicians to change the words as they do? — *Jim Schafbuch*

Not if that is what they are actually doing. The proper responsorial psalm from the day should be said or sung. However, there are exceptions. Liturgical norms state the following:

> The Responsorial Psalm ... should usually be taken from the Lectionary. It is preferable for the Responsorial Psalm to be sung.... However, in order that the people may be able to sing the Psalm response more easily ... Psalms ... chosen for the different times of the year ... may be used instead of the text corresponding to the reading whenever the Psalm is sung. If the Psalm cannot be sung, then it should be recited.... There may [alternately] be sung either the Responsorial Gradual from the Graduale Romanum, or ... Graduale Simplex ... or an antiphon and Psalm from another collection ... providing that they have been approved by the Conference of Bishops or the Diocesan Bishop.

> Songs or hymns may not be used in place of the
> Responsorial Psalm. (GIRM, 61)

As can be seen, an exception can be made, for reasons stated, to using the psalm for the day. In some parishes, the ability of the musicians and/or the people to learn and use different responses each week varies. Thus pastoral provision permits the use of certain seasonal psalms and refrains. But substituting hymns in place of the responsorial psalm is not permitted, and only texts approved by the bishops are to be used. It is possible that the words of the psalm that are sung may differ from what is in your prayer book, and appropriate, but only if the variant text is approved by the bishops.

For musicians, parishes, or pastors to make unauthorized changes to the texts of the psalm is strictly prohibited. Most commonly the forbidden changes involve altering the text to be "inclusive." But, theologically, certain texts in the psalms often refer to Christ, and altering the text loses the Messianic reference. Hence bad and unauthorized changes yield bad theology. It is properly prohibited.

Q. **It seems to me that, at Mass, priority should be given for the congregation to hear the priest and be involved with him in the preparation of the gifts and the prayers he says as he mixes the water and wine, etc. But it appears that more emphasis is given to singing at these times. — *William Dignan***

Liturgical norms of the Church seek to balance a number of things, such as the experience of Mass as a personal encounter with Christ and as a communal act of worship. It also tries to balance actions that pertain to the priest as opposed to what pertains to other liturgical ministers and the faithful who are gathered.

It is clear that you prefer less singing and would rather be directly engaged with the actions on the altar. However, in the prayers of the preparation of the gifts, the norms implicitly presume and favor that some sort of singing is going on. The celebrant is instructed to say these prayers inaudibly if singing is occurring; otherwise he may (not must) say them aloud.

Other prayers at that time are always to be said inaudibly by the priest, such as when he mixes the water and wine and bows to say the prayer that begins, "With a spirit of humility ... " The prayer that the Lord wash away his iniquity as he washes his hands is also to be said inaudibly, even if there is no music.

All of this is the way of demonstrating that during the preparation of the gifts the direct engagement of the faithful in the action is not the only or primary point. Hence congregational singing, taking up a collection, etc., are not distractions. The priest is performing these actions as a priest along with the deacon and other ministers, on behalf of the faithful.

As for hearing and seeing everything the priest is doing, this has value, but it is not the only value. Prior to 1970 the priest who was turned toward the altar whispered almost the entire Eucharistic prayer. (In the Eastern-rite Churches today, the priest often goes behind an iconostasis.) Though today this is seldom the case in the Ordinary Form of the Roman (Latin) rite, the principle still applies that the priest at the altar has gone up before God and is speaking to him and acting on behalf of the faithful in the person of Christ.

Q. I think that the reception of holy Communion is probably the most precious time a person can have to commune with the Lord. Why, then, are we forced to sing hymns the entire time Communion is being distributed, making it impossible for us to converse with the Lord?
— *David Tomko*

Liturgical norms state: "While the Priest is receiving the Sacrament, the Communion Chant is begun, its purpose being to express the spiritual union of the communicants by means of the unity of their voices, to show gladness of heart, and to bring out more clearly the 'communitarian' character of the procession to receive the Eucharist. The singing is prolonged for as long as the Sacrament is being administered to the faithful" (GIRM, 86). The instructions also state: "When the distribution of Communion is over, if appropriate, the Priest and faithful pray quietly for some time. If desired, a Psalm or other canticle of praise or a hymn may also be sung by the whole congregation" (88).

Note the emphasis on the "communitarian" nature of this moment. And while private prayer is not wholly excluded, neither is it extolled as the main point or purpose to be pursued after Communion.

The Sacred Liturgy is fundamentally a public and corporate act of worship of the whole Body of Christ together. It is not essentially a private devotion. The norms do permit a time after communion for silent prayer if this seems appropriate. The length of such time and the use of this option will vary depending on the needs of the congregation and other factors.

Your concerns are understandable, but they need to be balanced with what the Church teaches us the liturgy most fundamentally is. Consider that in the first Mass, at the Last Supper, the apostles did not go off and have private conversations with Jesus. Rather, they experienced him corporately, and the Scripture says that after partaking of the sacrament, they "had sung a hymn" (Mt 26:30). If we extend the first Mass to the foot of the cross, there, too, those who made it that far stayed together and supported the Lord and one another.

Private prayer and Eucharistic devotion are to be encouraged, but there is a context where this is best. Public prayer is also good and to be encouraged. It, too, has a context that should be respected for what it is.

Liturgy of the Hours

Q:When Psalm 1 is read in the liturgy, verse 5, which speaks of how the wicked will not survive judgment, is always omitted. The omission is strange because it sums up the message of the psalm. Why is the verse always omitted? — *William Pinto*

The verse was among numerous verses omitted in the 1960s due to their imprecatory quality. The "imprecatory psalms" (or verses) are so named because they call for a curse, or wish for God's wrath to descend on others. The verb imprecate means "to pray evil or invoke curse upon." A couple of examples of these psalms are: "Pour out your indignation upon them, / and let your burning anger overtake them" (Ps 69:24); "Let them be put to shame and dismayed for ever; / let them perish in disgrace" (Ps 83:17).

Prior to the publication of the Liturgy of the Hours, Pope Paul VI decreed that certain imprecatory psalms and verses be omitted. Therefore, approximately 120 verses, including three whole psalms, were removed. The introduction to the Liturgy of the Hours cites "psychological difficulty" and "spiritual discomfort" caused by these passages as the reason for their removal.

Your question echoes the concern of many that the removal of these verses is problematic. In the first place, it does not really solve the problem of imprecation in the psalter, since arguably one-third of the psalter contains such notions. Even the popular Psalm 23 expresses delight that our enemies hungrily look on while we eat our fill (see v. 5). Psalm 136 praises God, while pointing out he struck nations, saying, "To him who struck great kings, for his mercy endures for ever / and slew famous kings, / for his mercy endures for ever" (vv. 17–18). Thus removing the worst verses does not remove the "problem."

Moreover, it is troubling to assert that the inspired text of Scripture should be consigned to the realm of psychological difficulty. Rather, critics assert, it should be our task to seek to understand such texts in the wider context of God's love and justice.

Saint Thomas Aquinas teaches that such verses can be understood as predictions rather than as a wish that the sinner will be damned. Further, they can be understood as a reference to the justice of punishment, not simply as a gloating over the destruction of one's enemies. Finally, they can be seen as an allegory of the removal of sin and the destruction of its power (see *Summa* II-II, q. 25, a. 6, ad 3). So even troubling verses can teach important things.

Discussions of this sort will surely continue in the Church, and the imprecatory verses may one day be restored. For now, though, due to pastoral reasons, the Church has chosen to omit the most severe of the imprecations.

Q: **I was wondering why the Glory Be in the breviary is different from the regular one we all know.** — *David Gardner*

The breviary (also known as the Liturgy of the Hours) was revised by Rome in 1970. Strangely, the English translation of the conclusion of the *Gloria Patri* (the Glory Be) was different from the one most commonly known in the English-speaking world: "as it was in the beginning, is now, and ever shall be, world without end." The phrase "ever shall be, world without end" was truncated to "will be forever."

Thus the current translation of the prayer in the breviary is: "Glory be to the Father, and to the Son, and to the Holy Spirit; as it was in the beginning, is now, and will be forever. Amen." Exactly why this was done is not clear.

One explanation for the change is that it renders this prayer (which is repeated often in the breviary) smoother.

Another explanation is that some of the members of the translation committee argued it was more accurate. To be fair, the Latin is difficult to translate well into smooth English. The Latin ending is, *sicut erat in principio, et nunc, et semper, et in saecula saeculorum.* A literal rendering is, "as it was in the beginning, and is now, and is always, and unto ages of ages." This is basically a way of saying, "for a very long time," or more simply, "forever," which is what the breviary translation says. Hence, though awkward, the 1970 version is more accurate, though it folds the idea of the ages of ages into the word *semper* ("always").

All this aside, the version of the Glory Be known by the vast majority of Catholics is the traditional one, which ends "world without end." Thus there are many stumbles when people less familiar with the Liturgy of the Hours pray it together with those experienced in praying it.

Current plans are underway to retranslate the English Liturgy of the Hours, as was done with the Mass. It is expected that the Glory Be will be put back to the older form, since that will help avoid the many stumbles with two versions of the Glory Be known by the faithful.

Q. In the second sentence of the Glory Be, what does the phrase "as it was in the beginning" mean? Does it refer to the big bang, or to Adam and Eve, or something else? — *Jim Grady*

The phrase is an artistic way of saying God has always been glorious. Before time began or anything was created, God was glorious. God is glorious now and always will be glorious. Note the phrase "as it *was* in the beginning." In other words, at the beginning God already was glorious.

So, "in the beginning" as a phrase, while not excluding the big bang or Adam and Eve, is broader than a mere point in our created time. God was glorious before the big bang or Adam and Eve, and before any created thing was or existed.

The final phrase, "world without end," is not a particularly accurate rendering of the Latin, *per omnia saecula saeculorum*. The phrase is more literally rendered "through all the ages of ages." In other words, this is a reference to eternity, the fullness of time. God is ever and always glorious.

Q. I am a seminarian and am troubled by some of the older priests I have been assigned with for the summer who do not pray the Liturgy of the Hours. When I ask about it, they say it is monastic prayer and they are not obligated. This does not seem right, does it? — *Name withheld*

Priests are obliged to pray the Liturgy of Hours. Canon law says, "Priests, and deacons aspiring to the priesthood, are obliged to carry out the liturgy of the hours daily, in accordance with their own approved liturgical books" (Canon 276).

Further, every priest at his ordination to the transitional diaconate affirms the following promise: "Are you resolved ... in keeping with what is required of you, to celebrate faithfully the Liturgy of the Hours for the Church and for the whole world?"

Funerals

Q. • **Does the Catholic Church require music and hymns at funeral Masses?** — *Maggie*

No. A funeral Mass, like any Mass, can be entirely recited, with no music at all. However, individual parishes may rightly desire that funeral Masses not be merely recited. This is because many visitors (Catholic and non-Catholic) attend funeral Masses. Therefore, the parish may legitimately wish to use options in the Mass (such as the use of music) that best exemplify Catholic liturgical norms and something close to the best of what a parish can offer. Funerals are public liturgies of the Church and, as such, parishes cannot simply attend to the desires and preferences of the immediate family.

Q. • **During a funeral Mass recently, the celebrant invited those who were properly disposed Catholics to come forward for Communion. He asked all others to stay in their pews. This struck me as unkind and unnecessary. Could he not have invited them to come forward with arms crossed to receive a blessing?** — *Dianne Spotts*

The most certain answer is no. Holy Communion is a time for those who are going to receive Communion to come forward: that is its purpose. It is not really a time to confer personal blessings. There is a practice that has developed in many parishes where people do go forward for blessings, and while not sinfully wrong, the honest answer is such a practice is at variance from the norms and practice of the Church.

At funerals something does need to be said, given the large numbers of non-Catholics usually present. Perhaps the priest could simply and clearly invite practicing Catholics to come forward and omit telling others to "stay in their pews."

Q. •My sister was told by a parish in her area that they •would not celebrate the funeral of her husband, who is Catholic, because he was not a registered member. Is this allowed? — *Doris Chapman*

A Catholic parish should not decline funerals as a general norm. One of the corporal works of mercy is to bury the dead. Sometimes a parish has to decline a requested day and time due to scheduling problems or availability of clergy but can still negotiate another time. Though there can be pastoral encouragement to have a funeral in the parish where the person regularly attended, there may also be legitimate family reasons for holding the funeral at a parish where the person was not registered.

Q. •At a recent funeral of a friend, her ashes were •brought into the Church for the Mass. I thought this was not allowed? — *Madeline Kerek*

The practice you describe is permitted. In 1997, the U.S. bishops received permission from the Congregation for Divine Worship and the Discipline of the Sacraments for the celebration of funeral rites in the presence of cremated remains.

There are some adaptations to the rites, however. The priest may greet the remains at the door and sprinkle them with holy water, but the covering of the remains with the cloth (the pall) is omitted. The Easter candle may be placed near the cremated remains, but there was no mention of the priest incensing the remains. Otherwise, the funeral Mass is celebrated as laid down in the Roman Missal and the funeral ritual.

Prayers should be chosen that do not make reference to honoring the burying of the body of the deceased as indicated by the funeral norms. The prayers of final commendation at the end of the funeral Mass are largely followed in the normal way. It is uncertain at this point whether the remains are to be incensed or not.

It would seem this is permitted, but not required. The deacon or priest concludes the funeral Mass with an alternate dismissal listed in the rite, which makes no reference to the body.

The forbiddance of cremation by the Church in the past was due to the fact that many made use of it as a denial of the resurrection of the body. This is seldom the case today, but such an attitude must be ruled out before cremation is permitted. But note: "Although cremation is permitted by the church, it does not enjoy the same value as burial of the body. The Church clearly prefers and urges that the body of the deceased be present for the funeral rites, since the presence of the human body better expresses the values which the Church affirms in those rites" (Order of Christian Funerals, 413).

Q.•No priest or deacon could be at the burial of my husband at a national military cemetery, though he did have a Catholic funeral Mass. Should the grave be blessed?
— *Rose Belt*

The priest or deacon at the burial should bless the gravesite. If for some reason this did not happen, it can be done at a later time. Hence it may be good for you to ask a priest or deacon to come and pray the prayer of blessing with holy water. This is especially appropriate at non-Catholic cemeteries and military cemeteries. In Catholic cemeteries, the bishop has already generally consecrated the ground. But in non-Catholic settings this is not the case.

Be assured that if the grave was not blessed, this in no way affects your husband's status with God. But it is Catholic custom that burial sites should be blessed.

A related pastoral problem is that many cemeteries, especially national cemeteries, make it increasingly difficult for this custom to be fulfilled. For it is often the case that people are not able to go to the actual gravesite but are moved off to a separate chapel or pagoda somewhere nearby. This makes it difficult for the clergy to know where the gravesite is and bless it.

Q. Should priests, organists, altar servers, and sacristans be paid for participating in a funeral? — *Name withheld*

It varies according to the role. Priests are not paid for celebrating funerals. And while it is customary for many families to give the priest a donation or stipend, Church law does not require it. Such donations are generally small or a token symbol, since priests are well cared for by the parish already. While priests can and do accept such donations, any notion that what they receive is a "fee" should be avoided. Priests must be willing to celebrate liturgies and sacraments even when no stipend is offered. This is especially the case when working with and caring for the poor.

Organists and church musicians are another story. They can and should be paid. They have spent years in preparation and practice, and the monies they receive are usually part of their livelihood. Often, they must leave other obligations to participate in funerals and may have travel expenses. If families wish to engage their services, musicians and organists should be compensated. In cases where a family cannot afford to cover even basic music, the parish can help. But since elaborate music is not required for funerals, the requested fees should be reasonable.

As for servers and sacristans, the practice of donations is less common. In some places it is customary to give the servers a small donation; in other places not. Sacristans are seldom given donations. Servers and sacristans are generally presumed to be volunteers, and while a young server may appreciate a twenty-dollar bill, it is generally not expected. This is even more the case with adult servers who would likely be embarrassed by receiving a donation.

Q.:I am starting to hear about "green burials," where
people are buried in biodegradable boxes, etc. Do
such burials meet Catholic requirements? — *Name withheld*

It would not violate any Church norms, provided that the body is
reverently buried. Fancy caskets that seal in the body, concrete liners, etc., are not required by the Church. Charity, however, would
seem to bid us not to cast burial customs aside unnecessarily, in a
way that shocks. Some civil ordinances may require things such as
concrete liners as safety precautions to keep the ground in cemeteries from collapsing or becoming dangerously uneven. Further,
decaying bodies in unsealed caskets can raise health concerns. So,
consult local officials and ordinances.

PART IV

OUR
MORAL
LIFE

THE COMMANDMENTS

Q.•How did God sit in judgment on people prior to giv-
.•ing the Ten Commandments? — *William Bandle*

Your question needs to be addressed at two levels: temporally and
contextually.

Temporally, before the coming of Christ, no one was judged
in the sense that you describe, where God determined the eternal
destiny of each individual. Prior to Christ, all who died when to
Sheol, the place of the dead, and awaited the Messiah. Christ descended to Sheol and there gathered the righteous to himself (see
1 Pt 3:19). But the question remains, what was the context of judgment for those who lived apart from the Law of Moses or never
knew it? Among the Jews there was a tradition that those outside
the Covenant of Israel would be judged by the covenant and law
given to Noah.

The New Testament takes up a similar theme. For example,
in Matthew 25:31–46, Jesus indicates that the "nations" (Gentiles)
would be judged largely on their adherence to the corporal works
of mercy. Saint Paul appeals to what we call today "natural law"
when he says that the Gentiles would be held accountable for
what they can plainly see about God and his law in the things that
he has made (see Rom 1:18–20). And it would seem that the same
norms remain for those today who through invincible ignorance
have not come to Christ. God will judge them on what they could
reasonably know through reason and creation.

Q. In the 2016 movie *Silence*, a central premise is that intentionally stepping on a holy image, even if done out of fear or to save the lives of others, is apostasy. Is this a correct notion? — *James Macdonald*

The notion in the premise of the movie, at least as you state it here, is simplistic. And this is so for two reasons.

The first oversimplification involves the definition of apostasy. The *Catechism of the Catholic Church* distinguishes four sins against faith and the First Commandment: "*Incredulity* is the neglect of revealed truth or the willful refusal to assent to it. '*Heresy* is the obstinate post-baptismal denial of some truth which must be believed with divine and catholic faith, or it is likewise an obstinate doubt concerning the same; *apostasy* is the total repudiation of the Christian faith; *schism* is the refusal of submission to the Roman Pontiff or of communion with the members of the Church subject to him'" (2089).

Stepping on a holy image could be irreverence or disrespect, which, while serious, is less than apostasy per se. For the act to be formal apostasy one would have to indicate or mean, "I, by this act, intend to utterly and totally repudiate the Christian faith." Unless that intent is actively and consciously operative, simply stepping on holy images is not formal apostasy. For the premise of the movie to hold, it would have to set up this exact scenario.

A second oversimplification is that apostasy, like any mortal sin, requires not only that the act itself be grave (which apostasy is), but also that there be sufficient reflection and full consent of the will. From what you indicate in your summary of the movie, those who step on holy images are under significant duress. And this fear is not related merely to their own lives but the lives of others as well. Thus what they do may be sinful, but it is not necessarily mortally sinful. And this fact may also affect the very question of whether this is even apostasy. For, if faith cannot be forced by threats and fear, neither can apostasy be said to always occur when it is obtained under severe duress.

However, as the martyrs remind us, fear alone cannot excuse acts of irreligion and apostasy. To some degree we must leave the final judgment of such matters to God, who alone can see into the heart.

Q: Is saying "Oh my God!" when reacting to a situation or story taking the name of the Lord in vain? — *Janet*

While the phrase "Oh, my God" could be a prayer, it is not usually meant in this way in the situation you describe. More commonly it uses the divine name as a mere expression of surprise or exasperation. This is not a reverent or prayerful use of God's name in most circumstances. The word "vain" means empty, and in that case the phrase you cite would usually seem to qualify as using God's name in vain.

However, in assigning culpability (blameworthiness), it is good to remember that some have developed a bad habit of using this expression. As such, they usually commit the sin in weakness rather than malice — that is, not intending to show disrespect to God.

It should further be recalled that the Second Commandment, "You shall not use the name of the Lord in vain," has for its first meaning that we should never use God's name to swear falsely or curse others. Irreverence of God's name through casual use, such as you cite, is an extended meaning of the commandment. Therefore, we see that violations of the Second Commandment do admit some degree of seriousness. It is far more serious a sin to use God's name to swear falsely than to inadvertently use it to express surprise.

Still, one ought to avoid such vain or empty uses. One way to help break a bad habit that may have developed is to say aloud whenever they slip, "Oh, I mean to say, 'May the Name of the Lord be praised!'" This makes reparation and also helps break the habit.

Q. I was told by a fellow Catholic that the Church frowns upon tarot cards, palm reading, astrology readings, Ouija boards, etc., and that these are derivatives of Satanism. Thus we cannot participate in them. I think they can be okay or, at least, harmless. Is there a teaching on this?
— *G. Reiss*

Most of the things you mention are not foremost "derivatives of Satanism," but they can tend toward it. Fundamentally, the items you mention are sins against faith and violate especially the First Commandment, wherein God forbids us (for our own sake) to "have no other gods before me" (Ex 20:3).

Regarding such things, the *Catechism* teaches: "All forms of divination are to be rejected: recourse to Satan or demons, conjuring up the dead or other practices falsely supposed to 'unveil' the future. Consulting horoscopes, astrology, palm reading, interpretation of omens and lots, the phenomena of clairvoyance, and recourse to mediums all conceal a desire for power over time, history, and, in the last analysis, other human beings, as well as a wish to conciliate hidden powers. They contradict the honor, respect, and loving fear that we owe to God alone" (2116). Therefore, we are not to consult or partake of such things.

While one might argue that reading a horoscope is merely harmless fun, it still remains imprudent to make light of things which edge toward darkness. To set aside our trust in God is to implicitly summon other forces, powers, or demons to take God's place. It is never a good idea to invoke the occult. Exorcists are consistent in warning against any such practices and know by experience that most people who end up possessed have had some history of dabbling in occult practices. Such things open the door to demons and signal some form of permission for them to deepen a stronghold in the lives of those who invoke their occult powers.

The First Commandment is given us by God to protect us from entrusting ourselves to anything less than him. He alone can save us and supply us. Trusting in lesser things like wealth or power, or, even worse, occult practices and demons, brings great harm along with sorrow and dissatisfaction. Only God can heal us and be a true source for our trust and hope.

Q.•I am confused about the Ninth Commandment. •What does it mean to covet? What if two couples are really good friends and one man thinks if my wife dies and the man of the other couple dies, maybe his wife and I would get together. (Not that he would ever want either one to die.) Would that be coveting your neighbor's wife?
— *Name withheld*

There exists within each of us a whole range of appetites or desires. We desire everything from food, security, and temporal goods, to affection, friendship, sexual union, and a sense of being loved and respected. In themselves these desires are good, and they help protect and foster important aspects of us. However, since the human race labors under the effects of original sin, our desires tend also to have an unruly dimension. Frequently we desire things beyond what we know are reasonable or just. This is what coveting means.

Coveting does not include momentary desires that occur to us and which we dismiss as being unreasonable or inappropriate. Rather, coveting involves the willful entertaining of inappropriate or excessive desires.

The Ninth Commandment forbids coveting the wife (or husband) of a neighbor, which means the willful and excessive desire for the spouse of another, with the will to possess them. Coveting goes beyond adultery because, when one covets the wife of another, he seeks to end her spousal relationship with her husband to have her for himself. Adultery (which is sometimes committed in weakness, sometimes with persistence and malice) endangers a marriage by introducing infidelity. But coveting actively seeks to end the marriage in order to have the spouse of another for one's self.

What you describe is not coveting. It is more of a remote form of wishful thinking. But it is likely important to curb thoughts in this matter since they are not helpful in either the marriage or the friendship that is shared by couples. It might be rather harmless "what if" thinking. But it shouldn't be allowed to grow. It is also a mild form of fantasy, and indulging in too much fantasy is seldom helpful for living in reality and cherishing what we have.

SIN AND FORGIVENESS

Q: **The Church teaches that we are born with original sin. But if a mother is baptized and thus freed from original sin, how is it that her child is born with original sin?** — *Katey*

Human parents supply to their children only the fallen human nature that came from Adam and Eve. They cannot supply what is divine and supernatural.

Even in terms of human nature, parents are only able to supply the basic elements. So, for example, the child receives from his parents a brain and an intellect, as basic elements that come with human nature. But parents cannot transfer at conception their knowledge of language, or mathematics, or history, to the child. The child must acquire this for himself, with the help of others.

If this is the case with human nature, it is even more so with the supernatural life of grace. The mother may be baptized and free of original sin, but she cannot communicate this to her child, only God can. Therefore, the child must be brought to the Lord in baptism, and the Lord begins a saving work in which the child must grow.

Q. A Protestant coworker, whom I think is anti-Catholic, says that we Catholics focus too much on the Crucifixion and not enough on the Resurrection, that we focus too much on our sins, and not enough on the new life Jesus gave us in the Resurrection. How do I answer him? — *Name withheld*

Perhaps a first and philosophical point is that all of us should avoid setting up false dichotomies. The Cross and the Resurrection is not an either/or proposition, but a both/and reality.

Theologically, some simplify salvation, which, while a single reality, actually has two essential components: (1) the forgiveness (washing away) of our sins, and (2) the new life of the Resurrection. In other words, Jesus did not only forgive our sins, but also offers us a new life. And these two aspects make up the salvation which Jesus wins for us.

Saint Thomas Aquinas says, "The death of Christ ... is the cause of the extinction of our sins; but his resurrection, by which he returns to the life of glory, is the cause of our justification, by which we return to the newness of justice" (Commentary on Romans 4:3).

Therefore, the death of Jesus on the cross is the starting point of our salvation and justification since it removes sin. In the Resurrection is the manifestation of the new life which Jesus offers us, and which we are summoned to experience more deeply with each passing day. So, both the Cross and the Resurrection are essential in our salvation and justification: we die to sin, but we rise to new life.

I am going to guess that your coworker is an evangelical Protestant. Traditional Protestantism placed a significant emphasis on the Cross, as any look at an older Protestant hymnal will reveal.

Q. We are taught to make reparation for our sins. But how could we ever make reparation for homicide or abortion? — *Peter Tate*

Reparation (a word which means "to repair") for many, if not most, of our sins cannot be on a strict quid pro quo basis. This, of course, is why we need the Lord Jesus to atone for our sins. We cannot fully repair the damage our sins cause. However, we can make some amends and seek to heal some of the damage. We can return what we stole, or at least give the value to the poor. We can seek forgiveness when we offend, or speak words of love where we have caused harm with our speech. But as you point out, we cannot restore a life we have taken or undo all the damage of many of our sins. We can, however, seek to advocate for the dignity of life and work to save others or assist those whose life is endangered by destitution, etc.

Q. On the cross, Jesus said, "Father, forgive them; for they know not what they do" (Lk 23:34). But if we don't know what we do, how can we ever sin or be blameworthy for it? — *Jerry Conlin*

Jesus is speaking to a particular situation, and we ought not generalize what he says here. The ignorance he likely refers to here is that they do not know or understand his true identity. Did they really know that they were killing their Lord and Messiah? Likely not.

While it is true that the Lord gave many proofs of his identity by fulfilling Scripture and working miracles, along with the testimony of John the Baptist and the Father's testimony in their heart, many of his accusers and condemners still did not understand or come to faith. Many considered Jesus a blasphemer and felt quite justified in their condemnation.

Now this, of course, does not mean that they are without any sin at all, and as Jesus also said in the Gospel, "You will die in your sins unless you believe that I am he" (Jn 8:24). While those who kill

him and conspired to have him killed may be acting in some ignorance at the moment of the Crucifixion, the Lord is still calling
them to receive saving faith and come out of their woeful ignorance. Many, in fact, did come to faith later and repented (see Acts
2:37–42). Others seemingly did not.

Ignorance, and its relationship to culpability, speaks to what
a person could reasonably know and understand given their history, the condition of their heart, and so forth. Vincible ignorance
is ignorance we could reasonably have overcome. Invincible ignorance is that which a person could not reasonably have overcome
at the time of the sin. And while the Church makes these distinctions, only God can know the true inner condition of a person and
make this judgment. That is why the Church does not formally
teach that specific people are in hell. Only God can see into the
heart of a person to make that judgment.

Q. On the cross, Jesus said, "Father, forgive them; for
they know not what they do" (Lk 23:34). Does his
plea absolve all who took part in the Crucifixion? — *Cliff*
Journey

The Lord is certainly offering forgiveness and absolution. But as
with any offer of absolution or forgiveness, we must also receive
the gift by accepting it with contrition for our sins. In a certain
sense absolution cannot simply be granted (by way of an imposition or a mere declaration of sorts) since this does not respect
human freedom. If I were to stand before you and say, "I forgive you
and absolve you of the terrible things you did to me," you might
react with relief and joy. Alternately, you might react with anger
since you think you did nothing wrong. Hence the offer of absolution is one thing, the reception of it is necessary to complete the
act. Jesus is surely offering absolution; whether or not it was received by the participants was up to them.

Q. **I don't understand how mere humans are supposed to forgive everyone everything, but we are taught that God/Jesus only forgives us if we are repentant. How are we supposed to be more forgiving than he is?** — *Nancy*

I am not sure where you learned that the Lord Jesus only forgives if we are repentant. This is quite contrary to what he did on the cross. With the exception of John, Mother Mary, and several other women, we collectively mocked him, scorned him, and thought nothing of his sufferings. Yet in our most unrepentant moment, he said, "Father, forgive them."

The Scriptures also say, "But God shows his own love for us in that while we were yet sinners, Christ died for us. For if while we were enemies we were reconciled to God by the death of his Son" (Rom 5:8,10).

Perhaps you have in mind the judgment we will face. Many do think of the Last Judgment as God withholding forgiveness. However, the Lord makes it clear: "As I live, says the Lord GOD, I have no pleasure in the death of the wicked, but that the wicked turn from his way and live" (Ez 33:11). Also, God "desires all men to be saved" (1 Tm 2:4).

The Last Judgment is not about God's desire to condemn, or his refusal to forgive. Rather, the judgment in question is more about our final answer to the invitation of God to receive his offered mercy and accept the values of his kingdom. There are some who mysteriously reject the Kingdom and its values, who refuse the offered mercy of God or their need for it. Without pleasure, God accepts the final and lasting choice of some to dwell apart from him.

For us, forgiveness should not be seen so much as an imposed obligation, but as a gift to seek and receive from God. Forgiveness does not always mean we can go on in close relationships with people who may cause us great harm. It does not always mean that there should be no consequences for sin. Rather, forgiveness is letting go of the need to change the past. It is a gift from God that helps us to put down the weight of anger, resentment, and the desire for revenge that can consume and destroy us. Forgiveness is for us, not against us.

Q.**I recently repented of having stolen a few things of moderate value, one from work, and the other from an acquaintance. I was surprised (and I guess relieved) that the priest did not mention anything about making restitution. Is restitution required, and does this matter affect my absolution?** — *Name withheld*

Yes, restitution is required in matters of theft. The *Catechism* teaches that in view of commutative justice the reparation of the injustice committed requires the return of the stolen items to their owner (see 2412). Ideally, such restitution is made directly to the owner, and simple embarrassment does not excuse this.

However sometimes direct restitution is not possible. Perhaps the item is gone or used up. Perhaps the owner cannot be located or has died. Perhaps the actual owner is not known. Perhaps the one who stole is now unable to make the required restitution.

In such cases, some form of indirect restitution is necessary. Perhaps one is able to make restitution in kind, for example, through money worth the value of the damage, or by extra work if something was taken from an employer. If the direct owner cannot be found, perhaps a contribution to the poor or some contribution of value to the wider community involving the spiritual or corporal works of mercy can be done.

Restitution seeks to repair for the damage caused by theft in two ways. First, it restores to the owner, directly or indirectly, what was taken. Second, it cancels and closes off the benefits that the one who stole received, which they have no just right to go on enjoying.

In terms of absolution, the priest does not grant absolution provisionally. Absolutions cannot be worded: "I absolve you from your sins provided that you do X." However, if a priest were to hear that someone stole an item of significance but was refusing to make any form of restitution, he might reasonably conclude that they did not have the necessary contrition. If this were the case, he might find it necessary to withhold or delay absolution.

Q:A recently published book that claims to dispels "myths and maybes" of the Catholic Church says that "grave" sin is not "mortal" sin. Thus the author says that missing Mass is a grave sin, but it is not a mortal sin. Is this so? — *Thomas Simpson*

Grave and mortal mean the same thing in Catholic moral teaching. Hence missing Mass without a serious reason is a mortal sin (see CCC 2181).

It is true, today, that many moral textbooks and Church documents use the word "grave" more often than "mortal." There are likely pastoral reasons behind this. For it was a growing tendency for many poorly catechized people to think mortal sin referred only to killing someone. Hence the more common use of the word grave, meaning weighty or very serious sin, to refer to mortal sin. But, as you point out, this has led to other pastoral problems, wherein people do not often understand that grave and mortal mean the same thing.

The *Catechism* states, "Mortal sin is sin whose object is grave matter and which is also committed with full knowledge and deliberate consent" (1857), quoting Pope John Paul II's 1984 apostolic exhortation *Reconciliatio et Paenitentia*.

Q•Jesus is adamant that he did not come to abolish the
•law and the prophets in Matthew 5:17, yet Saint Paul
seems to say the opposite in Ephesians 2:15 ("by abolish-
ing in his flesh the law of commandments and ordinances"). Please clarify these two passages. — *Paul VanHoudt*

There are two approaches to understanding Jesus' words about
the Law in Matthew 5.

One is to emphasize that he says the Law will not be abolished "until all is accomplished" (v. 18). But according to this argument, in the passion, death, and resurrection all is accomplished.
Hence the Law can now change since what it pointed to has come
to pass. This approach neglects the first half of what Jesus says —
namely, that "till heaven and earth pass away" nothing in the Law
will be changed. By implication, the idea is that all will be accomplished only at the end of time.

Another approach is to distinguish what Jesus means by
the Law. The Jewish Law had three basic components: the moral
law, rooted in the commandments; the ceremonial law; and civic or customary law. The ceremonial law spoke to things like the
vestments of the priests, feast days, the manner of carrying out
sacrifices, etc. The civic or customary law spoke to how people
dressed, what they could eat, how they conducted business, and
even things such as the requirement to put rails on one's rooftop
to prevent falls.

Following this second approach, we understand Jesus is referring only to the moral law of God, which is unchanging. And this
makes contextual sense, since Jesus goes on to discourse only on
the moral law in the examples that follow in the remainder of the
chapter. Indeed, the moral law does not change. Murder, adultery,
lying, and theft are not going to become virtuous. They and the
rest of the moral precepts remain forever unchanged.

Clearly, Jesus and the apostles *did* alter the customary laws
(such as kosher) and the ceremonial laws (such as how and when
lambs are to be killed). Those things pointed to Christ and are now

fulfilled. Jesus is the Lamb who offers a perfect, once-for-all sacrifice; no need to kill thousands of lambs. Since Jesus came to give an inner transformation, no need to worry about unclean foods entering our bodies, or to call unclean what God has rendered clean, and so forth.

But God's moral law cannot change, since it is rooted in the unchanging nature of things that God has made and set forth. It is regarding this that Jesus says not even the smallest part of it shall be eliminated.

As for Saint Paul's comment in Ephesians, he is speaking to the way the Law is kept, not the Law itself. The context of Saint Paul's reflection indicates that he is speaking of how grace enables us to keep the law in a fulfilled and perfected way. Prior to grace, the law was to be kept by human effort. As such it taught and also condemned us because no one could really fulfill all the precepts and their implications. Jesus died to all that and, bestowing grace through a saving relationship with him, enables us to fulfill the law — that is, to fill it full. For example, by the Lord's grace we can love not only our neighbors and benefactors, but also our enemies and those who spitefully mistreat us. Law is now a picture of the human person transformed by grace, rather than merely a series of rules to keep us from our own feeble nature.

Q. I am a bit confused about the *Catechism's* treatment of acedia (sloth). What does the *Catechism* mean to teach by this sin? And how is it related to joy? — *Inigo Incer*

Yes, the more common word for acedia is "sloth," one of the seven deadly sins. Unfortunately, most people simply equate sloth with laziness. Although sloth can manifest as laziness, it manifests in other ways as well.

Fundamentally, sloth is a sorrow, sadness, or aversion toward the good things God is offering us. The *Catechism* teaches, "Acedia or spiritual sloth goes so far as to refuse the joy that comes from God and to be repelled by divine goodness" (2094).

The proper response to the good things that God offers us is joy. We should be joyful at the offer of a holy life, set free from sin and gloriously opened to the love of God and others.

But the sinful drive of sloth influences many to respond to this offer with sadness and aversion. Perhaps it would involve too many changes, and many fear and avoid change. Frankly, many like their sins, preferring to indulge their lower nature. Sloth therefore perceives God's gracious offer as a threat and moves to oppose it.

We do this in obvious and subtle ways. While sloth often manifests as a kind of boredom, aversion, or laziness toward spiritual things, one can also see it at work in the kind of frantic indulgence and workaholism common today. Indeed, many indulge in an excessive activism in politics, career, business, and other worldly pursuits. In no way are they lazy, but they often use frantic activism to avoid the spiritual contemplation of God or the things of God. The claim becomes, "I am too busy to pray, get to church, attend to moral and spiritual reflection, read the Scriptures, or study my faith." Such people are not lazy, but their aversion to spiritual things is slothful. It is a deep and sinful drive rooted in a disordered preference for passing worldly things.

We must ask for a joy for spiritual and eternal things and zeal to cultivate a deeper desire for God and the things of heaven, for our fallen flesh is strongly opposed to the desires of the Spirit (see Gal 5:17).

Q. Do you have any suggestions for a person who is guilty of sloth and laziness? On account of it, I am often sluggish and this keeps me from many of my responsibilities and duties to be a good and prayerful Catholic. — *Name withheld*

Sloth, which is one of the seven capital sins, is sorrow or aversion to the good things God is offering us. One who is slothful and hears that God can save them from sins and enable them to do many good works, instead of being happy and eager to embrace these gifts has a kind of aversion toward them. Perhaps they like their sins and would rather not be free of them. Perhaps the thought of good works seems burdensome. Therefore, the slothful person avoids God and the gifts that he offers.

While this often manifests through a kind of a laziness or inattentiveness, sometimes the opposite is true. Some slothful people immerse themselves in worldly activities such as business and career, and claim they are far "too busy" to pray, to think about God, or go to church. Therefore, at its heart, sloth is a problem about desire — namely, that we do not ardently desire God and the things he is offering.

I encourage you to pray the beatitude, "Blessed are those who hunger and thirst for righteousness, for they will be satisfied" (Mt 5:6). In other words, we ought to ask for the desire for God and what he offers.

Second, I would counsel that while praying for greater desire some small and initial steps be made toward God. Look for something you can reasonably do, which may not be highly desirable at first but can be reasonably accomplished. Before I was a priest, I worked in downtown Washington, and I made a Lenten resolution to go to daily Mass at my lunch break. At first, this seemed difficult and irksome. But gradually I grew to like it, and when Easter came I just kept going to Mass almost every day to experience its peace and the nourishment of God's word and his body and blood. Often life works like this. We ask for deeper desire and step out on our request by small actions which build.

Q. Is every lie intrinsically evil? I remember sixty years ago being taught that if a person was not entitled to the truth, one could, in fact, lead them away from the truth, by lying. For example, if I knew the hideout of Anne Frank and the Gestapo asked me if I knew her whereabouts, if I said I did not, would [that] be intrinsically evil? — *Ed Siering*

Permit a personal reply to this, with the understanding that reasonable people may choose to differ with aspects of my answer. I would answer that the approach that you cite is an unfortunately widespread notion related to a questionable concept called "mental reservation." I call it unfortunate because it seems to say that a lie is not a lie.

But in the common example you cite, you clearly would be lying since it meets the definition of a lie: to speak that which is untrue with the intention of deceiving. Indeed, the entire purpose of the lie is to deceive the officials by saying what is untrue. It will be granted that the situation described is dreadful and fearsome. But I, and many moral theologians, are not prepared to say it is not a lie simply because the situation is fearful and the authorities are bad people.

Perhaps the better approach is to say that it is a lie and that, as a lie, it is intrinsically wrong. However, when one is under duress or sees no clear way to avoid a consequent grave evil or injustice, the culpability (blame) for such a lie is lessened. It seems rather doubtful that God would make a big deal of the sort of lie you describe on Judgment Day.

But to call any lie good or justifiable is to harm a moral principle unnecessarily. Call it what it is: a lie. It is not good. And it is not permitted to do evil that good may come of it. With this in mind it is better to say that the lie described is a lie, lamentable but understandable. And given the duress, there was not likely much blame if any that was incurred.

Life sometimes presents difficulties that are not easily overcome. But to adjust moral principles to accommodate anomalies is to engage in a kind of casuistry that does harm to moral principles. Sometimes the best we can do is humbly shrug and say, "Well it's wrong to lie, but let's trustingly leave the judgment on this one up to God, who knows our struggles and will surely factor in the fearsome circumstances."

Q. **Killing someone and missing Sunday Mass are both mortal sins, punishable by eternity in hell. This seems to make the two sins equivalent. But in my mind, killing is far worse than missing Mass. Are they really equivalent?** — *James Becker*

No, they are not equivalent. There are degrees to mortal sin just like there are degrees to venial sin. First-degree murder is more grave than missing Mass, or viewing pornography, or any other grave sin that we might imagine.

It is true that killing someone and missing Mass are in the same category of mortal (or grave) sin. But they are no more equivalent than a rat is equivalent to, or the same as, a man simply because they are in the same category, mammal.

Your description of both sins as being punishable by eternity in hell also implies an equivalence by that fact. However, a distinction is necessary regarding the way you connect the notion of eternity to punishment. That one is in hell eternally is not due to punishment per se. Rather, the eternity of hell (or heaven for that matter) exists because our decision for or against God and the laws and values of his kingdom becomes a decision that is forever fixed at death. That hell is eternal is not by itself a gauge of the punishment involved.

We need not presume that everyone experiences hell in exactly the same way, any more than we can presume that everyone experiences heaven in exactly the same way. There may, in fact, be degrees of suffering in hell and degrees of glory in heaven.

While there are mysteries involved here, it makes sense that there are some saints who, on account of extraordinary virtue, have a greater capacity to appreciate God's glory in heaven. It also makes sense that for those in hell who have rejected God and his kingdom, there would be degrees of suffering experienced, related to how deep their rejection of the light is. The Scriptures indicate we are judged according to what we have done (see Rv 20:11–15). Therefore, there is at least implied some relationship of reward or punishment rooted in what we have done or not done. Jesus also speaks of places of special honor in heaven, indicating levels of some sort in the afterlife (Mt 20:23).

Q.**I would like to make a few comments regarding your frequent mentioning of mortal sin. It appears to me that a definition is in order, so as not to frighten people needlessly. For a sin to be mortal, three conditions must together be met: grave matter, full knowledge, and deliberate consent (see CCC 1857). I know a good number of people who don't attend Mass regularly or who look at pornography, but they are not aware that they commit a sin. Actually, it might be pretty hard for the average person to commit grave sin, for who would purposely turn against God?** — *Bernard Thyssen*

While rightly referencing the *Catechism* and providing a helpful reminder about what is necessary for one to be fully culpable of mortal sin, there are aspects of your comment that bespeak troubling trends in modern thinking.

First, there is the notion that people don't seem to know any better. The Scriptures, sacred Tradition, and the *Catechism* all speak of the conscience in every human person. The voice of God echoes in the depths of every human heart. While some suppress this voice, deep down it is still there. It is my pastoral experience that people generally *do* know what they are doing. When I speak to people who are missing Mass, or perhaps are cohabiting and fornicating, etc., they admit they know, deep down, what they are doing is wrong.

Second, the notion that mortal sin is rare also seems rooted in modern anthropology that minimizes human freedom and knowledge. While it is true, certain compulsions may marginalize or limit freedom, yet we are freer than most like to admit. In summoning us to a moral life and warning us of sin, the Lord is not simply setting up a straw man. He speaks to us as moral agents, who generally act freely, making decisions for which we are responsible.

You may call all this needless fear, but if so, the Lord never got your memo. Jesus often used vivid imagery to stir fear within us of the consequences of sin. As with any pastoral appeal, fear must be balanced with other appeals as well. But the modern attempt to remove all fear from the preaching of the Church has had poor results. Some degree of fear may be needful after all.

Q: **I have serious scrupulosity and have worked closely with several priests. I have been told if I follow their advice I will go straight to heaven when I die. How can they make this statement? I am in grave doubt.** — *Name withheld*

Since you do not state what the advice is, I cannot comment on that aspect. It is true that no one on earth, even a priest, can state unequivocally that a person will go straight to heaven when they die. The only exceptions might be someone who was baptized moments before their death, a baptized infant, or a young child who dies.

Serious scrupulosity is generally rooted in an unreasonable need for certainty regarding the state of one's soul before God. This causes the person to fret obsessively that he might be in mortal sin and will go to hell if he dies. In very serious cases obsessive thoughts can be so severe that the person experiences the return of the dread and fear moments after confessing, wondering if his very act of confessing was flawed. It is sometimes difficult for the priest to reassure such penitents, who become increasingly inconsolable as their fears and need for certainty grow. In the most serious cases, psychological intervention is required.

While strong confidence of salvation is surely available to the practicing believer, absolute and unequivocal certainty is not available to us. If it were, faith and trust in God would not be necessary. Thus the severely scrupulous person must be led to reject the unreasonable demand for certainty and feeling safe on human terms. He must be led to trust God's mercy for those who have sorrow for their sins.

Generally, this spiritual treatment for serious scrupulosity means that one must see a regular confessor who sets up strict norms for the penitent to follow such as how frequently he may approach the sacrament and how elaborate his descriptions of his sins may be. The confessor will often have to remind the penitent that he is not a judge in his own case, and that he should trust the confessor, who has the power of the keys and the task to assess how serious his situation really is. The point is to break the cycle and replace the inordinate demand for certainty with a trusting confidence in God.

I suspect that the priest you quote may have been using a kind of hyperbole (exaggeration) to emphasize that you should follow strictly the discipline and protocol he sets up for you, due to your scrupulosity.

Q. A family member who does not agree with many moral teachings in the Bible dismisses my mentioning of them by saying Jesus wants to unite us all and that I am divisive in quoting these things. — *H. K.*

Jesus does want to unite us, but he wants to unite us in the truth. Though he desires to unite us, he also said: "Do you think that I have come to give peace on earth? No, I tell you, but rather division; for henceforth in one house there will be five divided, three against two and two against three" (Lk 12:51–52).

In other words, Jesus acknowledges that his teachings will divide. His truth must cut away error and be the actual basis for unity rather than a contrived notion where no one upsets anyone else.

Jesus is spoken of in the Scriptures as a great cornerstone: "To you therefore who believe, he is precious, but for those who do not believe, / ... 'A very stone that will make men stumble, / a rock that makes them fall'" (1 Pt 2:7–8). Thus we see that division is unavoidable, not because of Jesus, but because of the rejection of his truth.

Q. I was talking to my theology teacher about the conscience. He seems to equate conscience with whatever a person thinks. But I know a lot of people (including him) who think some pretty strange and heretical things. Isn't conscience something more than merely what I think or opine? — *Name withheld*

You are correct. Conscience cannot simply be reduced to whatever I think. Frankly, it is often the role of conscience to challenge what we think. The *Catechism of the Catholic Church* describes conscience as a deep sense of right and wrong that God has inscribed in our heart. It is in effect the voice of God echoing deep within.

The *Catechism* says: "'Deep within his conscience man discovers a law which he has not laid upon himself which he must obey. Its voice, ever calling him to love and to do what is good and to avoid evil, sounds in his heart at the right moment.... For man has in his heart a law inscribed by God.... His conscience is man's most secret core and his sanctuary. There he is alone with God whose voice echoes in his depths'" (1776).

Surely, the conscience does interact with our intellect and reason, but of itself it is deeper and, one might argue, innate and preconscious. Here, too, the *Catechism* says: "Conscience is a judgment of reason whereby the human person recognizes the moral quality of a concrete act.... 'Conscience is a law of the mind; yet [Christians] would not grant that it is nothing more.... [Conscience] is a messenger of him, who, both in nature and in grace, speaks to us behind a veil, and teaches and rules us by his representatives'" (1778).

Since conscience involves the practical intellect and the virtue of prudence especially, it is proper to say that conscience can be "formed." But formed does not mean it is acquired from scratch. For, indeed, there is good medical and scientific evidence, which conforms to the teaching of faith, that the basic "sense" of conscience is present even in the youngest children, who can readily and innately grasp basic moral principles. The formation of conscience, therefore, involves the learning necessary to listen well to conscience and apply its voice to moral acts in each and every circumstance. Conscience is also formed when we acquire better and deeper knowledge regarding complex moral situations. We are able to incorporate that knowledge with our conscience as we make moral judgments.

Q. Our priest recently said that love does away with law and that if we love God rules are not needed. I am sick of all this mushy talk about love and relationship with God. We were taught the commandments, and it's time to get back to them. — *Name withheld*

Since the fuller context of the sermon is not here, it is difficult to know what was meant. There are obviously people today who substitute a vague "love" for parameters or rules, and this is incorrect and a form of self-deception. Love does have parameters.

However, there are reputable theologians who would agree that moral theology over the past five hundred years has become too solely focused on obligations, laws, and rules, and, as such, has become disconnected from grace and the moral renewal that is offered to us through relationship with Jesus Christ. The biblical, patristic, and scholastic tradition all emphasized that the heart of the Gospel was a transformative union with Jesus Christ that liberated us from sin and death. Therefore, the moral dimension of the Christian life flows from this powerfully transformative union.

As such, the moral vision of the Sermon on the Mount, the epistles, and early Church discipline were describing (not merely prescribing) what the transformed human person is like if they have met Jesus Christ and received the healing power of his saving grace.

How does a moral vision flow from relationship? Consider that we have all met people who have changed our life. Maybe it was a teacher who inspired us and who opened new ways of thinking for us or showed us gifts we didn't know we had. Perhaps it was someone who hired us or opened career paths for us we never imagined. Maybe it was our spouse who has helped to complete us. The rules or disciplines of the new things they showed us were not first — the relationship was first, and then we gladly moved forward in the new paths that were opened.

As to the concern that returning to a relational model will minimize the Christian life or make it vague, actually, and properly understood, it is the opposite. Consider that a man who loves his wife will surely follow the Fifth Commandment not to murder her. But he does far more: he loves her, cherishes her, and does not wish to be rid of her.

In the same way, law points to what is minimally required, but love asks, What more can I do?

Jesus' moral vision in the Sermon on the Mount is far more rigorous than the Law of Moses. For example, Jesus says it is not enough to refrain from the act of adultery or illicit sexual union. Even our thoughts are summoned to purity (see Mt 5:27–30). The love of God, rooted in a transformative relationship with Jesus, requires more, not less, and grace will accomplish it, if we actually walk with Christ.

Q. **The priest quotes Jesus at Mass, "Take this, all of you, and eat of it." There are no caveats like, "unless you are divorced," "unless you are gay," or any number of other qualifiers. Jesus gave the bread to Judas. Shouldn't the Church act as Jesus did and remove the caveats and qualifiers Jesus never had?** — *Bill McKenna*

The same Jesus you (rightly) extol as our model is the one who forbade divorce and remarriage, calling the second union an ongoing state of adultery (see Mt 19:1–11). He also forbade illicit sexual union of other sorts, calling it lust that risked the fires of hell (Mt 5:27–30). Further, through his appointed spokesmen, the apostles (Lk 10:16; Acts 1:8), he also made clear in numerous places — for example, Romans 1:17–24, Ephesians 5:3–20 — that fornication, adultery, and homosexual acts exclude one from the kingdom of God, as do other serious sins. So, the "no caveats" notion needs some amending, or at least clarification.

Whether Jesus gave Judas Communion or not is debatable — that is, which bread did Jesus give him — but let's just suppose that he *did* receive Communion. Note that the result for Judas was not sanctification, but it is suggested rather the effects of sacrilege. The Scriptures say, "Then after the morsel, Satan entered into him" (Jn 13:27).

And this sad effect on Judas is illustrative of Saint Paul's later teaching that it is a bad idea to receive holy Communion in a state of serious sin since it brings further condemnation and provides a deeper stronghold for Satan. Saint Paul writes: "Whoever, therefore, eats the bread or drinks the cup of the Lord in an unworthy manner will be guilty of profaning the body and blood of the Lord. Let a man examine himself, and so eat of the bread and drink of the cup. For any one who eats and drinks without discerning the body eats and drinks judgment upon himself. That is why many of you are weak and ill, and some have died" (1 Cor 11:27–30).

So, it would seem, despite your contention, there *are* what you call "qualifiers." The view that the words of the Lord, "Take this, all of you," should be understood univocally is not supported by other Scripture passages, which require certain things of those who receive. There surely is a general call to all to receive, but that call presupposes that we discern the body of the Lord and are able to receive holy Communion in a worthy manner — that is, free from mortal sin.

Q.I heard a priest mention the "sin of unbelief." But it occurs to me, how can God punish someone who sincerely fails to believe in him, or believes in another God? — *Janie Canou*

Unbelief can be understood in two ways. First, by way of pure negation, so that a person is called an unbeliever because he does not have the true faith through ignorance or some similar problem. Second, unbelief can be understood as opposition to the Faith, when someone has properly heard but then refuses or hates what he has heard. In this second sense, unbelief is a sin. Jesus says, "If I had not come and spoken to them, they would not have sin" (Jn 15:22).

Presuming the Faith has been accurately conveyed to us, and given the grace of God that draws us to faith, a response is required that will either be virtuous or sinful in some degree. The degree of the sinfulness will depend on many internal factors, many of which only God can weigh. Thus we must leave final judgments to God, but, in itself, this sort of unbelief is rightly placed in the category of sin.

Q: **I think the Catholic notion of mortal and venial sin is flawed. All sin is serious, and since it offends God, it is an infinite offense. The Catholic distinction leads to ignoring many sins and only focusing on some. All sin is a grave offense against God.** — *John Malvine*

It should first be noted that the distinction between mortal and venial sin is found in the Scriptures: "There is sin which is deadly.... All wrongdoing is sin, but there is sin which is not deadly" (1 Jn 5:16–17). It also stands to reason that there are sins that are more serious than others. Premeditated murder is certainly more serious than an act of careless gossip.

As for every sin being "an infinite offense" because it offends God, this is a colorful way of speaking that contains a kernel of truth but leaves too many distinctions behind. That God is dishonored by our sin certainly does elevate the magnitude of what we do. However, not everyone committing a sin seeks to directly offend God. Sometimes sins are committed in weakness, sometimes through forgetfulness, etc. And these sorts of things are not a direct attempt to dishonor God. The first three commandments specify sins that most directly dishonor God, whereas the other seven, while dishonoring God through disobedience, do so less directly.

God is just, so it does not follow that he would treat every offense as an infinite offense. Neither is God one who broods over personal injury. While sin does harm God's external glory, it does not inflict an emotional toll or dishonor his internal glory such that he would be robbed of beatitude. Further, God is able to look into the hearts of all to see their motivations and judge what they could reasonably know. Surely, then, God rewards and punishes in ways commensurate with what is done and does not consign all sin to the category of infinite offense.

As for the concern that distinguishing mortal and venial sins might lead us to make light of too many things, that is a danger. But the abuse of something does not take away its proper use. It is certainly true that certain things are more serious than others. But it does not follow that this means we ought to pay no attention to lesser things. Little things mean a lot and tend to build toward greater things. We do well to attend to them.

Q. **With all the mortal sins possible to us, why is there not a greater listing of these by priests so that we can avoid them?** — *Name withheld*

A simple list of mortal sins might be possible. It would be rooted in the sins enumerated in the Ten Commandments and those described in the Pauline epistles as excluding us from the kingdom of God if we die unrepentant. But a mere list isn't as helpful in moral reflection as might be thought. More than a list is needed.

The main difficulty centers on the distinction between considering an act in general and considering a specific occurrence of that act. Full moral assessment of a specific act requires us to look at three things: the act itself, the circumstances, and the intent of the one doing the act (see CCC 1750–54).

Regarding the act itself, this is the most objective of the three factors. But circumstances and intention are as varied as human beings and situations allow. Further, while circumstances and intention cannot make an evil action good, they do speak to the culpability (or blameworthiness) of the one doing the act.

Let's take missing Mass on Sunday as an example. The Church teaches that missing Mass on Sunday is a mortal sin (a truth found in the Third Commandment; see also CCC 2181). Such a declaration can look only to the act itself (missing Mass); it cannot speak to every possible combination of circumstances and intentions (or reasons) that play into the decision not to go to Mass.

Regarding circumstances, there could be three feet of snow that prevent one from reasonably attending Mass. There could also be illness, or the care of others who are ill, that prevents attendance. Or perhaps missing Mass is the result of inadvertence, such as oversleeping or being mistaken about the correct time.

Regarding intention, there can be any number of factors that determine the formation of one's intent. Perhaps a person is poorly instructed on their obligation to attend Mass. Or perhaps they know that we should go to Mass but are poor at weighing that obligation with, for example, going to a family gathering or completing an important project at work.

Thus, while missing Mass on Sunday remains a mortal sin, this presumes that the circumstances are such that a person could reasonably attend Mass and that the person understands the seriousness of the matter. This is not always the case.

No combination of circumstances or intention can ever make a sinful act good. Thus, with our example, missing Mass is always lamentable, whatever the reason or circumstances. Circumstances and issues related to the formation of intention can lessen one's blameworthiness to something less than mortal sin (even to no guilt at all), but it cannot make a bad thing good.

So, as you emphasize, the Church must continually hold before us the moral vision of Christ, giving emphasis to sins that are intrinsically more serious, because God's word says so. Sins against God such as blasphemy, idolatry, irreverence, ingratitude, and refusing to worship and honor him are serious sins. Sins against the human person, especially against human life (and the origins of human life in our sexuality) are serious matters. Sins against the truth — for example, lying — as well as sins against family, honor due to elders, obedience to superiors, coveting — that is, greed — and so forth may admit of lighter matter but are, of their nature, serious, since they are mentioned in the Ten Commandments.

PRECEPTS OF THE CHURCH

Q. **When I was young we learned six precepts of the Church. Someone told me that the list has been reduced to five. Can you clarify the current number and why the change was made?** — *G. Russell Reiss*

The word "precept" comes from the Latin *praeceptum*, meaning to warn, admonish or instruct (*prae*, "before," plus *capere*, "take"). As such, the precepts of the Church specified, historically, a kind of bare minimum that Catholics must observe in living the Catholic faith. *Prae* indicates that they were often given as an admonition to converts prior to their entry in the Church.

The number and specifics of the precepts have varied a bit over the centuries and places where they were given. They do not rise to the level of formal Church doctrine but are more in the nature of an authoritative pastoral admonition.

The *Catechism of the Council of Trent* did not mention them, though the current *Catechism* does (see 2041–43) and lists five:

1. You shall attend Mass on Sundays and on holy days of obligation and rest from servile labor.
2. You shall confess your sins at least once a year.
3. You shall receive the Eucharist at least during the Easter season.
4. You shall observe the days of fasting and abstinence established by the Church.
5. You shall help provide for the needs of the Church.

Older Catholics in England and America are familiar with a list of six which also included not to marry within a certain degree of kindred nor to solemnize marriage at the forbidden times. This sixth precept was not recognized in other parts of the world. When the universal *Catechism* was published in the 1990s, the more widespread list of five was used. The sixth precept is surely important, but it is spelled out clearly in other Church legislation related to marriage law.

Q.•In my younger days, the priest would remind us that **•missing Mass on Sundays or holy days was a mortal sin. I don't hear this anymore. Is it still a teaching of the Church?** — *Bill Messaros*

Yes, the *Catechism of the Catholic Church* says, "The faithful are obliged to participate in the Eucharist on days of obligation, unless excused for a serious reason (for example, illness, the care of infants) or dispensed by their own pastor. Those who deliberately fail in this obligation commit a grave sin" (2181).

The Lord Jesus also warns, "Unless you eat the flesh of the Son of man and drink his blood, you have no life in you" (Jn 6:53). Therefore, to miss Mass and stay away from holy Communion is a form of spiritual starvation. Further, we then fail to give God the praise, worship, and thanksgiving he is due.

It is a sad fact that this precept is underemphasized today. Priests, catechists, and parents must be clearer in teaching and witnessing to this requirement rooted in the Third Commandment. They must also teach why.

There is a modern tendency, not wrong itself, to emphasize "positive" reasons to do things rather than simply quoting laws. But the gravity of the offense against God's law should not go unstated. Obedience to God's law is good and brings with it many benefits and blessings, such as the instruction in God's word at

Mass and the astonishing blessing of being fed the Lord's body and blood.

Q. **.I wonder if the blessing of attending Mass would be greater if we didn't compel Catholics to attend. Further, keeping the Lord's Day holy is about twenty-four hours, not just one hour.** — *William Bandle*

I am not sure on what basis blessings would be greater. Perhaps you mean that being someone who joyfully attends Mass enhances both the experience of the one who attends and the communal experience of all who attend. This is fair enough. One can see how a congregation of wholehearted attendees could be more enriching, rather than a congregation of those who attend merely under some legal obligation and want to get the Mass over with as quickly as possible.

However, given our fallen human condition both individually and collectively, it is usually necessary that in important matters there be a number of things to motivate. Law is among them. For example, we may like to think that everyone will drive safely simply because they joyfully acknowledge the sacredness of the life of everyone around them and thereby will wholeheartedly comply with all traffic regulations. But to one degree or another, this is not always the case. Thus some fear of negative consequences for violating traffic laws must also be used to motivate compliance for at least some, if not many, drivers.

God knows how we are made and that, at times, we must be compelled to do that which is good and necessary for us. Removing the commandment which obliges to keep holy the Lord's Day would tend to signal that attending Sunday Mass was of lesser importance. But, of course, the Lord Jesus warns, "Unless you eat the flesh of the Son of man and drink his blood, you have no life and you" (Jn 6:53).

So, attending Mass, hearing the Word of God, and receiving the sacraments are critical medicines for us. Ideally, we should all run to them with great joy and relief that this help is available. But, practically speaking, due to sloth and other sins, many do not run with joy. Therefore, other motives must be used, and many must be warned of the critical need for these medicines; to freely neglect them is mortal sin.

As for your observation about striving to observe the Sabbath for twenty-four hours, not just one hour, you are correct. However, the way this is done may vary. Attending Mass is pretty straightforward — you've either done it or not. Rest and engaging in works of charity, however, will be experienced and fulfilled differently depending on one's circumstances and state in life. The *Catechism* wisely advises us to avoid too much legalism here (see 2173).

Q. **Our archbishop is closing the one and only Catholic church near the airport. Isn't there a requirement that there be a church in or very near an airport?** — *Name withheld*

No. It is, of course, a very nice convenience for travelers in larger airports that Mass might be offered, at least on Sundays. But given the shortage of clergy, and also the nature of modern airline travel with shorter layovers, security perimeters, etc., the ability of travelers to attend Mass at an airport is less nowadays.

Canonically, travelers who cannot reasonably attend Mass to fulfill their Sunday obligation may be exempted by their pastor from attendance on such an occasion.

Q. I am very careful to attend Mass each Sunday. However, next year I will make a nature trek in Nepal for sixteen days and will be unable to attend Mass. Can I go even though I will miss at least two Sunday Masses? — *V. Silva*

While Mass attendance is required of a Catholic each Sunday unless there is a serious reason to miss (see CCC 2181), when attendance is unreasonably difficult or impossible, one can be excused. Hence things like inclement weather, significant health issues, and travel, especially in remote locations, will often excuse one.

There are legitimate values in the journey you wish to make that may, in fact, help you to appreciate the glory of what God has created. It would be hard to argue that the trip would not be of sufficient value to permit a limited absence from Mass, if this cannot be reasonably avoided.

Catholics are, however, obliged to secure permission from their proper pastor (see Code of Canon Law, 1245), and thus you ought not fail to discuss the matter with him.

Q. My Saturday was busy and I ended up folding laundry on Sunday. Is this a violation of the Third Commandment? — *Name withheld*

As a general rule, there is a precept that we "refrain from engaging in work or activities that hinder the worship owed to God, the joy proper to the Lord's Day, the performance of the works of mercy, and the appropriate relaxation of mind and body" (CCC 2185).

That said, we also do well to avoid an excessive legalism against which Jesus himself taught when he said, "The sabbath was made for man, not man for the sabbath" (Mk 2:27).

While you might ordinarily seek to avoid folding laundry, etc., on a Sunday, such activity is not intrinsically wrong. Perhaps you find such an activity relaxing in the company of other family members. Perhaps, too, since the activity could not reasonably be accomplished on Saturday, it is an act of charity that helps the family to be prepared for the week ahead.

We do well to seek a proper balance between maintaining the principles of joyful rest on Sunday and avoiding excessive legalism.

Q.If I miss Mass for no good reason, may I receive Communion when I do go, even if I didn't get to confession? — *Name withheld*

The *Catechism*, in conformity with ancient teaching about the necessity of attending Mass, says, "Those who deliberately fail in this obligation commit a grave sin" (2181). Hence you ought to go to confession first. There are some reasons that one might miss Mass that are legitimate, such as serious illness, the care of the sick, or some lack of capacity due to weather or distance. Some also struggle with work schedules. But in this matter, they should consult with their pastor or confessor and also seek solutions.

Q.I am a transportation driver for an adult day-care center. My schedule is Monday to Friday. Do I have to work on Sunday if my supervisor asked me because they lack drivers or somebody called in sick? — *Ferdi Pac*

Ideally, and to the degree that we are able, we ought to avoid working on Sunday. However, *caritas suprema lex* ("love is the highest law"), and there will be times that charity may require us to assist others even on Sunday. This is especially the case in your situation since you are caring for the sick and/or disabled. In keeping the Lord's Day holy, exceptions are made for workers in critical jobs such as emergency care (fire and police), medical workers, and others who care for critical infrastructure and necessary tasks that need to go on even on Sunday.

Therefore, what your supervisor asks of you is not necessarily sinful, and if his request is reasonable, you ought to fulfill it. However, if the problem becomes a recurring pattern, it is not wrong for you to ask for other solutions to be sought so that your own religious sensibilities and requirements can be met.

Q. **I am eighty-seven years old, live in a retirement community, and can no longer drive. I attend the Mass which is offered here once a month and receive holy Communion when it is distributed each week by extraordinary ministers of the Eucharist. I watch Mass on TV. But someone told me that I am not meeting my obligation to go to Mass by watching it on TV. They say it doesn't count. Is this true?** — *Louise Rutherford*

Given your age and mobility issues, the general norms and rules do not apply. However, let's review the general norms and then look to your situation.

To say that a Mass "counts" implies that one meets an obligation by attending it. As a general rule, Catholics are obliged to attend Mass each Sunday. This is in fulfillment of the Third Commandment. The *Catechism* adds: "The Sunday Eucharist is the foundation and confirmation of all Christian practice. For this reason, the faithful are obliged to participate in the Eucharist on days of obligation, unless excused for a serious reason (for example, illness, the care of infants) or dispensed by their own pastor. Those who deliberately fail in this obligation commit a grave sin" (2181).

Simply watching Mass on TV does not fulfill the obligation. A Catholic who can reasonably do so must attend Mass at a parish church or oratory. However, these general norms do not always apply. For example, severe weather may lessen or cancel the obligation to attend Mass at a church. Likewise, poor health or the care of the sick, or some other acute and serious obligation can excuse one from the requirement to attend Mass.

In your case, given the difficulties that age has brought, it is difficult to argue that you have any obligation to attend Mass. Rather, the Church has obligations to you to ensure you receive the sacraments regularly.

As for watching Mass on TV, you are encouraged to do so. By doing so you hear the prayers and the readings and likely a short sermon. All this is good, even if it is not the same as actually attending a Mass. It doesn't have to "count" since you don't have an obligation to meet in the first place. So be encouraged. Thank you for staying united in prayer with the Church through the TV Mass and receiving holy Communion when it is offered in your community. Pray, too, for the conversion and return to regular Mass of those who could easily come to Mass but do not.

THE SANCTITY OF LIFE

Q. Saint Thomas Aquinas wrote that life does not begin until the second trimester. How should we answer this, especially in regard to abortion? — *Thomas Dincher*

The wording of your question is slightly inaccurate. Saint Thomas did not deny that life in the womb was, in fact, life. The teaching of Aquinas to which you refer is that an unborn baby receives a soul forty, or eighty, days after conception, depending on the sex of the child. (Note this is earlier than the second trimester.) Aquinas held this opinion based on Aristotle, who said a child has a soul when it first has a human "form" — that is, when the child looks human. The difference in sex was based on the point at which genitals could be observed on miscarried children, earlier for boys, later for girls.

While many link this position of Aquinas to the abortion debate, the date of ensoulment is not essential to the Church's position on the sinfulness of abortion. The Church roots her teaching in Scripture (see, for example, Ex 21:22–23; Ps 51:5; Ps 139:13–16; Jb 10:11; Is 44:24; Jer 1:5), Tradition, and natural law.

Saint Thomas never wrote directly on abortion. There are only a couple of indirect references in the *Summa* (IIa, IIae, q.64, a 8; q.68, a 11). But, surely, Saint Thomas was well aware of the Scriptures, as well as the ancient teaching of Tradition forbidding abortion at any stage. Beginning with the *Didache*, written in the late first century, which said, "Thou shalt not murder a child by abortion" (2:2), and continuing with Barnabas, Clement, Tertullian, Hippolytus, Basil, Chrysostom, Ambrose, Jerome, and many other early Christians, and also authoritative councils, the Church has consistently condemned abortion in no uncertain terms. Thus we ought not presume Aquinas, who never spoke on abortion directly, ever intended to contest the immorality of abortion at any stage.

Regarding his teaching on ensoulment, theologians do not hold such an opinion today, and most regard Thomas's positions as rooted in an earlier understanding of embryology. Clearly, natural science today demonstrates the existence of a genetically unique individual at conception.

Finally, even if one wanted unreasonably to hold that Aquinas supported early abortions, Saint Thomas, venerable and respected though he is, is not infallible and is not the magisterium. While his teachings are influential, they have not been universally adopted by the magisterium. One obvious example is that Saint Thomas was not supportive of the belief, then unofficial, of the Immaculate Conception of Mary.

Q. The Church condemns artificial birth control be-cause it violates God's will in our life cycle. Should not the same logic condemn mechanical interventions and organ transplants extending life as contrary to God's will in that cycle? — *Bill Bandle*

Using an artificial device such as a knee replacement or undergoing an organ transplant are procedures that seek to repair something which is no longer working properly. In the case of contraception, however, we are seeking to render dysfunctional something which is functioning properly and is a normal aspect of a healthy body. This is a rather big difference and renders your example more of a contrast than a comparison.

It is too simplistic to say that the Church condemns artificial birth control merely because it violates God's will in our life cycle. It is more proper to say that the Church condemns artificial contraception because it violates our obligation of safeguarding both the unitive and the procreative dimensions of the conjugal act. In other words, contraception violates the intrinsic meaning of human sexuality.

The replacement of a knee or a kidney, however, does not violate the essential meaning and purpose of the body. Rather, it helps to enhance the body's overall function, which has been diminished somehow, either by injury or disease.

There are, of course, limits to bodily interventions that we might make. There should be good reasons to replace organs or body parts, and our interventions should enhance the proper, God-given functioning of the body, not alter its intrinsic meaning. There are increasingly strange practices today involving exotic piercings and extreme "body art," some of which come close to mutilation and which may hinder the proper functioning of the body. So-called sex-change operations would also be excluded, since they seek to fundamentally alter what God has given.

Other things being equal, however, it is not inappropriate to make proper medical interventions to ensure proper and healthy functioning of the body.

Q: **I am an extraordinary minister of holy Communion and was called to the house of a man with a brain tumor who, it was said, would likely die soon. He was unconscious in the room and was being given no food or fluids, and according to his wife had been in this condition for days. In effect, he was being starved to death. What should I have done?** — *Name withheld*

Church teaching on this matter is clear. Nutrition and hydration, even by artificial means — for example, a feeding tube — cannot simply be terminated because doctors have determined that a person will never recover consciousness. The Congregation for the Doctrine of the Faith issued a statement in 2007 that emphasized that administering food and water to a patient in a persistently unconscious state is morally obligatory "to the extent to which, and for as long as, it is shown to accomplish its proper finality, which is the hydration and nourishment of the patient. In this way suffering and death by starvation and dehydration are prevented."

Exceptions may occur when patients are unable to assimilate food and water, or in the *rare* cases when nutrition and hydration become excessively burdensome for the patient because the fluids swamp the body.

Nutrition and hydration are not extraordinary care, since they are not excessively expensive and do not necessarily require hospitalization. Giving them is not a treatment that cures the patient, but is ordinary care aimed at the preservation of life.

A priest should certainly handle these sorts of cases. The priest, for his part, in encountering cases like this should ascertain the facts and be sure it is not a rare case where food or fluids would only intensify suffering because they cannot be digested and offer no help. Precluding such cases, he should then instruct and admonish the family to see that caretakers provide food and water (usually via a tube).

Unfortunately, if the family or caretaker with medical power of attorney refuses, there are very few legal remedies in most jurisdictions. Judges have usually ruled that food and water through a tube is not required care for those who are unconscious. Many do die prematurely on account of this flawed understanding of ordinary and necessary medical care. It is another tragic example of the world's rejection of the Church's teachings on life. It also endangers the mentally handicapped and others in need of care due to brain injury.

Q. **What is the Church's stance on artificial life support? May a Catholic be removed from it?** — *Gene Bozek*

If by artificial life support you mean something such as a ventilator, the use of such machines is not required when they are no longer therapeutic and the person is certainly dying. Neither is it required to revive a person who is approaching death each time their heart stops.

Allowing someone to die whom the Lord is certainly calling is morally very different from directly causing a person to die, which is what euthanasia advocates claim the right to do (usually by chemical injections).

One exception to the non-required use of artificial means: food and water, even if supplied by a tube, should still to be administered to those who are approaching death. Only in rare cases, where the major organs of the body have already shut down and can no longer process food or fluids, can this treatment be discontinued.

Q. I am ninety-three years old and have told everyone that I don't want any medical interventions if I get sick. They say I sound suicidal. Thoughts? — *Name withheld*

One ought to not speak too broadly when it comes to such matters. Generally speaking, the Church teaches that we are not required to employ excessive and burdensome treatments that are not really therapeutic. However, what is or is not therapeutic may vary. For example, a breathing machine that is merely sustaining a person who will never recover is not therapeutic. However, a breathing machine is therapeutic for a young person who has been injured and needs assisted in breathing temporarily.

Even for an older person such as you, certain treatments may be therapeutic, or might assist in your comfort. Food and water, even if administered by a tube, is helpful and therapeutic (except in the rarest of situations) and must be offered even to patients well into the dying process, according to Catholic teaching.

Rather than make a broad refusal of all treatments, you would do well to speak with a local priest, especially one skilled in medical and bioethical issues, and your doctor, to set up some reasonable protocols. It also helps to have someone designated with a medical power of attorney to speak for you in the event that you are incapacitated.

Generally, you are not required to employ extraordinary or excessively burdensome treatments. But particular circumstances are always going to be important and affect the determination of what is the moral and ethical thing to do, even at age ninety-three.

Q. Are the people who commit suicide doomed? Should we pray for them? — *Hugh Sweeney*

While suicide is a grave sin objectively speaking, the culpability (blameworthiness) of an individual may be reduced, even to a minimum, by severe mental anguish or mental illness that affects their freedom or ability to carefully reflect on what they are doing. Thus it is proper to pray for those who die by suicide.

Physician-assisted suicide is, however, a growing area where many may actually incur full mortal sin by arranging their own death. Presumably they reflect over a significant period of time and freely, apart from sudden mental anguish, plan and execute their own death in violation of the Fifth Commandment and the teachings of the Church. Regarding these types of suicides, it is reasonable to be concerned that they are, as you term it, "doomed." Still, we should always pray!

Q. You [have written that suicide is never justified]. What if, in the heat of battle, a soldier jumps on a grenade to save others. Is he not committing suicide? And did not Jesus say, giving one's life to save others is the greatest gift one can give? Is not what he is doing an unselfish act to save others? — *Larry Anzick*

The example you give in the question of a soldier jumping on a grenade to save others is not suicide. It is both intentionally and intrinsically different than suicide.

In an actual suicide, a person directly takes his own life. From the standpoint of intention, he seeks to purposely end his own life. Further, he does this for some perceived "benefit" for himself, usually the ending of his own suffering.

But the soldier you described does not directly intend to end his own life. His intent is to save his friends. Though he may foresee the possibility, even the likelihood, of his own death, from the standpoint of intention his own death is not what he intends, and he would rather not die.

What the solider does is also *intrinsically* different from suicide in that he does not act for his own perceived benefit, but rather for the benefit of others. Thus in no way can the soldier's act be considered suicide.

While those who attempt or accomplish suicide usually do so under some severe mental anguish, and deserve our sympathy, what they do cannot claim our approval. However, the soldier's act, which is selfless and heroically generous, does deserve a deep respect and admiration, for the reasons stated. It is those who lay down their lives for others that Jesus praises. Those who sadly take their life for their own sake or benefit act very differently and do not fall under the purview of Christ's praises here.

Q. **I am confused with something said in the *YOUCAT* (the *Youth Catechism of the Catholic Church* 387), which seems to forbid organ donation. Does this mean we can't be organ donors?** — *Maureen Normann*

The *YOUCAT* is a catechism aimed at youths, which was developed in conjunction with World Youth Day. While it is a valuable resource, it limits its answers to a very brief question-and-answer format. As such it does not always develop what it says. The hope is to connect young people with the larger *Catechism of the Catholic Church* and the *Compendium of the Catechism of the Catholic Church* published by the bishops.

The passage quoted above is a bit murky. However, *YOUCAT* later states more directly about organ donation: "Donating organs can lengthen life or improve the quality of life, and therefore it is a genuine service to one's neighbor, provided no one is forced to do it" (391). *YOUCAT* then points to the *Catechism* (see 2296), which develops the matter further.

On the American scene, organ donation is seen as altruistic and an almost unqualified good; surely, it can be such. However, remember, the *Catechism* (including *YOUCAT*) is written for a worldwide setting, where, in some places such as China, prisoners have been compelled to donate their organs. In other settings, the buying and selling of organs is becoming a problem. Hence the Church wants to encourage organ donation but balance it with the respect we should have for bodily integrity and the physical and emotional health of the organ donors. Increasingly the powerless and poor are being compelled to donate or are tempted to sell their organs.

The YOUCAT quote is likely aiming here in its analysis and clarifies later the good of donation in the right circumstances.

Medical Ethics

Q. I have been offered a job with a large pharmaceutical company, which, among other things, supplies materials for stem-cell research. Am I able to take such a job? — *Name withheld*

Part of the answer depends on an important distinction, which many lose, in the Church's teaching about stem-cell research. The Church does not oppose all, or even most stem-cell research. There are, for example, no moral issues with using stem cells harvested from adult humans or from umbilical cords after birth. It is only the use of stem cells acquired from human embryos which the Church opposes, because it requires the killing of human life in order to obtain them.

Therefore, the company in question may not be doing evil per se in supplying material for stem-cell research. Only those who wrongfully use stem cells acquired from human embryos commit wrongdoing.

However, let us suppose that it is clear to you that the company is certainly supplying some materials for the specific purpose of embryonic stem-cell research. The morality of you accepting employment with this sort of a company would vary based on a number of factors.

Let us presume, as is usually the case, that the pharmaceutical company is large and supplies a vast variety of pharmaceuticals for a wide array of medical purposes. In such a scenario, taking employment with such a company would only involve you in remote material cooperation. And such associations, while not ideal, are morally permissible.

However, if the position in the company would require you to promote embryonic stem-cell research, or to advance the sales of specific products related to that specific research, such work would involve a more direct material cooperation. In such a case, you ought not take the job, since it would involve you directly advancing and cooperating in a moral evil.

Q.: I have read that in some countries it is legal to sell blood and organs. What is the Catholic view of this practice? — *Bernie Askew*

Organs and blood should not be sold. No Christian can seriously propose such a thing. In the first place, it violates Scripture, which says: "You are not your own; you were bought with a price. So glorify God in your body" (1 Cor 6:19–20). We are not owners of our bodies, merely stewards. We should not sell what does not belong to us.

To be a steward means to use what belongs to another in a way that accords with the will of the true owner. Thus we are permitted in charity to donate blood and to donate certain organs while we live, and even other organs upon our death. These acts of charity conform to the will of the true owner of our body, God, who is love. Scripture encourages, "You received without pay, give without pay" (Mt 10:8).

The second reason not to sell blood and organs is the harm that it does to the poor. If they can be sold, the number of those who simply donate them will decline. And the price of purchasing them will surely be high. This gives the poor less access to healing remedies.

For these reasons, the buying and selling of organs and blood is an offense against Catholic teaching. It violates both the principle of stewardship and of charity.

Q. **I once heard that if an organ or limb is removed it should be buried. Is that true, and what are some practical ways to go about doing this?** — *Cathy*

There are no specific requirements for Catholics in this regard. Reverence for the body would certainly exclude discarding limbs or diseased organs with ordinary trash, but so would ordinary health regulations, for that matter.

The usual medical protocol when a limb must be amputated is to permit the patient the option of consigning the severed limb to a funeral home where it is cremated and buried reverently later.

Another common solution is to incinerate an amputated or severed limb or organ along with other medical and biological materials. In such cases the ashes are collected and buried. Having been rendered biologically harmless, the usual destination for such ashes is the local landfill. For this reason, some prefer to direct that something as precious as a limb be cremated by a funeral home with burial taking place in a part of a cemetery or other reverent location. While this is commendable, the Church does not require this of the faithful.

Q. **In Leviticus 19:28 God tells us not to lacerate or cut our bodies and to not "tattoo any marks upon you." Does this mean that if one gets a tattoo they are committing a sin?** — *Dixie Lynch*

The Catholic Church does not have a law forbidding tattoos. Neither does the Church see the requirements of the Old Covenant as binding in an unequivocal way. Certain verses in Leviticus involve fundamental moral law, but other verses state customary law or punitive laws that no longer bind. The determination of how to sort this out is complex but fundamentally involves later Scripture and Tradition. For example, many laws in the Old Testament involving dietary restrictions (kosher laws) were canceled by Jesus and the New Covenant (see Rom 14:20). Other laws stated in Leviticus and Deuteronomy are rooted in custom and involve certain references to clothing, or the trimming of beards, hair, and so forth. And these things fell away on their own and are not repeated in later legislation. Still other moral laws are stated and retained at every stage of biblical history and forbid killing, stealing, bearing false witness, fornicating, committing homosexual acts or adultery, and so forth.

The forbidding of tattoos in the text you state does not seem to have been retained in the moral code of the Bible in later stages. The reasons stated for not tattooing seem localized at the time of Leviticus, which links them to cultic practices of the pagans.

While the Church does not have an explicit teaching on tattoos, and does not teach that Leviticus 19:28 is still binding, that does not mean that getting tattoos is commendable. While it is not sinful per se, it is problematic that people choose to make lasting changes to their skin, often in dramatic ways that they later regret. Skin is not a canvas that we should etch all sorts of things on it. The Scriptures say: "Do you not know that your body is a temple of the Holy Spirit within you, which you have from God? You are not your own; you were bought with a price. So glorify God in your body" (1 Cor 6:19–20). Making permanent scarring on our body does not seem to respect the body as God has given it to us. Small ear-piercings and perhaps a small tattoo is one thing, but many large tattoos and piercings are excessive and seem at some point to cross over into a disrespect for our body, which really belongs to God.

As a pastoral stance, therefore, I recommend to one and all, don't get tattoos; just stay away from it. It may seem trendy now, but many of us who are older remember a time when such things were considered low class and foolish. In other words, trends and perceptions change. All the more reason not to make permanent changes to our body about things that are temporarily in vogue.

Q. Is there any official Church teaching about smoking? Is it a sin to smoke? I see bishops and priests smoke, so it made me wonder. What about secondhand smoke? — *Name withheld*

There is no official teaching forbidding smoking per se. There are, however, many general norms and moral principles that require us to exhibit proper care and respect for the body. For example, the Scriptures say: "You are not your own; you were bought with a price. So glorify God in your body" (1 Cor 6:19–20). The *Catechism* also teaches: "Life and physical health are precious gifts entrusted to us by God. We must take reasonable care of them, taking into account the needs of others and the common good. The virtue of temperance disposes us to avoid every kind of excess: the abuse of food, alcohol, tobacco, or medicine" (2288, 2290).

Given principles like these, and what we increasingly know about smoking and its effect on the body, it is difficult to conclude that smoking is merely a morally neutral act. It clearly causes grave and cumulative harm. Knowing this, and then willfully engaging in smoking, is to sinfully harm the body.

However, there are factors that may reduce one's guilt or blameworthiness in the matter. Some are strongly addicted to nicotine and struggle to be free. Many took up the habit of smoking before knowledge of its harm was as widely known or certain as it is today. Not so long ago, there was widespread social pressure to smoke.

Therefore, while it is difficult to conclude that smoking is anything other than gravely harmful and wrong, sufficient knowledge and full consent of the will are lacking in many. For this reason, the Church has a pastoral solicitude for those who struggle to be free of it. Obviously, if a youth were today to take up smoking, given all we know of its great harm, it would be hard for them to escape a more serious culpability as well as an assessment that the choice to do so was foolishness of the highest degree.

Should the Church come right out and say smoking is a serious sin? Perhaps, but as a general approach the Church moves rather cautiously in formally specifying new sorts of sins. Knowledge of smoking's harm is relatively recent, and most cultures have responded reasonably well to limit that harm. For now, there are plenty of general moral principles in Church teaching that can be applied, which allow people to connect the dots that smoking is wrong. Greater specificity of the sinfulness of smoking will likely emerge more from a consensus among the faithful working with their pastors than from an edict issued from Rome or a new entry placed in the *Catechism*.

As for the problems of secondhand smoke, all the norms above apply. And to this we must also add that those who willfully expose others to secondhand smoke not only sin against their own bodies, but the bodies of others. They also sin against charity and justice. Most today who still smoke seem reasonably aware of their need to not expose others to secondhand smoke.

Q: A Washington state law requires pharmacists to dispense abortion-inducing drugs against their conscientious objections. Otherwise they will be decertified. The Supreme Court has let this ruling stand. What is a pharmacist to do? — *Thomas Pohlen*

There is no obligation to follow an unjust or immoral law. If legal recourse is exhausted, it would seem that the point of civil disobedience has been reached. Fines will likely follow, which should not be paid. The pharmacists who refuse to comply may in fact lose their license or certification. This is difficult to be sure, but, remember that many early Christians lost their livelihoods as well.

Certainly, I would encourage Catholic pharmacists in Washington and elsewhere to consult their local bishop and seek diocesan legal advice. They will know the local scene and may know of other legal aspects. They will also know of other local efforts to resist the unjust law. Work together, not alone.

Q. **Is it morally permissible to divorce in order to be able to qualify for Medicaid assistance to pay for nursing-home costs? My wife has dementia and will soon need nursing-home care, which costs $120,000. My wife's savings would be wiped out in nine months, and then they will come for my assets, which would be gone in three years.** — *Name withheld*

You describe a difficult situation faced by many today. The brief space offered here cannot explore all the moral issues involved, but the bottom line answer is no, you should not divorce.

The well-known axiom that the ends do not justify the means applies here. And while the "end" of trying to save your money (presumably to give it to your children) is a good and understandable end, or goal, one cannot sin in order to obtain it.

What is the sin involved in what you ponder? Fundamentally, it is either to divorce, which God hates (see Mal 2:16), or it is to lie.

Regarding divorce, it is essential to recall the vow you made, which is very pertinent in exactly the case described here. The vow said, "I take you to be my wife, to have and to hold, from this day forward, for better, for worse, for richer, for poorer, in sickness and in health, until death do us part." Clearly, sickness and poverty were anticipated as a possible scenario in the vows you both made.

But one might argue: "We are not *really* getting divorced; it is just a legal move regarding civil marriage. We will still consider each other as spouses." But in this case, a lie is being told to the state for the purpose of Medicaid funds.

Either way, it seems that what is proposed is that one do evil (sin) that good may come of it. This is not a valid moral solution to an admittedly difficult and painful issue. In recent years, long-term-care insurance has been a solution to some of this, but for an older person, this new device is seldom much help since, if they have it at all, the premiums are high and the payoff low.

I pray it might be of some consolation to recall that the goal in life is not to die with a lot of money in the bank. The goal is to die in holiness. God has promised the Kingdom to those who are persecuted for the sake of righteousness, and for those who have done what is right even at high personal cost.

Q. **I am a student nurse, and I was wondering: When I am a nurse, if I have a patient who is serious about euthanasia and feels that it is the best choice for him or her, how should I respond? If I just let somebody else nurse that person, would I be indirectly allowing that person to die by "passing the buck"? The nurse is the patient's advocate, but what can I morally do, if the patient's wishes are incompatible with my morals as a Catholic, without stifling the patient's autonomy?** — *Kelley*

Your role as a patient's advocate cannot eclipse your vocation as a disciple of Jesus and a Catholic. You should not be asked to violate your conscience, and Church teaching on this matter, from the biblical tradition, is clear: We cannot cooperate directly in such an evil act, which euthanasia is, since it directly takes the life of another, usually by killing them through lethal injection.

If a patient speaks to you about his wish to be euthanized, it is best to avoid engaging in a debate. Rather, you would probably do best to say that you cannot recommend such a course for medical, social, and religious reasons.

Medically, euthanasia introduces grave distortions into medical practice by asking doctors and nurses to engage in an act of killing. But this is not the purpose of the medical community, which is oriented to bringing healing and care, not causing death. To ask the medical community to facilitate euthanasia shifts the focus and puts increasing pressure on doctors and nurses to recommend death to lessen costs, etc.

Socially, euthanasia endangers the lives of others since the so-called right to die soon becomes the duty to die. The physically and mentally handicapped, and others who are chronically ill or suffering, will increasingly find their dignity discounted and their lives accounted as "not worth living." Pressure to euthanize them will surely grow as it has in some countries which have legalized euthanasia already.

Religiously, euthanasia usurps God's role as the one who gives life and determines a person's years on this earth. As Christians, we are taught the need and the glory of the Cross. Suffering is not meaningless for a believer. Suffering, when given to God, produces glory and helps to set our focus on heaven (see 2 Cor 4:10–18).

As far as your patient's autonomy goes, that is more of a legal matter that will depend on the passage of certain laws, etc. You cannot force him or her to agree with you, but you have some rights to advise them as to what you think, and you cannot be required to cooperate with them. If they ask for another nurse, that would likely be their right, but you need not facilitate their request or find a pro-euthanasia nurse for them. Let them do the work and make the request to others. That way you are not "passing the buck." Rather, your stance must be to refuse to cooperate in evil, even if you cannot ultimately prevent it.

I hope this helps. Each situation will vary a bit, but these are some general principles to offer in what is currently a shifting legal landscape.

Q. My infant daughter is going to have her one-year checkup and will be receiving vaccines related to measles/mumps/rubella and chickenpox. I am concerned that some vaccines used today have been made using a process from cells of aborted babies. Can I have my daughter vaccinated? Do you have any further advice on what to do?
— *Hannah Kim*

Generally, Church teaching is clear that Catholics cannot directly cooperate in evil. However, remote material cooperation is permissible, and often impossible to avoid.

For example, few products we buy are wholly free from situations where injustice was involved in their production. Perhaps the products come from countries where unjust wages are paid, or child labor laws are poorly enforced, or working conditions are bad. And these injustices offend against human dignity and cause suffering. Yet it is not reasonable or possible for us to stop all buying and participation in a worldwide economy.

Thus while we cooperate materially in an economy that is based to some degree on injustice, nevertheless our cooperation is remote, and we do not directly intend or cause the injustices in the chain of production and supply. Further, alternatives to purchasing many needed products are not always reasonably available.

As you describe it, your permitting of the necessary vaccines for your daughter might include vaccines developed using cells from aborted children. However, it seems clear that your involvement in the matter is quite remote, and you do not directly intend to cooperate in abortion or the evils that flow from it. If you can reasonably find vaccines that are assuredly not part of any vaccine line even remotely connected with aborted children, you should do so, and request those vaccines. But clearly identifying such vaccines is not always possible, and the vaccinations are important for your daughter.

So, do what you can reasonably do to request better alternatives, but if they cannot be found, realize that your cooperation in any evils associated with the vaccines is remote and unintended.

Q. Is cosmetic surgery (simply to enhance one's appearance) morally acceptable? — *Bill Bandle*

Cosmetic surgery is not directly addressed in the Church's moral teaching. There are teachings related to it that require our attention and the application of prudential judgment to avoid sinful tendencies.

In the first place, we should, as you do, distinguish merely cosmetic surgery from corrective surgery. In the aftermath of an accident it may be necessary to repair certain damage, such as facial disfigurement or burned skin. Sometimes, too, there are birth defects — for example, a cleft palate — that require corrective surgery. In addition to repairing the physical functioning of the body, physical disfigurement can also have strong psychological effects, and the reparative effects may be helpful to restoring a sense of well-being and confidence.

Merely cosmetic surgery is focused more on the adjustment of physical characteristics that a person does not like. Since the changes to the body are permanent and there are risks associated with surgery, discernment is necessary. At the heart of our moral discernment is the concern for vainglory, where we attribute too much emphasis on appearance and have an excessive need to be praised by others. Modest jewelry, hair treatments, etc., are mentioned and tolerated in Scripture, but with cautions about excess (see 1 Tm 2:9; 1 Pt 3:3). If this is the case with simple and impermanent cosmetics, all the more so with permanent surgical changes.

Also of concern is the ingratitude for, or resistance or rejection of, the body God has given us. There can also be the tendency to forget that we are stewards of our body, not owners (see 1 Cor 6:19–20). Many today engage in excessive tattooing as if the skin were a canvas for self-reflection, while one's God-given appearance is increasingly set aside. As a permanent change to the skin, tattoos should seldom be sought and never rashly applied.

More strictly to be avoided are cosmetic surgeries and applications that impair the proper functioning of the body or which present risks to our health. Certain piercings of the mucous membranes of the lips and nose risk infection and can interfere with the body's proper functioning. Even more, tongue piercings, tongue splitting, and the like interfere with the proper function of the tongue, making eating, talking, etc., difficult.

One other area to be critiqued is the alteration of the body to make it more sexually alluring. While no one wants to feel unattractive, simply desiring to be appealing from a sexual point of view is a diminishment of the human person and can also be a form of immodesty or even seduction.

Of itself, cosmetic surgery is permissible, but there are many sinful drives and attitudes to be avoided. As such it should generally be a recourse rarely pursued, and then for serious reasons.

Q: **Is it morally okay to get a shingles vaccine shot? I read that the initial research in developing this vaccine involved embryonic stem cells.** — *Rita Malone*

Yes, given the circumstances you describe, it is acceptable to get the shot. While it is likely true that some research on the vaccine involved embryonic stem-cell lines, your own involvement and connection to that is very remote. There is probably no product that is not tainted in some way by sinful human actions.

We must refuse any direct cooperation with evil. We can also strive to avoid remote cooperation if it is reasonable to do so due to available alternatives. But in a world of sin, remote cooperation with sin, injustice, and evil is nearly impossible to wholly avoid.

SEXUAL MORALITY

Q.It has come to my attention that my twenty-two-
year-old son, who does not live with us, views a lot
of internet pornography. What can I say to him to dissuade
him? — *Name withheld*

Biblically and morally, pornography is sinful and unfit for a Christian. Jesus, for example, forbids a man to look with lust on a woman (see Mt 5:28–29), which, of course, is the precise purpose of pornography. Other passages forbid sexual immorality as well (1 Cor 6:9; Eph 5:3–5; Col 3:5). As these passages make clear, such sins are mortal and, unrepented of, exclude one from the kingdom of heaven.

Psychologically, pornography is unhealthy because it is unreal. It is rooted in fantasy — photos and movies are photographically enhanced, models are often surgically altered, etc. In a way, pornography is cowardly and appeals to those who cannot, or will not, take the risk to live in the real world and make the commitment to live and interact with a real spouse and all that entails.

In real life, sex is not had with a body, it is engaged in with a real person, who may not measure up to the fantasies and exotic wishes of pornography addicts. Real people have limits, preferences, moods, and do not simply disappear when sexual pleasure is completed. Thus pornography turns one inward, instills unrealistic notions, and often destroys interest in normal marital life.

Addiction to internet pornography is growing dramatically, and many are locked into terrible and descending cycles. It is a grave evil and takes a terrible personal and family toll. Many need significant help to break free. Often, a 12-step program under the strict care of a sponsor can help. Certain internet filter programs feature an accountability component which reports violations to a trusted friend or third party.

I pray your son will consider the grave spiritual, moral, and psychological ruin that can come from indulging this vice.

Q: •Is viewing pornography on the internet a mortal sin? •What is a good method to get away from what I know in my heart is wrong? — *Name withheld*

Of its nature, the viewing of pornography is a mortal sin. As with any mortal sin, one's culpability (blameworthiness) is affected by how freely one consents to the act, and the degree to which one fully knows and understands the gravity of the evil involved.

Internet pornography presents a very serious temptation to many individuals, as well as many pastoral challenges for the Church. The fact is, today, increasing numbers of people compulsively view this sinful material, and many are outright addicted to it.

As any confessor or pastor of souls will be able to attest, large numbers approaching the confessional and counseling are quite "stuck" in internet pornography. Many have seen their relationships and marriages greatly harmed, and some even end up with criminal charges related to the viewing of pornographic images of minors. This addiction is a slippery slope that leads to increasingly debased and degrading imagery. Pornography is indeed a snare, which lures its victims with promises of momentary delights, only to leave them quickly hungry for more. This is due to the increasingly insatiable lust that it ignites.

One of the more effective remedies that has emerged recently is a system of accountability, wherein one's internet activities are monitored and recorded, and a daily report is sent to someone of the pornography addict's choice. This "sponsor," of sorts, reviews the list and holds the addict accountable. Certainly, too, filters can be of some help to prevent tempting materials from appearing in the first place. These filters can be of great help to those who struggle more mildly with the problem. Sadly, though, many true pornography addicts know their way around such filters.

Finally, this salutary reminder: absolutely nothing we do on the internet is private. When we are on the internet, we are out in public, and our browsing habits are not difficult to discover for those who might wish to know. What's done in the dark can be brought to the light.

Take internet pornography seriously; it is a grave sin, which causes great harm, and is highly addictive to many people. The Scriptures say, "Shun immorailty" (1 Cor 6:18). And one does well to heed this prescription in a particular way related to internet pornography. Flee pornography; it is a snare.

Q: I accept the Catholic teaching on marriage and sexuality. However, I am often asked why the Church allows older couples to get married who cannot have children, since we teach that openness to procreation is essential for marriage and proper sexual activity in marriage?
— *Ruth Marie Appleby*

Catholic teaching on this matter indicates that the couple must be open to procreation, but the teaching does not require the impossible. In advanced age it becomes increasingly unlikely that a couple may conceive, but that is not of their making or under their control, and the situation occurs naturally. An older couple in this situation may still be said to be open to procreation. At a minimum, they are not intentionally excluding the connection between procreation and marital intercourse. As such, they are able to grow in conjugal love by it, but for natural reasons beyond their control cannot realize the procreative dimension.

The case is very different, however, for a couple that actively uses contraceptive drugs or devices, or engages in contraceptive behaviors. These are designed and intended to prevent conception. "Contra" means "against," and contraceptive practices are directly intended to preclude conception. That is the point of them, and why the Church indicates that recourse to them is sinful. A contracepting couple willfully breaks the connection that God intends. The older couple does not do so. Their incapacity to conceive occurs beyond their control, not as a result of their will.

In the case of same-sex "couples" there are many more issues than merely the incapacity to conceive. However, among the issues is the futility of their acts in terms of conception. In their case they cannot be open to conception; they are willfully unable to be open to it. From the beginning, they intentionally engage in acts that cannot possibly generate life and which knowingly violate even the most rudimentary biological facts necessary for conception. Those who engage in unnatural acts cannot then claim they are "naturally" incapable of conceiving and that they should not be equated with the situation of an older couple.

So, intent is the major issue here. An older couple does not engage in sexual acts that they willfully render sterile. Neither do they (or should they) engage in unnatural sexual practices that make conception impossible. This includes not only the use of contraceptive drugs and devices, but also other acts that are impolite to mention in a book of this sort.

Q. I think homosexual people are born homosexual. What is the Catholic Church's theological or scientific position on this matter? — *Charles O'Neill*

The *Catechism* states, regarding homosexual orientation, "Its psychological genesis remains largely unexplained" (2357). Hence the Church has no official doctrine that would either affirm or deny your assertion.

However, the moral requirements for a person of same-sex attraction do not vary based on the origin of the orientation. The *Catechism* teaches: "Basing itself on Sacred Scripture, which presents homosexual acts as acts of grave depravity, tradition has always declared that 'homosexual acts are intrinsically disordered.' They are contrary to the natural law. They close the sexual act to the gift of life. They do not proceed from a genuine affective and sexual complementarity. Under no circumstances can they be approved" (2357).

It is not unlike a diabetic, who may be so for genetic reasons, or by acquiring the condition (perhaps by overeating). The bottom line is the same: they must carefully regulate their diet. Thus, whatever the origin of homosexuality, the requirement is clear: one must embrace the life of celibacy that God enables.

Q. **Can Catholic actors accept roles that require of them nudity and enacting illicit sexual union on screen or stage?** — *Bill Bandle*

As a general rule, no. To do this is to engage in scandal in which one gives temptation to others and contributes to the lowering of moral standards. It is wrong to celebrate or encourage immoral activities.

There are, however, movies and drama that do comment on life and the human condition, which includes violence, treachery, corruption, sexual sins, and so forth. To treat of these matters in drama (as even the Bible does) is not per se wrong. What is wrong is to celebrate such sinfulness or seek to justify and normalize it.

Even more erroneous is to unnecessarily display what should not be seen. For example, to include a murder in a movie does not require us to watch a person brutally killed and dismembered. Likewise, to report a sexual infidelity does not require us to watch it pornographically portrayed. Subtlety and discretion are required to treat of topics like these.

So, Catholics actors should not transgress when sin is either celebrated or inappropriately displayed.

Q. Pope John XXIII, in an encyclical, stated that among the rights that belong to every person is the "freedom to form a family." Given the Church's stance on same-sex unions, and other non-Biblical family structures, with which I am in full agreement, doesn't Pope John's statement give tacit license that anyone could adopt in order to "form a family"? In other words, is not the expression "form a family" too vague? — *Janet Cooper*

As with any quote, historical context is important. Pope John XXIII lived in an era when single-parent families and cohabiting couples were rare, and same-sex unions were inconceivable. Back in the late 1950s and early 1960s, family meant a married father and a mother, and children. There was still a basic moral consensus, which could be presumed in using phrases such as "form a family."

Today, this is gone, and we must be much more specific. Thus, in reading Saint John XXIII, we must adjust to the context in which he spoke and cannot reasonably demand the precision that is necessary today. Neither would it be reasonable for our opponents on the marriage question to read into these remarks an approval for the current situation.

Q. What is the Church's official teaching about transgenderism and the demand that they can use locker rooms, etc., set aside for the sex other than what they were born? There does not seem to be a clear answer about all of this. — *Robert*

There is no such thing as being "transgendered" from any biblical or Catholic perspective. Thus there is no official teaching about something that doesn't even exist, let alone about the use of bathrooms. What we *can* do is apply Catholic principles to address the deep confusion that has arisen about something so clear and basic as one's sex.

The human person has a sex (not a gender, which is a term of grammar applied to nouns and adjectives), and God assigns our sex — either male or female. The Scriptures say that, in creating us, "God created man in his own image ... male and female he created them" (Gn 1:27). Our bodies are therefore a revelation of who and what God created us to be. No amount of clothes, cosmetics, or surgery can alter the fact that we are male or female right down to our DNA.

Transgenderism is one of the stranger manifestations of the sexual confusion of our times. It is a form of gnostic dualism from which a person can claim that he has an "identity" wholly separate from anything indicated by his body. In effect, he or she says: "I am not my body. I am only my thoughts and feelings." This amounts to a reduction of the human person and a stepping back from reality as clearly indicated by the body. It also denigrates the body and the witness it makes to us of who and what we are.

Yet the glory of the human person is to unite the two aspects of God's creation, the spiritual and the material. So precious is the bodily dimension of the human person that Christ took to himself a full human nature: body and soul. He did not simply come among us as a ghost or mirage. He walked among us as part of our full nature, offered his body on the altar of the cross, and raised up his full humanity and glorified it. To reduce our bodies to a mere tool, or a sort of prison (where a man is "trapped" in a woman's body), or to mutilate it surgically, is a grave offense against what God has wrought. Since our body is a revelation from God of who and what we are, to ignore its voice or overrule what God says through it is a sign of the pride of our days.

The *Catechism* teaches: "Man and woman have been created, which is to say, willed by God: on the one hand, in perfect equality as human persons; on the other, in their respective beings as man and woman. 'Being man' or 'being woman' is a reality which is good and willed by God.... In their 'being-man' and 'being-woman,' they reflect the Creator's wisdom and goodness" (369).

Those who struggle with their sexuality as given by God deserve our sympathy and care. But in no way can we participate in confirming them in a very great error and one of deep confusion. Only the truth as God has declared it will set us free. We therefore must resist and teach against the "gender ideology" of our times, which seeks to replace what God has created with vain imaginings that both confuse and demean the true glory of the human person.

Q. **[I recently learned that] some bishops are allowing some divorced and remarried Catholics to receive Communion, citing a papal endorsement. What does this papal endorsement state?** — *Diane Reinke*

Church policy on Catholics who are divorced and remarried remains unchanged. As a general rule, divorced and remarried Catholics are not able to receive Communion or absolution in confession. This is because they are living in an invalid marriage, where at least one of them has been married to someone else before.

In accord with what Jesus teaches in Matthew 19, Matthew 5, Mark 10, and other times in the Gospels, those who divorce and then remarry are in a state of adultery. And since their marriage is ongoing, and regular conjugal relations are presumed, Catholics in this state are not usually able to make a firm act of contrition, which includes the promise to avoid adulterous sex in the future. Hence they cannot receive absolution, nor can they be offered holy Communion.

In relatively rare situations, some Catholics are able to live with their current spouse in a kind of "brother-sister" relationship where sexual relations are not part of the picture. Sometimes this is due to mutual agreement between the spouses, and sometimes it is due to health-related issues that preclude sexual activity and will not change in the future. In such rare cases, a Catholic is able to make an act of contrition, receive absolution, and be restored to holy Communion.

Of itself, a request to review current Church policies is a legitimate matter to consider in any number of areas. As most priests know, many people today find themselves in complicated situations. Many, for example, have returned to the Church after many years away, often in irregular marriage situations. Some can be quickly and easily rectified. Others, because current or former spouses are uncooperative, create difficulties in people being restored to the full sacramental life of the Church.

Are there ways that we can more efficiently deal with these situations and at the same time respect the Lord's clear teaching in Scripture? Perhaps, but it is unlikely that there can be any major changes in Church policy in this regard. However, there can be great improvements in explaining our pastoral stance to Catholics who are often confused by what the Church teaches and why.

Q.•In Matthew 19, Jesus forbids divorce [with] an exception — for unchastity. Please explain what the Lord means here. — *Name withheld*

The particular verse you reference reads as follows in the New American Bible: "And so I [Jesus] say to you, whoever divorces his wife (unless the marriage is unlawful) and marries another commits adultery" (Mt 19:9).

The phrase "unless the marriage is unlawful" is a rendering of the Greek *me epi porneia*, which most literally means, "except for illicit sexual union." The Greek word in question is *porneia*, which refers generally to any illicit sexual union. Depending on the context, it most often means premarital sex, but can also refer to incest and more rarely to adultery and/or homosexual acts. I say "more rarely" because adultery and homosexual acts have their own proper Greek words and descriptions that are normally used (*moichao* for adultery and *paraphysin*, etc., for homosexual acts).

Some, especially from the Protestant tradition, think *porneia*, as used here, means "adultery." They hold that divorce and remarriage is allowed if one (or both) of the spouses committed adultery. But this seems unlikely, since, if the Lord meant that, he could have used the more specific word for adultery (*moichao*), which he uses later in the very same sentence. It also seems a strange logic that a second marriage would not be considered adulterous if the first marriage is rendered adulterous by one or both parties.

Catholic teaching and understanding regarding the word *porneia* in this verse holds it to mean "incestuous relationships." This makes historical sense. The Jewish world had very clear under-standings about permissible marital unions, forbidding marriage where the bloodlines ran too close, such as siblings, first cousins, etc. But as the Gospel was spread into the Greek and pagan world, there were differing and unacceptable notions about who could marry whom.

Because of these many strange marital practices, the so-called Matthean exception seeks to clarify the Lord's teaching. The phrase "except for unlawful marriage" (sometimes also rendered "except for unchastity") clarifies that those who are in marriages that are illicit, due to incestuous and other invalidating factors, should not stay in them. Rather, these are not marriages at all, and can and should be set aside in favor of proper marriage.

Q. Can Catholics have gay friends? If so, under what circumstances? — *Charles McKelvy*

Yes, though as you indicate, circumstances are important. In the first place, there are different kinds and degrees of friendship. Some friendships are close and personal, others are more peripheral. Some friendships are of a professional or business nature, whereas others are more rooted in family and community ties. Some friend-ships involve very personal sharing, whereas others involve only a general acquaintance.

Clearly, it is easier to overlook many things with people with whom we are only acquainted, or with whom we simply have professional relationships. In these situations, our obligations to give and receive fraternal correction is less. But in close friendships, more is expected and required. Generally, close friendships presume many shared values and similar respect for the truth. When such things are lacking in significant areas, close friendships are going to be strained.

Close friends also have greater obligations to instruct and admonish one another (see, for example, Jas 5:19; Gal 6:1). Hence it is not the proper nature of a close relationship to simply overlook significant matters. If I have a close friend and I know he is viewing pornography regularly, or living with a woman outside of marriage, I have an obligation as a Christian to seek to correct him. If I have a close friend who is destroying his life with alcohol or drugs, I have obligations to admonish him and assist him to seek help.

All of these principles apply to someone with a homosexual orientation. If I have a close friend with this orientation and he or she is living celibately, this is fine, and I should seek to offer encouragement in this regard. If, however, they are straying into illicit sexual union and/or advocating the so-called gay lifestyle, same-sex unions, and so forth, I would have an obligation to instruct and admonish. It is difficult to see how a close relationship could continue if the individual were to utterly reject such correction about such a significant manner. The first concern for close friends ought to be each other's salvation, not merely their feelings.

While many prudential factors must be weighed in terms of how best to fraternally correct, close friendships must be rooted in the truth and cannot really be called close friendships without reverence for the truth. If a Christian were too weak to engage in this instruction, then it would seem that the close friendship is not really experienced as a friendship between equals, but rather a friendship wherein the other person has the upper hand. In this case one might consider the admonition of Scripture, "Bad company ruins good morals" (1 Cor 15:33), and seek healthier friendships. For, once pressured to silence, many Christians give tacit approval, and the truth is no longer respected or proclaimed.

Q. How does one respectfully turn down an invitation to a wedding involving a same-sex couple? — *Name withheld*

The approach to be taken is like that of an invitation to any marriage that is invalid. As a general norm, Catholics should not attend such ceremonies. Examples of this include wedding ceremonies held in a place other than a Catholic Church without permission when either the groom or bride is Catholic. Likewise, when either the groom or bride has been married before, and the Church has not or cannot recognize the nullity of prior unions.

A same-sex wedding is invalid since God, in establishing marriage, indicates that the suitable partner for a man is a woman (see Gn 2:18). God further teaches that this is why a man shall leave his father and mother and cling to his wife, and the two of them become one flesh (Gn 2:24). So, marriage is one man and one woman who cling to each other in a lasting, stable union, and who are open to bearing children if this be possible and God grants it (Gn 1:28).

To attend a wedding we know to be invalid is problematic since attendance indicates approval and celebration of what is taking place. We cannot rightly give approval or celebrate that which we know to be wrong.

With all this in mind, I might suggest the following text to decline such an invitation:

> Thank you for your kind invitation. I will need
> to decline, however, and hope you will under-
> stand my reasons. Since attendance at a wedding
> indicates support and approval of the union, I
> must truthfully decline to be present. For sin-
> cerely held religious reasons, I cannot accept or
> indicate support for the notion that two people of
> the same sex validly wed one another. I realize we
> disagree on this, but I am bound in conscience to
> follow scriptural norms through which I believe

God has spoken to us with authority. I am happy
to discuss this with you in the future if you wish.
For now, please accept my gratitude for your kind
invitation and my sincere regrets that I cannot
attend for the reasons stated.

Unfortunately, we live in times where many are intolerant of
sincerely held religious beliefs. We do well to remind such people
that our beliefs regarding the nature of marriage and the wrong-
ness of sexual sin, including homosexual acts, stretches back thousands of years and is reiterated at every stage of biblical revelation.
We can also remind them that those who seek tolerance should be
prepared to offer it as well.

Q. I am a fifty-year-old man and was raised Catholic.
But I have been married twice, divorced, and then
lived with a woman. I now live alone, and my Catholic
friends tell me to return to the Catholic Church! Other than
my job, I do lots of unpaid volunteer work. Is that good
enough to go to heaven if I die suddenly? What should I
do? — *Name withheld*

Your friends are right; return to the Catholic Church. What this
means practically is that you should go to confession and resume
receiving holy Communion. In situations like yours, where one has
been away from the Church for some time and struggled to live
some of the teachings (in this case, teachings on holy matrimony),
you would do well to meet with your parish priest or some other
priest your friends can recommend. Simply going to confession
one Saturday afternoon and then resuming Sunday Mass with holy
Communion is technically permissible. However, it is more fruitful
to spend some time discussing your life and struggles in the context of a longer confession and/or counseling session with a priest.

In order to make a good confession, you must bring with you a purpose of amendment to live a chaste life and follow the teachings of the Church on marriage. Perhaps the priest can discuss these with you, help you understand your struggles of the past, and assist you with the proper vision going forward. Dating and future marriage is not for you right now, until and unless annulments can be granted.

Praise God for your friends who encourage you. Regular prayer, the Word of God, sacraments, and walking in fellowship with the Church are essential help in finding our way through the desert of this world into the promised land of heaven.

As for your question about good works, we cannot "purchase" forgiveness from God. Good works cannot replace true repentance and returning to Christ, whose mercy is free. However, good works can reflect a repentant heart and help to cleanse us from our sinful tendencies. So, you are commended and encouraged to continue in the good works you have undertaken! May God bless you and your journey back into the practice of the faith and the reception of the sacraments.

Q. Several of my cousins live together with others and are having sexual relations outside of marriage. They think that it is no problem for them to go to holy Communion since, to their mind, it is either not wrong at all or only a venial sin. Are there texts in the Bible or *Catechism* I can point them to? — *Doris O'Hare*

The situation you describe objectively involves mortal sin, in which case one must cease and receive absolution in confession before returning to holy Communion. Saint Paul instructs and warns: "Whoever, therefore, eats the bread or drinks the cup of the Lord in an unworthy manner will be guilty of profaning the body and blood of the Lord. Let a man examine himself, and so eat of the bread and drink of the cup" (1 Cor 11:27–28).

In many places, the Scriptures teach that fornication (sex before marriage) is a mortal sin. Saint Paul warns that fornicators will not inherit the kingdom of God (see 1 Cor 6:9; Eph 5:5; Heb 13:4, among others). Jesus, too, indicates that we should be more willing to put out our eye than to sin by lust and thus enter hell (Mt 5:27–30).

The *Catechism* speaks of fornication as a grave offense: "Fornication is carnal union between an unmarried man and an unmarried woman. It is gravely contrary to the dignity of persons and of human sexuality which is naturally ordered to the good of spouses and the generation and education of children. Moreover, it is a grave scandal when there is corruption of the young" (2353).

Therefore, your cousins, if they are committing acts of fornication, are committing the kind of serious (mortal) sin that requires confession with a firm purpose of amendment prior to receiving holy Communion. Living together (even without having sexual relations) is imprudent (as a near occasion of sin) and might cause scandal. However, of itself and without illicit sexual union, it is not something that would necessarily require confession.

Q .I was surprised to hear on a radio show an advocate for the gay community say that the story of Sodom and Gomorrah is not about homosexuality at all; that the sin for which God destroyed that city was greed and a lack of hospitality. What do you think of this? — *Christina Jensen*

It is a strange but unfortunately common notion among the advocates you describe and others. If the assertion that the destruction of Sodom and Gomorrah has nothing to do with homosexual acts is true, then the Holy Spirit writing in the Letter of Jude was never told. There it is written: "Sodom and Gomorrah and the surrounding cities, which likewise acted immorally and indulged in unnatural lust, serve as an example by undergoing a punishment of eternal fire" (Jude 1:7). So, clearly the destruction of those towns is not merely about greed or a lack of hospitality.

This does not mean that homosexual practices were the only sin of those ancient towns. Ezekiel adds: "This was the guilt of your sister Sodom: she and her daughters had pride, surfeit of food, and prosperous ease, but did not aid the poor and needy. They were haughty, and did abominable things before me; therefore I removed them, when I saw it" (Ez 16:49–50).

It is proper to see that there were many sins in those ancient towns, but among them were fornication and homosexual acts. Any straightforward, non-ideological reading of the story in Genesis 19 will show that homosexual acts are not only mentioned, they are central to the story. At the moment of critical tension, the townsmen, young and old, stand outside Lot's door and demand: "Where are the men who came to you tonight? Bring them out to us, that we may know ['have sexual relations' in some translations] them" (Gn 19:5). So, the text is rather straightforward.

The *Catechism of the Catholic Church*, while reminding us that persons with same-sex attraction are to be accepted with respect, compassion, and sensitivity, also cites Genesis 19 among other texts in the assessment of homosexual acts: "Basing itself on Sacred Scripture, which presents homosexual acts as acts of grave depravity [see Gn 19:1–29; Rom 1:24–27; 1 Cor 6:10; 1 Tm 1:10], tradition has always declared that 'homosexual acts are intrinsically disordered.'... Under no circumstances can they be approved" (2357).

Q. My sister-law is hostile to the Church and says that we are obsessed by sex and abortion and don't care about the things Jesus did, like helping the poor. Is there an effective answer to this sort of charge? — *Name withheld*

The charge that the Church is "obsessed" with sex and abortion (and many add today, homosexuality) is not sustainable.

Any look at the *Catechism* will show a holistic concern for the human person, ranging from our call to faith, accepting our dignity in being made in the image of God, how God reveals himself to us, how he saves us, liturgy, prayer, and spirituality, and the whole scope of the moral life, including care for the poor and justice.

The U.S. bishops and the pope speak on a wide range of issues, including immigration, trafficking, education, the economy, etc. And, yes, they do also speak to life issues, and issues of sexuality and marriage.

Anecdotally, most practicing Catholics not only fail to see an "obsession" about sex in the Church but note with frustration a certain silence from the pulpits of their parishes regarding many of the critical issues related to sex, family, and life. So, it is difficult to see how the charge of obsession in the Church with these issues can prevail. If there is obsession with such issues, it is more likely to be found in popular culture — in movies, music, in the news; in recent years in strident demands for the legal recognition and support of abortion, cohabitation, pornography; and now in the promotion of same-sex unions and the redefinition of marriage.

To such strident and increasingly absolute demands, the Church must surely make a response. But it is a response to an already existing issue or trend that is arguably revolutionary and passionately demanded, along with legal penalties for conscientious objectors. Hence the culture looks to be very obsessed itself.

Jesus surely did care for the poor. The Catholic Church, too, has long been known for extensive care for the poor, the sick, and the dying. The corporal works of mercy are widely practiced and advocated in the Church.

But Jesus also spoke on many occasions to other moral issues, such as lust, divorce, greed, anger, the requirement of faith, etc. Any survey of the Sermon on the Mount (Matthew, Chapters 5 to 7) and other places will reveal that. Jesus ought not to be reduced to a mere social activist who only cared about the poor and social justice. He spoke and taught on many issues.

Q: My son is away from the Church and angry with many things about our teaching. Though he is not gay, he has friends who are, and he tells me the Church is bigoted against homosexuals and that Jesus never said anything about homosexuality and doesn't care. What is the best way to answer him? He is quite hostile, and it's hard to have a reasonable discussion with him. — *Name withheld*

In situations where there is hostility to the teachings of the Church, I find it helpful to use the Socratic method. This method, going back to the ancient Greek philosopher Socrates, uses questions as a basis to explore an issue and teach.

To your son's statement that the Church is bigoted, you might ask: "Why do you say that? Can you tell me more what you mean by bigoted?" This sort of question puts the onus on the other to make a case for the charge and to explore some of his own premises. Depending on the answers, you can ask follow-up questions.

Keep the questions open, respectful, and nonconfrontational in tone. The point of this method is not "gotcha" questions or moments. It is an attempt to get whom your talking with to reflect more deeply on his own view. This does not mean that your questions must always be vague. Thus, to the second point that Jesus never said anything about homosexuality, you might ask, "Why do you think that Jesus' silence means approval?" And clarify: "For example, he said nothing about rape. Does this mean Jesus approves of rape?" He might counter that rape is bad. And you can say: "I agree, but Jesus didn't mention it. So that's why I'm asking whether Jesus' silence means approval. Does it?"

Wait respectfully for an answer. Even if the silence continues a while or there are protests at being asked a question, or there are attempts to change the parameters, just politely return to the question.

Occasionally, it helps to reset the parameters of the conversation by saying something like: "I am trying to understand your view, I am trying to listen; that's why I am asking questions. I don't think

I agree with you, but I am trying to understand why you think the Church is bigoted and wrong."

Even if he walks away, you have left him with questions that are valid and may help him to clarify what he thinks and why. You have also respected him by asking about his views, not merely rebuking them. Sometimes it is good to seek understanding of why a person holds a view so it can provide a basis for common ground, which gives a way back to the teachings of the Church rather than deepening the divide.

Q. I am a Catholic priest and have begun work at a parish where many who are civilly married receive Communion every day, and some are even extraordinary ministers of the Eucharist. They seem to have no doubts about their status. Pastorally I wonder how best to handle this situation without causing a large outcry. I also heard the confession of a dying person recently in an invalid marriage and wondered if I should. — *Name withheld*

It sounds as if you have been given a congregation that has been poorly catechized and even misled by previous clergy. Even in congregations that have not been misled, many Catholics have a poor grasp of the Church's marriage law.

One thing I have found helpful is to place a brief post in the bulletin explaining the need for Catholics to be married in the Church, not before a justice of the peace or in some other non-Catholic setting. I try to explain succinctly and invite people who think they may need further information or a validation to contact me. I usually do get calls, and the meetings begin. Some situations can be resolved simply by the renewal of vows. Other situations are more complex and require an annulment or counseling. But at least a process is underway to resolve issues. This process is discreet and personal.

But there is a need to instruct the entire congregation on these matters, and priests have an obligation to teach on what is required for a valid marriage. Usually this will cause controversy, because many have been misled to think that the Church is unjust and unmerciful in this stance. But it is the teaching that we seek to uphold (see Mt 19:1–12; Mt 5:31–32; etc.), along with the teaching of Saint Paul that we are not to receive the Eucharist in a state of unrepented sin lest we bring condemnation on ourselves (1 Cor 11:27). Many may bring a hostile attitude to the subject, but we have to teach and win people over to the truth of the Gospel even if it means suffering for us.

In the danger of death (*in periculo mortis*) situation you describe, especially when a person is actively dying (*in articulo mortis*), a priest is generally able to absolve if the person manifests repentance. This is because they are not likely to return to the sexual activity of an invalid marriage given the circumstances of death being near at hand.

Q: **I was trying to instruct my son that masturbation is wrong. And when I went to the *Catechism*, it did say that masturbation is intrinsically and gravely disordered. But then it says this: "To form an equitable judgment about the subjects' moral responsibility and to guide pastoral action, one must take into account the affective immaturity, force of acquired habit, conditions of anxiety, or other psychological or social factors that can lessen, if not even reduce to a minimum, moral culpability" (2352). What does all this mean? Is masturbation a sin or not? Mortal or not?**
— *Alice Hawley*

It is a sin. However, in assessing a moral act, three things are considered: the act itself, the circumstances, and the intention of the person who acts (see CCC 1750). And while the circumstances and intention of the person who commits the act can never make a bad action good, they can affect the culpability (blameworthiness) of the person.

The *Catechism* speaks to the circumstances and intent in the paragraph you cite. It sometimes happens that one does what is sinful under the burden or sway of circumstances that limit their freedom, and this reduces the level of their guilt.

Self-mastery in the area of sexuality comes with difficulty for many, especially in the area of their thought life. Integrating sexuality in a way that is healthy and proper is an aspect of maturity which many lack well into adulthood today due to cultural circumstances which mislead and tempt. Some people also develop a habit of masturbation in youth and have difficulty breaking it in adulthood. While many are able to avoid fornication and pornography by taking due precautions, it is not possible for them to be free from their own body or to simply shut down their imagination or thoughts. Self-mastery in this area is more complex and difficult.

None of these factors make masturbation a good thing. It remains a sin, and sin always causes harm. Considered simply, in itself, masturbation is a mortal sin. But it does not follow that everyone who masturbates is guilty of mortal sin each and every time, for the reasons stated.

While it is unusual for the *Catechism* to include a pastoral note of this sort, it was deemed necessary to include it here. Many struggle in this area and are affected by shame and unhelpful fears rooted in a merely legalistic notion of mortal sin, all of which can discourage growth. The penitent needs some room to breathe, and the pastoral sense of the Church acknowledges this in the passage you cite.

That said, since masturbation is a sin, it should be confessed. The penitent should work with a confessor to, as the *Catechism* says, "guide pastoral action." The confessor can advise on a plan of action that regards the sinfulness of the act but also helps the penitent not to lose their sense of dignity or capacity to grow because of excessive shame or paralyzing self-reproach.

Q: If one spouse indicates an unwillingness to have more children, would the other spouse be free to refuse all sexual intimacy? — *Name withheld*

You raise and link two issues that must first be treated separately. In the second matter, refusing all marital intimacy, except for a grave cause, is a violation of the rights of one's spouse. When a man and a woman marry, they exchange, among other goods, what canon law calls *jus in corporis*. This refers to a right to expect a reasonable recourse to sexual intimacy.

Saint Paul speaks of this when he writes: "The husband should give to his wife her conjugal rights, and likewise the wife to her husband. For the wife does not rule over her own body, but the husband does; likewise the husband does not rule over his own body, but the wife does. Do not refuse one another except perhaps by agreement for a season" (1 Cor 7:3–5).

Other things being equal, the ongoing refusal of marital intimacy is an injustice to one's spouse. There are, of course, certain times when a spouse may reasonably and temporarily withhold requests for intimacy (such as health, significant fatigue, inconvenience, etc.). The right to intimacy refers to a reasonable expectation of intimacy, not an absolute one.

In the second issue you raise, there is a spouse who is no longer open to the good of children. In itself this is problematic. One may seek to delay the birth of another child, but this must be for a serious reason — for example, serious health or financial issues — and not involve contraceptive acts (rather abstinence during fertile periods).

In the example you cite, presuming the reasons to avoid pregnancy are serious, it would be wrong for one spouse to fully withhold marital intimacy, for the reasons stated, even if the spouse is not open to another child. A husband or wife cannot, however, be required by their spouse to use illicit forms of contraception, and they should not directly cooperate in such action.

But even this does not mean that they may, or must, refuse all sexual intimacy. Most moral theologians hold that in circumstances where one spouse makes sinful use of contraceptive measures, the other spouse is not required to refuse intimacy and does not incur sin as long as they state clearly their objection to the practice and do not cooperate in any direct way. For example, a husband may not be able to stop his wife taking a pill that suppresses ovulation, but as long as he does not cooperate with it and states his concerns, he does not incur sin by having recourse to the marital act.

ETHICS IN SOCIETY

Q. **I have had a long association with the Shriners Hospital and their work of providing largely free medical care for the poor. I want to remember them in my will, but recently discovered that they are associated with Freemasonry. As a Catholic, can I remember them in my will?**
— *Name withheld*

Catholics are not permitted to join the Masons or to engage in specifically Masonic activity or ritual. However, what you describe would seem to fall under the category of remote, material cooperation. What you seek to support is the common humanitarian work of caring for the sick and the poor, an activity in keeping with Catholic vision. I am presuming your intention is not to support Freemasonry per se, and surely not its potentially anti-Catholic views. I say "potentially" since not every Mason or Masonic organization, especially in America, is specifically focused on being anti-Catholic, as was, and often still is, the case in Europe. Further, it seems you also have some personal history tied to the particular hospitals in question and are grateful for the care they have exhibited.

Presuming that this is your intention rather than to support Freemasonry directly, it is permissible for you to donate under the circumstances stated. It remains the case, however, that Catholics are not free to join the Masons or to directly support Freemasonry.

Q. If a nation such as North Korea or Iran launches a nuclear weapon that causes major destruction, does the targeted nation have a right to respond in a way that virtually obliterates that nation? When it comes to nuclear war it seems hard to imagine a proportionate response. — *Name withheld*

The simple answer to your question would be no. The targeted nation could not simply retaliate in kind, and certainly not seek to obliterate the offending nation.

Some sort of military response might well be called for, even full-scale war. This would presume that the criteria for just war have been met — namely, that the damage and threat are grave, lasting, and certain (which would be the case in your scenario); that other means of ending the conflict have been tried or are not possible; that there is a reasonable hope of success in turning back the threat by military means; and that the use of arms must not produce evils and disorders graver than the evil to be eliminated (see CCC 2309).

Even within a war, a nation must use means to distinguish between combatants and noncombatants. Hence choosing to wipe out whole population centers, indiscriminately killing combatants and noncombatants, is not a moral option. Indiscriminate obliteration cannot be condoned under any circumstances (see CCC 2314).

It will be admitted, given the existence of large-scale nuclear devices, the most effective means to deter such attacks is complex and debatable. A short answer such as this can-not possibly explore all the points debated in the deterrence of nuclear threat. Here let it be noted that the *Catechism* expresses strong moral reservations regarding the modern "arms race" (2315).

To return to the main question, if a nation were lamen-tably to be attacked by a country in the way you describe, that nation is not thereby justified in indiscriminately retaliating by wiping out whole cities or in annihilating that country.

Q. **I am a contractor who did some work for some cous-ins. They cheated me out of a significant amount of money. Strangely, I still get invited to family functions by them as if nothing happened. But I don't want anything to do with them. Does forgiveness require me to accept invi-tations and be friendly?** — *Name withheld*

Forgiveness involves letting go of the need to change the past. Through forgiveness we are able to let go of resentments, our de-sire for revenge, and wrathful anger that often accompanies hurts or injustices we experience.

In most cases forgiveness does permit us to resume or stay in relationships with people. In many situations the hurts are slight, and the issues are more of the moment, rather than involving on-going and unhealthy aspects of our relationships with others.

But there are times when it is simply not wise to continue in relationships, whether business or personal, in which there is ongoing sin, injustice, or harm. A woman may forgive her husband for the repeated physical abuse he has inflicted on her in the past. She may understand that his anger comes from the fact that he himself was abused as child. She may, by the grace of forgiveness, harbor no anger or resentment. But it does not follow that forgive-ness means she should resume a common household with him. This might further endanger her and her children. It might also deepen the husband's pathology and delay him getting the help he needs.

In your case, there may be reasons for you to stay clear of the family members who cheated you. It may be the best way to just let go of what happened. You would not be rude or wrathful to them, but it also does not mean you are required to be jovial and pretend that nothing happened.

On the other hand, what is to prevent a forthright conversation between you all about what happened? Too often when there are hurts or injustices, the parties go to their corners and stew or harbor resentments rather than seek to discuss and find greater understanding.

I cannot, from this distance and with limited information, say what is best for you. I can only establish the principle that forgiveness does often mean that the parties involved share this gift in order to further and deepen the relationship. But, as stated, there are exceptions to this, and forgiveness does not always require resuming unhealthy situations which really benefit neither party.

Q: While the *Catechism* technically permits the death penalty, it, and the bishops, foresee its use as rare, if ever. If capital punishment is forsworn in all cases, a criminal often lives to commit another atrocity. Is society not left helpless? I write as one who has been robbed at gunpoint.
— *Danny House*

There are many complexities in discussing the death penalty because there is some tension between the traditional doctrine regarding it and the modern pastoral setting.

Unlike abortion, capital punishment is not an intrinsic moral evil, for a couple of reasons. First, in certain settings the use of the death penalty has served the common good, ensuring that dangerous criminals are no longer able to cause harm. In punishing grave offenders, others can be deterred from capital crimes, too. Second, the Scriptures do not forbid the practice. Even in the New Testament, Saint Paul speaks to the state's right to punish grave offenders in this way, and even indicates that, in so doing, it acts as a minister of God's justice on the wrongdoer (see Rom 13:4).

The Church cannot simply overrule the Scriptures and declare intrinsically evil what God permits in certain circumstances. However, that the Scriptures permit the death penalty in certain circumstances does not mean that it is always wise or prudent to promote such punishment.

In the modern pastoral setting, recent popes and the bishops of the world have taught that recourse to the death penalty should be rare if ever. A significant part of this prudential judgment is rooted in concern for what Saint John Paul II called the "culture of death." The culture of death is a mindset wherein the death or non-existence of human beings is increasingly proposed as a solution to problems. Abortion, euthanasia, and quick-recourse warfare or other violent means, along with the anti-life mentality of contraception, are widely promoted in our culture as ways to solve problems. The Church stands foursquare against such thinking.

Even though the death penalty has received reluctant approval in the past, the current pastoral setting seems to require that the Church stand consistently against yet another way that death is proposed as a solution to the regrettable problem of crime.

I regret the criminal assault you experienced. I too have been held up at gunpoint and was beaten. More needs to be done to keep serious and threatening offenders off our streets. However, given the wider pastoral setting, it is the consensus of recent popes and the world's bishops that standing against all facets of the culture of death is an important pastoral posture to maintain, even if our tradition does permit the death penalty in very rare circumstances.

Q **.** A coworker is a member of a very fundamental-**ist** Protestant denomination and says the Catholic Church changed her teaching, which once forbade usury, and now permits it. He says the Bible forbids usury? Is this so? — *James Bulware*

Usury must be defined. Perhaps the clearest definition of usury as understood by the Church was given by the Fifth Lateran Council in 1515: "For this is the proper interpretation of usury; when one seeks to acquire gain from the use of a thing which is not fruitful, with no labor, no expense, and no risk on the part of the lender."

In the past, when more of a barter economy existed, those lending money were few and often took advantage of others. This was rightly condemned as usury. In current economic conditions, however, money is used more widely, which can be fruitful in diverse ways. One incurs expense when lending money since it could have been used in many other fruitful ways. Also, there is risk incurred when one lends.

But the wider use of money also means the lending market is rather competitive and interest rates are more commensurate with actual risk and opportunity costs. Reasonable reparation, in the form of interest, for these costs and risks is not immoral per se. Thus ordinary market interest rates do not usually merit the term "usury."

So, usury is still condemned by the Church, but given changes in the marketplace, usury is no longer synonymous with the mere charging of interest, but only with excessive interest that does not reflect the actual costs to the lender.

Q. My son and I own different large parcels of land adjacent to each other. His land is in another jurisdiction and is exempt from sales tax; mine is not. We want to purchase a work vehicle that we will share. Is it wrong for me to give him the money and have him buy it entirely so we can avoid the tax? — *John S.*

Morally speaking there does not seem to be a problem here. Let me hasten to add that I am not a civil or tax lawyer and do not know all the ins and outs of what "Caesar" might demand. But in moral terms it is not wrong to take advantage of opportunities and options presented by civil law. People look for tax shelters all the time. Presuming they are legal, it is not wrong to use them, even though paying just and certainly required taxes is annexed to the Fourth and Seventh Commandments.

What you could *not* do in the situation you describe is lie to get the tax break. For example, suppose the duly authorized local state authorities stipulate that the vehicle is housed primarily or exclusively in the state, but you have no intention of doing this and will keep it entirely on your land outside the state. Even if you consider such questions intrusive, you could not lie to obtain the tax break. But neither do you need to wholly disclose that you will share or borrow the vehicle from your son unless the state reasonably requires such information.

Q**.** In the *Catechism of the Catholic Church* it states that it is morally obligatory to exercise the right to vote. But this seems false since for most of history there have been no systems of voting and, even today, there are many who cannot vote. How can the *Catechism* claim that voting is a moral obligation? — *Jenna O'Neil*

The part of the *Catechism* you reference reads as follows: "Submission to authority and co-responsibility for the common good make it morally obligatory to pay taxes, to exercise the right to vote, and to defend one's country" (2240). This delineation of duties takes place in a section that also mentions other duties, such as the duty to collaborate with and justly criticize those in authority, exercise solidarity with other citizens on matters of importance, have grateful charity and proper patriotism for one's country, and to work for the common good.

The *Catechism* speaks to a worldwide audience wherein people live under different forms of government. Further, as you note, it speaks out of a long historical tradition that transcends merely modern forms of government. As such, its principles should be understood in the general manner in which they are stated. The principles must be adapted to specific situations.

To speak of a moral obligation to "exercise one's right to vote" presupposes that one has a right to vote. The *Catechism* does not and cannot impose an obligation on those who have no right to vote.

Further, the moral obligations specified in this section of the *Catechism*, while generally binding, are not absolute. For example, the general obligation to participate in the defense of one's country might be overruled or ameliorated if the engaged war is an unjust one. We should generally observe civil laws, but not when they are unjust or contrary to God's law. If, for instance, due to social unrest and threats of violence one cannot reasonably vote without grave risk, they are morally excused. Not every moral obligation is absolute.

Q :Can you tell me what the best kind of government
  •is? I read that some Catholics think a monarchy is
best; others say democracy. What should Catholics think?
— *Roy*

The *Catechism* says little specifically about forms of government
and speaks more broadly in the following terms: "Every institution
is inspired, at least implicitly, by a vision of man and his destiny,
from which it derives the point of reference for its judgment, its
hierarchy of values, its line of conduct. Most societies have formed
their institutions in the recognition of a certain preeminence of
man over things. Only the divinely revealed religion has clearly
recognized man's origin and destiny in God, the Creator and Redeemer. The Church invites political authorities to measure their
judgments and decisions against this inspired truth about God
and man.... 'The Church respects and encourages the political
freedom and responsibility of the citizen'" (2244–45).

In continues: "It is a part of the Church's mission 'to pass
moral judgments even in matters related to politics, whenever the
fundamental rights of man or the salvation of souls requires it. The
means, the only means, she may use are those which are in accord
with the Gospel and the welfare of all men according to the diversity of times and circumstances'" (2246).

Therefore, we have general observations and limits ascribed
to forms of government, but nothing so specific as the number and
types of legislatures, deliberative bodies, leadership structures, or
constitutional contents.

Since the modern democratic republics common today were
largely unknown in biblical times, and due to the hierarchical
structure of the Church and the biblical teaching on families, some
today favor monarchy (or a modified version of it) as the best fit
for Catholic teaching, especially if the monarch is of the Faith. But
this is probably going too far and is more specific than Catholic
teaching prefers.

While some systems are better than others, all have short-comings that require the voice of the Church and of faith and natural law to set limits and occasionally voice opposition.

Atheistic forms of government that seek to silence the voice of faith are excluded since they deny a natural right of man. Secular or nonsectarian forms of government are permissible as long as they do not deny the influence of faith altogether or limit the religious liberty of citizens.

Other principles of Catholic social teaching are operative in assessing forms of government. In particular, solidarity and subsidiarity are significant. Governments have obligations to promote and enhance solidarity among citizens so that all are included and cared for equitably, and so that legitimate needs are met. Subsidiarity is the principle that government should be carried on at the lowest and most local level possible — that is, things should not be handled federally that can be handled locally or at the level of the state government. Nevertheless, federal or national government is at times necessary for larger things such as national defense, national standards, and the like.

Beyond these norms, reasonable people, as well as nations and cultures, will differ as to the exact form of government that is best and to the particulars within those forms.

PART V

THE
CHURCH

The One True Church

Q: Are all religions equal? — *Sister M. Gemma*

No, they are not. Religions and faith traditions other than that of the Catholic Church are deficient in two possible ways: first, by the defect of incompleteness. While they may have elements of the truth, they do not possess the whole truth revealed by God for our salvation. As such they are less helpful than Catholicism. Second, they can be deficient by the defect of error — that is, they teach false and erroneous doctrines or promote an erroneous understanding of Scripture and revealed truth.

While it is popular today to say that all religious traditions are different and equal ways to the same God, this violates many rational principles, such as the principle of noncontradiction. For example, it cannot be simultaneously true that Jesus is Lord and that Jesus is not Lord but only a good man. That Jesus is Lord is true, and all other claims to the contrary are false. What is true is of value, and what is false is not. Thus all religions are not equal.

Q: My daughter says she loves Jesus but doesn't like the Church (for lots of reasons). She doesn't see any problem with this and doesn't think going to church is necessary. Is there anything I can say to her? — *Name withheld*

The Church is the Body of Christ (see Col 1:24; 1 Cor 12:27; Rom 12:4–5). Therefore, to declare love for Jesus but disdain his body is inauthentic. We cannot have Jesus without his body. How would your daughter feel if someone said to her, "I love you, but your body is awful, ugly, and I can't stand it." She would not appreciate this and would discard any artificial distinctions between her and her own body. It is the same with Jesus. Perhaps if she can be taught to understand the rather insulting quality of her position, she will reconsider.

Certainly, there are sinners and imperfections in Jesus' body, the Church. But even Jesus was found in the company of sinners. Many in Jesus' time were scandalized by the associations he maintained. But he is found where he is found, not merely where we want him to be. So, if your daughter loves Jesus and really wants to find him, she needs to join the rest of us poor sinners.

Q. **What is the Church's current position on the statement "no salvation outside the Church"?** — *Paul*

Given the nature of your question, it is best to paraphrase the *Catechism of the Catholic Church*, which teaches on this matter. This doctrine means that all salvation comes from Christ the head, through the Church, which is his body. Based on Scripture and Tradition, the Church understands herself as necessary for salvation, since the Church is the Body of Christ and one cannot truly have Christ apart from his body, the Church. And not having Christ means not being saved. They cannot be saved who, knowing that the Catholic Church was founded as necessary by God through Christ, would refuse either to enter it or to remain in it.

This affirmation is not aimed at those who, through no fault of their own, do not know Christ and his Church. Those who, again, through no fault of their own, do not know the Gospel of Christ or his Church, but who nevertheless seek God with a sincere heart and, moved by grace, try in their actions to do his will as they know it through the dictates of their conscience — these, too, may achieve eternal salvation.

Although in ways known only to himself, God can lead those who are ignorant of the Gospel to that faith without which it is impossible to please him. However, the Church still has the obligation and also the sacred right to evangelize all men (see CCC 846–848).

Q. •I have always understood that the baptized are •members of the Body of Christ. But in Bible study last month, the deacon taught from Colossians that Jesus "holds all creation together in himself." So how can we Christians claim any special status? — *Geraldine Kramer*

The Letter to the Colossians says: "In [Jesus] all things hold together. He is the head of the body, the Church" (1:17–18). So, Christ does hold all things together in himself, but only the Church is his body.

Perhaps by analogy you and I could have something in or associated with our body that is not our body per se. For example, I could have food in my stomach that is in me, but not of me.

The analogy falls short, however (like all analogies do), since I do not cause the food in my stomach to exist or "hold together." But Christ, as God, is the ground of all being and is "being itself." Saint Paul rightly says that in him all things "hold together" (the Greek is *synesteken*, meaning to be sustained, consist, or to stay together), for without the Lord they would not exist at all.

However, despite this immanent (close) relationship of Christ to all of creation, only the Church, consisting of baptized members, is the Body of Christ. For by grace, a baptized Christian becomes one with Christ, "becomes a 'son of light,' indeed, he becomes 'light' himself" (CCC 1216; see also Jn 1:9; 1 Thes 5:5; Heb 10:32; Eph 5:8).

Therefore, the Christian is not only sustained or held together by Christ, but becomes one with him, a member of his very body, dying with him and rising with him, ascending with his entering the Holy of Holies in heaven. Only the baptized are said to receive this glory and to be a member of Christ's body.

Q.How does the Catholic Church reconcile CCC 841, which says, "The plan of salvation also includes ... Muslims" (who deny the Resurrection), with 1 Corinthians 15:14, which says, "If Christ has not been raised ... your faith is in vain"? — *John Clubine*

God surely wants to save all and has set plans in place to do so through the preaching of the Gospel. That the plan of salvation aims for all does not mean that all are in fact saved. If one were to knowingly reject Christ after having him effectively preached, they may well forfeit their salvation. However, not all have had Christ effectively preached, and the Church leaves the final determination to the Lord of how culpable they are of their seeming rejection of Christ.

Q.I am having difficulty in resolving the teachings of the saints and the subject of Islam. The saints say that no one can be saved apart from the Church, and some called Islam superstitious and so forth. I cannot square this with the *Catechism*, which says God's plan of salvation includes Muslims. — *David Pair*

The *Catechism* teaches, "The plan of salvation also includes those who acknowledge the Creator, in the first place amongst whom are the Muslims; these profess to hold the faith of Abraham, and together with us they adore the one, merciful God, mankind's judge on the last day" (841).

It remains the teaching of the Catholic Church that no one who knows the Church and Christ are necessary for salvation and yet rejects them may be saved. However, when and how a person "knows" enough to be blameworthy of this sin of unbelief is not always clear.

There is a distinction made between vincible and invincible ignorance. Invincible ignorance is that which cannot be reasonably overcome, given the circumstances. As such, one is not fully culpable for acting contrary to what they did not know. Vincible ignorance is that which could have been overcome with a reasonable effort but was indulged anyway. This sort of ignorance is more blameworthy and brings forth varying degrees of punishment depending on the degree of resistance to the truth.

Church teaching therefore recognizes that there are sometimes obstacles that keep Muslims from recognizing the need for Christ and the Church. Many are taught from their youth that Christians are blasphemers for our teaching on the Trinity. In certain areas, it is unlawful to practice the Christian faith. Such Muslims can be saved if they sincerely seek God but remain in substantial and invincible ignorance as to the need for Christian faith.

This does not mean that they are automatically saved, or even likely saved, only that salvation is possible for them, since we know God to be just and not the sort who would condemn others for what they could not reasonably know. Surely, they would have to undergo purgation after death.

As for the saints, we cherish their lives and example. However, they are not the magisterium. We are not required to square Church teaching with them. Rather their views need to be squared with Church teaching. Further, the saints often lived in and spoke to situations more specific than what the general norms of the Church address.

Q•A priest wrote in our local paper that we should humbly accept that our church, whatever our denomination, does not have the whole truth. But I thought the Catholic Church was the pillar and foundation of the truth. — *Lucy Hart*

Here, too, the subtleties of language are important in understanding how questions are answered. The Catholic Church maintains, for demonstrable reasons, that we possess the fullness of revealed truth and the full means to salvation given by God. We hold this in distinction to other denominations and religious traditions, which may have elements of the truth but are lacking the fullness of these and are usually admixed with error.

That said, we do not claim to know *everything* there is to know about God. God is more glorious than everything we could ever say or know about him. It is perhaps in this vein that the priest wrote his remarks. Nevertheless, one might wish for greater precision when discussing these issues, as your puzzlement demonstrates.

Q•Could you please tell me why many within the Church refer to Pentecost as the birthday of the Church, in light of CCC 766? — *Arleen, Ross*

The *Catechism* citation you note says: "'The origin and growth of the Church are symbolized by the blood and water which flowed from the open side of the crucified Jesus.' 'For it was from the side of Christ as he slept the sleep of death upon the cross that there came forth the "wondrous sacrament of the whole Church."' As Eve was formed from the sleeping Adam's side, so the Church was born from the pierced heart of Christ hanging dead on the cross" (766).

Hence there arises your question as to why Pentecost is often called the birthday of the Church. I would generally be among those who do not prefer that attestation for the reason you cite. Calling Pentecost the birthday of the Church is more of a pious custom and not an official teaching or declaration. The image is used since, in a way, the Church comes forth from her initial formation in the "womb" of Galilee during Christ's public ministry. She comes forth now to begin her mission to the ends of the earth.

The problem with this image is that the Church that comes forth is no infant. She has been formed and is now clothed with power from on high to begin a mission, having been schooled, prepared, and enabled. The image of birth falls short here since birth bespeaks a helpless infant in need of complete formation. But the Church at Pentecost was far more mature.

One might argue that in the image of Eve coming forth from Adam's side, she came forth as an adult, not an infant, and thus "birthday" here can be understood in that manner. This may be fair enough, but it is not the usual manner in which we speak of birthdays. At some point an image with too many qualifiers suggests a possible flaw in the image itself.

What Pentecost surely is, is the commissioning of the Church to go forth unto all the nations. She has been formed, purified, taught, equipped, and enabled to go forth with joy and confidence. On the day of Pentecost, a fire fell on the Church, and those who had been frightened, confused disciples went forth with confidence and holy boldness, their minds made clear.

THE CHURCH'S AUTHORITY

Q. Why don't the bishops excommunicate self-proclaimed Catholic politicians who not only dissent from Church teaching but actively work to undermine the Church's mission? — *Maurice*

When it comes to excommunication or denying holy Communion to someone, we are dealing not only with Church law, but also with the prudential application of that law. It would seem that most bishops currently consider the application of these penalties to be imprudent and/or counterproductive.

In the Scriptures we see that Jesus himself gives various answers as to how to deal with sinners in the Church. On the one hand, he offers that for unrepentant sinners who will not even listen to the Church, they should be considered as a tax collector or Gentile — that is, excommunicated (see Mt 18:17). But elsewhere, Jesus tells a parable about field hands who urged the owner to tear out the weeds from the field, but the owner cautioned that to do so might also harm the wheat. He then said, let them grow together to the harvest (Mt 13:30).

So here we see that prudential judgment is necessary, and that many things must be weighed. Currently, many bishops have expressed concerns that to excommunicate or apply other public penalties would make "martyrs" of these public figures and further divide the Church.

What is clear is that the pastors of such politicians and other wayward Catholics should meet with them privately to call them to repentance. If their repentance is lacking, they should privately be urged to stay away from holy Communion and be mindful of their final judgment before God.

Q.: I am a former Catholic who left out of annoyance at all the layers and structures we find in the Church these days. I wonder if the apostles would recognize the simple and humble Church they had, compared with the pompous and ceremonial Church of today. — *Jonathan Fischer*

Well, I am not so sure. It's kind of like asking if Orville and Wilbur Wright would recognize the simple wooden and cloth plane they flew, compared with the modern jetliner of today. To some extent they certainly would see the basic structure, but they would also marvel at all the magnificent developments that their simple idea ushered in.

I rather doubt they would wag their finger and insist we go back to planes made of cloth, wood, and gasoline motors. It seems more reasonable that they would admire the developments that had ensued, all of which built on the basic ideas that they set forth.

I think it would be similar with the apostles. It is clear that doctrine has developed over the years, as have liturgy and other necessary structures in the Church. But these things developed from the structures that were already present from the beginning. The seed of truth has become the mature tree. The hierarchal structure, established by Christ himself, has expanded to meet the needs of a worldwide Church.

You are free to consider things you don't like as pompous, but others see such things as dignified and appropriate. God and the things of God are rightly to be honored with some degree of ceremony and respect.

Q. Pope Francis granted parish priests permission to absolve the sin of abortion. Why was this necessary? Can you explain why a priest was instructed not to forgive sins? Why should the woman be required to go to a bishop?
— *James Reaux*

Your question requires some distinctions to answer it clearly. It is not that a priest cannot absolve the sin of abortion. The issue concerns lifting the excommunication that may be incurred when one procures abortion. If this penalty was incurred by the penitent, priests traditionally had to consult the bishop before lifting it, and then absolve the penitent. It was not the case that the penitent herself (or himself) had to go to the bishop. It was the priest who was required to ask for the permission to lift the excommunication.

Canon 1398 states, "A person who actually procures an abortion incurs a *latae sententiae* (automatic) excommunication." This means that at the very moment that the abortion is successfully accomplished, the woman and all formal cooperators in the act — for example, the abortionist, nurses, those who pay for it — are excommunicated.

The penalty of excommunication is assigned this sin due to its serious nature. But for the penalty to apply, it requires that the person was older than sixteen, knew the penalty at the time of the abortion, and was not compelled to obtain an abortion. Thus not everyone who obtains or cooperates in an abortion incurs the penalty of excommunication. The priest will usually ask the penitent if they knew of such a penalty at the time of the abortion. Most indicate they did not know.

There are other sins that have penalties that a priest cannot lift before granting absolution. Among them are desecration of the Blessed Sacrament, physical violence against the pope, a priest's direct violation of the secrecy of the confessional, a priest's attempt to grant sacramental absolution to his partner in sexual sin, and a bishop's ordaining another bishop without an express mandate from the pope.

Though abortion is very serious, it has become sadly too common. To expedite granting absolution, most, if not all, U.S. bishops had granted the faculty to lift the excommunication to their priests many decades ago. While it is probably rare that most penitents from abortion incurred the penalty, priests will usually read the formula lifting the excommunication aloud or discreetly. This is done out of caution and to cancel any doubts. The absolution is then granted.

A common form for lifting the excommunication is: "By the authority granted me, I lift from you the bond of excommunication so far as your needs require, in the name of the Father, and of the Son, and of the Holy Spirit. Amen."

Q. **Does the pope have the authority to overturn pronouncements of previous popes, for example, in matters of contraception and the ordination of women? —** *Alice O'Hara*

We must distinguish between different types of law and teaching. There are certain laws and precepts that are ceremonial and customary practices, or merely disciplinary rules. These can be changed, and are changed, from time to time. For example, things such as the kinds and types of vestments and other regalia worn by the clergy and other merely ceremonial aspects of the liturgy can be changed. Disciplinary norms such as curial structures, canonical penalties, etc., can also be changed.

But in matters of defined doctrine by the magisterium regarding faith and morals, rooted in Scripture and apostolic Tradition, or from previous popes and councils, the pope is bound to uphold them. There are some technical debates about what is definitively taught that are too complex to set forth in this short answer. But the two matters which you cite are certainly teachings to which the pope is bound and may not overturn.

THE CHURCH'S

HIERARCHICAL STRUCTURE

Q. **:** The Catholic Church teaches that Peter was given primacy among the apostles, yet Peter considered himself a fellow elder and thus did not view himself as one superior to the other apostles. So, aren't local churches to be led by a plurality of elders? — *John C.*

The text you cite is 1 Peter 5:1, where Peter exhorts the leaders of the Church to be zealous shepherds. But what you see as equivalency may simply be fraternity.

For example, when my archbishop writes a letter to the priests of his diocese, he begins, "My dear brother Priests." Now, the archbishop is a priest, and shares that in common, as a brother, with all the priests of this diocese. But his salutation is not a declaration that there is no difference, or that he does not also have authority over us as the cardinal archbishop.

In the letter you cite, Peter begins by writing of himself, "Peter, a servant and apostle of Jesus Christ" (1 Pt 1:1). Hence your point that he thought of himself merely as a fellow elder does not seem supported. Further, the Catholic Church's position on the primacy of Peter does not rise or fall based on one text. Our teaching is based on a number of foundational texts and also on sacred Tradition.

We see that Christ singles Peter out and calls him "the Rock," giving him the keys of the kingdom of heaven, a sign of special authority (see Mt 16:19). He also assigns Peter the special role of uniting the other apostles when the devil would sift (divide) them like wheat (Lk 22:31–32). Peter is also singled out by Jesus at the lakeside and told to "tend my sheep" (Jn 21:16).

In the Acts of the Apostles we see Peter living the office Christ gave him. He is always listed first among the apostles. He preaches the first sermon. He convenes the brethren and directs the replacement of Judas. He works the first miracle, pronounces sentence on Ananias and Sapphira, is led by the Spirit to baptize the first Gentiles, and presides over the Council of Jerusalem, bringing unity to its divided deliberations.

Relying not only on a wide biblical tradition, the Catholic Church also bases her understanding of Peter's office on the broad and consistent testimony of the Fathers of the Church and other witnesses to the practice of Christian antiquity. These sources attest that Peter and his successors were accorded special dignity. Their authority to rule over the whole Church in a unique and singular way is confirmed by these sources.

Q.•An Orthodox family member insists that Peter has no special authority and that whatever authority he received, the other apostles received, too. Is this so? — *Name withheld*

The authority of the Petrine office originates in Jesus' appointment of Simon Peter in the Gospel of Matthew when he gives Peter the keys of the kingdom of God (see 16:19). Keys in the ancient world were a sign of authority. Keys grant access; they open and close doors. Further, Jesus speaks of Peter's capacity to bind and loose. And while the apostles as a group were later given the power to bind and loose, Peter alone received the keys. His authority has unique and universal qualities.

Q. A Protestant coworker said to me recently: "Who needs a pope? We have Jesus and the Bible and don't need some man to tell us what to do." How do I respond? — *Name withheld*

At the heart of the office of the papacy is the uniting of the faithful around a visible vicar (or representative) of Christ. Denominations and groups which left the Church and severed their ties to the pope demonstrate this very fact by their subsequent disunity.

The historical fact is that tens of thousands of denominations have emerged in the wake of the Protestant movement that broke from the Catholic Church and rejected the pope's authority. This rupture began in the sixteenth century. And though they claim that Scripture is the only source of authority and unity, the remarkable disunity among these non-Catholic denominations belies their claim. Simply put, if no one is pope, everyone is pope.

It is not enough to say, "The Bible clearly teaches A," because too easily another person will say, "No, Jesus and the Bible actually say B." Both camps are invoking the Bible and what they sense Jesus and the Holy Spirit are saying to them. So now what?

What usually happens is just what has happened among Protestants over the past five hundred years: divisions into new denominations or branches of denominations. They all claim the authority of the Bible and the inspiration of the Holy Spirit but cannot agree even on essentials such has how one is saved, and if once saved are they always saved? They cannot agree whether baptism is necessary for salvation, on eschatology, etc. In more recent decades Protestants also have had serious divisions regarding the moral issues of our time: abortion, same-sex unions, the morality of same-sex acts, euthanasia, etc. These are very serious divisions, and there is no real way for denominations in the Protestant tradition to resolve them. They claim Scripture alone is an adequate source of authority and unity. But without an authentic and authoritative interpreter, their own history shows that Scripture can divide as often as it unites. A text, even a sacred text, needs an interpreter that all agree can authoritatively deal with differences.

And this is a central reason why we need the pope. Jesus said to Simon Peter in Luke's Gospel, "Simon, Simon, behold, Satan has demanded to have you, that he might sift you like wheat, but I have prayed for you that your faith may not fail; and when you have turned again, strengthen your brethren" (Lk 22:31–32). To sift is to divide. And knowing the devil's intent, Jesus' solution is to pray for one man, Simon Peter, so that Peter would unite and thereby strengthen the brethren. Peter and his successors therefore represent (not replace) Christ, and through the grace of Jesus' prayer they accomplish the necessary work of uniting the Church. This ministry of unity is shown in many events in the Acts of the Apostles.

Q. **Jesus tells the apostles in Matthew 19:28 that they will sit on twelve thrones and judge the twelve tribes of Israel. There are lots of reasons to believe that Judas won't be in the lineup for this job (see Jn 6:70; Mt 26:24). What does the Church teach us on who is sitting on that twelfth throne? Matthias? Paul? Judas? —** *Paul VanHoudt*

Matthias would be the most likely candidate. We read in the Acts of the Apostles that he was elected to fill the office left vacant by Judas. The lengthy passage begins, "In those days Peter stood up among the brethren (the company of persons was in all a hundred and twenty), and said, 'Brethren, the Scripture had to be fulfilled, which the Holy Spirit spoke beforehand by the mouth of David, concerning Judas, who was guide to those who arrested Jesus'" (Acts 1:15–16). The passage concludes with the addition of Matthias to the apostles: "And they cast lots for them, and the lot fell on Matthias; and he was enrolled with the eleven apostles" (1:26).

Saint Paul, while surely in possession of the title "apostle" (along with Barnabas), was not, strictly speaking, numbered among the Twelve. Saint Paul had, in fact, seen the risen Lord on the road to Damascus, so he can be considered a witness to Jesus' resurrection. Saint Paul says of himself: "Last of all, as to one untimely born, [the Lord] appeared also to me. For I am the least of the apostles, unfit to be called an apostle, because I persecuted the Church of God. But by the grace of God I am what I am" (1 Cor 15:8–10).

The term apostle fell away from use as the number of those who met the criteria established by Saint Peter dwindled through age and martyrdom. The office of apostle continued in the office of bishop. The Greek word *episkopus* literally means "one who oversees." So, we note that the first apostles moved about as evangelizers and founded many local churches, but bishops, though successors to the apostles, had a more settled duty of overseeing a local church.

Q. We call our priests "Father." But Jesus teaches in the Bible that we must call no man on earth "father" (Mt 23:9). How can I explain why we Catholics use this term for priests? — *Name withheld*

If the purpose of Jesus were to banish the use of the word "father" in reference to human males, then it would seem the other New Testament authors never got the memo. In the New Testament alone there are 195 uses of the word father(s) to refer to earthly human males. It seems clear that understanding Our Lord's words as an absolute banishment of the term for any but God is not supported by the practice evident in Scripture itself.

The Catholic practice of calling priests "Father" has several meanings.

In one sense, it is meant as an affectionate family term. Parishes are like a family and use family terms such as "brother" and "sister" for men and women religious, "mother" for the superior of a group of religious sisters, and "father" for priests.

Priests imitate biological fathers in a spiritual way. Just as fathers give life, food, encouragement, and instruction, so priests give us these things in the spiritual order. They confer spiritual life by God's power at the baptismal font, give food through the Eucharist, and meet other spiritual needs through the other sacraments and by instruction and encouragement. Thus, by analogy, we call priests father.

Saint Paul referred to himself as a father: "For though you have countless guides in Christ, you do not have many fathers. For I became your father in Christ Jesus through the gospel" (1 Cor 4:15). Again, "For you know how, like a father with his children, we exhorted each one of you and encouraged you and charged you to walk in a manner worthy of God" (1 Thes 2:11–12). And, "Timothy ... as a son with a father he has served with me in the gospel" (Phil 2:22). We can see how calling priests father, in this sense, is not against biblical principles. Saint Paul himself makes use of the term in this way.

When discussing calling no one on earth your father, Jesus is emphasizing that God is preeminent. No earthly father, biological or spiritual, can ever overrule or take the place of the heavenly Father. God is ultimately the Father of all fathers, and we can never call any man father like we call God Father.

Q. **I have written to my bishop for several years now about liturgical abuses in my parish and get no response. It seems to me that bishops don't care about their flock anymore. How can I, a lowly layperson, possibly get through to my bishop?** — *Name withheld*

The insularity of many leaders is a common human problem that has gotten worse in the modern age. This is due to the pace of life, to increasing demands to be many places, to be on top of many issues, and to communicate in countless ways. As a result, many leaders require staff who help them manage the many requests for their attention. Bishops are usually not an exception to this. Balancing the needs of the common good and the needs of particular individuals is difficult to get perfectly right. And thus many, as you articulate, are frustrated at a lack of response or ability to talk directly to bishops, or even pastors of large parishes.

I would encourage you to address your concerns at the lowest level possible before going straight to the top. Most dioceses have deans who help oversee a group of parishes. Dioceses also have personnel directors who oversee the priests. Sometimes just finding a sympathetic priest who can help you navigate the diocesan structure may produce a better result.

Q: .Our bishop is closing our parish. My grandparents were among those who built and paid for this parish. By what right does the bishop close what is ours? — *Name withheld*

Canonically, there are some solutions that permit the lay faithful to take possession of a building slated for closure, undertake its maintenance, and keep them open as chapels, etc., under the supervision of the local church. Frankly, though, most congregations that have reached a critical state where closure is deemed necessary are not able to undertake such solutions.

While there are legitimate canonical issues, and the lay faithful have canonical rights at the closing of parishes, I am not a canon lawyer and would like to answer your question pastorally. From a pastoral point of view, it seems evident that bishops do not close parishes, people close parishes. Some wish to explain the widespread closing of Catholic parishes, especially in the Northeast, as mere demographic shifts. And while there are demographic issues, the fact remains that with the Catholic population almost double what it was in the 1950s, many parishes filled to overflowing back in that era now sit increasingly empty.

This is a teachable moment, and we must accept some very painful facts. When only 25 percent of Catholics go to Mass nationwide, and when Catholics stop having many children or effectively handing on the Faith to their children, this is what happens.

The Church simply cannot maintain parishes and other institutions such as schools and hospitals when Catholics are largely absent. Pastorally speaking, people, not bishops alone, close parishes. Many parishes, schools, seminaries, and convents now sit largely empty. And as they begin to go empty, bills are unpaid, maintenance is deferred, and the situation eventually becomes critical. Dioceses do not have endless amounts of money, or priests and other personnel, to staff and maintain increasingly empty, no longer viable parishes. Decisions have to be made.

Pastorally, one would hope that long before things get utterly critical bishops — working together with communities that are going into crisis — can speak honestly and work for solutions. But this is not simply the responsibility of the bishop; it is the responsibility of all the people of God to have such honest discussions.

Thus we are left with a difficult but teachable moment about what happens when the Faith handed down to us is largely set aside by the vast majority of Catholics. It's time to evangelize and make disciples, as Christ commands.

Q. **What do you think about women being ordained to the priesthood? I think if Christ wanted women in this role, he would have ordained his mom.** — *Allen Eberle*

Your answer is not far from the point. People often give the Church exaggerated power, as though she can do anything she pleases, but, as the last three popes have all stated, the Church has no authority whatsoever to confer priestly ordination on women. This is because Jesus, though he broke many conventions of his day, nevertheless called only men to be apostles. And in the call of the apostles is the origin of the priesthood.

The Church can no more alter the matter and form of this sacrament than she can use beer and pretzels for consecration instead of bread and wine. There are just some limits we must observe.

Q: Why does the modern Church not have deaconesses? (Scripture and some of the ancient Church Fathers mention them.) It seems they would fill a void, given the shortage of priests. — *Dolores Chauffe*

The references to deaconesses in the early Church are complicated, and much debated. Saint Paul does speak of certain women as having a ministry of service. And in his discussion about deacons in 1 Timothy 3:11, Paul does say, "The women likewise ... "

But what he means here is unclear. Does he mean that women were ordained deacons? Or is he referring to the wives of deacons? And even if they were deaconesses, did they receive the ministry by the laying on of hands? It seems not. Though Acts 6:6 mentions the first deacons having hands laid on them, there is no reference to this in terms of the women.

In the Greek text of the New Testament, the word *diakonia* can refer to the office of deacon (*diakoni*) or more generically to a ministry (*diakonia*) of service. Some speculate that an essential task of deaconesses was to attend the baptism of women, since baptisms were conducted disrobed. For modesty's sake women conducted the baptisms of women.

At the end of the day, however, we are left with a great deal of speculation if we simply examine the scriptural text. But we do not simply attend to the scriptural text. We also look to the practice of the early Church. And regarding this, there is no evidence that the clerical office of deacon was ever conferred on women by the laying on of hands.

There is little doubt that women can and do serve in many capacities in the Church today. It is true that women can provide great service (*diakonia*) to the Church. But it does not follow that they must be ordained to the clerical state of deacon to do so.

Q **.** **Why does one see the names of cardinals with their title between the first and last name — for example, Timothy Cardinal Dolan? Sometimes I also see it the other way, Cardinal Timothy Dolan. Which form is more correct?** — *Jim Perron*

The more correct and common practice is to place the title between the first and last names — that is, Donald Cardinal Wuerl. However, this is a matter related to pious custom, rather than a strict juridical requirement.

How the custom developed is not fully clear. But most interpret the practice as a form of humility. Those who acquire lofty titles in the Church often like to remind themselves that, before God, we are all just his children. Indeed, of all the titles a clergyman could ever require, such as Reverend, Monsignor, Excellency, Eminence, etc., the greatest title he actually has is a title that he shares with every other baptized Christian: Child of God.

Similarly, whatever leadership status anyone attains in the Church, one never loses the status of being a disciple. Saint Augustine famously stated to his people, "For you I am a bishop; with you, after all, I am a Christian" (Sermon 340).

Q **.** **Our priest seldom wears clerical attire. He often comes over to the church in athletic clothes. Is this right?** — *Name withheld*

A priest should generally wear clerical attire. Canon law says, "Clerics are to wear suitable ecclesiastical dress, in accordance with the norms established by the Bishops' Conference and legitimate local custom" (Canon 284).

The norms of the U.S. Conference of Catholic Bishops state: "Outside liturgical functions, a black suit and Roman collar are the usual attire for priests. The use of the cassock is at the discretion of the cleric" (Index of Complimentary Norms).

Thus clerical attire ought to be worn. There can be common-sense exceptions — for example, when playing sports, at a picnic, on a day off, etc.

THE CHURCH'S TEACHINGS

Q: My father constantly holds up the example of Saint Thomas the Apostle who doubted that Jesus had risen, even when the others said so. He says this is why it is okay that he should question everything, that doubt isn't wrong, even regarding the teachings of the Church. — *Tom O'Neil*

Yet, the Lord rebukes Thomas; he does not praise him for his stubbornness or resistance to believe. He instructs Thomas, "Do not be faithless, but believing" (Jn 20:27).

Consider, too, the enormous blessings Thomas missed in failing to gather with the others — that is the Church — that first week when Christ appeared. He missed seeing the Lord in his risen glory. He missed being reassured in the darkness of doubt and loss. Agony and grief were extended for him because he blocked his blessings by failing to gather with the Church.

It is also likely, at least for most of us, that the longer we remain in negative tendencies, the more difficult they are to break. So, Thomas's adamant "I will not believe" in response to the declaration of the early Church, "We have seen the Lord!" is not praised.

For those of us who are baptized, the Church is an object of faith. We affirmed at our baptism and say each Sunday in the Creed,

"I believe in one, holy, catholic, and apostolic Church." To refuse to believe what the Church professes and declares to be revealed by God is for us, therefore, a sin against faith.

Thanks be to God, Saint Thomas's journey does not end with his refusal. At some point he relents and is gathered with the community of the early Church the following Sunday. The Lord, in his mercy, grants Thomas's request to see and touch the wounds, but teaches that this is an exceptional mercy: "You have believed because you have seen me. Blessed are those who have not seen and yet believe" (Jn 20:29). Thus the mandate to believe without seeing is emphasized, and Thomas's insistence on seeing is rebuked.

It is true that Thomas's journey yields an extraordinary testimony: "My Lord and my God!" (v. 28). God does sometimes permit our stubbornness to believe to yield even stronger faith in the eventual believer — for example, Saint Paul and Saint Augustine. God can write straight with our crooked lines. But he shouldn't have to.

The story of Saint Thomas ends happily, but it does not follow that the story of every doubter or denier of the Faith will end happily, and your father is under the same mandate from Christ that any believer is: "Repent, and believe" (Mk 1:15).

Q. **The true presence of Christ in the Eucharist is central to our Catholic faith, and many converts I know of say it was essential to their conversion. If this is so, why is the true presence not mentioned at all in the Nicene or Apostles' Creed? Should it not be added at the end where we state things like our belief in the communion of the saints, the resurrection of the body, and so forth?** — *Jerry Roventini*

Well, there are many things that are not mentioned in the Nicene Creed. There is no mention of the Ten Commandments or of grace; neither are we told what books belong to the New Testament, or that we should care for the poor, and so forth. The Creed is not a catechism; it is a statement of certain key doctrines that were being disputed at the time it was composed in the fourth century.

The Nicene Creed was written largely in response to debates about the divinity of Jesus Christ and the doctrine of the Holy Trinity. While there are a few concluding statements related to ecclesiology and eschatology, the Nicene Creed remains preeminently a statement of faith in the one God: Father, Son, and Holy Spirit. The belief in the true presence of Jesus Christ in the Eucharist was not widely disputed at the time. And to the degree it was, the need to definitively teach on the divinity of Christ was an important foundation to lay in order to establish his true presence also in the Eucharist.

In the Sacred Liturgy many signs and words indicate the true presence. The words of the consecration, which are Jesus' own words, say, "This is my Body ... my Blood." The priest later says, "Behold the Lamb of God ... who takes away the sins of the world." There are also signs of the true presence through our reverent acts of kneeling and genuflecting. And, as Communion is distributed there is the simple creedal declaration and response: "The Body of Christ." "Amen." Therefore, in the wider liturgy of the Mass and devotions such as adoration, the Church proclaims and teaches her belief in the true presence.

While it would not intrinsically hurt to add it to the Nicene Creed, one might wonder where it would stop. Further, since the Creed is shared by the Catholic and Orthodox Churches, adding to the ancient Creed (especially after the *filioque* controversy when the Western Church added the simple word "and") might harm attempts at unity.

Pope Paul VI wrote a longer "Credo of the People of God," which did speak to the Eucharistic presence, but it is too long to recite at Mass.

Q. •Should the Church emphasize the salvation of souls •rather than social justice and ecology issues? — *Robert Bonsignore*

While we need to do both, your question centers on emphasis. It is true that some do overemphasize social justice, though others neglect it. Christ one day looked at a paralyzed man and said, "Your sins are forgiven" (Lk 5:20). He had sized up the man's biggest problem as his sin, not his quadriplegic condition! On another occasion Jesus was asked to intervene in a matter where a brother was not acting justly in distributing proper shares of the estate. Jesus objected to being drawn into such matters and warned the complaining man to avoid greed (see Lk 12:15). So, our first priority is to deal with the salvation of souls and to avoid sin in our own heart. Beyond this, however, we cannot neglect the admonition of Jesus to feed, clothe, and care for the poor (Mt 25:31–46).

Q. •I don't think the Church teaches that the saints are •omniscient. Therefore, my question is how are they made aware of our prayers, which are directed to them? — *Harold Whalen*

Our communion with the saints is accomplished in and through Jesus Christ, who is the head of the body, the Church. All the members of Christ's body, those here on earth (the Church militant), the saints in heaven (the Church triumphant), and those in purgatory (the Church suffering), are members of the one Body of Christ and are united by him and through him who is the head.

To use an analogy, my right hand has communion with my left hand, not because my hands have their own capacity to work together. Rather, my right hand and my left hand have communion and can work together only in and through the head of my body, which unites and directs them. And so it is with the members of the Body of Christ. In this regard, Saint Paul teaches when one member suffers, all members suffer; when one member is glorified, all members are glorified (see 1 Cor 12:26). There is thus a communion of all the members in the one body.

That the saints are aware of us and pray for us before the throne of God is attested in Revelation 5:8, wherein the four living creatures present the prayers of the saints before the throne of God, and where the incense — which is the prayers of God's saints — is brought before the throne. There is also the ancient tradition of the Church from apostolic times wherein the martyrs and heavenly saints are invoked for help of every sort.

Let us be clear that such communion with the saints does not occur apart from Jesus Christ, but, rather, it is facilitated by him through whom and in whom all things are and subsist, and who is the head of the body, the Church, uniting his members.

THE CHURCH IN SOCIETY

Q. **I keep hearing that the Church is declining in numbers, but every year I see that the number of Catholics in this country is larger. Which is it, are we going up or down?** — *Alfreda Johnson*

To understand the numbers, it is helpful to make a distinction between nominal and practicing Catholics. Nominal Catholics are those who call themselves Catholic but are not practicing or living the faith in any real sense. This number is going up as our population continues to grow. And that growth is mainly from immigrants, the majority of whom are at least nominally Catholic. Thus the overall number of Catholics is growing.

But to be a nominal Catholic is not necessarily to be a practicing Catholic. And though here in America the overall number of Catholics is growing, the number of practicing Catholics does seem to be declining overall. Sadly, only about 25 percent of Catholics go to Mass each Sunday (down from close to 80 percent in the 1950s). And an even smaller percentage agree with all the teachings of the Church and practice their faith daily to a significant degree.

Q: What factors do you ascribe to anti-Catholicism in our country. — *Peter Tate*

As with many sociological and cultural issues, there are likely many reasons and layers to the problem. Historically, people were much more serious about their religious beliefs than most are today. And this instilled a conflictual interaction in the past. Culturally, huge waves of mostly Catholic immigrants came to this land in the early twentieth century. Many of them were also very poor and did not speak much English at first. Until that time, America was a largely Protestant country. People generally do not like change, and this was a huge one for America.

Most of the conflict today stems from anger that the Catholic Church does not affirm the departure from moral and biblical norms that much of our culture has embraced. Given our size and influence, we are a special target of wrath from secular sources.

OTHER CATHOLIC RITES

Q. A friend who grew up in the Russian Orthodox Church married a man from the Roman Catholic Church. They had a Catholic wedding and she now practices Roman [Latin-rite] Catholicism. She said she did not have to do anything to become Catholic. Is that correct? — *Thomas Pohlen*

No. She should speak to her pastor and request formal acceptance into full communion with the Catholic Church. There are also some protocols that are observed in receiving members from the Orthodox churches that will need some attention (see Code of Canon Law for Eastern Churches; Canons 35, 896–901). While she would not need to receive sacraments, her formal reception into the Catholic Church is covered by these norms and protocols, which exist to show respect for the rite from which she came. If she wishes to practice the Latin rite, that can be done; but there are procedures to be followed.

OUR PROTESTANT BRETHREN

Q. Some experts say that the Catholic Church is responsible for the Protestant Reformation. Is this true? — *Paul McHale*

There is an old saying: "A one-sided pancake is pretty thin." That is to say, where there is human conflict, there are going to be different views and plenty of blame to go around.

To be sure, the emergence of Protestantism did not come out of nowhere. The "protest" of Protestantism was a response to alleged Catholic errors and excesses. Not all the errors that were alleged were errors at all, but were in fact the true faith received from the apostles. There were, however, certain endemic problems in some areas of the Church which were deplorable. These included poorly trained clergy and corruption involving benefices (where bishops and priests "collected" parishes, took income from them, but didn't serve them, appointing instead poorly trained replacements). The offering of indulgences, while not erroneous doctrine, suffered from grave excesses of individual clergy and the drive to fund the rebuilding of Saint Peter's in Rome.

However, what really drove Martin Luther and others was their rejection of key Catholic doctrines from antiquity and the refusal of the Church to accept their notions. Each of the main Protestant leaders rejected various teachings, including the authority of the pope, the understanding of Scripture, teachings on Mary and the sacraments, and the very nature of the Church itself.

Neither can we ignore the intersection of faith and politics as being a key ingredient in the Reformation. Emerging differences in culture and the rise of secularism and nationalism surely had a lot to do with the growth of movements opposed to the Church's authority, even concerning doctrine.

So, the disarray within the Church contributed significantly to the problem that led to the Protestant Reformation. But Protestant leaders also contributed, along with a rapidly changing culture, as the medieval synthesis broke down and, arguably, Christendom itself began its decline in Europe.

But deeper blame must ultimately fall to those who broke union with the Church Christ founded. Leaving the Church and founding rival institutions cannot be a valid solution to problems within the Church. When Christ prayed for unity at the Last Supper (see Jn 17:21), he certainly did not have in mind the tens of thousands of divided denominations the Protestant movement has unleashed. Sin and scandal are nothing new in the Church, but we must always recall that Jesus was found in the company of sinners and that the Church he founded is his body. We cannot find the true Christ by walking away from him and severing our union with his body, the Church.

Q. **Evangelicals have been telling people in my area that Catholics are not Christians. Would you give me some points that I can make to prove them wrong? Catholics are Christians!** — *Robert*

Of course, you are right, Catholics are Christians. In fact, we are the very first Christians. And we who call ourselves Catholic are no less Christian than Lutherans who call themselves Lutherans, or Methodists who call themselves Methodist, etc.

A primary argument is historical. The Protestant denominations are all less than 500 years old in terms of their founding. The human founders of these denominations, such as Martin Luther and John Calvin, broke away from Catholicism, and/or one another. Thus their existence is a relatively recent historical phenomenon in the more than 2,000 years of Christian history.

The Catholic Church — to include Latin-rite (Roman) Catholics and Eastern-rite Catholics — was not founded by mere human beings, but by the Lord Jesus Christ, and built on the rock of Saint Peter. In Acts 11:26, we are told, "In Antioch the disciples were for the first time called Christians." This declaration and description was made of the Church more than 1,500 years before any Protestant denominations ever existed.

Therefore, the Catholic Church has borne the title Christian long before any breakaway groups ever used the term to describe themselves. We do not deny they are Christians, and neither should they deny that of us, for the reasons stated. Catholics are Christians to be sure, the *first* Christians.

Q. I hear the term "evangelical Christians" used a lot, but I am not sure to what or whom this refers. Can you enlighten me? — *Name withheld*

Non-Catholic Christians have usually been termed "Protestants" in the English language, because they were collectively "protest-ing" something in Catholic teaching or practice. But, of course, Protestantism is a very diverse group of tens of thousands of differ-ent denominations which span the theological spectrum — liberal to conservative.

Thirty years ago, Protestant denominations were largely broken into two groups: (1) more socially conservative "funda-mentalists" and (2) more liberal (both socially and theologically) "mainline" denominations, such as Lutherans, Methodists, Presby-terians, and Episcopalians.

The fundamentalists tended to draw their numbers from the more conservative Baptist congregations and a wide variety of independent and nondenominational groups. What tended to divide fundamentalists from mainline Protestants was how the Scriptures were to be interpreted. Fundamentalists tended toward a more literalist adherence to the text that was more suspicious of applying historical context or other interpretive principles for un-derstanding the text. The mainline denominations moved rather dramatically toward such interpretive keys, so much so that many of them have arguably moved beyond the text itself and, as such, have no problem permitting things which biblical texts unambig-uously forbid, such as homosexual acts, homosexual marriage, di-vorce and remarriage, women clergy, etc.

During the 1970s and 1980s, there was a protracted campaign in the media and the wider culture to discredit fundamentalism as rigid, pharisaical, and out of touch. Fair or not, the fundamen-talists began to adopt the term "evangelical" in response. While today's evangelical Christians are not simply synonymous with the fundamentalists of the past, the term fundamentalist has largely been replaced by the term evangelical.

Today, despite theological differences between evangelicals and Catholics, there is a lot of common ground on moral issues. This has led to greater understanding and evangelical Christian denominations today are now some of the most fruitful sources of converts to the Catholic Church. They bring with them a great love for the Lord Jesus and a great love for Scripture, and they seek the more stable historical, theological, and sacramental framework of the Catholic Church in which to live their faith.

These closer relations have led to the description of "evangelical Catholicism." This term expresses an emphasis on the scriptural and apostolic origins of our holy faith. At the heart of evangelical Catholicism is the concern to avoid becoming too self-referential, to always remain centered on Christ.

Q.I have been asked recently if I am Christian or Catholic? What kind of question is this, and how should I answer it?! — *Name withheld*

You are right to be annoyed and take offense. Catholics are Christian, indeed, the original Christians. We have been here for 2,000 years and are the Church founded by Jesus Christ himself.

It is sadly true that there are some who polemically and rhetorically ask, "Are you Catholic or Christian?" as if the two categories were mutually exclusive. They are not. It would be like asking a certain man, "Are you male or human?" And, of course, the answer is both, and the question as stated is offensive. The same answer is true here: Catholics are also Christians.

Unfortunately, not all Christians are Catholic. And this is a countersign, because Christ founded one Church, and he has one body. He prayed for unity, not endless divisions. He did not found tens of thousands of different disputing denominations. He established one Church, which he founded and unified around his vicar: Peter and his successors, the popes, who are designated to unify and strengthen the others whom the devil would sift (separate) like wheat (see Lk 22:31).

The word "Catholic," while often used as a proper noun, is also an adjective. It comes from the Greek and means "according to the whole." And this is understood in at least two ways. First, the Church is Catholic because we preach the whole counsel of Christ, not just certain favorite passages of Scripture or popular viewpoints. We are called to preach the whole Gospel, whether in season are out of season.

Second, the Church is catholic because we are called to a universal outreach to all nations. We are not just a church of a certain race or nation, or a certain city or town. We are called to go on to the ends of the earth and make disciples of all nations. The Church has a catholic — that is, a universal — mission to everyone.

Thus the Catholic Church *is* the Christian church, and all Christians are called to be Catholic. It is for this unity that we must lovingly strive.

Q. **What do evangelicals mean by the mantra, "Jesus is my personal Lord and Savior"? I was asked [if Jesus is my personal Lord and Savior] by an evangelical. I answered yes, but he gave me a skeptical look. —** *Name withheld*

They usually mean that they have personally encountered the Lord Jesus in prayer, repented of their sins, and accepted him into their lives.

But many Catholics rightly wonder at the word "personal" and are suspicious that this can too easily mean a Jesus of our own making rather than the Jesus revealed in Scripture and the teachings of the Church. Further, there is suspicion that personal can mean that it is adequate to know and meet Jesus apart from his body, the Church. Clearly, these are deficient understandings of Jesus, who does not merely relate to us personally but also corporately through the members of his Church united in the faith through baptism.

This may explain the skeptical look from the evangelical you encountered. Many think the Catholic understanding has too many moving parts and violates their own rather simple (and I would argue un-biblical) notion that getting saved is a mere manner of reciting a "sinner's prayer." Never mind that this sinner's prayer is found nowhere in Scripture and that Scripture prescribes that we repent and be baptized, become disciples, and be taught whatever Jesus has commanded (see Acts 2:38; Mt 28:18–20; Mk 16:16). The skeptical look also likely stems from an attempt to draw you into his world and way of thinking. Your quick affirmation as a Catholic likely threw him off guard since he realizes that you mean something a little richer than he has in mind.

All that said, there is a Catholic way to say that Jesus is our personal Lord and Savior. That he is our Lord and Savior is clear. To call him personal is to attest that we have encountered him personally in prayer and through the ministry of the Church. He is not some stranger we have merely heard about on the pages of a book. He is, in fact, someone we have encountered. He ministers to us in the Liturgy and sacraments, speaks to us in his word and in our prayer, and he is changing our lives. But in calling him our personal savior, we do NOT mean that he has saved us apart from his body, the Church. Some think they can have Christ without the Church, which we cannot do. We may know him personally, but never alone.

Q. •The Lutheran Study Bible states that the meaning •conveyed by Matthew 16:18 is that the Church is not built on the authority of the man Peter but on the faith in Jesus Christ that he proclaimed in Matthew 16:16. A friend cited this as a reason not to subscribe to papal authority or the primacy of the Catholic Church. Can you shed any light? — *Art Osten, Jr.*

There are two central points in refutation of this interpretation of your friend. First of all, it violates the rather plain meaning of the text of Matthew 16:16–18. Had the Lord meant to indicate Peter's faith rather than Peter himself, he would surely have said so. The Lord's address to Peter here is clearly personal. He uses the Greek singular "you" (*su*) in saying to Simon, "You are rock." If the Lord had meant to indicate faith, he would have said, "You are Simon and upon the faith you have shown I will build my Church."

So, the first answer to this interpretation is that it requires of us a highly speculative and fanciful notion that the Lord does not really mean what he is plainly saying, but rather something very different which requires lots of explanation to understand. But the Lord is not speaking in riddles here, such that we must engage in elaborate notions to understand what he plainly is saying. He speaks directly and clearly. The word "faith" is not used. He is speaking personally and directly to Peter and calls *him* a rock, indicating that his Church will be built upon the rock he is clearly referencing: Simon, now called by his new name, Peter.

The second problem with your friend's theory is that it also sets aside other biblical teachings regarding Peter. This is not the only text in which Peter is singled out by the Lord to be a source of unity and strength for the others. In Luke's Gospel we read that Jesus says, "Simon, Simon, behold, Satan demanded to have you, that he might sift you like wheat, but I have prayed for you that your faith may not fail; and when you have turned again, strengthen your brethren" (22:31–32). Note, therefore, the Lord's solution to the fact that the devil wants to sift (divide) the apostles like wheat. The Lord's solution is to pray for one man, Simon Peter, and through him to hold his brothers together in one. Simon Peter is to be a firm foundation for their unity.

Further, we see Peter's role as leader and unifier rather consistently demonstrated throughout the Acts of the Apostles. It is he who directs the early Church to fill the vacancy left by Judas, which he calls an office. He sets forth the criteria and calls for candidates and discernment. It is Peter who preaches the first sermon at Pentecost. Peter is always mentioned first in any list of the apostles or disciples. It is Peter to whom Saint Paul submits his teaching for review, lest he be running his course in vain (see Gal 1:18—2:9). It is Peter who arises at the first Council in Jerusalem over the question of how to treat Gentile converts. And when he rises, all fall silent and hear him declare that the Church should not require the Gentiles to follow Jewish ways. This resolves the vociferous debate, and even James, likely opposed to Paul and Barnabas (and very influential in the early Church), acquiesces, asking for some concessions which he is granted (Acts 15).

Through all this, we see that Peter's leadership is indicated not only in Matthew 16, but also in Luke, and that, just as Jesus directed, Saint Peter took up this role in the early Church. So, your friend's view does not hold up either in terms of the specific context of Matthew 16 or in terms of the wider context of the New Testament.

Beyond the Bible, the consistent witness of the early Church, among the Fathers and others, was that the successor to Simon Peter continued to have centralizing and unifying authority in the Church.

UNFORTUNATE SCANDALS

AND DIVISIONS

Q. Are Catholics who reject the Church's teachings on the Mass, the Trinity, the virgin birth of Christ, abortion, etc., no longer Catholics, or are they one for life because of their baptism? — *John Clubine*

Regarding baptism, the *Catechism of the Catholic Church* affirms the following: "Baptism seals the Christian with the indelible spiritual mark (character) of his belonging to Christ. No sin can erase this mark, even if sin prevents Baptism from bearing the fruits of salvation. Given once for all, Baptism cannot be repeated" (1272).

That said, your question also seems to touch on how deep one's communion is with Christ and his Church. If one were to reject the teachings you mention, they would in effect seriously harm, even sever, their communion (unity) with the Church. At times the Church must ask those who intentionally dissent to assess their own communion with the Church, and to no longer celebrate a communion that is seriously impaired by refraining from receiving holy Communion. In rare cases the Church my see a need to formally declare an excommunication exists.

However, even in such cases, given the indelible mark that baptism confers, one can never utterly lose the status of belonging to Christ. By analogy, even if a son or daughter of yours were to wander far from you, live in total contradiction to what you believe, and even curse you to your face and act so badly that you had to erect legal protections for yourself, none of this would change the fact that they are still your son or daughter.

Q. One of the common objections my adult son raises about going to church is that all the sin and hypocrisy in the Church is intolerable to him. Any advice on what to say about this? — *Name withheld*

Well, of course, this is one of the objections that Jesus had to face from the Pharisees: "This man receives sinners and eats with them" (Lk 15:2). It's a remarkable thing that Jesus is found among sinners and hypocrites. He is not found in the perfect places of our imagined "church." He is not simply found in the places or company that is considered desirable; he is found where he is found — among sinners. Indeed, one image for the Church is Christ, crucified between two thieves!

As for hypocrisy, we do well to wonder if any human being on this planet, save for the most heroic saint, is utterly free from this ubiquitous human problem. Surely your son cannot consider himself wholly free from it, can he?

In terms of mission, the Church is a hospital for sinners, and that means sinners will be found there. But so will the medicine of the sacraments, the wisdom of Scripture, healing, encouragement, and admonishment, too. And, yes, sinners ... even some in critical condition. We know our sin. That is why we have confessionals in every parish. Pray God we always have room for one more sinner.

As for those who seek Christ apart from the Church — that is, apart from his body — that is not possible. Christ is found with his body, the Church. He associates with sinners and holds them close. He incorporates them into his body through baptism and seeks them when they stray.

Tell your son that Jesus loves sinners and is not too proud to be in their company and call them his brethren. Join us!

Q. **Pope Francis talks a lot about the poor. But then why doesn't he just sell off all that Vatican art and give the money to the poor?** — *Jack Rogers*

Simply put, it is not his to sell. All that art belongs to all the people of God, now living and those to come. The poor like beautiful churches, too. If there seems a lot of art in the Vatican and elsewhere, remember that the Church is 2,000 years old, and these gifts have accumulated over the centuries. Simply selling it would gain little money overall and would be a betrayal of the stewardship the Church owes to this beautiful patrimony. Beware the poverty of Judas (see Jn 12:6).

Q. **I have been a Catholic all my thirty-five years. But I am becoming increasingly angry at how the Church abuses its power and, among many things, excludes gay people from getting married. Well, I pretty much know you won't agree, but I have to speak out.** — *Name withheld*

You exemplify an interesting phenomenon in the modern world, which often exaggerates the notion of Church "power." The Church does not have unlimited power to do as it pleases or craft a different faith than has been received from the Lord and the apostles.

In terms of divine moral law, the Church has no authority whatsoever to overturn the biblical teaching against homosexual acts, or to redefine the parameters of marriage as given by God in the Scriptures and sacred Tradition. The Church is the servant of the Word of God (see CCC 86), not an all-powerful entity that is able to tear pages from the Bible, cross out lines, or overrule it. The sinfulness of homosexual acts (and also illicit heterosexual acts, such as fornication and adultery) is consistently taught at every stage of biblical revelation to the last books.

Hence I would urge you to reconsider that what you call an abuse of power is actually a humble recognition by the Church of the limits of her power.

Q: In the History Channel show *How Sex Changed the World*, it spoke about the Church's role in prostitution and said that 20 percent of the "customers" were clergy. Is there any truth to this? — *Susan Marron*

When one hears claims about Church history that are less than flattering — or shocking — two balancing perspectives are helpful.

On the one hand, one ought not to become too alarmed or defensive of claims that there has been sin in the Church. Anytime there is one human being in the room, there is bound to be sin. And the Church is very big and very old. The "hospital" we call the Church includes many saints, but it is also a hospital for sinners.

On the other hand, not all claims of sin in the Church are fair or presented in proper context. And some claims are outright lies or exaggerations. It is highly unlikely that 20 percent of the clientele of prostitutes, as recounted in the television show you mention, were clergy. There are and have been great sinners among the clergy. But as recent scandals (sadly) show, the percentage of offending clergy is quite small (though even a small number is too many and can cause great harm).

Other claims against the Church regarding the Inquisition and the Crusades also tend to present these issues out of historical context and backload current sensibilities to times that were far more brutal, and where stable governments and modern jurisprudence did not yet exist.

So, we must have balance when discussing these issues. Jesus has always been found among sinners, to the scandal of some. We do not make light of sin, we simply seek fairness.

Q.•Given the harm that alcohol causes, I find it strange •that the otherwise strict Catholic Church allows for Catholics to drink. Call me an old-time Protestant, but I find your silence on this scandalous. — *Name withheld*

Strict prohibition of alcohol is difficult to maintain, given the biblical data. The Bible and cultural mores have generally steered a middle course between prohibiting drunkenness but also allowing, even praising, the "gift of wine."

Saint Paul advises Timothy, "No longer drink only water, but use a little wine for the sake of your stomach and your frequent illnesses" (1 Tm 5:23). The context of advice like this was that water was seldom pure in the ancient world. And though the ancients knew little of bacteria, they knew by experience that wine (likely the alcohol in the wine) could assist in avoiding illnesses. Surely the alcohol assisted by killing at least some of the bacteria that thrived in impure water sources such as wells and dirty streams. Frankly, by modern standards, the ancients drank significant amounts of wine for these health reasons, though they often mixed or diluted it with water.

However, Paul also warns of not indulging in too much wine or being given over to drunkenness (see 1 Tm 3:3,8; Ti 1:7; 2:3). In Ephesians 5:18, he says plainly, "Do not get drunk with wine, for this is debauchery." So, we are pretty clearly dealing here with a call to moderation and sobriety, but not a total abstinence. And if the Catholic Church is strict in matters, she is strict in what God's word says, not in mere human prudence.

Note, too, that Jesus made wine in abundance (over sixty gallons) at Cana, and used wine at the Last Supper as one source (or matter) of the sacrament of holy Communion. The Book of Psalms says that God gives "wine to gladden the heart of man" (104:15). And Proverbs, "Give strong drink to him who is perishing, / and wine to those in bitter distress" (31:6). So, there seems to be a medicinal and "cheering" effect that God's word permits and encourages, at least in certain settings.

But again, none of this should be taken to advise drunkenness, which is a sin of gluttony, and which robs us of our most important faculties of intellect, judgment, and even our will.

Q. Jesus embraced the sinner. The Church reconciles women after abortion and has prison outreach. Why won't the Church embrace homosexuals? — *Name withheld*

For the record, the Church does have an outreach to homosexual persons known as Courage. It emphasizes living the virtue of chastity by teaching that homosexuals can live celibately. While many do accept this outreach, it is also true many homosexuals reject this call to live celibately.

It is, of course, challenging for the Church to reach out to those homosexuals who insist that the only way we can "properly" minister to them is to accept wholeheartedly and uncritically what God teaches is sinful. Jesus embraced sinners, but he also called them to repentance. Proper ministry and love are rooted in the truth of what God reveals. Scripture consistently and at every stage defines homosexual acts as gravely disordered and sinful. It also condemns fornication, adultery, and incest.

Q. Why is the Society of St. Pius X (SSPX) consigned to obscurity? Why are they treated so harshly when they just want to worship in the traditional way? — *Dennis Yebba*

It is more complex than that. The Church permits the Traditional Mass and the older forms of the sacraments. In most dioceses these traditional forms are celebrated in a few parishes regularly. I routinely celebrate the Traditional Latin Mass and conduct sacraments in the older forms when requested to do so.

The Society of St. Pius X was founded by Archbishop Marcel Lefebvre in 1970 in the diocese of Fribourg, Switzerland. At that time it was not a schismatic group, but it was controversial be-cause it adhered to the older forms of the Mass and sacraments as they were celebrated prior to the Second Vatican Council. The group, more specifically its clerical leaders, were excommunicated when bishops were ordained without permission of the Holy See.

This issue of the SSPX goes more to a question of authority (bishops were ordained without permission, etc.) and of their diffi-culty in accepting some of the Second Vatican Council's teachings that extend beyond liturgy. These problems are too extensive to detail here. However, the Vatican has been working consistently to restore the SSPX to proper canonical status. Negotiations contin-ue. Pray for unity!

PART VI

PRAYERS
AND
PRACTICES

PRAYERS

Q.What do we mean when we speak of "our exile" in the prayer Hail, Holy Queen? — *Dionilla*

Biblically, "exile" refers to the fact that, after original sin, Adam and Eve were banished from the Garden of Eden (see Gn 3:24). Hence we are exiled from there and live in this "valley of tears," another expression that occurs in the same prayer.

Since the death and resurrection of Jesus, we can also say that exile refers to the fact that we are not living in our true home. For Christ has opened the way not merely back to the Garden, but to heaven. Heaven is now our true homeland. This sinful and suffering world is not our home, and thus our time here can be considered a kind of exile as we await our summons to our true and heavenly homeland.

Finally, speaking of this world as an exile and valley of tears is a sober recognition that life in this world is often difficult. And though we may ask God for certain relief, true and lasting joy can only come when we leave this exile for our true home with God.

Q.Didn't Mary's consent occur before she conceived by the Holy Spirit? But in the Angelus prayer, "She conceived of the Holy Spirit" comes before "Be it done unto me according to thy word." Shouldn't the order be the other way around? — *Tim*

Some theologians argue that Mary conceived in her heart before she conceived in her womb (though this is not likely what is meant in the first strophe of the Angelus prayer).

More specifically, liturgical prayer accesses chronological time with reference to the fullness of time. Thus at Christmas, though referencing Jesus' infancy, we still gather with him in the

Upper Room and at the foot of the cross, and thereby celebrate him as the risen, glorified Lord at Christmas Mass. Though we focus on one aspect of his temporal work, we always have the whole in mind.

The same can be said for the Angelus prayer. We are not simply declaring the event of the Incarnation in a strict, chronological way, but in a way that theologically expresses all the components understood wholly: God's initiative, Mary's assent, and the fact of the Word becoming flesh.

Q. **I am wondering about the difference between praying before the Lord when there is Eucharistic Adoration versus simply praying before the tabernacle? Is one better than the other? I always stop by my church and do adoration before the tabernacle because my schedule is not always good for me because of work.** — *Name withheld*

The Church does not assign an essential difference between praying before the tabernacle and exposition where the Lord is displayed in the monstrance in Eucharistic Adoration. A Vatican document on the Eucharist says: "Exposition of the blessed sacrament, either in a ciborium or a monstrance, draws the faithful to an awareness of the sublime presence of Christ and invites them to inner communion with him. Therefore, it is a strong encouragement toward the worship owed to Christ in spirit and in truth" (*Eucharisticum Mysterium*, 60).

Both forms of adoration are commended. But while there is not an essential difference, there can be a subjectively different experience. In adoration with the Blessed Sacrament exposed in a monstrance, there is a visual aspect that helps many to stay more focused. In this sense one may argue that Eucharistic Adoration before the monstrance is "better." But as you point out, personal factors such as schedules or a preference for quieter, briefer, or more solitary visits can also influence what is better.

The bottom line is that the Church encourages devotion to the Blessed Sacrament. Such devotion, through visits, adoration, signs of respect through kneeling, genuflection, and signs of the cross as one passes a Catholic Church, all acknowledge the sublime presence of the Lord in the Most Blessed Sacrament.

Q.•I hear people speak of meditation and contemplation. Is there a difference, or are these just synonyms? — *Jenny Foster*

Some people do use these terms interchangeably, but in the more precise language of spiritual theology they are distinct.

Meditation is a type of prayer where our experience of God is "mediated" in some manner, usually by means of a text, a work of art, or simply our memory or imagination interacting with our understanding. We think on something which then inspires our affections for God.

Contemplation describes a prayer that is deeper and more directly attentive on God without the mediation of words, images, or obvious thinking. It is *cor ad cor loquitur* (heart speaking to heart). It is a loving, simple, and fixed attention of the soul on God. Contemplation is the prayer of deep union.

Contemplation is not a technique that can be learned (though one can dispose himself to it). Contemplation is the gift of God to those who have advanced through the fundamental stages of the purgative way and are ready to receive deeper illumination.

Q.• Does the Catholic Church disapprove of yoga for exercise or to assist meditation? — *Rita Malone*

The Church generally distinguishes between the physical postures of yoga and the philosophy or religion from which they come (see the Congregation for the Doctrine of the Faith, "On Some Aspects of Christian Meditation," 26–28). The adoption of a physical position, even if originating in a religious system other than Christianity, is permissible provided the posture is sought apart from the religious tradition from which it originated. There is a custom by which the Church has "baptized" even pagan practices down through the centuries that were not intrinsically linked to paganism.

Therefore, each person engaged in the practices must ask if the yoga postures can be independent of non-Christian religious teaching. Perhaps they are used for physical health or to reduce stress while not embracing to any degree the religious teaching behind the posture. If so, yoga is theoretically possible.

However, many who have experience with yoga indicate that this complete severing of yoga from its roots is difficult. The main point of yoga is to manipulate internal forces in order to achieve a particular physical or mental state. Some supporters of yoga reply by saying, "These are just natural forces." But the existence of these forces is dubious from a natural perspective, and they are said to exist because a non-Christian religious tradition says so. It is seldom a good idea to seek to manipulate "forces" that are not taught to us by the Lord or even by natural law.

While the question of yoga has not been definitely answered by the magisterium, prudence would likely advise against its use. The saints got along fine without it, and if one seeks to find a good prayer posture, a little experimentation on one's own should suffice. The key point in prayer is to be comfortable so as to focus on the Lord, not on our body or on certain forces said to exist by non-Christian philosophies and religions.

Q. Saying the Rosary and repeating the Hail Mary fif-ty times seems strange and irrational to me. Are we supposed to concentrate on the prayer we are saying and the mystery all at one time? Please help me understand. — *George Frohmader*

The *Catechism* speaks of the Rosary as an "epitome of the whole Gospel" (971). In other words, it is a summary, or an embodiment, of the entire Gospel because it encourages the faithful to meditate upon the fundamental events of salvation history and the life of Christ. The Rosary has also been called the "Gospel on the string." These images help to emphasize that the central work of the Rosary is to meditate on the Scriptures, and that Mary's work, above all, is to lead us to a deeper faith in Jesus.

There are some who find the Rosary a helpful way to pray. Others find it difficult and distracting. The Church, while encouraging the Rosary, does not require it. It is a fact that people are suited to different prayer forms. Saying repeated Hail Marys is appreciated by many as a kind of rhythmic background for meditation on Gospel passages, which is the key point of the Rosary, and this aspect of it should be central in our thoughts.

Q. As I pray the Rosary, I sometimes have so many in-tentions that I cannot remember them all and it takes a long time to try and recall. Sometimes I just lift my hands or my book of intentions. Is this okay? — *Loretta Leonard*

God knows our weaknesses. We cannot always remember everyone for whom we should pray, or everything for which we should pray. Saint Augustine says that more things are accomplished in prayer by sighs and tears than by many words. Thus, while precluding outright laziness or a refusal to resist any mental distractions, we can count on God's merciful awareness of our prayers and concerns for others, even if these things escape us in the moment.

Q. **My pastor does not allow us to celebrate Christmas during Advent, tells us not to decorate our homes, and forbids any parties on church grounds until December 25. Is this right?** — *Phil*

The liturgical environment has stricter rules than Catholics are necessarily obliged to follow in their own homes. While it may be ideal that our homes perfectly reflect the liturgical cycle, practically speaking, many Catholics begin decorating earlier in the month of December.

As for celebrations on church grounds, that is a matter of pastoral judgment. Frankly, most pastors are rather relaxed about this, understanding that cultural influences, even if less than ideal, can be respected out of regard for the legitimate wishes of people to celebrate conveniently. I would encourage you to listen carefully to your pastor's teachings and strive to keep Advent as much as possible. But it does seem that some leeway in these matters is acceptable.

Q. **Before I drive, I usually say a prayer for safety. Recently, I had a minor but expensive accident. Should I be angry at God?** — *Hugh Sweeney*

Prayers for protection and safety are good and recommendable, but they are no guarantee that we will evade all harm or travail. It is part of God's will for all of us that we share in the Cross since some degree of suffering is healing for us. The remedy of the Cross is the "strong medicine" which teaches humility.

Saint Paul says that suffering produces glory (see 2 Cor 4:17). Saint Peter says that suffering purifies our faith and makes it genuine (1 Pt 3:14). Saint James says that suffering produces endurance (Jas 1:2–3).

I am sorry for your accident, but God can and will bring good out of it. Scripture assures, "We know that in everything God works for good with those who love him, who are called according to his purpose" (Rom 8:28). Notice the text says "everything," not just the good things, works together for good if we trust God. So, even this can be a gift in a strange package. If we are faithful, all is gift.

EUCHARISTIC ADORATION

Q: **Is it ever acceptable to leave Eucharistic Adoration when you are the only one present? Also, one location I know has a veil available to cover the monstrance when one is the last to leave. Is this acceptable?** — *Joann Capone*

The Blessed Sacrament, when exposed for adoration in the monstrance, should not be left unattended. The whole point of exposition is that the Most Blessed Sacrament be adored by the faithful. There is also the concern to prevent desecration or theft of the Blessed Sacrament. Consecrated Hosts are sometimes sought by satanic cults.

You are correct, most adoration chapels have provisions if one must leave the presence of the Lord and no one else is there. In some places, there are doors that can be closed over the monstrance. In other places a veil is placed over the monstrance. If one must leave for the restroom and the monstrance cannot be conveniently covered, this is okay, but only for a moment or two. In such cases the adoration chapel ought to be secured by a lock of some sort — for example, a combination lock or a key-code entry.

Clearly, pastors must make some of these options available since people do run late or forget to keep their commitments to pray. He should not assume that all will be well simply because a schedule is published.

Q.My friends and I debated the culpability of fall-ing asleep during adoration. Is it acceptable to fall asleep accidentally? How about intentionally, after we have finished our prayers? — *Teresa Fenn*

Something done accidentally is not matter for sin, unless it is the result of woeful neglect. To intentionally choose to nap, however, is not the purpose of adoration. Adoration implies an attentive, loving, and conscious worship of the Lord. To the apostles who slept in his presence he said: "So, could you not watch with me one hour? Watch and pray that you may not enter into temptation" (Mt 26:40–41).

The Lord knows our weakness but counsels us to be sober and watchful.

SACRAMENTALS AND BLESSINGS

Q. I was taught there were seven sacraments (including marriage) that give grace, and also that there were things called sacramentals that do not give the grace the way that the sacraments do. Why then, in my Church bulletin, do I read about classes being offered to prepare people for "sacramental marriage"? — *Rosemary Easley*

In this instance, "sacramental" is being used as an adjective, not a noun. Hence it is not wrong to speak of sacramental marriage. But, your bulletin could be clearer by saying Sacrament of Marriage (or Matrimony).

That said, your distinction between the nouns "sacrament" and "sacramental" is sound. Sacramentals include things like blessings, blessed objects, holy water, medals, etc. They bear a resemblance to the sacraments. But sacraments, as efficacious signs, absolutely confer the grace they announce, presuming the recipient is properly open to receive them. Sacramentals are signs that prepare us to receive grace and dispose us to cooperate with it, but they are much more dependent on our disposition to be fruitful. More can be read in the *Catechism of the Catholic Church* (see 1667–73).

Q. What does the I.N.R.I. on the top of crucifixes mean? — *Name withheld*

"INRI" is an abbreviation for *Jesus Nazarenus, Rex Judeorum* — Jesus of Nazareth, King of the Jews. In Latin, the I and J are usually interchangeable, and ancient Latin did not use the J. That is why it is INRI, not JNRJ.

It was common for the Romans to hang a *titulus*, or sign, above the crucified to indicate the charges against him. Scripture says that Pilate put the charges in Latin, Greek, and Hebrew. Pilate placed this title above Jesus in scorn and mockery rather than faith. He also likely knew it would irritate the Jewish leaders, which it did (see Jn 19:21). Yet even in his ridicule, Pilate spoke truth. Jesus is King, not of the Jews only, but of all things.

Q: If a rosary is broken but repaired, does it lose its blessing? — *Ed Stewart*

No, it does not lose its blessing. If the majority of the beads were replaced, etc., it would not be wrong to have it blessed again, but blessed objects remained blessed.

In rare cases, blessed or consecrated objects can lose their blessing through association with a gravely sinful act. For example, if a murder takes place in a consecrated Church, it is the usual practice to re-consecrate the place.

A related question is what to do with blessed objects that are no longer usable. Generally speaking, they should be burned or buried, but not discarded in the regular trash. Old and tattered Bibles, holy cards, scapulars, and the like can be burned and buried. If burning of them is not possible, simple burial will do. Things that cannot be burned such as ruined medals, statues, or rosaries, should be buried. If possible, before blessed or religious objects are buried it is permissible to shred, smash, or in some way render them less recognizable. This helps to avoid the possible scandal of others happening upon them and not realizing that they were buried for pious reasons as no longer usable, and not merely discarded.

Q. •A friend insisted that I should bury a statue of Saint Joseph upside down in my yard to assist the sale of the property. He said it really works. When I balked at this [as] superstitious, he took offense. I have similar troubles with some of the prayer cards and novena promises that go about. Am I being too strict? — *Patricia Barry*

The *Catechism of the Catholic Church* defines superstition in the following manner: "To attribute the efficacy of prayers or of sacramental signs to their mere external performance, apart from the interior dispositions that they demand" (2111).

The practices you describe do have troublesome aspects. This becomes the case especially when the prayer or practice starts to have lots of moving parts. For example, it becomes not enough to pray, asking Saint Joseph's help, but one must bury a statue of him in the front yard, facing the proper direction, and upside down as well. This not only seems impious (since burying a statue is not really a proper use of it), but also seems to have no connection to selling a house. One might ask, why not just ask Saint Joseph to pray for a quick sale?

At least things like candles and the wearing of medals are external reminders to us and others of our prayer and devotion. But even these could become superstitious if one thinks that the mere performance of an external act will accomplish the goal. Further, if one frets over the fact that they forgot to wear a medal one day, or could not light a candle of a certain desired color, or place it in a particular spot in church, he or she is straying into magical thinking and superstition.

Some will argue that burying a statue is just a harmless and pious custom. Perhaps. Reasonable people will often differ on where to draw the line between legitimate prayer practices and superstitious ones. This is because one cannot always see the internal disposition of the one who prays.

But when prayers and practices start to have a lot of specific requirements or guarantees — for example, "never known to fail"

— the risk and likelihood of superstition is increased. If a certain prayer said a certain number of times is "never known to fail," does this not amount to a claim that we can force God to say yes to us? But this is a sin against faith, since we must trust God to give the best answer. Sometimes "no" is the best answer.

Superstition is a common human problem rooted in fear. Often anxious or desperate people fall into this sort of thinking. But the only real solution is to develop a quiet trust in God, who knows what we need before we ask. Novenas, medals, candles, and statues can be consoling reminders that God and others love us, but they cannot alone substitute for faith.

Q: **What is the meaning of candles that people light in church when they put in an offering?** — *Adelaide Murphy*

These are referred to as votive candles, and people purchase and light them to symbolize their prayers or devotion. The candle continues to burn for some hours or days (depending on the size) and thus signals the prayer and love of the person who lit it, long after they must go.

Biblically, the root of this practice is the notion of a "burnt offering." In the Old Testament, things of value (usually sacrificed animals) would be burned and thereby offered to God. The smoke was a symbol of the sacrifice of praise ascending to God.

Catholics who light candles are making an offering to God of prayer and praise. The fire of the candle symbolizes ardent love. The consuming of the candle symbolizes the oblation (offering) of something of value to God: our time, our praise, our resources, and so forth. The lingering quality of the candle symbolizes the fact that our prayers, praise, and concerns continue in our heart even when we must leave the church. The flickering light also seems to say, "Remember me Lord, remember my prayer and those for whom I pray."

Electronic votive candles do not as clearly show these symbols, but the idea is still the same.

Q: •Where did the practice of blessing ourselves with •holy water on entering Church come from? In my parish, sand replaces water during Lent. — *Karl Jones*

In the ancient Church, one usually entered the sanctuary through the baptistery, and the custom of blessing oneself with the water naturally was a reminder of baptism. In later centuries, as church buildings grew larger and doors multiplied, small fonts were placed near those doors and the tradition continued.

The practice of placing sand in the fonts for Lent is a tired aberration and not prescribed by any norms. At no point in the liturgical year is it appropriate to cease remembering our baptism.

Q: •I don't bless myself with holy water when I enter the •church; the water looks dirty. Is this wrong? — *Name withheld*

No, you are not required to bless yourself with holy water as you enter the church. It is a reminder of baptism and a request for purification as we enter the holy place of God's house. You are encouraged to spiritually ask mercy and recall baptism, but the water is not necessary.

For obvious reasons, the holy water near the church doors needs to be changed frequently. You might wish to speak to your pastor or an usher about the problem. Also, in the past, blessed salt was often mixed with the holy water, to keep down bacteria levels, etc. This practice is still permitted and should be encouraged.

Q: • I bless myself with holy water when I enter and leave the Church. Several people said I should not bless myself more than once a day, since I am already blessed. Is there a rule about this? — *Name withheld*

There is no rule in this regard. It is a matter of personal piety, and you are free to follow the practice you describe. Perhaps those who say this to you have some liturgical principles in mind, but they are overextending the norms or absolutizing them.

Generally speaking, there were some efforts when the ordinary form of the Mass was introduced in the 1970s to downplay or eliminate extra Signs of the Cross that had come into the Mass by custom. For example, there was the tendency to make the Sign of the Cross after the *Confiteor*, and many priests began and ended the sermon with the Sign of the Cross, etc. There was a conscious effort by some liturgists to emphasize that the Mass began and ended with the Sign of the Cross, and that other merely customary introductions should be eliminated to give emphasis to those prescribed moments of blessing.

Further, some liturgists thought that other pious customs, such as the priest giving a blessing to the servers or others in the sacristy after Mass, should cease. After all, they reasoned, had he not just blessed them at the end of the Mass? Did this request for a blessing in the sacristy not suggest that the blessing at Mass was inadequate?

It was also this premise that made some think that, while blessing oneself with holy water on entering was a proper and even necessary sanctifying action, to do so on leaving gave the impression that the blessings received in Mass were not adequate or that people had actually lost sanctity during the Mass.

While such concerns are not without some merit, as you can see there is also the possibility that we think a little too much about some things and can end up getting fussy or even pharisaical.

Teaching that the blessings at Mass are real and powerful blessings, not mere ritual actions, may, in a constructive way, lessen the *felt* need for extra blessings after Mass. However, to assume that people are denying the efficacy of the Mass by the pious customs described here is a stretch. You remain free to bless yourself any number of times a day, as long as superstitious notions are avoided.

Q. **How does one properly dispose of old and worn priestly vestments? One lady in the altar guild took the vestments and made throw pillows. This does not seem right.** — *Julia Sullivan*

No, making pillows isn't right. Once something is dedicated to sacred use, it should not then be converted to ordinary use.

Older vestments are often sent to missions. But if they are too worn, they ought to be burned and the ashes collected and buried in an out-of-the-way and appropriate place.

This is a general rule for all sacred, blessed objects and sacramentals. Sacramentals, such as scapulars and prayer books, should be burned and then buried. Larger sacramentals that don't burn should be altered so they no longer appear to be a sacramental. For example, a statue can be broken up into small pieces and then buried. Broken rosaries can be further disassembled and burned or buried. Objects made of metal can be melted down and used for another purpose.

Q. **Who can give blessings? There are laypeople in my parish giving blessings, which does not seem right.** — *Sr. Mary Gemma Younger*

Context and content are important in answering a question like this. In the liturgical setting, only a priest (and sometimes the deacon) should be conferring blessings, since they are present and available for such. Thus the practice observed in some places of laypeople who are distributing Communion also giving blessings is inappropriate. The priest should be sought for this, apart from the Communion line.

However, in other settings, laypeople may give certain blessings in certain ways. For example, a parent can bless a child, an elder may bless a youngster, etc. In doing this, however, they ought to avoid priestly gestures such as making the Sign of the Cross over others. Perhaps tracing the cross on the forehead, simply laying a hand on the head, or no gesture at all would be better.

In settings where laypeople are praying for one another — for example, in a prayer for healing or deliverance — similar rules should be followed, avoiding overt priestly gestures and being content to lay hands or make no gesture at all.

In the rare instances where laypeople lead formal liturgical gatherings, such as the Liturgy of the Hours, they must not only avoid gestures, but also follow prescribed texts which merely ask God's blessing on the assembled believers, and not imply they are bestowing such blessings.

Finally, there are certain specific prayers and blessings that can only be given by a priest. The norms are too specific to be given here in a general answer. But most blessings of objects and sacramentals are reserved to clergy, and the laity ought to be content to offer simple prayers, asking blessings for one another only in appropriate contexts.

Q:•At a local nursing home, a religious sister, who is •very traditional and wears the full habit, conducts a Communion service. During Communion, non-Catholics are also brought forward and she traces the cross on their forehead and says, "God bless you." Is this allowed? — *Pat Reagan*

The conferral of a blessing, even with the Sign of the Cross, is not forbidden to the non-ordained in all circumstances. For example, parents should be encouraged to bless their children, even to trace the cross on their forehead. In some settings and cultures, elders often bless youngsters. Laypeople even bless themselves whenever they make the Sign of the Cross.

However, in the liturgical setting you describe, some parameters should be observed. The moment of the distribution of holy Communion, whether at a Mass or a Communion service, is not really the moment for people to seek other sorts of blessings. In a Mass, the priest will give the general blessing at the end of the liturgy with the Sign of the Cross over the whole congregation. Hence all those present will, in fact, receive a blessing.

There are, however, pastoral concerns of how best to deal with a practice that has become widespread and is not done in bad faith. Frankly, most pastors overlook the practice and, when requested, confer blessings in the Communion line. Even if they do dissuade their parishioners from the practice, many visitors still often come forward requesting blessings. Thus the matter may better be resolved at the diocesan or national level.

While the situation you describe is wrong, Sister is probably trying to make the best of a difficult situation, where people expect such blessings, even if they are not Catholic. Finding a teachable moment to gently instruct the faithful is not always easy given the presence of many visitors.

Nevertheless, the goal to move toward is to teach that the distribution of holy Communion is not really the time to seek other blessings. An additional confusion is created when, though priests and deacons are present at Masses, laypeople at other Communion stations are often giving out what appear to be priestly blessings. Finding a gentle way to clear up the confusion becomes increasingly important.

Q. •At Mass, when the priest offers the bread and wine, •we say, "Blessed be God forever." But how is it possible for us to bless God? He does not need our blessings, and he blesses us. — *Name withheld*

Linguistically, the response you cite translates the Latin *Benedictus Deus in saecula*. The *benedictus* in Latin literally means to speak well or favorably about someone or something (*bene* [well] plus *dictus* [say or speak]). What we mean by "blessed" and the phrase "Blessed be God forever" is, "It is well that God should be forever praised." We are not claiming to confer some sort of grace or favor upon God, as is often the meaning of the word "blessing" in English.

Theologically, though, we can distinguish between God's intrinsic glory and his external glory. As you point out, there is not one thing we can add to or take from God's intrinsic glory. God is glorious and blessed all by himself, and he has no need of our praise.

However, we can help spread God's external glory by praising and acknowledging him before others, as well as by reflecting his glory through lives of holiness, generosity, and conformity to the truth. In this sense, we can also understand the phrase "Blessed be God forever" to mean: "May God's external glory and blessedness be extended and experienced in all places and times. May God be blessed (praised) everywhere, and unto the age of ages."

QUESTIONS ABOUT MARY

Q: An evangelical Christian in my office saw a holy card on my desk of the Blessed Mother. He was rather dismissive of it and my Catholic faith. Sadly, I got angry. But I did not really know how best to answer him. He understands we don't worship Mary, but still says we ought to focus only on Jesus. Any thoughts? — *Name withheld*

In discussing such a matter with evangelical Protestants, it's best to stick with Scripture. While there are many Scriptures we could quote, it seems the most fundamental passage to set the stage for the discussion is from the Gospel of Luke. There, Mary, under the influence of the Holy Spirit and rejoicing with her cousin, Elizabeth, says: "From henceforth all generations shall call me blessed. For he that is mighty hath done to me great things; and holy is his name" (1:48–49, KJV).

Now, if the Word of God is inspired, and it *is*, then we should be asking a few questions of our own to our good brothers and sisters in the evangelical tradition. Since Scripture says that all generations would call her blessed, aren't we Catholics fulfilling exactly what Scripture says? And if *we* are thus fulfilling Scripture, how are *you*, and why do you criticize us for doing it?

It is not to the detriment of God to call Mary blessed, any more than it is a slight against an artist to praise a masterpiece by him. Mary is God's masterpiece, and as the text says, she is blessed because God who is mighty has done great things for her. In calling her blessed, we bless the artist, who is the Lord himself.

At some point, we need to start answering questions by asking a few of our own in a kind of Socratic method. And thus a simple and humble question to ask our critical evangelical brethren is, "How do you fulfill what Scripture says of Mary, that 'all nations will call me blessed'?" We should ask this with humility, but in silence await, and insist upon an answer.

Q. Why has Mary never been given the title "Co-redemp-trix"? Answer: Mary is not divine. She had to be a very special person since from her physical body Jesus came, but she is not divine. — *Jean McKinney*

Usually, I get the question, and am supposed to give the answer. But I see you have done both! However, your answer does need distinctions applied.

The title "Co-redemptrix" (redemptrix is a feminized form of redeemer) has been used of Mary, even by popes, in the past. It can be understood of her in a proper theological sense that does not divinize her or make her an equal partner in the work of redemption.

The problem in understanding the term emerges in the changing meaning of the prefix "co" which, to most modern ears, indicates an equality of status. Co-president, co-commander, or co-chair would usually indicate two people who equally share in an office or function.

However, the prefix "co" does not always indicate equal status. For example, a co-pilot is not equal to the pilot, he is subordinated to the pilot. If I tell you to "cooperate" with God, I am not indicating you are equal to God but rather that you should submit to God's work (or operation) in your life.

In this second sense, Mary can rightly be called a co-redemptrix, since the Lord chose to work very closely with her in the work of redeeming us. As you point out, he took his sacred humanity from her, was nourished and cared for by her, and he allowed her to signal the beginning of his public ministry (see Jn 2:1–11). Also, she was with him at the foot of the cross, having the title "woman," a reference to Genesis 3:15, where God indicates that Satan and the woman would be enemies and that she would be instrumental in his defeat, since her seed (Son) would crush Satan. The same theme is developed in Revelation 12.

Mary does not save or redeem us; Jesus does. But the Redeemer, Jesus, so closely associates her in his work that she can be said to co-operate in the work of redemption. Thus the title Co-redemptrix, properly understood, can be ascribed to her, with "Co" here referring to her as a subordinate partner.

The reason the title has not been formally declared is likely due to the very misunderstanding of the term your question illustrates. Too many would think "co" meant equal, not subordinate.

Q. On the solemnity of the Annunciation, I wondered about Mary's "yes" and her choice to agree or refuse God's request. Did she really have a choice? She was conceived without original sin, therefore was she not predestined by God to be the mother of his Son? If she really had a choice, would she have been born without original sin? — *Jeannine Aucoin*

Your example presupposes that God, knowing beforehand what we will do, therefore forces us to do it. But this supposition is wrong. One can imagine that we mere humans may know what is going to happen before it does, but we see that our knowledge does not rob the participants of freedom. Suppose you are sitting on a hill and see below that two trains are heading toward each other on the same track. Your knowing what is about to happen does not remove the freedom of the engineers. They continue to act freely even though you know what will soon happen.

God's knowledge is surely more sweeping. But the truth remains that we are not preprogrammed or forced to do what God knows we will do. Rather, we act freely, and God, who lives outside of time and sees the whole sweep of time at once, has merely set forth his plans in accord with his knowledge of what we will do. Mary freely said "yes," and Judas freely said "no." God, not forcing, but knowing, their free choices from all eternity, set his plans in accordance with that.

Q ● Since Mary was conceived without original sin, does ● it follow that she was spared a chief punishment of that sin — namely, pain in childbirth? — *Ed and Mary Ruzauskas*

It is a widely held view among theologians that Mary did not experience the pains of childbirth. However, the Church does not formally teach this as doctrine or dogma.

Those who assert a painless childbirth cite the Fathers of the Church, who with few exceptions taught a painless, miraculous birth where Christ emerged from Mary's womb but not through the birth canal. They also reference Isaiah 66:7, which, while an allegory of Jerusalem, is also a Messianic reference: "Before she was in labor / she gave birth; / before her pain came upon her / she was delivered of a son."

Theologians who do not see a need to affirm a painless childbirth cite other scriptural texts. The Gospels indicate some sort of labor on Mary's part (painless or not) and not merely a miraculous appearance that Mary experienced passively (see Mt 1:25 and Lk 2:7). Further, Revelation 12:2, while an allegory, is also a reference to Mary, which says, "She was with child and she cried out in her pangs of birth, in anguish for delivery."

So, the question of Mary having pain or not in childbirth is not a settled dogma or doctrine, only that she remained a virgin before birth (*ante partum*), after giving birth (*postpartum*), and in the birthing process (*in partu*). But as for the birthing process, we need not assert her virginity (*in partu*) in a merely physical way, for virginity is to refrain from the sexual act. It does not necessarily follow that for Christ to be born in the normal way violates Mary's virginal state.

As for your question that if she was preserved from this since she was free from original sin, it does not follow, since both she and Jesus suffered many things that came due to original sin, even though they were free of it. I am aware that much of this issue is wrapped up in piety, and many are easily troubled by different views. But the honest answer to your question is that, while Mary's perpetual virginity is dogma, how this affected her physically or was manifest in her physically is not dogmatically taught.

Q. The Legion of Mary handbook describes Mary's relationship to God the Father as "that of daughter." Is this correct? — *Robert Bonsignore*

Mary is rightly called the daughter of God in terms of her relationship to God the Father. She, as a creature like us, calls God her Father. In terms of her relationship to the Son, she is rightly called the Mother of God, since Jesus is God. In terms of her relationship to the Holy Spirit, she is often called the spouse of the Holy Spirit.

Q. Does the definition of the word "assumption" (to presume or take for granted) originally stem from Protestant objections to Catholic teachings on Mary's assumption? In other words, did they use the word to mock our teaching, saying that we merely assume she was taken to heaven? — *Marvel Kaderlik*

The use of the word "assumption" to refer to Mary's being taken up to heaven predates the Protestant period by hundreds of years.

The word assumption, meaning to take up, comes from Latin roots: *ad* (to, toward) plus *sumere* (to take or put on). Thus the dogma of the Assumption refers to Mary being taken up to heaven, soul and body. The Lord takes her to himself. While it is true that in the modern English sense assumption refers to something we presume or take for granted, that is not its original or only meaning.

Assumption is different than ascension, since to ascend is to go up by one's own power. Mary does not go up to heaven by her own power as Jesus did. She is taken there by the Lord. An ancient story and tradition about Mary, going back to apostolic times, states that when her earthly time ended, her body, not just her soul, was taken to heaven. Whether she died first and her body was entombed or instead was taken up at the moment of death is not certain. There are two different traditions. But both traditions are clear: her body was taken up, and there are no relics of her to be found in antiquity or now.

While this event is not recorded in Scripture, Saint John, in the Book of Revelation, describes Mary as the Ark of the New Covenant. The ancient Ark of the Covenant was a box covered in gold that carried the presence of God in Israel. Mary is the Ark of the New Covenant because she carried the presence of God in Israel bodily, first in her womb, later in her arms. When John looks to heaven, he sees God's temple in heaven and the Ark is there. Subsequent verses speak of a great sign in heaven, a woman clothed with the sun carrying the Messiah in her womb and perpetually giving birth to him in our lives. These tightly woven verses have many layers of meaning. But for our purposes, John sees Mary bodily, as the Ark of the New Covenant. He sees her in the temple that is heaven, not in a tomb.

This is not a "proof text." The Church teaches Mary's assumption because we have always done so. But the scriptural text of the Book of Revelation shows that this teaching is not contrary to Scripture.

Q • In the Fátima devotions, we are told to make the five first Saturdays in reparation to Mary. But, though I am devoted to Mary, I wonder how I can make reparation to Mary for my sin when the sins I have committed have been against God and those around me? Is it not to God that reparation needs to be made? — *Margaret Mantia*

The word "reparation" means to repair damages that we or others have inflicted. Even in secular language the word is used when one nation or group is asked or expected to make reparations — that is, pay damages or support restoration to another nation or group to whom they have unjustly harmed.

At Fátima itself, Our Lady said, "I shall come to ask ... that on the first Saturday of every month, communions of reparation be made in atonement for the sins of the world." Yet it wasn't until December 10, 1925, that she made her formal request to Sister Lucia, one of the seers. In particular, she asked that the faithful go to confession, attend Mass, stay fifteen minutes after Mass, and pray the Rosary on the first Saturday of five consecutive months.

Many people later asked Sister Lucia why five Saturdays were requested, since other devotions emphasize nine days. It was Our Lord himself who answered that question when he appeared to Sister Lucia on May 29, 1930. He said it was because of five offenses against the Immaculate Heart of Mary — namely, speaking against or ridiculing her Immaculate Conception, her perpetual virginity, her divine and spiritual maternity, the rejection and dishonoring of her images, and the neglect of implanting in the hearts of children a knowledge and love of his Immaculate Mother.

In this sense we, by our devotion, make reparation — that is, we seek to repair, by our devotion, for the effects of the sins of irreverence, omission, and unbelief. Since it is Our Lady who is dishonored, we make these reparations to her in the strict sense. But in a wider sense we also make reparation to the Lord who is offended by irreverence to his mother, as any son would be.

Q. **Are Catholics bound to believe in the apparitions of Mary, such as those at Lourdes, Fátima, and Medjugorje?** — *Name withheld*

No. When an apparition is "approved" by the Church, it is simply proposed to Catholics by the Church as worthy of belief and for edification. But there is no requirement to believe any particular apparition.

The apparitions at Lourdes and Fátima have been approved as authentic, but Medjugorje has not. Catholics are thereby cautioned to temper their devotion to this apparition until such time as it is approved, but they are not forbidden from believing in or even visiting Medjugorje. Official Church-sponsored pilgrimages there, however, are discouraged until approval may come.

Q. **It is my understanding that private revelation cannot be binding on the faithful and that apparitions of Mary fall in that category. If that is the case, then why are several Marian apparitions given memorial, or even feast, days on the Church's liturgical calendar? Our Lady of Guadalupe is even a mandated feast in the American Church. Does this not bind the faithful?** — *Name withheld*

As you point out, the feasts of Our Lady of Fátima and Our Lady of Lourdes are optional memorials. Therefore, it is difficult to describe them as mandated or binding on the faithful. However, the feast of Our Lady of Guadalupe is mandated (though only in the Americas) and cannot be set aside in favor of the celebration of a simple weekday Mass or some other votive Mass.

But it is a stretch to say that this results in a mandate that binds the faithful to accept the teachings and miracles related to Guadalupe. For though the feast is mandated liturgically for December 12, the faithful are not obliged to attend.

Why does the Church set the feast of Our Lady of Guadalupe as a required feast? Such things are done in the order of charity and in order to promote unity. Certain feast days are important because they are deeply tied to nations, peoples, or groups. In such cases, feasts are mandated so that priests do not arbitrarily omit them in such a way as to show (even if unintentionally) dishonor to a feast that is very important to the faithful in his region.

Some feasts and nonoptional memorials are also mandated since a particular saint has great significance in the universal Church. For example, Saint Catherine of Siena has a memorial that is not optional due to her significance in Church history. But it does not follow that one is required to accept her *Dialogue* as given by the heavenly Father or to accept every teaching or image she wrote of.

Other saints who founded religious orders also have obligatory memorials due to their significance. And some regions have mandated feasts that other areas do not. For example, Saint Joan of Arc is obligatory in France, but not in the United States. Here, too, her feast, obligatory in France due to its national significance, does not require one to accept that Saint Joan actually had the visions or locutions of saints that are said of her.

One should see the ranking of feasts and their obligatory nature in the order of charity and unity rather than as a proclamation that every detail of every saint or event is thereby doctrine that binds all the faithful.

Q.•Our diocese is holding a procession in honor of Our Lady of Guadalupe on Sunday December 7. Is not Sunday reserved to Our Lord? In years when Marian feasts fall on a Sunday they are usually moved to Monday. — *Daniel Barth*

Outdoor processions and devotions do not have to follow the same strict calendar norms as the Mass. I suspect the procession was timed to be when many did not have to be at work.

It is unlikely that Our Lord is offended by our honoring of his mother, and there is nothing inherently disrespectful in celebrating Mary whom God himself chose to work with, and whom Jesus honored and revered as his mother. A non-Catholic offended by this practice might be reminded that Catholics fulfill the Scripture, which says, "All generations will call me blessed; / for he who is mighty has done great things for me" (Lk 1:48–49).

ANGELS

Q.•What was St. Thomas Aquinas' evidence for saying there are nine choirs of angels? — *Samuel*

Saint Thomas states the source himself in the *Summa Theologiae*: "The authority of Holy Scripture wherein they are so named. For the name 'Seraphim' is found in Isaiah 6:2; the name 'Cherubim' in Ezekiel 1 (Cf. 10:15–20); 'Thrones' in Colossians 1:16; 'Dominations,' 'Virtues,' 'Powers,' and 'Principalities' are mentioned in Ephesians 1:21; the name 'Archangels' in the canonical epistle of Saint Jude (v. 9), and the name 'Angels' is found in many places of Scripture" (I, Q 108 Art 5, sed contra).

Some today are critical of this citing from various unconnected Scriptures and wonder if the terms are not interchangeable. But

Saint Thomas carefully sets forth the sensibility of the names of the nine choirs, which speaks to their property, eminence, and participation in the divine economy. His reasoning is complex, but it has a depth that many of his dismissive critics lack.

In effect, Saint Thomas argues as to the fittingness of the names since they bespeak ranks and functions as well as properties. In this way, they are not simply different names used in different places of Scripture to designate the same reality. There are real distinctions in the names of the ranks, which indicate nine distinctions or ranks, also termed choirs, not in the sense of song, but in the sense of groups or ranks.

Q. **I was surprised to learn that "the practice of assigning names to the holy angels should be discouraged." Please explain this. What if I was told the name of my angel in prayer?** — *Rose*

A document written in 2001 by the Congregation for Divine Worship and the Discipline of the Sacraments entitled *Directory on Popular Piety in the Liturgy: Principles and Guidelines* says, "The practice of assigning names to the Holy Angels should be discouraged, except in the cases of Gabriel, Raphael, and Michael, whose names are contained in Holy Scripture" (217).

While the congregation does not offer reasons for discouraging the practice, I will offer a couple.

First, there is the understanding of what a name is. For most of us in the modern Western world, a name is simply a sound we go by. But in the ancient biblical world, and even in many places today, a name has a far deeper meaning. A name describes something of the essence of the person. This helps explains the ancient practice of the Jews to name the child on the eighth day. The delay gave the parents some time to observe something of the essence of the child, and then, noting it, they would name the child. Indeed, most biblical names are deeply meaningful and descriptive. But it is presumptive to think that we can know enough of the essence of a particular angel to be able to assign a name. Therefore, assigning a name seems inappropriate.

The second reason is that assigning a name indicates some superiority over the one named. Thus, in the case of children, parents, who are superior over their children, rightly name them. However, in the case of angels, they are superior to us. And even though we often speak of them as serving us, they do this on account of their superior power and as guardians. Thus God commands us to heed their voice (see Ex 23:20–21).

So, naming an angel does seem problematic, and it is to be discouraged. As for the name being revealed to you, let me respectfully offer that this is not likely the case, since it seems unlikely that an angel, or the Holy Spirit, would act contrary to the directive of the Church, herself graced to speak for Christ.

Q.•On the feast of the Guardian Angels (October 2), I •was wondering how the angels can know what we are thinking, and if they are able to read our minds? Also, how do we hear them? — *Charles Genaro*

As for angels reading our thoughts, it is not likely they can. In the field of demonology a similar question exists, and most demonologists conclude that demons, while very intuitive and good observers, cannot actually read our minds. I presume the same basic thing about the angels, too. However, angels might have the additional advantage that God reveals to them our thoughts on some or all occasions. But all this is speculative. No scriptural or dogmatic statement on the matter comes to mind.

There is also the great mystery of how angels (or demons) can hear or see us. Talking and hearing are usually terms that refer to a physical process of vibrating air being perceived by our eardrum. Seeing involves photons touching our retina. But angels do not have bodies and thus have no ears or eyes. So even if we talk out loud, how can they hear us, or for that matter how can they see us? This is mysterious. Perhaps, then, our thoughts can be projected in some manner, such that a being that is pure spirit can perceive them.

An analogy comes to mind. Even we humans, possessed of physical senses, do not see everything physically. For example, we do not see subatomic particles, even with a very powerful microscope. Rather, we come to know their existence by the use of our intellect and reason. We may see some of their effects — for example, by using math — but fundamentally we "see" them by reasoning to their existence and developing an understanding based on what we already know. The same thing is true for metaphysical concepts such as justice and mercy. We do not see them physically, though we may see their effects. Rather we see these concepts by reasoning to their existence. They are real, though metaphysical, and we see through our intellect and our spirit (which supplies our ability to grasp metaphysical concepts).

Further, how can we hear and listen to the voice of our angel as God clearly tells us to do in Scripture (Ex 23:21)? Since angels do not have bodies, we cannot hear their voice in a physical sense. Yet somehow they are able to interact with our soul (I suspect they do this particularly through our conscience) in a way that reaches our intellect.

It is clear that Scripture and Tradition take for granted that angels can and do interact with us, but how they do so is mysterious.

Q. •Our priest, in a homily, referred to the angels as "re-
•flections of God" and made the comparison to the
facets of a diamond — God being the diamond and the angels his facets. Does this sound right? — *Name withheld*

Angels do reflect God's glory, as do all creatures to some degree.
But angels are creatures, distinct from God, they are not a part (or
facet) of God.

Some sympathy for the preacher may be in order, however.
Sometimes analogies go wrong in live preaching. I suspect what
Father meant to say was that angels reflect God's glory in differ-
ent ways. The seraphim are the "burning ones" before the throne of
God, manifesting God's fiery glory and love; the cherubim manifest
God's glory and will toward creation; and so forth.

I rather doubt your priest thinks of angels as part of God. I
think his analogy slipped or morphed, and that by facets he does
not mean to imply the angels are of the same substance as God, but
that they reflect his glory differently.

Q. •When does a person receive his guardian angel — at
•birth, or when one is baptized? — *Michael Missaggia*

The *Catechism of the Catholic Church* teaches of the guardian angels, "From its beginning until death, human life is surrounded
by their watchful care" (336). Hence an angel is assigned from the
moment of conception. That the unbaptized also have an angel assigned seems likely as well and is deduced from the fact that the Old
Testament speaks of the unbaptized Jews as having or being in the
care of angels (see, for example, Ps 34:7; 91:10–13; Jb 33:23–24; Zec
1:12; Tb 12:12).

Q.I was having a friendly debate with a family member over whether or not the unbaptized have a guardian angel? Is there a teaching on this? — *Name withheld*

The traditional (but not unanimous) teaching from many of the Fathers of the Church (such as Clement, Tertullian, Origen), as well as Saint Thomas Aquinas, is that every human person has a guardian angel assigned at birth. However, after baptism the angel plays a new and richer role.

Prior to baptism, and for all non-Christians, though an angel is assigned, they have little power other than to protect from the most savage attacks of demons and to provide some influence. But at baptism, the angel becomes able to tap into the power and grace of Jesus Christ. Origen said: "If I belong to the Church, no matter how small I may be, my angel is free to look upon the face of the Father. If I am outside the Church, he does not dare" (*Homily on Luke*, 35).

So, baptism unlocks the greater powers of the angel to help. One can also see that a human person rescued from original sin and increasingly healed from its effects by grace is someone with whom a guardian angel can work more richly.

Q.Is it true that a guardian angel is assigned to every person? If this is so, do our prayers go right to God, or through our guardian angel? — *Bob Penders*

The Church teaches that each believer has a guardian angel. The *Catechism* says, "Beside each believer stands an angel as protector and shepherd leading him to life" (336). And this fact also flows from what Jesus says: "See that you do not despise one of these little ones; for I tell you that in heaven their angels always behold the face of my Father who is in heaven" (Mt 18:10).

Regarding the second part of your question, it can reasonably and rightly be argued that angels do serve as intermediaries in our communication with God. The very word angel means messenger, and it is clear that God often mediated his message to us through angels.

Regarding our prayers going to God, it is not unreasonable to presume that angels serve in some way to mediate these messages. However, it does not follow that God does not know or hear us if we don't tell our guardian angel something, or that the only way a message can reach God is through his angels. God is omniscient, knowing all things in himself.

While Jesus does not forbid us to pray to our angels, when he teaches us to pray, he tells us to pray to our Father, who is in heaven. Though angels may help to serve as intermediaries for these prayers, we ought to have our attention on God. Consider, for example, that if we spoke to someone through a translator, we would not tell the translator to say something to the other person, we speak directly to the other person and simply allow the translator to do his or her work.

Exactly how the angels serve as intermediaries in our prayers to God is somewhat speculative, but the point is to focus on God and pray to him in a natural way. To whatever manner and degree God has our angels serve as intermediaries is really not important for us to know. What is important is that God hears us, that he knows our needs and what we say, and that he loves us.

Q. **How does the Church reconcile the role of our guardian angels with the fact that so many children are vulnerable today to things like pornography and many things contrary to the Faith? There are so many attacks, and children seem so vulnerable. Where are the angels in all this?**
— *Name withheld*

Your question is a profound one, touching on the deep mystery of evil — in this case, moral evil (as distinct from natural evils such as disasters, disease, etc.). In terms of moral evil, the answer is focused on the reality of human freedom. The Lord is quite serious about permitting human freedom, and only rarely steps in to prevent our free acts. Without freedom there can be no love. God seeks sons and daughters who freely love him, not slaves who are forced to obey him by being overpowered and overruled.

In terms of the angels, therefore, their care for us does not routinely veto free human acts. In one of the early books of the Bible, the Lord describes the work of the angels in the following way: "Behold, I send an angel before you, to guard you on the way and to bring you to the place which I have prepared. Give heed to him and listen to his voice, do not rebel against him, for he will not pardon your transgression; for my name is in him. But if you listen attentively to his voice and do all that I say, then I will be an enemy to your enemies and an adversary to your adversaries" (Ex 23:20–22).

We see that the main role of the angel as described here is to guide, lead, and influence, more than merely to protect us. The blessings we obtain from an angel is the fruit of obeying his voice. The protection is not some sort of automatic force field set up around us to keep out all trouble and screen out bad influence.

Human freedom is largely reserved by God from direct intervention. Our own sins and abuse of freedom are the sad cause of the ills you describe. And while angels can help, it is generally restricted to exerting good influences that touch our conscience and warn us of sin. God summons us to obey the voice of our angel, but the choice to actually obey remains ours, and it is not something even God will force, let alone our angel.

Q. Did God let all the angels know the details of the passion, death, and resurrection before time began?
— *Peter Tate*

It is a common tradition in the Church (but not a biblical or defined teaching) that God revealed his plans for the Incarnation to the angels. But that tradition does not usually hold that the Lord revealed to them a detailed description of the passion, death, and resurrection.

The traditional understanding is that Lucifer, one of the highest ranking angels, was so angered at the thought that God would join himself to the human family, instead of the angelic ranks, that he rebelled against God and took about a third of the angels with him. In the ensuing war in heaven, Saint Michael the Archangel and his ranks prevailed, and Satan was cast out of heaven and fell to the earth.

Though the angelic rebellion is related in the Scriptures (see Rv 12:1–17; Lk 10:18; and, allegorically, Is 14:12–15), the details are often symbolic and do not indicate the exact reason for the rebellion of the angels.

We should be cautious in assigning too much knowledge to the angelic ranks, fallen or not. In Scripture, Satan shows a significant degree of uncertainty at the time of the Incarnation. He seems vaguely aware that God's plan for redeeming man is underway, but the details elude him. Jesus is able to make a stealthy incursion into Satan's domain of this world. Satan, sensing something, stabs wildly in the dark, killing the Holy Innocents, but Jesus escapes. During the temptations in the desert, Satan once again seems to be testing Jesus to find out if he is the Lord.

So, if Satan is unclear as to the Incarnation, it is not likely he knew the details of the Paschal Mystery either. Indeed, if Satan really knew in detail the plans for the passion, death, and resurrection, it seems unlikely he would take the bait, knowing he would lose.

All of this indicates that it is unlikely that God, before time and the rebellion of the angels, gave all the angels detailed knowledge of the Paschal Mystery. It may well be true that certain angels — for example, Gabriel — who were included in the events received knowledge in greater detail, but we cannot be sure.

THE SAINTS

Q. **If I can pray to God about anything I want, what is the purpose of praying to saints and Mary and asking them to pray for me?** — *Jason*

What if you could do both? It is not as though one sort of prayer excludes another.

Your question might well be applied to any number of scenarios. Why would I ask you to pray for me? Or, why do I often say to someone, "I will pray for you!" And why does Scripture call us to pray for one another (see Eph 6:18)? Why does Paul ask others to pray for him (Rom 15:31)? If Jesus is on the main line, and we can talk directly to him, why pick up line two?

Yet it is our instinct to do exactly that. Scripture commends both forms of prayer.

Sometimes God wills to answer us directly; sometimes he answers through another's prayer. At the wedding at Cana (see Jn 2:1–11), though Jesus surely knew the need for wine, mysteriously he chose to let his mother sway his decision. So why not pray both ways and let God decide?

Q. **The Bible says you shall have no other gods before me. Since we have a personal relationship with God, why would I need a go-between? Why do Catholics see praying to saints as more effective than praying to God directly?** — *Katy Hinsch*

Part of your concern is the understanding of the word "pray." Pray, like all words in the English language, has undergone some change in meaning and emphasis over the centuries. Most modern people, when hearing the word pray, think of an act of worship, and worship, of course, is directed only to God.

Originally, however, to pray simply meant to ask. Even today, in the world of law, lawyers will often conclude a legal briefing with request: "The defendant prays that the court will do such and such." Many older Catholic prayers stretch back centuries, and Catholics frequently use the word pray in this older sense. To pray to a saint is to ask him or her something, not to engage in active worship.

As for your wonderment about going to anyone other than straight to God, it should be clear that we are always able to go to God, and should do so. However, there is also a human instinct to ask others to pray for us. Saint Paul often asked others to pray for him, or for the Church, or for world leaders, etc. Saint Paul (and the Holy Spirit speaking through him) did not consider asking others for prayers to be a futile or a pointless thing to do. Communal prayer helps to build up the Body of Christ and helps us grow in mutual charity.

Biblically, it does seem there are some who have special influence with God. While this is mysterious, it is illustrated in Scripture. Moses, for example, as well as Abraham and others, were able to specially intervene and get God to reconsider or delay his plans for punishment. Mary, too, at the wedding feast at Cana, was able to get Jesus to make wine for the young married couple, though he seemed reluctant at first to do so. Scripture says, "The prayer of a righteous man has great power in its effects" (Jas 5:16). So, while our personal prayer is effective because God loves us, it does seem that God also wills that we seek out others to pray to as well, especially those noted for holiness.

Q•**:** It is my understanding that we do not know the time or circumstances surrounding Saint Joseph's death. However, my children's religion textbook shows Saint Joseph in bed surrounded by Jesus and Mary, and mentions an angel calling him home to heaven. What do we really know about the death of Saint Joseph? — *Lori Yarsky*

Your initial observation is correct. We know nothing about his death. The depiction you describe of Saint Joseph in bed with Jesus and Mary present is a common one. However, it is merely an imagined scene. It is likely given in the children's book merely as a plausible answer to the sorts of questions children ask. One may ponder the prudence of making things up, but it seems harmless enough.

There is a fairly consistent tradition that Joseph was an older man, perhaps a widower, when he was wed to Mary. If so, it makes more sense that he simply died of the effects of age, rather than by some dramatic cause. This may be why the Scriptures do not record what was a normal occurrence.

The story about the angel is not something I have ever heard. Here, too, one can hope it is presented more as what might have happened, rather than as factual. It seems clear enough that the angels do have a role in escorting us to judgment and, we pray, eventually to heaven. But there is no factual account of such an event after the death of Saint Joseph.

Q. I don't think Saint Joseph gets the recognition he de-serves. We rightly speak a lot of mother Mary, and certainly of Jesus. But Joseph is often relegated to the background. Why is this so, and should it change? — *Jeannine Aucoin*

More should be said of Saint Joseph, especially nowadays when fatherhood is in such crisis. Saint Joseph was a strong man who was willing to sacrifice career and personal comfort to protect and care for his family. He listened to God and did what he was instructed to do in the obedience of faith. Here is a powerful model for men and fathers today. I often preach on Saint Joseph when I give men's conferences.

That said, the lack of emphasizing Joseph extends to the Scriptures themselves. This is not due to any neglect of Saint Joseph personally, but it extends from the emphasis that the true Father of Jesus is God the Father. Thus Joseph's role as foster father steps to the background after the early infancy narratives.

Nevertheless, your point remains valid. We ought not be overly forgetful of Saint Joseph. Even if what we know of Joseph from the Scriptures is limited, what we do know is powerfully inspiring and should be highlighted.

Q. Does the Catholic Church ever declare Jews or non-Catholic Christians to be saints? For example, I have in mind Old Testament figures like Moses and Elijah. — *Robert Noonan*

Actually, Moses and Elijah are termed saints, most commonly in the Eastern Churches (Saint Moses, Saint Elijah, et al.). Non-Catholics are not officially declared saints, more out of respect for their denominational status and not because the Church considers sanctity nonexistent outside the realm of official Catholicism.

There are some ways that non-Catholics are honored short of official and personal canonization. Saint John Paul II officially recognized Dr. Martin Luther King as a martyr of the faith. Saint Charles Lwanga and those martyred with him were not all Catholic (some were Anglican), yet on their feast day no distinction is made.

Q. When we invoke Michael the Archangel, we call him Saint Michael. Isn't the term "saint" only applied to human beings? — *Robert McBride*

The word saint means holy. Saint Peter more literally rendered is "Holy Peter." And while we usually apply the term saint in our tradition to canonized men and women in heaven, this is not exclusively the case, as you note. The angels are holy, and thus are rightly called saints.

Since we know the names of only a few of them, we generally speak of them merely as angels. But for the three names we know from Scripture, we do assign the title "Holy." Thus Saint Michael, Saint Gabriel, and Saint Raphael are rightly termed saints, since they are most certainly holy and among the highest multitudes in heaven.

Q. How did the feast day of Saint Valentine end up associated with romantic love? — *Matt*

There is not an obvious connection between a third-century cleric and martyr and romantic love. There are actually two men from the early Church known as Valentine. The first is the Roman priest Valentine. He was decapitated in AD 268 for the crime of trying to convert a member of Emperor Claudius the Goth's household. He was also a renowned healer. The second Valentine is Bishop Valentine, who was also a renowned healer and was also turned in for converting people to Christianity. He was imprisoned and an attempt was made to force him to sacrifice to pagan gods. When he refused, his persecutors tried to club him to death. When that failed, he was beheaded, in 273.

One current and credible theory of the romantic connection to Valentine is that it comes from the poet Geoffrey Chaucer. Chaucer wrote in a poem, in 1375, that it was on February 14 that birds sought out their mate: "For this was sent on Seynt Valentyne's day, When every foul cometh ther to choose his mate" (from "Parliament of Foules"). And since no record exists of romantic celebrations on Valentine's Day prior to this poem, it may be the source of the holiday we know today. Beginning in the fourteenth century, courtly love among the nobles and wealthy began to be celebrated on February 14. The practice gradually spread.

Another largely discredited theory held that Valentine's Day was created as an attempt to supersede the pagan holiday of Lupercalia, celebrated near the Ides of February in Rome.

So, as best as we can conclude, Saint Valentine's feast day came to be associated with romantic love through Chaucer's poem. It was really more the day of the feast (February 14) than Saint Valentine himself where the connection was made, since it was on that day that a popular notion held that birds mated up.

Q. Why do we no longer celebrate the feast of Saint Christopher? He is such a popular and important saint. — *John*

The general answer is that we know so little about Saint Christopher that even his name may be incorrect. Our reference to him is really more of a title than a name: "Christ-bearer."

But to whom was this title applied? Was it possibly Saint Menas, himself known only in legends? It is said that Saint Menas was a very tall man for his time, and that he carried a small child across a swollen river. The child was later revealed to be the Christ Child who had mystically appeared. But this is only a theory. Devotion to a "Christopher" spread widely as the patron saint of travelers. And since most people travel, his fame spread. But the fundamental legend is so vague that we are not sure a saint by the actual name of Christopher ever existed. Catholics are still free to maintain devotion to Saint Christopher. God surely knows who he is.

As far as the feast of Saint Christopher, it had a very brief time on the official Roman calendar. The old Tridentine calendar permitted Mass to be celebrated in honor of him, but only in private (smaller devotional) Masses. In 1954, his feast was included on the regular calendar and could be celebrated more publicly and widely. But in 1970, when the Calendar of Saints was widely reorganized, his feast once again fell away, since so little is known of him and the feast was not known in antiquity.

Christians today are free to retain devotion to Saint Christopher, and there are some parishes that remember him locally through the use of votive Masses.

RELICS

Q: **There are many relics of the true cross about. Where did they come from? How do we know they are true? And is there a large chunk of it somewhere?** — *Joseph Vasut*

The largest relic of the true cross is said to be in the Monastery of Santo Toribio de Liébana, Spain, and it is twenty-five by fifteen inches. Relics of the true cross originated when Saint Helena (the mother of Emperor Constantine) was shown the hiding place of the wood and nails. From there, tiny slivers were eventually spread throughout the world.

The authenticity of each relic is difficult to directly verify. Usually, the authenticity is indirectly given when the relic exhibits power to heal or is effective against demons in exorcisms and the like. As such they self-authenticate. But very ancient relics such as the true cross must ultimately be accepted with faith, rooted in evidence of their power.

Q: **An organization has been sending me what they term "relics" of Padre Pio. It is a small square of cloth encapsulated on a small plaque of the saint. I do not wish to receive these items, which are sent to solicit money, but I am reluctant to just throw them in the trash. How am I to treat these items?** — *Chris Wroblewski*

It sounds as though you are describing a third-class relic. A first-class relic is a part of the body of a saint, usually a fragment of a bone or perhaps a lock of hair. A second-class relic is some article owned by a canonized saint, usually an article of clothing or some other personal object associated with the saint. A third-class relic is something, usually a cloth of some sort, which is merely touched to a first- or second-class relic.

One may serenely dispose of third-class relics. Most piously and properly this is done by burning or burying it. Merely pitching such things in the trash is probably to be avoided, though there is no absolute Church norm related to the disposal of third-class relics.

The practice of mailing or placing these third-class relics in the hands of the faithful may, at times, seem annoying. But here, too, there are no absolute Church norms forbidding such a practice, or of mailing third-class relics. This is quite different from first-class relics, of which significant Church norms and laws are involved.

Q:I am confused by the admonition of the Church on burial and against spreading ashes in light of the practice of dividing the remains of saints and scattering them throughout the world. — *Jenifer*

There are important differences between the practices. Relics usually involve small portions of the body, such as bone fragments, to be reserved for veneration. Thus the entire body of a saint is not "scattered" throughout the world, or even scattered locally as with strewn ashes.

Second, the relic of the saint is retained for veneration as a kind of physical and visual memory, whereas scattered ashes are spread in order to disappear and return to the elements. And while some may find this meaningful, the result is that any physical reminder of the person is lost. This is quite different from a relic.

Third, with a relic, the physical presence of a small portion of the body is treated with reverence, much as a gravesite would be, and prayers are often said in its presence in acknowledgment of the given saint. In the case of scattered ashes, neither the ashes nor the place of their dispersal receives the same kind of veneration, and may in fact be tread upon by human beings unaware of their presence and by wild animals.

While it will be admitted that burial practices have some variance across cultures, the current practice of the Church, out of respect for ancient Christian practice and current sensibilities, is to insist that human remains of any sort be buried or entombed. A January 2012 newsletter for the U.S. bishops' Committee on Divine Worship had this to say about the disposition of cremated bodies: "The cremated remains should be buried in a grave or entombed in a mausoleum or columbarium [a cemetery vault designed for urns containing ashes of the dead]. The practice of scattering cremated remains on the sea, from the air, or on the ground, or keeping cremated remains in the home of a relative or friend of the deceased are not the reverent disposition that the Church requires."

Q.I have inherited a first-class relic. Are there any norms for what I should do or not do with the relic?
— *Kathy Keffler*

Other than a brief mention in Canon 1190 forbidding the sale of relics, there are surprisingly few directions on the care of relics.

Certainly, relics are meant to be reverently kept, and ought not be simply cast in a drawer or some forgotten place. Ideally, they are put in an ostensorium, a display vessel easily purchased in most Catholic bookstores, shrine gift shops, or catalogs. Relics ought to be displayed in a suitable place of prayer in one's house. It would be best if the location was uncluttered of other more worldly things like souvenirs, collectibles, etc. If the possession of relics is not conducive to one's spiritual life, they ought to be given to another who might benefit or be placed in the care of the local parish.

Relics are meant to remind us of the saints, their stories, and what God can do even with weak human flesh. They should summon us to prayer and trust. But they ought not to be regarded superstitiously as if their mere presence could ward off all suffering or work independently of the will of God. The great wish and prayer of any saint is that we know and love God and that we be conformed to his will and plan for us.

Q.I just returned from a pilgrimage to Quebec City and visited the Shrine of Saint Anne de Beaupre. In the basilica, there is a reliquary containing the forearm of Saint Anne, mother of the Virgin Mary. I have faith, and believe, but I wonder how we could have such a relic and know that it is authentic. Is there some light you can shed on this? — *Jeannine Aucoin*

The veneration of relics is both commended by the Church and regulated by the Code of Canon Law (see 1186–90).

Among the practices of the Church in more recent centuries is to insist that relics be authenticated. Various individuals within the Church do this, for example, the postulator of the cause for sainthood of a man or woman, or the general superior of a religious congregation who has custody of the body of a saint from their community. They supply a modest amount of relics from the body of the saint or blessed and attest to the validity of the relic. Proper evidence is submitted to one of various Roman curial offices, and a certificate of authenticity is issued from there. In addition, the reliquary in which the relic is placed has a wax seal affixed to it which also has a stamp of authenticity.

In this way, the Church seeks both to authenticate the relics in question and to protect the faithful from fraudulent claims. The system works reasonably well for the relics of more recent saints. However, it is obvious that a relic of Saint Anne, the mother of Mary, would predate any such system.

Clearly, the Basilica of Saint Anne has ecclesiastical permission to display the relic, but how can we be certain of its authenticity? In a direct sense we cannot, if by certainty is meant direct physical and documented evidence of the origin of the bone, traced directly to the known burial site of the saint. No sort of evidence exists for a relic like this.

However, indirect evidence may exist in the documented handing down of the relic from antiquity. Another indirect evidence of authenticity is the healings and conversions that the relic brings by God's grace. Indeed, there is a long history of numerous healings taking place at the Basilica of Saint Anne in Quebec City. Many crutches and other testimonies of healings are found in the church. And, in this sense, many, especially older relics, are validated by the experience of the faithful.

While the faithful are not required to believe in relics, the veneration of them is both permitted and commended by the Church. Many testify to the consoling presence and healing power that relics bring, much like a mother who lost a child is consoled by the presence of a lock of that child's hair and feels somehow connected to that child.

FASTING AND ABSTINENCE

Q: **I have heard that Advent used to be a time to fast, much like Lent. Is this so, and what should we do?** — *Steven Acton*

This is true. Advent was once treated more like Lent than it is today, though perhaps with less intensity. The use of purple vestments and the elimination of the *Gloria* in Mass speak to the older practices as well. For the record, there were also other days in the past, such as "ember days" at the change of the seasons, that involved some fasting or abstinence. That said, current Church documents do not call Advent a penitential season per se, and penitential practices are not currently required of Catholics in Advent.

In my own life, I usually do give up something for Advent. Since there is no requirement to do this, it increases the devotional (loving) aspect. Even in Lent, abstaining from some lawful pleasure is a personal devotion, not a strict requirement of the Church. There is only a very mitigated fast on Ash Wednesday and Good Friday, and an abstinence from meat on Fridays of Lent.

So, a small token of penitence in Advent, and even more so in Lent, is to be encouraged. It is less observed today, but should not be forgotten.

Q. At a Friday funeral in Lent, the visiting priest told the faithful that, since food had been prepared that contained meat for the luncheon after the funeral, we could be dispensed from our obligation and eat it. But the pastor came to the reception and publicly reprimanded the visiting priest for doing this. We all wondered if we had done something wrong by eating it. — *Sandy Vignali*

From a juridical point of view, it does not pertain to a visiting priest to dispense congregants from observing specific aspects of the precepts of the Church. When dispensations can be granted (such as in a case like this), that is usually the prerogative of the bishop or pastor. Hence the visiting priest was wrong to do this.

However, one is left to wonder as to why the pastor chose to publicly indicate his irritation, especially at the particularly awkward moment when the very meal was being enjoyed. One might wish he had discussed his concerns discreetly with the priest who transgressed the proper jurisdictional norms.

As for the assembled people of God, they did nothing wrong: They acted in good faith, presuming they had the dispensation needed.

Q. What is the rule about eating meat on Fridays? Is it only a Lenten requirement? — *Name withheld*

Currently, Latin-rite (Roman) Catholics in the United States are directed not to eat meat only on the Fridays of Lent (and Ash Wednesday). On other Fridays of the year, Catholics in the United States are free to substitute other observances to commemorate the Lord's passion, and the requirement to refrain from meat (under pain of sin) no longer binds.

The bishops still encourage abstaining from meat on all Fridays and direct that if that is not chosen some other abstention or practice is to be observed. Here, too, this is not directed under pain of sin, but rather by way of encouragement so that Catholics freely undertake an observance of the Lord's passion that best suits them. They should also avoid scrupulosity in their own case or harsh judgments of others.

Note that Catholics in other parts of the world may have other norms from their bishops, and Catholics from Eastern rites also follow norms set by their bishops. Among Latin-rite Catholic bishops in the United States, some find the current norms too vague and lament the loss of a more common Catholic practice. Future years may see more specific norms such as recently were restored in England.

Q: **The Church abolished most of the norms regulating "meatless Fridays" and declared Fridays outside of Lent merely as "a day of penance." Does the penance have to be performed on Friday, and are there any parameters to observe?** — *Peter Stein*

Generally, the penance should be performed on the Friday, though exceptions can be made due to other obligations such as attending family or civic celebrations. Strictly speaking, one can work out deferrals or dispensations in regard to Friday observances with their pastor, but practically most simply work through this on their own.

The thinking back in the 1970s, when "meatless Fridays" were substituted with a day of penance, was to offer other observances to people on Friday. Simply giving up meat and going to Red Lobster was hardly a penance for most, though the law was being observed technically. Hence the new norm became to permit any range of penances, from giving up other things to taking on special prayers or works of charity.

But as your question implies, it is difficult to follow an uncertain trumpet, and many Catholics simply drifted from any Friday observance with such wide-open parameters. Psychologically, it would seem that having a clear focus is necessary to assist in such practices. Hence some bishops' conferences are going back to meatless Fridays.

Here in America that is not yet the case, though there is some discussion ongoing. For now, you are largely free to determine how to observe Friday, presuming it has a penitential character. It could be to abstain from something good, or to take on some pious or charitable work.

TITHING

Q.•Can you cite a scriptural reference [that] supports •tithing? — *Norbert Gorny*

The Book of Malachi says: "Will man rob God? Yet you are robbing me.... In your tithes and offerings. Bring the full tithes into the storehouse, that there may be food in my house; and thereby put me to the test, says the LORD of hosts, if I will not open the windows of heaven for you and pour down for you an overflowing blessing" (3:8,10)

In the New Testament, Jesus references tithing when he says, "Woe to you, scribes and Pharisees, hypocrites! for you tithe mint and dill and cummin, and have neglected the weightier matters of the law, justice and mercy and faith; these you ought to have done, without neglecting the others" (Mt 23:23). Note that in this text, while the Lord speaks of weightier matters than tithing, he says, regarding tithing, that we should not neglect it.

The Church does not require an absolute adherence to the biblical tithe — that is, giving one-tenth of our income to the Church. Nevertheless, there is a precept that Catholics contribute to the mission of Church. While details are left to the individual conscience, tithing is a long and ancient tradition. As Malachi 3 explains, tithing is not merely an obligation; it also opens the doors to many blessings.

Q. I overheard a Baptist coworker explaining to his wife that the pastor was requiring him to submit his W-2 form so that his tithe could be properly monitored. Is this right? — *K. Tanty*

Tithing — that is, giving 10 percent of one's income to the Church — is a commendable practice and rooted in Scripture. But for a pastor to insist on tax documents seems far too intrusive. It is not something that would be tolerated in the Catholic Church.

Not only is the pastor intruding into private matters of a congregant, but it also manifests a lack of trust, where a pastor ought to assume that a parishioner has discerned their proper level of giving with God. Accountability has its place, but investigations rooted in suspicion rather than trust seem wholly out of place in a Christian denomination.

INDULGENCES

Q. Indulgences used to be designated by time value: one hundred days, five hundred days, etc. Now, only the terms partial and plenary are used. Why the change? — *Peter Stein*

This change to "partial" or "plenary" occurred in 1968 when the *Enchiridion of Indulgences* was issued. There are several reasons this was done.

First, the designation of "days" did not originally reference time in purgatory. The origin likely had more to do with the penitential practices of the early Church, which were often lengthy and somewhat severe. Given this, one could visit Confessors of the Faith while in jail, or if he or she had once been jailed, for the practice of the Faith. These Confessors of the Faith were held in high esteem by the early Church, so such a visit, and the promise to say prayers, often resulted in time being knocked off one's penance by the bishop. Where and when this designation of days, weeks, and years came to be applied to the souls in purgatory by the faithful is not exactly clear.

The second problem in designating time values to indulgences is that we are not certain that purgatory runs on an earth clock. How time passes there, or if there *is* time, or how time here relates to time there, is all uncertain.

The third problem is that the merit of a prayer or action depends not only on the action done, but on the dispositions and state of the soul of those who undertake them. Exactly how fruitful the saying of a Rosary is may not be something we can simply gauge by assigning a number.

Most prayers are not sacraments but sacramentals. Even indulgenced acts related to the reception of the sacraments do not pertain to the sacrament itself, but to the fruitfulness of the reception of it and the application of those fruits to another. Therefore, we are not speaking of something that works automatically (*ex opere operato*), but rather something that depends for its fruitfulness to a large extent on the disposition of the one who does it (*ex opere operantis*).

Most people did find the old system of days, weeks, and years to be helpful in gauging the general fruitfulness of certain acts or prayers. These days, however, the Church seems to prefer to leave matters such as this less clearly specified for all the reasons stated. And while common sense might value the Rosary above a brief prayer or aspiration, even here it is sometimes best to leave things up to God, who sees not only the appearance, but looks into the heart.

Q. I am told that on All Souls' Day, if we make six visits to six churches and say designated prayers, the souls in purgatory for whom we pray go straight to heaven. What do you think of this? — *Name withheld*

There are many danger signs in the practices you describe. We ought to be cautious about various spiritual practices or exercises that have many different moving parts or complex requirements. We ought to be even more suspicious of unqualified and overly certain promises of success.

At the heart of indulgence practices is a proper notion that prayer has salutary effects. However, prayer should not be reduced to superstitious practices. We cannot force God's hand; neither should prayer be likened to magic, which seeks to manipulate reality. Every pious practice and prayer is always submitted to God's will, and through these things we commend ourselves to God's good graces, knowing that he will answer in ways that are ultimately best for all involved.

Q. Why are indulgences seldom preached or taught? Even in RCIA we tend to emphasize the relief of going to purgatory more than the idea that we should avoid going there. Indulgences are a game changer, especially the Apostolic Pardon given to the dying granting a plenary indulgence. — *Christine Gubbins*

Pastoral strategies often involve complex issues at the intersection of culture, faith, and what people can reasonably retain with all the proper distinctions in mind. Indulgences are a particularly complex issue and involve careful theological concepts of merit, faith, works, grace, and sanctification.

While plenary indulgences are a great gift of God to the Church's treasury of merit, they are difficult to obtain, since one must be free from attachment to all sin. The complexity and diffi-

culty of attaining plenary indulgences probably explains the sub-
dued emphasis you cite.

You are right that more should be said of the power of prayer
and holy works in helping us to avoid the need for purgation at all.
But most people die far from the perfection promised by the Lord
and required for full entrance to the heavenly realms (see Mt 5:48;
Rv 21:27).

EXORCISMS

Q. •I noticed that Pope Francis is giving greater recog-
•nition to exorcists and exorcism. My own pastor,
**however, sees this as a problem and seems to be a critic of
exorcism. Why would a priest be critical of this?** — *Name
withheld*

It is indeed a good thing that the pope has given encouragement to
the ministry of exorcism. It is proper that we recover an important
part of our spiritual tradition which has been significantly lost, especially here in America during the past forty years.

While I cannot read the mind of the priest critic you cite, we
might do well to interpret his remarks as concerns rather than
outright rejection. For, as in most areas of pastoral life, there are
pitfalls and exaggerations to be avoided.

Those who practice deliverance ministry, to include the ministry of formal exorcism, are quite aware that demons often interact with a host of spiritual, emotional, and mental struggles in
people's lives. And many people (not all) who approach the Church
are often desperate for solutions and hope for something simple
and quick. Alas, it is not usually simple or quick. Deliverance ministry more often involves a lengthy and multifaceted approach,
which includes deliverance prayers (and more rarely the prayers

of major exorcism) along with the sacraments, spiritual direction, and in some cases psychotherapy and psychiatric interventions. We want to avoid a kind of magical thinking, wherein it is supposed that the mere recitation of the prayers — without undertaking other avenues of spiritual growth — will bring quick results.

Another pastoral struggle involved in deliverance ministry is that many people today often ascribe exaggerated powers to demons, and at the same time underestimate the power of angels, of sacraments, of prayer, of the Word of God, and of the grace of Jesus Christ. For example, someone might say, "I was cursed by an ancestor and that is why I am locked in this mess." Okay, but what of the fact that you have been baptized, claimed for Christ, and blessed on countless occasions in the liturgy and by the reception of sacraments?

Those who seek deliverance ministry (to include exorcism) must seek to grow in faith in the power of the sacraments, and of steady growth in the spiritual life. All of us must lay hold of the truth that Jesus Christ is more powerful than any demon, including Satan himself, and thereby not give way to exaggerated or superstitious fears.

Hence, like most other things in the spiritual life, growing in faith and holiness is at the heart of the solution. The prayers can help and should be offered. Cynicism about exorcism and ascribing it to the "lunatic fringe" of the Church is neither healthy nor true to our spiritual tradition. But exorcism is not magic; it is a journey in faith.

Q. In our diocese, it is very hard to get an exorcism performed. I thought that Rome had insisted that this ancient rite be restored and made more available. — *Name withheld*

Your summation of Rome's stance is correct but incomplete. The faithful do have a right to pastoral care when demonic possession is suspected, and each diocese ought to have some way of addressing the concerns.

But step one is always to assess each case to determine if there is true possession or perhaps a lesser form of demonic oppression. Sometimes, too, there are natural causes related to behavioral problems and mental or spiritual struggles.

True demonic possession is rare, and the Rite of Exorcism indicates that the exorcist must not too easily conclude possession. There must be significant certainty, based on expected signs, that a person is possessed. Performing major exorcism on a person who is not possessed can cause great harm psychologically, spiritually, emotionally, and even physically. Given the rarity of possession and the intensity of exorcism, it should, like surgery, be considered only for cases that are clear, serious, and admit of no other cause or solution.

I cannot judge the situation in your diocese, and whatever procedures are used to determine possession are going to be discreet. It is certainly to be hoped that, in any diocese, if true possession is identified, an exorcist is appointed. Likewise, in the majority of cases where there are lesser forms of demonic oppression, some sort of deliverance ministry is needed and helpful.

Q•**I am an eighty-six-year-old Catholic, and I am trying to remember the three signs of demonic possession that I was taught. I seem to recall that they are coldness, objects moving by themselves, and the third I can't remember. Can you help me remember?** — *Michael Valko*

These would not be the signs that an exorcist is instructed to look for. The Old Rite of Exorcism stated three signs, and the new rite (of 1999) added a fourth. The signs are these: "Speaking a number of words in an unknown language or understanding someone speaking [in it]; making known distant and hidden events; showing strength beyond the nature of the individual's age or condition ... vehement aversion to God, the Most Holy Name of Jesus, the Blessed Virgin Mary and the Saints, the Church, the Word of God, sacred things and rites, especially sacramental ones, and from sacred images" (*De Exorcisimis*, 16)

These aversions and capacities are manifest in the person when in the possessed state. Those who are possessed are not in the possessed state all day, every day. Rather, they go in and out of the state, usually with increasing frequency as the possession gets deeper.

To determine possession, the exorcist is instructed in the preface of the Rite of Exorcism not to easily believe a person is possessed. He should rule out natural causes, to include physical and psychological causes as well as spiritual, along with poor religious instruction which may cause some individuals to easily conclude diabolical causes and overlook other sources, such as their own sin and the influence of the world.

Usually the exorcist will pray over someone thought to be possessed using certain selected prayers and look for the four signs. Merely detecting aversion to sacred things is usually not enough. He will usually look for at least one of the other signs as well.

Not finding sufficient cause to conclude possession does not mean there is no diabolical influence. If one is not possessed, they may be suffering a lesser form of attack known as oppression. In such cases, deliverance prayers and ongoing spiritual care are called for rather than major exorcism.

Q.Why doesn't the Church speak more about exorcism and have exorcists speak out more about possession? — *Name withheld*

Major exorcism is a matter of supreme discretion and confidentiality. The identity of the diocesan exorcist is not generally made known, except to those who need to know.

While procedures in dioceses vary a bit, it is most common that the exorcist works with a team that includes at least one other priest, a medical doctor, and a properly trained psychotherapist who all assist in the assessment of whether a person is actually possessed.

If major exorcism is considered advisable, the exorcist proceeds with it, but only with the explicit approval of the bishop, who must concur with the judgment to go ahead with the major exorcism. Here, too, the exorcist should never work alone, but with at least one other assisting priest and an appropriate team. It is almost never the case that exorcism is a one-and-you're-done scenario. Generally, exorcisms are conducted over a series of sessions, sometimes weeks or months apart.

If one suspects demonic possession, the first place to begin inquiry is always with the parish priest or another trusted priest. If that priest has reason to suspect possession (rather than obsession or torment), then he should contact the diocese and request consultation with the appointed exorcist.

PART VII

OTHER
TOPICS

HUMAN ORIGINS

Q.A friend at work says Catholicism cannot be reconciled with evolution. What is the teaching here? — *Arthur Johnson*

There is no formal Church teaching which requires Catholics to accept or reject the scientific theory of evolution — namely, that present and more complex forms of life may have evolved from simpler or more basic forms of life.

However, there are some aspects related to evolutionary theory that tend to run afoul of certain Church and scriptural teachings. First, many evolutionists insist upon a type of "blind evolution" through which genetic mutations happen as completely random acts. This form of evolution rules out any intelligent or intentional cause behind the evolutionary process. Such an insistence runs contrary to Scripture's assertion that God intelligently and intentionally creates all things and guides whatever evolution does take place.

There really isn't a reason that evolutionists must insist the process behind evolution is utterly blind and random. It is possible simply to observe evolution, without rendering an opinion as to the exact cause of it. The cause, currently unknown to science, is frankly beyond the realm of what science is designed to study. To insist that evolution is an unguided and blind process is actually a metaphysical claim. But physical sciences study only the physical world; they are not designed to study the metaphysical. Frankly, there's a lot of evidence that things evolve in this world in an orderly, not random, way.

The second problem related to evolution is more technical and complex. It is the problem of polygenism versus monogenism. Polygenism emphasizes that human beings emerged from some group of hominids. Monogenism would hold that we all emerged from one set of parents (whom the Bible names Adam and Eve).

While Catholics are not absolutely forbidden from holding poly-genism, the Vatican has warned over the years that it is difficult to square this teaching with the doctrine of original sin. That doctrine teaches that original sin comes from one man, Adam, not from a tribe of early human descendants of hominids who erred.

The bottom line of all this is that, while Catholics are free to accept or reject the fundamental scientific theory of evolution, we cannot accept the theory uncritically and with no distinctions at all. There are aspects related to the theory such as those described above which require critique.

Q. **I get frequent questions from parishioners about the need to "reformulate" our Genesis-based under-standing of Creation and the Fall, based on scientific find-ings of the age of the universe and its origin. How do you answer critiques that point to this apparent conflict be-tween faith and science?** — *Rev. Donald Wright*

I am not sure that we have to reformulate anything. The Genesis account does not propose to us a literalistic and scientific account of the origins of the cosmos. The Genesis account of the Fall "uses figurative language, but affirms a primeval event" (CCC 390).

So, the accounts of Creation and the Fall are describing ac-tual events and God's sovereign acts, but use figurative and poetic language. For example, what does it mean in the Genesis account to speak of a day when the sun and moon are not created until the fourth day? How can evening come and morning follow before there is a sun (see Gn 1:8)? Thus "day" may indicate an era or period of time.

Further, there are actually two accounts of creation in Genesis (see Gn 1:1—2:3; and Gn 2:4–25). The two are quite different, revers-ing the order of creation. So, Scripture speaks to the truth of God as creator and sustainer of all things but does not propose to us a strict, univocal account of the details.

There need not be an intrinsic conflict between what Genesis affirms and what science, using its terminology, affirms. That said, Darwinism's notion that the process of evolution is utterly blind and due to random mutations (rather than guided by an intelligent design) is not something a Catholic can accept. I would argue that this is not even a proper scientific thesis, since it cannot explain the non-entropic way in which matter has gone from simplicity to complexity. Neither can it explain the intricate design at every level of creation.

Q.**You recently wrote that Adam and Eve are (theologically) considered the first human beings. And though God gave them rational souls, he may have developed the physical aspect of man through evolution. However, it seems interesting that some of the hominids that precede Homo sapiens seem to have some rational tendencies, such as burying the dead and fashioning tools and the like. Does this mean their brains were developed enough to know more values such as [right and] wrong? —** *Steve Brestic*

Exactly what they knew is somewhat speculative. Even some nonrational animals today show some signs of social behaviors such as organized hunting, etc. Reward and punishment can also condition animal behavior. However, this does not mean they are engaging in moral reasoning or accessing metaphysical concepts such as justice, right, and wrong. Further, moral reasoning and accountability presuppose freedom. Be we do not presuppose freedom in nonrational animals, and thus we do not hold them morally accountable for their actions.

It was probably the same with these early hominids. Anthropologists will properly debate the "emergence" of the rational intellect and moral reasoning within their field, but theologically we posit the beginnings of this with the direct creation of the rational souls of Adam and Eve, which prescinds from matters of brain development, etc.

Q: Can a Catholic hold to the theory of evolution? — *Joe*

It depends on what is meant by evolution. If evolution merely means that creation took shape over a long period in stages, that is fine. But evolution is often presented by proponents insisting the whole process is utterly blind and caused by entirely random mutations. This insistence is not acceptable for a Catholic who should hold that God has intelligently and purposefully designed all things and still carefully guides and sustains all creation.

Frankly, the insistence that evolution is a blind, random process is not even good science, since science cannot prove this or speak to the primary causality of all things. That is a metaphysical question beyond the realm of the physical sciences.

Q: If we teach that life begins at conception, why do we account our age from the day of our birth? — *Victor Bunton*

We should recall that our modern understandings of fetal development have come a long way. So has our capacity to account for time in a more accurate way. Yet even with our more developed understanding of conception and fetal development, and our more accurate calendars and timepieces, it is not always easy to fix the exact date of our conception (and it might be a little rude to ask a lot of questions to do so).

I was born July 10, 1961, but all I can say is that I was conceived sometime in early October 1960. Birth, however, is a pretty clear demarcation. It is the day when everyone could see me and refer to an agreed-upon calendar date on the wall. While not denying that life begins at conception, fixing our age by the day of our birth is currently more practical and certain.

Q: •As I understand it, Catholic teaching tells us that •when Adam and Eve fell, creation also fell. But if nature had no say, why did it fall at all? — *Peter Tate*

Saint Paul indicates that creation was indeed affected by the fall of man: "For the creation was subjected to futility, not of its own will but by the will of him who subjected it in hope; because the creation itself will be set free from its bondage to decay" (Rom 8:20–21).

This was indicated also by God when he spoke to Adam: "Cursed is the ground because of you; / in toil you shall eat of it all the days of your life; / thorns and thistles it shall bring forth to you" (Gn 3:17–18).

Creation was indeed affected by our fall — God himself thus affected it. We are living in paradise lost, a created world that still manifests God's glory, but also the unruliness of sin by its chaotic and painful qualities.

However, your question seems to point more to the "fairness" issue: Why should nature be affected poorly by the sin of man? At one level let us be clear: It does not pertain to creation to "decide" one way or the other. Neither does it pertain to creation to merit reward, deserve punishment, or perceive injustice and be harmed in such a manner. The earth was given to us, and thus it is part of our punishment that our surroundings were affected by our sin.

In this sense, it is a simple ecological fact that our bad behavior can and does affect our world. Human sin can affect the world in any number of ways, including pollution, the squandering of resources, the loss of beauty, and the ruination of local ecosystems.

Theologically, creation is affected by our sin foremost because we are the pinnacle of material creation. To us God gave the mandate, "Be fruitful and multiply, and fill the earth and subdue it;

and have dominion over the fish of the sea, and over the birds of the air and over every living thing that moves upon the earth" (Gn 1:28). Having a degree of dominion, or headship, man affects everything under him. Where the head goes, the body follows.

Q. **It is said that Adam and Eve had preternatural gifts. What does "preternatural" mean, and what were these gifts?** — *Robert Bonsignore*

The term preternatural in traditional theology refers to something that is rare but nevertheless happens by the agency of created beings. It is distinct from what is supernatural, which refers to acts of God. Today preternatural acts are sometimes called marvels.

The word preternatural comes from the Latin *praeter* (beside) and *natura* (nature). The word supernatural comes from the Latin *super* (above) and *natura* (nature). Thus theologians emphasize that only God has the power to disregard the laws of nature, which he has created. Only he can do supernatural things. Demons, however, and more rarely humans, may be able at times to manipulate the laws of nature, but not supersede it. They cannot really move from the preternatural to the supernatural and work genuine miracles.

That Adam and Eve are said to have had preternatural gifts refers specifically to three gifts they had: bodily immortality, integrity, and infused knowledge. These are called preternatural because they are not strictly due to human nature but do not necessarily surpass the capacities of created nature as such.

Bodily immortality means that they would not have died. Integrity meant that there was a harmonious relationship between flesh and spirit since their passions were completely subordinated to their reason. Infused knowledge refers to the fact that their intellects had knowledge granted them by God immediately, rather than in the usual way, through the senses by learning and experience. Hence they knew of God and his laws more intuitively since the knowledge was infused (poured in).

Q. Did people 10,000 years ago have a soul, or did it just start with Adam and Eve? — *Francis Phielx*

The wording of your question presents a couple of difficulties in presenting an answer. First of all, we're not sure exactly when Adam and Eve lived; it may have been a good bit longer than 10,000 years ago. The shorter time frames for human history often emerge from a literal reading of biblical dates and time frames, which is not necessarily required of a Catholic.

Nevertheless, whenever Adam and Eve lived, your question still stands. But here, too, the wording of your question presents the need for a distinction. We would not speak of the hominids that existed before Adam and Eve as people, or persons. According to widely accepted Catholic and philosophical tradition, a person is an individual substance of a rational nature. Hence human beings who have a rational soul are persons; so are angels, and so are the three members of the Blessed Trinity. Animals, however — to include primates — are not persons, for they have no rational soul.

If it is true that we in some way physically emerged from prehistoric primates (a widely held scientific theory), we could not speak of them as having a rational soul until God acted to directly create Adam and Eve, infusing them with a rational soul. Even if our animal or physical nature may be said to have evolved, the human soul is directly created by God, and we are now dealing with a new reality: no mere advanced primate, but the creation of the human persons Adam and Eve.

With these distinctions in mind, the answer to your question is: No, the primates who existed prior to Adam and Eve had no rational soul. However, they may, like all living things, be said to have had a nonrational soul. This is because, philosophically, the soul is the animating principle of a living thing. Hence animals have a type of soul.

What makes humans different is that we have a rational soul, sometimes referred to as the spirit. On account of this, we are able to think and grasp metaphysical concepts like justice, beauty, meaning, and truth. It is the spiritual aspect of our soul that makes us capable of relating to God.

Q. What does the Church believe about extraterrestrials? — *Elena*

The Church has no direct teaching on this matter. As such, Catholics are free to speculate. But, using Catholic and scientific principles, some of the following parameters and distinctions may be interesting or helpful.

First, we ought to define "extraterrestrials." If by this term we mean persons, then it is clear that there are myriads of extraterrestrials, since angels are persons. We are human persons, but they are angelic persons. And, since it is the teaching of the Church that God makes use of his angels to guide all his creation, then angels are everywhere in the universe, assisting in God's governance of all things.

If by extraterrestrials you mean biological life of any sort, all the way from simple paramecia to more complex life forms, it seems likely that there is some of this sort of life out there, especially less complex forms of life.

If, however, you mean humanlike creatures with physical bodies and rational souls, the likelihood drops significantly, but is not zero. Some today argue for thousands or even millions of places where humanlike life could emerge. Others say such places are exceedingly rare. Both sides use statistics.

Those who think there are many earthlike planets capable of sustaining humanlike life-forms point to the vast size of the universe with billions of galaxies, each with billions of stars and presumably a lot of planets. They argue that, statistically, there must be many stars with planets like our own.

Others, however, point out that for the earth to be what it is, and to be able to support our kind of intelligent life, is not just the result of a few factors. It is the result of hundreds, even thousands of factors. The sun must be stable, and just the right kind of sun without too much of the wrong radiation. The planet must have an orbit that is closer to a circle than a steep ellipse (earth is only three degrees from a perfect circle, whereas most of the other planets in our solar system have a steep ellipse that brings them relatively closer to the sun and then farther away. The atmosphere must have just the right kind of gases. It must be a volcanic planet that generates those gases and also generates a magnetic field that deflects the most harmful rays of the sun. The earth also benefits from Jupiter and Saturn nearby, catching comets and other space debris. The earth also has a good balance of land and water, and the continents are rather evenly distributed. This limits deserts and other weather extremes. Earth also has a steady rotation on a good axis that permits seasons, and the proper distribution of rain, and an almost perfect relationship with the moon so that tides are steady and ocean currents are assisted. The list could go on for a long time. However, the statistical probability of all these same sorts of things coming together in this or similar combination on distant planets is rather low. There is just a kind of "God-given" perfection to earth that is hard to replicate statistically. Scientifically, this is called "rare earth theory."

All that said, there are no theological problems with holding that there is intelligent, humanlike life on other planets. But even if there is, we would still have to ask: Do they have free will? Do they have a conscience? Has God revealed himself to them? How? Did they sin and need redemption? Did God join their race or family by becoming one of them? Will they go to heaven? If so, why has no one who has had a vision of heaven ever seen them there?

At any rate, the speculations could become numerous. As for us now, God has not revealed anything specifically about life elsewhere. Evidently, he does not think we need to know too much about this. Thus we do well to spend only a little time wondering about it.

SUFFERING

Q. A member of my family is an atheist, hostile to faith, and likes to challenge me to explain how a loving God permits suffering. Is there an answer I can give? — *Name withheld*

It is perhaps too absolute to say the Church has "an answer" to suffering and why God permits it. The full answer to this is ultimately mysterious and has many aspects hidden from our view.

To be sure, we do have elements of an answer, which God reveals to us, or which human reason can supply. One element of an answer is the existence of human freedom. One way God could prevent a lot of suffering would be to cancel human freedom whenever it was abused. But God, it would seem, does not usually see fit to do so, and his respect for our freedom is very consistent.

Another aspect of an answer is that suffering often brings growth and opens new possibilities. Perhaps God sees these fruits and thereby allows some degree of suffering.

But again, these insights are only *part* of an answer. They do not constitute a full or complete answer to the great mystery of suffering and why God allows it. These insights tend to bring up even more questions. Fundamentally, we must accept that we do not have an absolute answer to the problem of suffering.

While it is fine that atheists raise this issue (for it is a valid question we all have), their demand for an absolute answer is not reasonable. We must also ask them to consider that not everything has a simple answer.

If they demand that I must absolutely answer the question, "Why is there suffering?" then I would like to ask them to give an absolute answer to these questions: Why is there love? Why is there generosity, a passion for justice, self-sacrificing heroism? Frankly, why is there anything at all?

If you and I must account for suffering — the negative side of our existence — then perhaps our critics should account for the existence of love. If they are honest, they will perhaps admit that while they can give a partial answer, they cannot fully account for these things.

The bottom line is, not everything can be absolutely answered. An unreasonable demand for answers from us, when they cannot supply answers to our questions either, is not itself a rational or adequate refutation of the existence of God.

Q: **I have grown exhausted and frustrated in waiting for God's healing in important matters. These are not frivolous concerns, and I am growing weaker in faith.** — *Name withheld*

I am sorry for your struggle and hope you will seek personal counsel with a priest or spiritually wise fellow Catholic. There is a great mystery to suffering and to God's apparent delay in alleviating our difficulties. I have learned, however, that I gain wisdom from struggles and have grown more from them than from what pleases me. I am hard to save, and sometimes God must use strong medicine.

It is true that God does sometimes delay. But he has his reasons. Some of them I have learned; some reasons I will have to wait to learn in eternity. Faith is less about getting what we want and more about accepting what God wills.

Q: **Given God's mercy, how do we explain devastating earthquakes and other natural disasters? It certainly tests our faith!** — *Gerald Olesen*

Part of the answer is that we cannot really know the full answer, since there is so much we don't see or understand. This was the basic answer that God gave Job, who asked the meaning of suffering in his own life. In effect, God challenged Job to explain how the stars were made, or the seas, or any other natural wonder (see Jb 38–39). And if Job could not understand those things, how could he think he would understand the meaning of suffering?

In seeking to understand the suffering of natural disasters you mention, recall that in the natural order there is a cycle of life, and in a remarkable way many of the troubles of creation also bring blessing. The molten and fiery center of our planet is responsible for earthquakes and volcanoes, but it also has a critical role in creating a magnetic field around the earth that protects us from the harmful radiation emitted from the sun. Volcanism also provides us with rich soils and gases in our atmosphere that are necessary for life. Therefore, were God simply to answer our prayer and stop some of these upheavals, other blessings might be lost, and the loss of life might be far worse, perhaps even total.

The point is, we see very little of the whole picture. God is like a master artist whose canvas is all of creation. We cannot see the entire picture — one dark pixel of the painting might alarm us, but if we could see the whole painting we would see that it is an interplay of light and darkness that makes for a beautiful masterpiece.

We might also recall that God offered us paradise, but Adam and Eve (and humanity has certainly ratified their choice) sought to live apart from that sheltered paradise, which existed only through trusting and obeying God. Hence we now live in "paradise lost," a place that still manifests God's glory but also the harm caused by original sin. For Adam's sin affected not only him, but the whole of creation. God said to Adam, "Cursed is the ground because of you" (Gn 3:17). And while it is not certain if the Garden of Eden would have had no natural upheavals, it seems fair to say that our sin intensified the chaos of creation in some mysterious way.

Q. My daughter-in-law was watching *The Bible* on TV, [and she] said she did not understand why Jesus had to suffer so much. I am not sure how to answer why his Father made him go through so much. — *Rose Haynick*

One of the difficulties in understanding why Jesus suffered for sinners is that many of us, especially in the modern world, tend to think of sin only in legal terms, as the breaking of some abstract rules. But sin causes real harm and has real effects, and these must be healed. Something actually has to happen.

For example, let us say that you see me near the edge of a cliff and warn me to take three steps to the right. But out of rebellion, I take three steps to the left and slide down the great cliff into an abyss. I lie there, injured and utterly incapable of ever rescuing myself. Let us then say, in my humiliation and pain, I cry out and ask you to forgive me. In your mercy, you say yes. And that is forgiveness. But in order for me to be healed and restored, you will now have to expend great effort to come down the steep cliff, care for my wounds, and carry me out of the abyss.

As I hope you can see by this analogy, my transgression was not simply the breaking of a rule. Deep and devastating effects happened in my life, and I was incapable of restoring myself. And this was our state; we were dead in our sins (see Col 2:13). We were incapable of ever restoring or healing ourselves.

Jesus, therefore, not only brought us God's forgiveness, but also extended the effort and agony to come down, heal our wounds, and lift us up. This was a great and painful effort. Our sinful disobedience had brought us suffering and death. Jesus took up that suffering and death in order to restore us, even elevate us to a higher place.

The horrible suffering of Jesus shows us very clearly how awful sin really is, how it disfigures, wounds, and even brings us death. These are realities, and Jesus takes them up in order to heal them and carry them away for us. We tend to make light of sin today. It is no light matter, and to remember that, we do well to look to any crucifix and see what love cost him.

Q **.** I cannot understand why a just and holy one like Je-
. sus had to die on the cross instead of God just doing away with Satan and evil. — *Roy Roberts*

The approach undertaken by God in addressing sin is one that is respectful of human and angelic freedom. Were God simply to come and do away with the choices made by angels or humans that he did not like, we would not really be free, since God would simply overrule our choices.

Adam and Eve were warned by God that great suffering and death would come from eating of the Tree of the Knowledge of Good and Evil. Nevertheless, tempted by the fallen angel Satan, they rejected what God said.

But God, accepting that they opted for the way of suffering and death, instead of canceling their decision or its consequences, took up suffering and death himself. Jesus, by his obedience to the Father, and though sinless, endured the full fury of suffering and death and never ceased saying yes to his Father. In so doing, he opened a way for us that does not cancel our original choice, but actually uses its consequences as a way back for us, through the way of the cross.

Q. If the Lord answered all prayers he heard, there would be no sickness, problems, etc. But since there is sickness and problems, one wonders if we should pray, and if God was really serious when he said, "Ask and you shall receive." — *Hugh Sweeney*

We always receive an answer from God. Sometimes the answer is "no." It does not follow that if God answered our requests there would be no trouble, since we do not know how to pray or what to ask for all that well. God wants us to ask, and he tells us in many ways to pray and ask for what we need. But he also tells us to trust that he knows what is truly best for us, not just what is apparently best. We simply cannot know all the implications for ourselves or others when we ask. But God does. And sometimes no is the best answer.

Q. Why do animals suffer? It is apparent that nature has always featured death, even before the fall of man. Therefore, I don't see how the Fall could explain why animals suffer. — *Pat*

If one draws simply from the Book of Genesis, then the answer is that death, violence, and chaos in nature all resulted from original sin. Not only were Adam and Eve affected by what they did, but all creation, too. God told Adam, "Cursed is the ground because of you" (Gn 3:17). In other words, paradise is no longer; death has entered the world, and sin is its cause.

Scripture links suffering and upheaval in creation to sin, but the relationship may not be as simple as cause and effect. Perhaps it is enough to say that our sin intensified the chaos of creation, but was not its only cause. As you observe, scientific evidence is strong that long before man or sin there were great upheavals in creation, and that animals, such as dinosaurs, killed one another for food, and that there was death, even mass extinctions.

Therefore, that animals suffer is linked to sin, but mysteriously to other things, too. Consider that there is a circle of life that seems apt for the world. God fashions and refashions using this cycle. Last year's leaves serve as nutrients in the soil for this year's growth. Hurricanes distribute heat from the equator toward the poles. Animals feed upon other animals, but also keep their populations in proper balance. There is a genius in the system that must be appreciated, even if it shocks some of our sensibilities.

And while it does seem clear that animals do suffer physical pain and experience fear, it may be that a lot of the suffering we impute to them may be a projection. Much of human suffering is rooted in our sense of self and our awareness of death. An animal does not necessarily go through all this. They may instinctually respond to danger in the moment and have little or no emotional feelings at all other than fear, which stimulates fight or flight. It is hard to say.

Ultimately, in matters like these, it may be best to admit that we do not have all the answers and are summoned to reverence the mystery that is before us. And suffering, be it human or animal, is a great mystery.

Q. **Since God knows all the harm that wicked people and demons cause, why does he permit them to exist at all, or, knowing the evil they would do, why not destroy them before, or even after, they do it?** — *Name withheld*

While a brief answer such as this space allows cannot possibly plumb the depths of the questions you raise, a few observations should be made.

First, it does not pertain to God to annihilate any rational creature he has made. Angels and men have an immortality that pertains to their souls; for humans, one day, to our bodies as well. Having given the gift of existence to persons (angelic and human), God never withdraws his gift. While it is true that demons and the human souls in hell have definitively rejected his love, God does not thereby cancel the love he has extended to them. He continues to sustain the life even of his enemies, though they choose to live apart from him and what he values.

Second, your question tends to put God within serial time, where time passes incrementally from future to present to past. So, the question occurs to us, "Why would God, at some time in the past, knowing what a person would do in the future, bring them into existence today?" But God does not live in or relate to time in this manner. For God, past present and future are all equally present. And thus, while God's inner life is mysterious, it is clear to us that God does not deliberate in the manner we do. Time does not unfold for God like it does for us. So, to some degree, even the way we phrase our questions is invalid. God does not ponder A, look forward to B, and then does C.

But let us for a moment assume God did act temporally in this way, and that at some point in the past God, knowing that a person would do horrible things in the future, considers their existence today. Let us say that, seeing the bad things they would do, he simply vetoes their existence.

What does this do, then, to human freedom? In effect, it cancels it. Why? Because if in knowing that a person will choose badly, God preemptively vetoes their existence, then the whole process of choosing God and his kingdom values is front-loaded, and none of us who do exist is really free. Freedom would only be theoretical, since no existing person actually can or ever did say "no." If we are not free to say no, we are not really free to say yes to God and love him.

Many more things related to the questions you raise could be said. But for now, let it be enough for us to say that the answers are caught up in the mysteries of God's love, time, and human freedom.

CATHOLIC TERMS AND CONCEPTS

Q: **.I have difficulty sorting out the differences between
•words we often use in the Church. How are words like
intellect, mind, heart, and conscience distinct? Or are they
all speaking to the same thing?** — *Bob Tisovich*

The intellect is that capacity of persons, both human and angelic,
to know beings (or things) in their essence and particularity. The
word intellect comes from the Latin *intellectus*. Its roots are from
inter (between) and *legere* (choose, discern, or read). Our intellect is
able to move beyond mere sensory data and knowing to a knowing
that is able both to group and distinguish things. So, by our intellect we can see this or that particular tree, and also abstract a form
called "tree-ness" in which things of that similar quality participate.
In this way we can see how things are both similar and distinct; how
things relate and how things fit together into a whole.

The word mind includes the intellect but is broader, especially in its biblical meaning. Biblically, the mind (*nous* in Greek)
is where "I" live; it is at the core of our being. It is that place where
memory, imagination, and knowing interact. It is that place where
we ponder, discern, and, interacting with our will, decide. It is that
deepest part of us where we can be alone with our thoughts and
with God.

Scripture will sometimes use the words mind and heart interchangeably, though heart will usually include more of a sense of
affections, aversions, and desires as well as thought.

The conscience is described rather experientially by the
Catechism as that place where "man discovers a law he has not laid
upon himself but which he must obey. Its voice, ever calling him to
love and to do what is good and to avoid evil, sounds in his heart
at the right moment.... For man has in his heart a law inscribed
by God.... His conscience is man's most secret core.... There he is
alone with God whose voice echoes in his depths" (1776). Thus the

conscience, though we must be formed to recognize its voice ever more clearly, echoes within us and informs and influences the mind and the heart, urges the will, and assists the intellect.

Q.**:** **A coworker of mine who claims to be an atheist is dismissive of anything beyond modern science and claims there is no scientific evidence for the soul, and that we are really just advanced apes. What can I say in answer to this?** — *Jason Reid*

It sounds like the coworker is a proponent of something called "scientism," which holds that the physical sciences can now, or one day will, wholly explain all reality, and that there is no reality beyond physical matter. The problem with such a claim is that it breaks the very rule it announces. For, to say there is no reality beyond the physical world is a metaphysical claim; it is a philosophical stance that the physical sciences cannot prove. In other words, he or she is using a nonscientific premise to try and prove that physical science gives a comprehensive explanation for all things.

That there are nonmaterial realities is not difficult to demonstrate. Justice, mercy, humility, beauty, and so forth are not physical, but they are real. And while these concepts surely interact with our physical brain, they themselves are metaphysical — that is, nonphysical. We would not be able to see justice and humility out having lunch together.

That we can grasp things beyond the physical world and discuss them points to the existence in us of a nonmaterial and rational soul. For, since action follows being, that we can apprehend nonmaterial concepts and make use of them points to a reality and faculty about us.

That human beings are different from animals (by having a rational soul) is demonstrable by mere observation. Though we physically resemble animals in many ways, there are dramatic differences. Animals do not build cities, form bicameral legislatures, or debate the common good; they do not write poems or collect accumulated knowledge in libraries; animals do not invent or show ingenuity, and show no appreciation for beauty, truth, or concern about death. Apes do not debate; they do not write on the topic of causality and engage their coworkers in nonmaterial topics such as justice or fortitude. They do not appreciate a Beethoven sonata or ponder an impressionistic painting. There is no "life of the mind" evident in them at all. And even if one may wish to show some rudiments of this in higher animals, the human person is so dramatically beyond these rudiments that we cannot reasonably conclude that the differences between human beings and animals is anything but vast.

All these differences point to the existence of the rational soul. In other words, we are more than merely advanced apes; we clearly have different faculties altogether. Perhaps in making such a claim your coworker bears some burden of proof. Perhaps he might be asked to prove that the soul does not exist, using science.

Q: I read a quote by Saint Augustine, which says, "Beauty is indeed a good gift of God; but that the good may not think it a great good, God dispenses it even to the wicked." Could you please explain further what this means? — *Name withheld*

Saint Augustine states this in *The City of God* (see XV, 22). Essentially, what Augustine is teaching is that we can become too focused on lesser goods and thereby neglect higher goods.

Physical beauty, though somewhat differently defined by people, does exist, and is a pleasant gift of God to behold. But we can esteem it too much, failing to realize that spiritual beauty, truth, goodness, holiness, and God himself are far greater gifts. Hence God signals the limits of physical beauty by often bestowing it on those who may seem undeserving of it, to teach us that physical beauty is a limited good.

Saint Augustine continues, "And thus beauty, which is indeed God's handiwork, but only a temporal, carnal, and lower kind of good, is not fitly loved in preference to God." The problem is not with beauty, but with us. Augustine adds, "When the miser prefers gold to justice, it is through no fault of the gold, but of the man; and so with every created thing."

Q. **I am a convert from the Evangelical Church, and my RCIA teacher told me that the seven days of creation in Genesis is a primitive mode of speaking and does not really mean seven days. Is this true?** — *Shelly*

The *Catechism* discourages the word "primitive" in reference to Scripture (see 304). A better Catholic approach is to describe the creation account as a poetic account, rather than a modern, scientific one.

If we try to hold to a purely literal reading of all the details, we have difficulties. For, if a "day" is a 24-hour cycle of the sun, it is surprising to read that the sun and moon were not even created until the fourth day. Further, if the account is purely a literal, scientific one, there is the problem that there are two accounts of creation in Genesis 1:1—2:3 and 2:4–25. The two are very different.

What is essential for us to hold from these accounts is that God made everything out of nothing, and he did so in wisdom and love, guiding every step. Though transcendent, he remains present and active in all he has made.

So, seven days is likely more poetic than scientific.

Q. I was taught that, once mankind was put out of paradise due to original sin, two distinct impediments to his return existed. First, he needed redemption, and this was supplied by Jesus on the cross. Second, he needed sanctification, and this is supplied by man in this life. A priest recently told me I was wrong. Am I, and how? — *David Bearss*

Your terminology and theology need a bit of refinement. You are correct in asserting that we were put out of paradise due to original sin. You are also correct in saying that Jesus has redeemed us — that is, he has purchased our salvation by his once-and-for-all perfect sacrifice on the cross.

However, man does not supply sanctification. Only God can sanctify so as to save us. It is true that works do accompany the gift of our faith. But these works are not so much the source of our sanctification as the result of it. Our works are God's gift to us. Scripture says, "For we are his workmanship, created in Christ Jesus for good works, which God prepared beforehand, that we should walk in them" (Eph 2:10). So, for us, all is gift, all is grace. Sanctification is a work of God in which we cooperate, and our merits are due to grace, not to our actions.

Finally, it is not God's will that we merely return to some earthly paradise. Rather, in his immense love, and despite our grievous fall, God has now willed to open heaven itself to us. Therefore, our redeemed state is greater than even our original state (before the Fall).

Q: We are taught that faith is a gift from God and that no one can come to Jesus unless the Father draws him (see Jn 6:44). But this seems to imply that God decides who will be saved and that we are not really free. — *Ben Johnson*

Not necessarily. If someone were to open their door and call to me to come into their home, I would be drawn by their voice. And the open, unlocked door would be a necessary component supplied by them for me to enter. However, none of that would compel me to enter, such that I lose my freedom.

Further, the notion that God does not will to save some seems to be set aside in 1 Timothy 2:4, which says, "[God] desires all men to be saved and to come to the knowledge of the truth."

There is, to be sure, a mysterious interaction between God's sovereignty and our free will, but we cannot resolve it by picking our freedom or God's sovereignty. We must hold both revealed truths in balance.

Q: I know that Saint Augustine wrote about predestination, and that John Calvin wrote about double predestination. Can you explain what they both taught and what the Church says about it? What are some things to think about as we reconcile free will with God's omniscience? — *Graham*

Predestination is a proper biblical concept which indicates that God chose us and called us before we were ever made to be his own. It does not deny that we freely chose him, but insists he first chose us, and thereby enabled us to choose him.

Scripture says, "Even as he chose us in him before the foundation of the world, that we should be holy and blameless before him. He destined us in love to be his sons through Jesus Christ, according to the purpose of his will" (Eph 1:4–5; see also Rom 8:29–30).

Predestination, understood in a way that does not cancel human freedom, is thus biblical and proper. Double predestination, however, as articulated by Calvin and others who followed him, is not biblical. Double predestination teaches, in effect, that some are destined by God from before their birth to go to heaven or hell and have no real choice. In other words, God sovereignly ordains the eternal destiny of every human being — the lost as well as the saved. Thus the damned are fated and destined to hell from before their birth.

But this is contrary to Scripture. God says, for example, "Have I any pleasure in the death of the wicked, says the Lord GOD, and not rather that he should turn from his way and live?" (Ez 18:23; see also 1 Tm 2:4). So, double predestination is wrong: God does not desire, will, or force anyone into hell. Only by freely choosing against heaven and the values of the kingdom of heaven does a person depart to hell — it is really each person's choice; God merely affirms it at the judgment.

An analogy that is sometimes used regarding predestination and double predestination is in reference to sports. In the NFL draft, certain players are chosen by certain teams. In this sense they are predestined to play for a certain team. However, they are not doubly predestined because they are not absolutely forced to play for that team. Though they might have to pay some financial penalties, etc., they are free simply to refuse to play for that team and insist on being available for another team. If they were legally forced to play for whatever team chose them, no matter what they thought or wished, this would be an example of double predestination. It would be akin to the Calvinist notion that people are chosen to go to heaven or hell no matter what they think or do.

What Calvin's double predestination is trying to do is to preserve the sovereignty of God. But it does so at the expense of another truth, the freedom of the human person. And this is the essence of all heresy: it takes two truths that are sometimes in tension and, in order to resolve the tension, discards one truth and embraces the other. The word heresy is rooted in a Greek term meaning to choose.

Orthodoxy, however, holds the balance and accepts the tension. The tension is embraced in humility that accepts the fact that the tension between God's sovereignty and our freedom is created by our own human limits in understanding.

Part of the mystery of predestination is that God lives outside of time and sees it comprehensively. God knows and sees the future and the past, along with the present, as one moment. But the fact that he knows something does not mean he causes or forces it. Even humanly, I might be able to see two trains moving toward each other on a track and know they are going to crash. But my knowing this does not mean I cause this.

Q. **I am trying to ponder how God knows all things and yet we have free will? Better minds than mine have thought about this, but how does that work exactly? How does predestination fit into all of this?** — *Charles*

Merely to know something is not the same as to cause something. Consider, for example, a married couple who has been going to the same restaurant every Friday for all forty-five years of their marriage. Now, every Friday, without fail, the husband orders apple pie a la mode for dessert. On a certain Friday, the waiter comes to get the dessert request. The wife knows exactly what the husband will order, and sure enough he does order apple pie a la mode. But her knowing this does not cause him to order it; she simply knew ahead of time what he would order, but he himself is the cause of his order. And it is similar with God. The mere fact that he knows what I will do does not of itself cause me to do it. I am no less free because God knows ahead of time what I will decide.

Now, of course, the interaction of God's knowledge and sovereignty with our freedom is also connected to the mystery of time. Time does not unfold for God like it does for us. For God, past, present, and future are all the same. God lives in a comprehensive *now*, where my yesterday is no less present to him than my future. God does not wait for me to do things. All of time is equally present to him. This sort of experience of time is very mysterious to us. We must therefore bring with us a great deal of humility when we speak of concepts such as predestination.

However we describe predestination, we cannot understand it in such a way that it cancels human freedom. The Scriptures do clearly teach that we make free choices for which we are responsible. And when Scripture does use the word predestined, it is not the same as predetermined. We are free. While God always knows what we will freely do, his knowledge does not replace our will.

Q: **I am trying to understand if soul and spirit are one and the same. Or is the spirit a separate part of our being?** — *Linus Langer*

Although Scripture sometimes uses the terms spirit and soul interchangeably, the human person remains properly described as having two essential parts: body and soul. The spirit is an aspect of the human soul, not a third part altogether.

In philosophical terms, the soul is the animating principle of any living thing. It is what makes it different from dead things. As such, animals and even plants have a soul, understood as this life-giving principle.

Human beings, however, have spiritual and rational souls. And this is demonstrable by the fact that we ponder the meaning and purpose of things, share knowledge, grow in understanding, and have built great bodies of knowledge in libraries and the development of the sciences. We have rationally deciphered not only many realities of the physical world but also the metaphysical world in comprehending things like justice, beauty, honor, and so forth.

It is this aspect of the human soul that is called the spirit, which distinguishes us from animals and other living things and gives us what theologians call a *capax Dei*, a capacity for God. It is through the spiritual aspect of our soul that God addresses us and that we have the capacity to hear him, understand, and make a response as free and responsible moral agents. In this aspect of our soul, we are capable of loving God and choosing him. It is also in the spiritual aspect of our soul that freedom is fundamentally operative.

This specialized aspect of the human soul is called the "spirit." To be clear, the human spirit is not the same as the Holy Spirit, the third person of the Blessed Trinity. He indwells the baptized and interacts with our human spirit, but the Holy Spirit is not the human spirit.

That said, neither are soul and spirit "one and the same" as your question sets forth, for the part of something is not the whole of it. Similarly, I and my hand, or I and my ability to think, are not one and the same, for I am more than one of my capacities or aspects.

Q. **According to Catholic teaching, what are ghosts? How does that fit with the particular judgment and purgatory?** — *Pauline*

Ghosts are not widely attested in Christian tradition. They tend to be more an element of folklore. However, Scripture does make mention of them. Saul conjured up the presence of Samuel through the witch of En-dor (see 1 Sm 28). Jesus was able to speak to Moses and Elijah on Mount Tabor, and when he appeared in his resurrected glory the disciples thought they were seeing a ghost (Lk 24:37). However, Church documents and rituals are silent when it comes to speaking of or dealing with ghosts. Some demonologists accept that human souls can appear from purgatory or from hell. And among hagiographers (those who study the lives of saints) there are also attested some apparitions of saints.

We can accept the existence of so-called ghosts, but the Christian tradition generally holds that such apparitions are rare. Demonologists caution that we should never speak to or seek contact with the dead so as to obtain knowledge from them. So-called divination (conjuring the dead) is most often saturated with superstition and fraud, and it is dangerous. Even with canonized saints, we should not easily seek simple communication from them. These apparitions are rare, and we ought only pay attention to approved apparitions.

In certain cases where recently deceased loved ones "appear," we must first rule out natural causes for their appearance. Sometimes sleep disorders and other mental struggles related to grief are at the roots of these appearances. However, when such causes have been reasonably set aside, the usual solution is to pray the Office of the Dead for them and offer Masses for the repose of their souls. It is possible the Lord has allowed some reminders to be sent to us that we should pray for the souls in purgatory. But, if recently deceased loved ones appear and do anything other than ask for prayers, most demonologists assume it is a trick of demons, and that in no way should conversations with such apparitions be undertaken.

Q.I have read prayers that ask blessings for the healing of body, soul, and spirit. I always thought that soul and spirit [are] the same thing. Are soul and spirit different, or are they the same? — *Jo Hadley*

Soul and spirit are often used interchangeably in modern English, and also to some extent in the Scriptures. The human spirit is not some third part of the human person, separate from the soul. Rather, as an aspect of the soul, the human spirit (as distinct from the Holy Spirit) is that aspect of our soul that opens us to God. Some theologians speak of this openness of our spirit as giving us *capax Dei* (a capacity for God) — that is to say, since our souls are spiritual and rational, we have the capacity to know and interact with God.

Also, the spirit is that aspect of our soul which most distinguishes us from the animals.

In this distinction of soul and spirit, the *Catechism* says the following: "Sometimes the soul is distinguished from the spirit: St. Paul for instance prays that God may sanctify his people 'wholly,' with 'spirit and soul and body' kept sound and blameless at the Lord's coming. The Church teaches that this distinction does not introduce a duality into the soul. 'Spirit' signifies that from creation man is ordered to a supernatural end and that his soul can gratuitously be raised beyond all it deserves to communion with God" (367).

Q. **If God made us to know him, love him, and serve him, why did he make some who will never be able to do this because they do not have all their faculties? —** *Thomas*

Your question seems to define "knowing" in merely intellectual terms. Yet knowing, in terms of faith, is something richer than a mere intellectual grasping of God.

Further, we cannot know fully the inner life of the mentally disabled. The same can be said for infants and very young children. I have a small memory of my early childhood, when I was perhaps five years old. I recall that I had great intimacy with God, who spoke to me simply and with love, and I to him. As I grew older, and my brain grew "bigger," my heart also seemed to diminish, and I lost that experience of intimacy with God. I have spent my later years trying to recover that early intimacy.

I do not offer this memory as proof that little children (or, by analogy, the mentally disabled) all have this intimacy, but only to indicate that there are mysteries in how God relates to us that cannot be simply reduced to high intellectual knowing.

It would seem, rather, that God relates to us in ways appropriate to our state. It would also seem we should at least be open to the possibility that the mentally disabled may have an intimacy with God that we of "able mind" can only admire as we seek to become more like little children, "for to such belongs the kingdom of God" (Mk 10:15).

Q. Is it right to say that we get our body from our parents and our soul from God? — *Robert Bonsignore*

This is perhaps too fine a distinction. Every good and perfect gift comes from above, from God. Hence our whole existence is given and sustained by God. It is perhaps more proper to say that God uses the secondary cause of our parents to fashion the material part of us we call the body, but he directly creates our soul. We ought not separate too strictly body and soul, which are both God's workmanship. Even regarding the body Scripture speaks of God as knitting us together in our mother's womb (see Ps 139:13).

Q. Why does the Catholic Church think certain terms and the spiritual gifts — for example, apostle, evangelist, speaking in tongues, healing, miracles, etc. — ended with the apostles? — *Steve Kwilos*

It is not taught by the Church that the charismatic (spiritual) gifts ended. Vibrant praise, speaking in tongues, and even words of prophecy are still evident. These gifts, and others, still exist and are often manifest in the Church, especially in charismatic Masses or prayer services. There are many healing Masses and prayers of deliverance.

The title "apostle" did give way and seems to have been restricted to those who had seen and walked with the Risen Christ. Perhaps out of deference to the apostles, the term shifted to "bishop," but the office remains the same. Though the apostle Saint Paul did not walk with Christ, he did see him in risen glory when he was struck down on the road to Damascus. The title "Evangelist" was used only of the four Gospel writers in any formal sense. And since no new gospels are to be written, that title is restricted in Catholic circles.

Q. The Church teaches that lay Catholics share in the priestly, prophetic, and kingly offices of Christ. Can you provide a fuller understanding of these offices and what limits or distinctions are in order? — *Mary McCarthy*

The *Catechism* affirms, "The anointing with sacred Chrism ... signifies the gift of the Holy Spirit to the newly baptized, who has become a Christian, that is, one 'anointed' by the Holy Spirit, incorporated into Christ who is anointed priest, prophet, and king" (1241).

The common priesthood of believers and the ministerial or hierarchical priesthood, while being ordered to one another, differ in essence. It is not simply a difference in degree, but a difference in kind.

Biblically, priests are those who offer sacrifice to God. Thus in the common priesthood of all the baptized believers are to offer their own life as a sacrifice to God, serving God and caring for all God's people. The whole life of a believer should be a sacrifice pleasing to God, as we offer our time, talent, and treasure. All the faithful are also called to offer a sacrifice of praise by taking part in the Sacred Liturgy, and in prayer in vivid and conscious ways, exercising roles in the Sacred Liturgy that are proper to the laity.

Prophets are those who speak for God, who are God's voice in the world. As prophets, believers must first hear and heed the Word of God and, having done so, proclaim the authentic Word of God to this world by what they say and do. Clearly, the prophet must proclaim only that which befits sound doctrine, only that which the Lord has revealed to his Church in the Scriptures and sacred Tradition.

Kings are those who exercise authority. And thus the baptized believer must first of all take authority over his or her own life. Believers must rule over their unruly passions, over disordered drives of the soul and body, and so forth.

Having gained self-mastery, Christians are also called to exercise lawful authority in this world. Of course, this must begin in the family with parents. But the royalty of the baptized must extend beyond merely the family into the whole world, as believers seek to extend the kingship of Christ throughout the entire social order.

Q.I was asked how people who lived in Old Testament times were really any different from New Testament Christians. We seem just as sinful and foolish, but also as virtuous as they were. I did not know how to answer this. What is the basic difference? — *Stewart Johnson*

The essential difference is grace. The prophet Ezekiel records God's promise to ancient Israel: "I [the Lord] will sprinkle clean water upon you, and you shall be clean from all your uncleannesses, and from all your idols I will cleanse you. A new heart I will give you, and a new spirit I will put within you; and I will take out of your flesh the heart of stone and give you a heart of flesh. And I will put my spirit within you, and cause you to walk in my statutes and be careful to observe my ordinances" (Ez 36:25–27).

This power that causes us to keep God's law is a gift of the Holy Spirit dwelling in us. This is, after our salvation from sin, the chief difference between those who lived before and after Jesus. It is the key difference between the Old and New Covenants.

Your observation that many things and people seem largely unchanged is a reminder, however, that grace is not a magic spell or something that forces our will. It makes great sanctity possible, but it does not force this upon us. We must be willing to cooperate with the indwelling Holy Spirit. The lives of the saints show what grace can do in us when we do not impede or refuse the Spirit's graces.

It is a sad truth that many do not really expect a great deal from their faith and their relationship with Jesus Christ. The normal Christian life is to be in a life-changing, transformative relationship with the Lord. It is to see sins put to death and virtues come alive; sorrow give way to joy; fears give way to confidence; and so forth. But most people do not expect much, do not seek much, and thus experience very little because they do not seek it. The Letter of James says, "You do not have because you do not ask" (4:2).

Saint Paul reminds us: "Therefore, if any one is in Christ, he is a new creation; the old has passed away, behold, the new is come. All this is from God, who through Christ reconciled us to himself" (2 Cor 5:17–18). And this describes the normal Christian life. Yet, sadly, many do not seek it or even know to ask for it. The blame for this is manifold, but it must surely lie first with those who have the task of preaching and teaching. It is for us to paint this picture and teach the souls under our care to desire it and ask for it.

If we seem no different than the people of the Old Covenant, that is on us, not God. The saints also call such a premise to mind and show what God can do with grace.

Q. •I have to be honest that I get a little annoyed some-
•times by the rather constant refrain of the New Evangelization. What is new about it, and why use the word new for an ancient faith? — *Name withheld*

Irritation of this sort is perhaps understandable when a phrase gets picked up and used widely in multivariate ways and thereby becomes more of a slogan than something informative.

That said, the New Evangelization is officially used to mean several rather specific things. First, it is new in the sense that we, as a Church, are not announcing the Gospel to a culture that has never heard of Jesus. Rather we are re-proposing the Gospel to a culture that has rejected or diminished it. We cannot afford to do business as usual. We must use new approaches and behave in new ways. We can no longer be content to sit within our four walls and talk about the Faith among ourselves; we must go out. We cannot simply think of evangelization as opening the doors and hoping people come in. If there ever was a kind of cultural inertia that brought people to the Church, that is not so now. It is clear that we must go into the community, into the culture, and re-propose the Gospel.

The New Evangelization also appreciates that we cannot simply say what we believe; we must explain *why* and show its reasonableness. Perhaps in previous times it was sufficient to argue from authority, but these days people want to know why, not just what.

Third, evangelization is "new" in that we must vigorously engage in all the new ways of communicating that have exploded on the scene today. We must creatively engage all these new forms of communication, along with the traditional modes of communication, such as writing, cinema, radio, and so forth.

Q: I get confused about the various uses of the words continence, chastity, and celibacy. Are they the same thing? — *Name withheld*

The words are related but also have distinct meanings.

Continence, in the wider sense, simply means self-control, especially related to the body. It comes from the Latin *continentia*, which means a holding back. However, over the years the word has also developed the more specialized meaning of sexual restraint or of the complete abstaining from sexual intercourse. In this case, it is similar to the state of living celibately.

Celibacy, too, has a strict and wide meaning. Its wider meaning refers to anyone who lives in an ongoing state of refraining from sexual intercourse. And, in this sense, anyone who is unmarried should live celibately. However, a person could eventually marry, and celibacy would cease. More strictly, celibacy refers in the

Church to a vowed, perpetual state of refraining from sexual relations that religious and priests undertake. Here, of course, the
celibate state is ongoing and expected to be maintained for life.

Chastity is the virtue whereby we refrain from all unlawful
sexual activity and intercourse. It is a virtue all are called to have,
but its manifestation will vary based on one's state in life. Married
people are to be wholly faithful to each other sexually. Single people are to refrain from all sexual union.

Q.•A fellow Catholic maintains that at some time in the past the Catholic Church believed in reincarnation. Is this true? — *Maria-Luisa Berry*

As regards the matter of so-called reincarnation (the belief that we
have had previous lives in other bodies, or will come back in other
bodies or forms), the view is clearly excluded in Scripture and by
Christian anthropology.

Scripture says, "It is appointed for men to die once, and after
that comes judgment" (Heb 9:27). "Once" is pretty clear: there are
no previous deaths or lives, nor shall we face death again. Once
cannot mean many.

In addition, Christian anthropology excludes the notion of
reincarnation. This is not the place to set forth a full anthropology,
but in this space it is sufficient to state that the soul is the form of
the body, and it does not pertain to the same soul to form different
bodies. I am my body and soul together. My body is not a mere ap-
pendage or container that can be shed or exchanged.

Finally, whenever someone claims the Catholic Church once
taught something, a good follow-up request is, "Show it to me in
writing." For many make unsubstantiated claims, and the pressure should not be on us to defend against something that never
happened, but for them to demonstrate clearly the truth of their
charge.

Q. •I recently read that Pope Francis has said that many •Catholics are sacramentalized but unevangelized. What does this mean? It seems to me that it denigrates the sacraments. — *Thomas Keene*

I am unaware that Pope Francis has used this phrase. However, it is a rather common expression today among priests and theologians. It describes the unfortunately common reality of many Catholics in the pews who have received all their sacraments, and may even faithfully attend Mass each Sunday and go to confession at least once a year, but have never really met Jesus Christ or encountered his presence powerfully.

Sadly, many Catholics, often due to poor catechesis, reduce the sacraments to rituals, rather than to living and real encounters with the Lord Jesus, who himself is the true celebrant of every sacrament. The purpose of all the sacraments is to sanctify us and, in particular ways, to lead us deeper and deeper into a life-changing and transformative relationship with Jesus Christ. They are to put us in living, conscious contact with Jesus, so that we see our lives being changed.

But the common experience of many Catholics is that sacraments are only vaguely appreciated in this way. Many see them as tedious rituals, rather than transformative realities. Too many seek the shortest Mass, almost as if it were more like a flu shot, a kind of "necessary evil" to be dispensed with as quickly and painlessly as possible. Confession, too, is avoided.

Very few Catholics come to Mass expecting to be transformed. In a way, people put more faith in Tylenol than the Eucharist since, when they take Tylenol, they expect something to happen; they expect the pain to go away and healing to be induced. But too many Catholics do *not* expect anything like this from holy Communion.

This is what it means to be sacramentalized but unevangelized. It is to be faithful to the pew and to the sacraments, but to lack the evangelical zeal, joy, and transformation one would expect from a more fruitful reception of the sacraments. It is to go through the motions but not really get anywhere. It is to receive Jesus but not really experience him in any meaningful manner.

Pastors, parents, and catechists need to work to overcome what amounts to a lack of deep faith in and experience of Jesus. Far from denigrating the sacraments, the phrase seeks to underscore the truer and fuller reality of the sacraments, which are not mere rituals, but powerful realities if received fruitfully.

Q. In a sermon, the priest said Satan hates us. It occurred to me to ask, why does Satan hate me? What did I ever do to him? — *John Smoot*

To be sure, there are very deep mysteries involved in the motives for Satan's hatred. We struggle to understand our own human psyches, let alone the psyche of a fallen angelic person.

However, an important clue to Satan's hatred is contained in the third temptation he makes to Jesus in the desert. Showing Jesus all the kingdoms of the world, he says, "All these I will give you, if you will fall down and worship me" (Mt 4:9).

Here we see the curtain pulled back, and we glimpse for a moment the kind of inner torment that dominates Satan. He seems desperate to be adored. He cannot bear that he is a creature, and that there is another, who is God, ever to be adored.

In his colossal pride he hates, first of all, God. And, by extension, he hates everyone and everything that manifests the glory of God. Even more, he hates those who seek to adore God rather than him. In his venomous pride, he seeks to destroy the Church, which declares the glory of God and reminds us that God alone is to be adored. Surely, he hates and seeks to destroy those who even try to adore God, and who do not accord him, Satan, the worship and pride of place he ravenously hungers for.

Hence, as the text from the temptation in the desert shows, Satan is tormented by pride, and his torment is filled with deep hatred for all who worship God and all who draw others to the worship of the one, true God.

Q. The *Catechism* says, "that man might become God." Please explain. — *Jim Jeson*

The *Catechism* here references a quote from Saint Athanasius, and also a clarification by Saint Thomas Aquinas. It is true that Athanasius speaks boldly, as saints often do! But as both Athanasius and Thomas were careful to do, distinctions are necessary.

The exact quote from the *Catechism* is: "'For the Son of God became man so that we might become God.' 'The only-begotten Son of God, wanting to make us sharers in his divinity, assumed our nature, so that he, made man, might make men gods'" (460).

Note that in the second sentence, a comment by Thomas on Athanasius's statement, the word "gods" is not capitalized. And this is to make it clear, as Athanasius would agree, that we do not become a god as separate and distinct from the one, true God. Rather, we partake, or participate, in the divine nature.

To partake or participate comes from the Latin word *particeps*, meaning to take up a part of something, but not the whole. Though we come to share in aspects of the divine nature, we do not do so in a way that is separate from being members of Christ's body through baptism. We access this share in a part or aspect of divine life and nature only in union with Christ, only by entering into communion with Jesus at baptism and thus receiving divine sonship.

PART VIII

THE
LAST
THINGS

DEATH

Q. Where do our souls go after we die? Do all go to heaven? — *Audrey*

The first destination is the judgment seat of Christ: "It is appointed for men to die once, and after that comes judgment" (Heb 9:27). And again, "For we must all appear before the judgment seat of Christ, so that each one may receive good or evil, according to what he has done in the body" (2 Cor 5:10).

From here, there are three possible destinations. Many do go to heaven, the ultimate destination of all who believe in the Lord and, by his grace, die in love and friendship with him, and are perfected. But most of the heaven-bound likely first experience purgatory, where those who die in friendship with God, but who are not yet fully perfected in his love, are purified and then drawn to heaven (see 1 Cor 3:12–15).

Finally, some go from judgment to hell, for by their own choice they rejected God and the values of the Kingdom. It is wrong, as some do, to dismiss hell as an unlikely possibility, since the Lord Jesus taught frequently of it, and warned that many were on the wide road that led there.

Q. A Jewish friend insists that, according to his religion, there is simply no afterlife. Is this true, and consistent with the Old Testament? — *Charley McKelvy*

The views of the Jewish people regarding the afterlife vary to some degree. Unlike the Catholic Church, there is no central teaching authority among Jewish people. Thus, in a short answer like this, we cannot fully treat what all Jewish people believe about the particulars of the afterlife. But it is fair to say that most believing Jews do believe in an afterlife. It is also fair to say that the concept of the resurrection of the dead developed in Judaism over the centuries and became clearer in the later books of the Old Testament as God brought the ancient Jews to a deeper understanding of what he was offering.

To say that there is nothing in the Old Testament about it requires the dismissal of a good number of texts from the prophets, psalms, and the wisdom tradition that speak quite vividly of the dead rising (see, for example, Is 26:19; Jb 19:25–27; Dn 12:2; Ez 37:12; Hos 13:14; 1 Sm 2:6).

At the time of Jesus, the Sadducees did reject the resurrection of the dead, holding that, at death, one simply ceased to exist. Part of the reason for this was that they only accepted the first five books of the Bible and claimed that in them there was no mention of the dead rising. Jesus sets aside their view by invoking the encounter of God with Moses at the burning bush in the Book of Exodus, one of the first five books of the Bible. There, God called himself the "God of Abraham, of Isaac, and of Jacob" (3:16). But if God "is not God of the dead, but of the living" (Mk 12:27), as the Sadducees would surely insist, then somehow, to God, Abraham, Isaac, and Jacob are alive.

And while your Jewish friend is not likely to accept the authority of Jesus, this text goes a long way to show that declaring there's nothing in the Old Testament about resurrection, especially in the first five books, is not an interpretation immune from critique. It further illustrates that at the time of Jesus, while the Sadducees rejected the resurrection of the dead, most other Jews — such as the Pharisees and also followers of Jesus and others — *did* accept, teach, and expect the resurrection of the dead.

Therefore, it seems safe to consign your friend's remark as the opinion of one Jew, or some Jews, but not all Jews then or now.

Q. Many of our Protestant brethren say that before Jesus comes there will be a rapture wherein all the faithful will be taken up. When I tell them that the Bible says that he will come, seated upon a cloud, and will send his minions to gather the elect from the four winds (see Mt 24:30–31), and I ask them who will be left to gather if everyone has previously been raptured, they say it will be the Jews. What is the Church's teaching on this? Will there ever be such a thing as the Rapture? — *Rich Willette*

The notion of the Rapture (a Latin word that means to be snatched away) is a novel concept among certain (not all) evangelicals. It is a notion less than 150 years old and finds no real support in the biblical text, as you point out. Fundamentally, the theory asserts that before the final tribulations of the end times, faithful Christians will be snatched away. Rapture theorists disagree about the exact moment of the snatching. Some say it will be pre-tribulation, others midway through the tribulations, some even say post-tribulation. As you can see, it's a bit fuzzy.

The root text for evangelicals who hold to the Rapture theory is a text from the First Letter of Paul to the Thessalonians: "For this we declare to you by the word of the Lord, that we who are alive, who are left until the coming of the Lord, shall not precede those who have fallen asleep. For the Lord himself will descend from heaven with a cry of command, with the archangel's call, and with the sound of the trumpet of God. And the dead in Christ will rise first; then we who are alive, who are left, shall be caught up together with them in the clouds to meet the Lord in the air; and so we shall always be with the Lord. Therefore comfort one another with these words" (4:15–18).

Now, the context is the second coming of Christ. There are not two second comings taught in Scripture, but rapture theory posits two, the one described in First Thessalonians and another one, some 1,000 years later. Note, too, that in First Thessalonians there is no mention of some being left behind. There is no mention of a 1,000-year reign in this text. Nor does Saint Paul indicate that what he is describing here is a different coming of Christ, distinct from other texts in the Gospel where Christ describes his own second coming.

Thus we are left with a text that simply does not support what the rapture theorists say. They further strive to unnaturally stitch this account with other texts in the Book of Revelation. The result is a highly debatable account of the last days that even rapture theorists hotly debate in terms of the details. The whole enterprise amounts to an attempt to shoehorn biblical passages into rapture theory that more clearly call it into question.

To say the elect are merely the Jews is speculative at best and fanciful and contrived at worst.

As for Catholic teaching on these matters, the *Catechism* summarizes it as follows: "Before Christ's second coming the Church must pass through a final trial that will shake the faith of many believers. The persecution that accompanies her pilgrimage on earth will unveil the 'mystery of iniquity' in the form of a religious deception offering men an apparent solution to their problems at the price of apostasy from the truth. The supreme religious deception is that of the Antichrist, a pseudo-messianism by which man glorifies himself in place of God and of his Messiah come in the flesh" (675).

You can read more at this same point in the *Catechism*.

Q. What is the Catholic view of the Rapture, which is held by some Protestants? — *Terry Morrison*

The Catholic view would reject the notion of the Rapture as held widely by certain evangelical Christians. The word rapture (from the Latin *rapiemur*) means to be caught up or snatched away. Those who hold this view claim 1 Thessalonians as their source, where Saint Paul writes: "And the dead in Christ will rise first; then we who are alive, who are left, shall be caught up together with them in the clouds to meet the Lord in the air; and so we shall always be with the Lord" (4:16–17).

The problem is that Saint Paul clearly applies this being caught up to the definitive and final Second Coming of Christ. Scripture also teaches that the period just before the Second Coming will include a great deal of tribulation and suffering for the faithful (see Mt 24:9–14). Then Christ will come in glory and the final Judgment will take place at once (Mt 24:29–31).

But those who hold to the Rapture remove it from this context and insert a lot of views that the text does not support and that Saint Paul never taught. Many evangelical Christians insert into the 1 Thessalonians text a notion that unbelievers will be left behind on earth and that a 1,000-year period will ensue, which will be a kind of earthly golden age during which the world will become thoroughly Christian. Thus they separate the Second Coming and the Last Judgment by a thousand years and teach that Christ will physically reign on earth.

To prove this view, they make questionable use of other biblical texts, mainly from the Book of Revelation. They also use many dubious notions — referred to as premillennialism and a complex brew of pre-, mid-, and post-tribulationism — which are too complicated to detail in a short article. So complex are all these interwoven theories that the Rapture enthusiasts hotly debate the details among themselves.

The Catholic approach is to rest on the firmer ground of sacred Tradition (current notions of the Rapture are less than 150 years old) and a plainer teaching of the Scriptures. These unite as one event the Second Coming, the Last Judgment, and the faithful being caught up into heaven to be forever with God while the unfaithful depart immediately to hell.

Q: At a funeral, the priest consoled a grieving family of a man who had died in rather serious sin by reading the parable of the lost sheep, and said that precisely because this man was a lost sheep Jesus would take him home. It seemed he was saying the man was saved simply because he was lost. Is this true? — *Name withheld*

No. The image of the lost sheep indicates Christ's desire and effort to save all of us. However, merely being a lost sheep is not an indication of being saved. Rather, we must have a willingness to be found. Hence the Lord's desire to save us does not cancel our freedom.

Funerals are difficult moments, and both clergy and people attending are in a sensitive place. But while there is an instinct to console, it is not really possible or proper always to give clear assurance that the beloved who has died is with God. Our best stance is to pray with confident assurance that the Lord loves our deceased more than we do and wants to save them.

That said, no one warned of judgment and the possibility of hell more than Jesus. In many parables and teachings, he clearly indicated that many were in serious danger of being lost (see Mt 7:13–14; Lk 13:24). This is not because he is mean or severe, but because we have hearts that can be obtuse and stubborn. We can harden our hearts against God and the values of his kingdom. There are many in our world who do not want to love their enemy, live chastely, forgive those who have hurt them, or esteem and love the poor. But these are kingdom values that are celebrated in heaven, along with the praise of God and the celebration of his whole truth. The narrow way (Jesus' words) to salvation is the cross, and there are many who are unwilling to embrace its demands or conform to the challenging values of the Kingdom.

So, the Lord seeks the lost but will not compel them to answer. We who live should pray for the departed and ask mercy on their behalf and a speedy purification for those who are saved but in purgatory. Funerals are also moments to cultivate a proper urgency to attend to our own salvation and become more firmly committed to seeking the Lord who alone can save us.

Q. **I recently read a book by an author who had a near-death experience and claims that God told him that one's belief system was irrelevant. This seems like New Age indifferentism. Can you comment on near-death phenomena and what he says?** — *Bob Tisovich*

Near-death experiences (NDEs) seem to be a rather widely reported phenomenon with certain common features. One has an "out-of-body" experience with a reported capacity to see oneself as if looking down. There is usually some experience of a light to which the person is drawn, sometimes down a tunnel. There is usually some sense of peace and joy, but also a sense that now is not the time and one is "sent back." In rarer cases, some who have had NDEs report being in the heavenly realm, seeing loved ones, and so forth.

While it cannot be denied that NDEs are reported with enough frequency that likely they do happen, NDEs are problematic in certain ways.

First, they can reasonably be explained naturally as consciousness fades. The Church usually looks for natural explanations and seeks to rule them out before quickly asserting a supernatural cause or affirming a report of visions.

A second, and more significant, problem with many (not all) NDEs is that they would seem to violate or skip over certain biblical and Church teachings regarding the last things. One aspect that is missing in most of them is judgment. Scripture says, "It is appointed for men to die once, and after that comes judgment" (Heb 9:27). Saint Paul also speaks of us passing thorough fire to have our works tested and purified after death (see 1 Cor 3:13). The teaching on judgment and purification are seemingly absent in many, if not most, NDE reports.

Even more problematic are NDE reports which speak of being able to walk around heaven, see loved ones, etc. Heaven is not attained in bypassing the judgment seat and the purification which most, if not all of us, will need. Scripture says of heaven: "Nothing unclean shall enter it" (Rv 21:27). So, such reports seem dubious, if Scripture is a reliable guide; and it obviously is.

Your question refers also to a book by an NDE survivor who claims that in his discussions with "God," God didn't care what spiritual tradition one had. But this is in contradiction to Scripture, which teaches there is no other name given by which we are to be saved than Jesus (see Acts 4:12). So, New Age Gnosticism does not save one, and it would seem that the real God *does* care.

But here, too, is another societal ill of our times: the rejection of the authority of the Word of God in favor of often-trendy visionaries. Death awaits us all, and we do well to simply heed the Lord's warning to be ready by living sober, holy, and devout lives.

JUDGMENT

Q. **No soul may see God unless it has been totally purified, which is why we must go to purgatory before heaven. But since purgatory ends on the Day of Judgment, what happens to the souls of the people who are still alive on Judgment Day? How are their souls purified?** — *Amy O'Donnell*

This level of detail is not supplied to us by the biblical texts. Nor are such details defined in the magisterial teachings of the Church. Hence we are in the realm of speculative theology when it comes to such matters.

We ought to begin by saying that the Day of Judgment will not be a day like any other. There are many unknown factors, especially related to the mystery of time, that underlie our speculations. For example, will Judgment Day really be a day of twenty-four hours? Or will it be a moment in time that happens like a flash? Perhaps it will be a longer period of some indeterminate length? Will time even exist, as we know it now, at a moment like that?

There is also a premise in your question that is not certain — namely, that purgatory ends on the Day of Judgment. We do not know this. Perhaps purgatory, or the process of purgation, may exist for a time after the Last Judgment. But here, too, is another question. What does it mean to say that something exists "for a time," once time as we know it no longer exists?

Perhaps the best we can do with a question like this is to say that it is not for us to know such details, and that God will accomplish the purifications and purgation necessary in ways known to him.

It would certainly seem that such purification would in fact be necessary based on Scripture, which says of heaven, "Nothing unclean shall enter it" (Rv 21:27). While purgatory or the process of purgation is set forth in Scripture for us who die now, how God will accomplish this for souls in the rarefied conditions of the Second Coming is known to him, but not revealed to us with enough specificity to answer your question without speculation.

Q. How will God judge non-Catholics at the time of their death? — *William Bandle*

Scripture says, "Man looks on the outward appearance, but the Lord looks on the heart" (1 Sm 16:7). Thus God, who knows our hearts, will judge us first and foremost based on what is there. Not all in this world have had the same opportunity to come to know the Lord, his body the Church, and the help of the sacraments. God knows this and will judge accordingly. Jesus says, "And that servant who knew his master's will, but did not make ready or act according to his will, shall receive a severe beating. But he who did not know, and did what deserved a beating, shall receive a light beating. Every one to whom much is given, of him will much be required; and of him to whom men commit much they will demand the more" (Lk 12:47–48).

Therefore, for non-Catholics who may have lacked some of the knowledge or sacramental assistance God has provided, God who is just will look into their hearts and judge them based on what they could reasonably have known and what they did based on that. To say that God looks into the heart does not mean that he merely looks to a person's feelings or disposition. Rather, as Scripture says elsewhere, we will be judged also by our deeds (see, for example, Rom 2:6–11). Did our deeds correspond to our understanding of what was expected or not?

The degree of a person's knowledge of God's will and the obedience to that knowledge through righteous deeds are key on the Day of Judgment. This does not simply mean all non-Catholics and other nonbelievers get a pass. The ignorance they have of full Catholic teaching must be what is called "invincible ignorance." Invincible ignorance refers to a lack of knowledge that a person could not reasonably overcome. If one is simply lazy, or makes easy excuses in terms of seeking the truth, surely God will also take this into account.

The Lord alone sees into our heart; the Lord alone will be our just judge.

Q: **In the reading at Mass today, Jesus says that whoever disobeys the Son will not see life, and that the wrath of God remains upon him. Why present God in such mean-spirited terms?** — *Name withheld*

The wrath of God does not mean that God is angry or in a bad mood. God is not subject to moods or fits of anger. In God there "is no variation or shadow due to change" (Jas 1:17).

The wrath of God says more about us than God. It describes the total incompatibility of our sinful state before the holiness of God. Without the transformation effected by grace, we cannot endure the presence of God, which, though glorious, is too much for us to take unless God purifies and prepares us by grace.

Perhaps a couple of analogies will help. As we know, fire and water do not mix. There is a conflict between them, and we can hear that conflict in the sizzle when water is spilled on a hot stove. There is a conflict (or wrath) between the two substances. They cannot be in the same place at the same time. If fire is allowed to represent God, then you and I are going to have to become fire to endure his holy presence. God must bring us up to the temperature of glory for us to endure and enjoy the "weather" of heaven. No wonder that God sent his Holy Spirit like tongues of fire at Pentecost.

If we are not transformed by the Lord's grace, then the presence of God will seem harsh and wrathful, not glorious and beautiful. But the problem or wrath is in us, not God.

And this leads to a second analogy. In our homes, we are happy to have lights shining brightly in the evening hours. Upon waking from sleep in the dark morning hours, however, if someone turns on the lights, we may protest, "The light is harsh!" But the light is not harsh, it is the same light we enjoyed earlier. The light has not changed, we have. In a similar way, the wrath of God is more in us than in God. It is our experience of him, not who God is in himself.

Since it is admittedly complex, the concept of the wrath of God requires a more careful study than merely reading it in a literalist way.

HELL

Q. **We learn that God loves us unconditionally. But then why is there hell? That doesn't seem unconditional.**
— *Peter Smithers*

Perhaps you would agree that if someone loves someone else, that love would not include him forcing his will on the other. And while it is certainly true that the Lord wills to save everyone, he does not force us to accept him. God is not a slave driver, but rather he is Love, and love invites us to freely accept his offer of an eternal relationship.

While some people think that everyone wants to go to heaven, generally they have a heaven in mind of their own design. The real heaven is not merely a personally designed paradise; it is the kingdom of God in all its fullness. Heaven therefore consists of the celebration of charity, worship of God, truth, chastity, forgiveness, esteem of the poor, love of one's enemies, humility, etc. Yet there are many who reject some or all of these values. Why would a loving God force people to enter into the eternal place that celebrates things they reject?

Hence the existence of hell is not opposed to God's love. It is in conformity with the respect necessary for our freedom to accept or reject the relationship of love. Mysteriously, many come to a place in their life where they definitively reject God and the values of the kingdom he offers.

Q. How are we to understand scriptural teaching about the fire of hell? Do persons who wind up in hell literally burn continuously and forever? How is that possible?
— *Name withheld*

Most of the Fathers of the Church and theological tradition understand the fire of hell to be an actual, physical fire. But questions like yours remain. Even further, what effect would physical fire have on the fallen angels consigned to fiery hell but who have no physical bodies with nerve endings from which to feel a physical fire?

Saint Thomas summarizes the theological tradition that sees the fire as an actual, physical fire that God uses to limit the fallen angels and fallen souls. He says that it is the "seeing" of this fire that torments them: "But the corporeal fire is enabled as the instrument of the vengeance of Divine justice thus to detain a spirit; and thus it has a penal effect on it, by hindering it from fulfilling its own will, that is by hindering it from acting where it will and as it will.... As the instrument of Divine justice, [fire] is enabled to detain [a spirit] ... and in this respect this fire is really hurtful to the spirit, and thus the soul, seeing the fire as something hurtful to it, is tormented by the fire" (*S.T. Supplement*, Q 70, art 3, *respondeo*).

So, seeing this fire torments by setting forth in fallen angels and fallen souls a seething indignation that must come to a fallen spirit who is hindered and can no longer live the lie of following its own will in order to find satisfaction. The fire is a limiting fire that attests to the fact that nothing outside God will satisfy, and that roaming about seeking satisfaction in anything other than God must now end. The fire burns and is unquenchable, for only God can quench it. But since the fallen have forever refused God, he cannot quench it in them without violating their "no" to him and his kingdom values.

Many modern theologians have moved away from insisting that the fire of hell is a physical fire and prefer to emphasize more the figurative or symbolic nature of the image. For even now, we often speak metaphorically of how our own passions can "burn like fire." We speak of burning with lust, or of seething with anger, or being furious (fury being related to the word for fire). We speak of the heat of passion, of boiling over with anger, or of seething with envy. Even good emotions like love can burn like fire if they are not satisfied.

And thus the fire of hell, even if physical, speaks also to deeper spiritual struggles. We were made for God, and God alone can satisfy us. To choose anything less than God is to remain gravely unfulfilled and to burn with a longing that has refused to seek its proper goal — that is, one burns with desire but has rejected the one thing necessary to satisfy that desire. The fire seethes and the fury grows.

The second part of your question seems to presume that the fire of hell is a fire consuming the body. You wonder how a limited body could be consumed by fire forever. But we need not presume the fire to be a consuming fire. A fire may cause pain without necessarily consuming.

Q. **If the condemned in hell are there for all eternity, why is Satan allowed to run amok in the our world, out of hell? Isn't he supposed to be suffering in hell along with his minions and other condemned? It seems as though he is having a good time creating havoc and not suffering one bit.** *— Robert Flint*

While some texts in Scripture speak of Satan and the fallen angels as being cast into hell (see 2 Pt 2:4; Jude 6), other texts speak of the fallen angels (demons) as being cast down to the earth (Rv 12:8–9; Jb 1:7). Thus, though consigned to hell, it would seem that some or all of the demons have the capacity also to roam the earth. However, Satan is also described as being chained and in prison (Rv 20:1–3). This is likely a way of indicating that his power is limited in some sense. But it is not a denial that he still exerts considerable influence through other fallen angels, which can and do roam the earth. Near the end of the world, Scripture says that Satan will be wholly loosed and come forth to deceive the nations for a while, and after this brief period he and the other fallen angels will be definitively cast into the lake of fire and their influence ended (Rv 20:10).

Why God permits freedom to demons to wander about the earth is mysterious. We know that God permits evil as a necessary condition of freedom for the rational creatures he has created. Angels and humans have free and rational souls and, if our freedom is to mean anything, it must be that God allows some angels and men to abuse their freedom, and even become a source of evil and temptation for others.

As such, this life amounts for us to a kind of test, wherein God permits some degree of evil to flourish, yet not without offering us the grace to overcome. Further, there is the tradition implied in the Scriptures that for every fallen angel there were two angels who did not fall (see Rv 12:4). Therefore, our lives are not merely to be accounted as under the influence of demons, but also under the influence and care of angels.

It is also clear that, on account of temptations and trials, our "yes" to God has greater dignity and merit than if we lived in an essentially sin-free zone or paradise.

It would be too strong to say, as you have, that demons and Satan do not suffer at all. Demons, like human beings, suffer defeats as well as victories. They have things that delight them, and things that disappoint and anger them. Anyone who has ever attended an exorcism can attest that demons do suffer a great deal, especially when the faithful pray and make pious use of sacraments and sacramentals such as holy water, relics, blessed medals, rosaries, and so forth. Faith and love are deeply disturbing to demons.

Q. The *Catechism* says that fallen angels have irrevocably rejected God (see 391–393). Why is that choice irrevocable? Why is their sin unforgivable? Can they not repent? — *Eric*

They cannot and will not repent, and thus forgiveness is not possible for them.

In this life, you and I are *in statu viae* (in the state of journeying). Thus we can and do change and make decisions that gradually form our character. But this is not so for the souls of men and angels who are caught up into eternity. For something to be everlasting demands that its essence be fixed or unchanging.

St. Thomas considers the angels by saying: "Everlasting stability is of the very nature of true beatitude; hence it is termed 'life everlasting'…. Sacred Scripture [also] declares that demons and wicked men shall be sent "into everlasting punishment," and the good brought 'into everlasting life.' Consequently … according to Catholic Faith, it must be held firmly both that the will of the good angels is confirmed in good, and that the will of the demons is obstinate in evil…. [And] as Damascene says (*De Fide Orth.* ii), 'death is to men, what the fall [from the heavens] is to the angels.' Now it is clear that all the mortal sins of men, grave or less grave, are pardonable before death; whereas after death they are without remission and endure forever" (*Summa*, I, Q 64, A 2).

Saint Thomas further reasons, with an epistemology that is complex to untrained philosophers: "Man by his reason apprehends movably, passing from one consideration to another; and having the way open by which he may proceed to either of two opposites. Consequently, man's will adheres to a thing movably, and with the power of forsaking it and of clinging to the opposite; whereas the angel's will adheres fixedly and immovably."

Thus, for the angels and the souls of men and women who have passed from this changing world, their decision for or against God and the values of his kingdom is forever fixed.

Q. •I heard a priest say that God is so much love that he •does not think people will live in hell for eternity, [but] that all will be enlightened to full truth at one point, and then they will all choose heaven. What do you think?
— *Julie Robinson*

The position of the priest would be a pretty exact form of Origenism, which was condemned by several councils in the early Church. The term Origenism is tied to the theologian Origen, who lived in the third century and proposed that in the restoration of all things (often called the *apokatastais*), Satan and all the condemned would reconsider their stance and be reconciled to God. It is related to another view today called "universalism," which holds that most if not all will be saved in the end.

Such notions are emotionally understandable and seek to emphasize God's abiding mercy. But they set aside Jesus' own words that hell is a reality that "many" (not none or few) will inherit. So, the priest in question errs because he declares a view condemned by several councils and at odds with Scripture. The understandable hope that all will be saved in the end cannot withstand the charge of being wishful thinking.

The understanding of the Church is that the angels' decision for or against God and his kingdom values is fixed and unalterable. Thus demons will never repent, and good angels will never fall. Further, the same would seem to be true of human beings upon our death — that is, our decision for or against God and his kingdom is forever fixed. The saints in heaven will not fall, but neither will the souls in hell change their rejection of God and what he offers.

Some of the Church Fathers used the image of clay on a potter's wheel. As long as it is moist, it is able to be shaped and reshaped. But when subjected to the fire of the kiln, its shape is forever fixed.

If hell is eternal, as Jesus teaches it is, then the eventual emptying of hell by a change of heart in the condemned is in opposition to this teaching of the Lord himself. Jesus spoke of hell as a place of exile, "where their worm does not die, and the fire is not quenched" (Mk 9:48).

Q. Are there any teachings about what Jesus did when he went to hell, as described in the Apostles' Creed?
— *Robert Lusby*

It is important to distinguish the hell of the damned from the place of the dead, which the ancients termed variously as "Sheol," "Hades," or "Hell." Since the *Catechism of the Catholic Church* answers your question quite thoroughly. Here are some excerpts:

> [Jesus] descended [to hell — that is, to the realm of the dead] as Savior, proclaiming the Good News to the spirits [of men] imprisoned there [see 1 Pt 3:18–19].

> Scripture calls the abode of the dead, to which the dead Christ went down, "hell" — *Sheol* in Hebrew or *Hades* in Greek — because those who are there are deprived of the vision of God.... Jesus did not descend into hell to deliver the damned, nor to destroy the hell of damnation, but to free the just who had gone before him.

> The "gospel was preached even to the dead." The descent into hell brings the Gospel message of salvation to complete fulfillment. This is the last phase of Jesus' messianic mission, a phase which is condensed in time but vast in its real significance: the spread of Christ's redemptive work to all men

of all times and all places, for all who are saved
have been made sharers in the redemption.

Christ went down into the depths of death so that
"the dead will hear the voice of the Son of God,
and those who hear will live" [1 Pt 4:6].... Jesus ...
[delivered] all those who through fear of death
were subject to lifelong bondage." (632–35)

An ancient Holy Saturday sermon says: "Greatly desiring to visit those who live in darkness and in the shadow of death, [Jesus] has gone to free from sorrow Adam ... and Eve, captive with him. [And finding them he says,] "I am your God, who for your sake have become your son.... Awake O Sleeper. I did not create you to be a prisoner in hell. Rise from the dead, for I am the life of the dead" (c. second century).

PURGATORY

Q: Does Satan have any access to the souls in purgatory? — *Kathy Cain*

The souls in purgatory are not accessible to the devil or demons; they are safe in God's hands, in what amounts to the "vestibule" of heaven. There, they undergo final purifications, which only lead to heaven (see 1 Cor 3:13–15).

Further, at death, our final disposition for or against God (and for or against his kingdom) is final; it is definitive. This places the souls in heaven and those in purgatory beyond the reach of the devil. Sadly, it also places heaven beyond the reach of those who have finalized their decision against it. At death the judgment or verdict is in, and it is irreversible (see Lk 16:26; Heb 9:27; Jn 8:21; Jn 10:27–28).

We do well today to be more sober about this definitive aspect of death, and to realize that our cumulative decisions build toward a final disposition by us that God will, in the end, acknowledge.

Q. **You said in a previous answer that purgatory oper-ates outside of space and time. Does that mean that, for the millions of souls that may be there, they don't re-quire any space? Also, if there is no time in purgatory, why was I taught as a child that I could pray and get a person one hundred days indulgence, etc.?** — *Philip Hoos*

I don't recall using the expression "purgatory operates outside of space and time." However, regarding the need for physical space, it does not follow that purgatory would require this. Why? Because there are souls in purgatory, not bodies. Our souls are not physical and do not occupy physical space any more than a thought occu-pies physical space. This does not absolutely mean that the Lord does not have purgatory in a certain location. But where that lo-cation might be, and how large it is, etc., is not revealed to us. The point is, physical space is not per se required for purgatory.

Regarding time in purgatory, it would seem there probably *is* time in purgatory. Why? Because there is the change of purifica-tion occurring. One understanding of time is that it is a measure of change, or "movement" in the philosophical sense. However, whether time is experienced in purgatory as it is here, or how time here relates to time there, is mysterious.

As for the old system of giving prayers a sort of ranking based on the number of days of indulgence granted — for example, one hundred days, five hundred days, etc. — that was not a reference to the number of days in purgatory. Numbers like that go back to an early period in Church history when penances were often quite lengthy. The prayers of certain fellow Christians (especially Confessors of the Faith who had suffered imprisonment, etc.) could be used to reduce the length of certain penances for other Christians. The system of days and years then came to be used as a kind of gauge of the relative merit of certain prayers and pious actions but were not a reference to days in purgatory. The system of assigning numbers (such as one hundred days indulgence) was set aside in 1970 in favor of simply declaring an indulgence to be partial or plenary. This change was made in large part due to just this sort of confusion about the true meaning of those numbers.

Q: **I have Catholic family members and friends [who] say that purgatory does not exist and that the Church no longer teaches it. Several of them insist that their priest told them this. What is the truth here?** — *Gregory Rolla*

That any Catholic today, especially a priest, would say that purgatory does not exist is lamentable. This claim was sadly common in the 1970s and '80s. But much work has been done in the Church to reiterate the truth of this perennial teaching and the need to pray for the dead.

Purgatory is a dogma of the Faith, consistently taught and believed through every age of the Church. It is set forth clearly in the *Catechism of the Catholic Church* (see 1030–32).

Scripture sets forth the need and the existence of some sort of purifying process for most. Jesus promises that when his work is complete, we will be perfect as the heavenly Father is perfect (see Mt 5:48). Saint Paul prays that God who has begun a good work in us will bring it to perfection (Phil 1:6). Scripture attests that nothing imperfect or impure shall enter heaven (Rv 21:27).

Yet most of us will admit that completed, godlike perfection is rarely observed in those who die, even the very pious. Though I can reasonably conclude that I love God and am not aware of mortal sin on my soul, I am far from godly perfection (ask anyone who knows me).

For this reason, the *Catechism* states, "All who die in God's grace and friendship, but still imperfectly purified, are indeed assured of their eternal salvation; but after death they undergo purification, so as to achieve the holiness necessary to enter the joy of heaven" (1030). Also, "The tradition of the Church, by reference to certain texts of Scripture, speaks of a cleansing fire" (1031).

Thus Saint Paul teaches that our works will all be revealed and tested by fire. And some of our works, though built on the foundation of Christ — that is, not conceived in mortal sin — are ignoble, so they will be burned away, but the pure works will bring reward. "If any man's work is burned up, he will suffer loss, though he himself will be saved, but only as through fire" (1 Cor 3:15).

Therefore, we see that some sort of purgation after death is taught by Scripture, which also lays the foundation of the need for it. Further, instinct of the faithful to pray for the dead and the solemn teaching authority of the Church testify to the truth that purgation (and thus purgatory) is a needed gift of the Lord to us.

HEAVEN

Q: **Does the Church teach that in heaven we will recognize and communicate with one another? If so, what will an infant or aborted baby have to say? Will they be a fetus or infant eternally?** — *Fred Matt*

In answering questions about what our state in heaven will be like, it is important to recall that we are dealing with mysteries beyond our experience. We cannot simply transpose earthly realities to heavenly ones. We must also recall that we are engaging in speculative theology in these matters.

With these cautions in mind, we do well to use a basic rule employed in the final section of the *Summa* by St. Thomas (or one of his students) in speculating on these matters. In pondering what our bodies and other aspects of our interrelatedness will be like, we can reason that most perfection has neither excess, nor defect.

Age is one of these aspects. In terms of physical life, we can speak of being young and immature physically, and thus we manifest a sort of defect of age. And we can also speak of being past our physical prime, and thus we speak of an excess of physical age. Thomas thereby speculates that we will have resurrected bodies that will appear to be about the age of thirty, an age, which manifests neither defect nor excess, and is also the same approximate age at which Christ died and rose. It is his resurrected quality that models our own (see Phil 3:21).

Hence it would seem that in heaven, when our bodies rise, we will not see infants or elderly among us, but we will all manifest the perfection of physical "age." Similar reasoning can be applied to other aspects of our physical bodies, such as disease, missing limbs, or other defects. It seems that these defects will be remedied. However, one might speculate that some aspects of our physical sufferings might still be manifest, though not in a way that would cause us pain. For we see in Christ's resurrected body the wounds of his passion. But, now, they are not signs of his pain, but rather of his glory, and so, too, perhaps for some of our wounds.

As regards our interrelatedness, this too would be perfected. We will not only recognize and communicate with one another, but we will do this most perfectly as members of Christ, since our relationship to Christ, the head of the body, will be perfected.

Q. The *Catechism* states that [the] faithful who die after receiving baptism "will be in heaven," and that "before they take up their bodies again" (1023). Could you please explain and elaborate on just what this means? — *Jim Grady*

Currently, prior to the Second Coming, when we die, our bodies lie in the earth, but our soul goes to God. Those deemed worthy and capable of heaven, after any necessary purifications, are admitted into heaven.

Only at the Second Coming will our bodies rise, when, as Scripture attests, "the trumpet will sound, and the dead will be raised imperishable, and we shall be changed" (1 Cor 15:52). Our body which rises will be truly our body, but gloriously transformed as Saint Paul details in the same place in Scripture (see 1 Cor 15:35–40).

What this most fundamentally means is that Christ did not come to save only our souls, but the whole of us, soul and body. One great dignity of the human person is that we unite both the spiritual and material orders of God's creation in our very person. This glory will be restored to us at the Second Coming.

An additional meaning of this truth is that we must reverence both our soul and body through the spiritual and corporal works of mercy, and we must fulfill the mandate to glorify God in our body as well as our soul.

Q. In our Catholic faith we believe in the resurrection of the body. Scripture states that in the Kingdom there is neither male nor female. Does this mean that our body will not be resurrected in its full earthly form? — *Dion Hankinson*

It seems that you're referring to what Paul writes in Galatians 3:28: "There is neither Jew nor Gentile, there is neither slave nor free, there is neither male nor female: for you are all one in Christ Jesus."

Here Saint Paul is indicating that there is no difference in terms of dignity. In other words, whatever distinctions there are between us, even essential distinctions, there remains the truth that we are all equal in dignity before God, whose children we are. But this equality in dignity does not mean there is no difference in essence. Clearly, being male or female is a distinction that goes to the very depths of our being, including our soul. Therefore, when our body rises, we will indeed be male or female.

Perhaps, in the context of your question, it is also good for us to reflect on a common modern error that reduces sexual distinctions to a merely incidental, surface quality about the physical characteristics of the body. But this is not so. The soul is the form of the body. That is to say, it is the identity of the soul and its capacities that give rise to the design of the body. Hence a person's sex is not simply an incidental quality of their body; it is an aspect of their person that extends from the depths of their soul. Human persons do not just *have* a male or female body, they *are* male or female.

The most extreme form of reducing sex to a merely incidental quality of the body is illustrated in those who engage in so-called sex-change operations, as if simply altering the body surgically could change a person's sexual identity. It cannot. Scripture says, "male and female [God] created them" (Gn 1:27). Our identity as male or female extends to our inmost being and cannot simply be shed like clothing is.

Q.**I recently lost my husband of thirty-six years and long to be reunited with him one day. Will we know each other in heaven?** — *Name withheld*

I am sorry for your loss. You most certainly will know each other in heaven, and in a far more perfect and intimate way than you ever could on earth.

There is a tendency to read too much into Jesus' words that in heaven people neither marry nor are given in marriage. The first meaning of Jesus' words is that we cannot merely compare heaven to earthly realities. Heaven is richer. Second, sexual intimacy will no longer have purpose and we will live more like the angels.

But marital love is perfected in heaven, not discarded. Your knowledge, understanding, love, and intimacy with your husband (and family members) will be deeper, richer, and stronger in heaven, not less.

Q.•I want to be sure I go to heaven when I die. What exactly should I do? — *John Hahn*

A short biblical answer to your question is supplied by Peter in the Acts of the Apostles. Having heard a sermon that he preached on Pentecost, many were struck to the heart and cried out, "What shall we do?" Peter's response: "Repent, and be baptized every one of you in the name of Jesus Christ for the forgiveness of your sins; and you shall receive the gift of the Holy Spirit" (Acts 2:38).

But this is not simply to be understood as a ritualistic observance that we fulfill on one day; it is meant to usher in a whole renewal of the human person. Thus we ought to look at all three things Peter indicates in some more detail.

First, the word translated as "repent" is *metanoia*, which means more than to clean up our act. It means to come to a whole new mind, rooted in what God teaches and reveals, with new priorities and the ability to make better decisions.

Next, to be baptized is not only to be cleansed of our sins, but also to see our old self put to death, and for Christ to come alive in us. Baptism ushers in the beginnings of a lifelong healing process that must continue by God's grace. Baptism also points to all the sacraments of the Church. For, having been brought to new life, we must also be fed by the Eucharist and by God's word, we must see the wounds of sins healed in confession, and we must be strengthened for a mission by confirmation. Baptism also makes us a member of the Body of Christ, which means we are called to walk in fellowship with all the members of Christ's one body, the Church.

Saint Peter also speaks of receiving the gift of the Holy Spirit. Thus we are taught that our dignity is to be swept up into the life, love, and wisdom of God. We are called to be sanctified by the Holy Spirit, to see sins put to death and many virtues come alive.

Finally, something needs to be said about your use of the word "exactly," which might imply there is some very simple formula for getting saved. As can be seen, there are many dimensions to the work of God in saving us. Therefore, we are to walk in a loving covenant relationship with the Lord and his body the Church. And like any relationship, this cannot simply be reduced to a few things. We must trust the Lord and walk in a relationship of love and obedience to him. We are to do this in fellowship with his Church, through the grace of the sacraments, obedience to the Word of God, and prayer (see Acts 2:42).

Q.: I have been wondering, especially after reading the Book of Revelation, is there Mass in heaven? I suppose there is no need for it, but could there be? — *Name withheld*

Your impression of a great Mass in heaven is well-founded. One of the chief descriptions of heaven is that it is a liturgy. For indeed, God is praised by the multitude of angelic and human persons in heaven. Our earthly liturgy, in fact, is modeled on the heavenly liturgy. When John sets forth the vision of heaven he had beginning in Revelation 4, he describes hymns, incense, priests in long white robes, a book (or scroll), the Lamb of God standing on a thronelike altar, candles and lampstands, and the list could go on.

Heaven is like a great Mass. The first part of John's vision in Revelation focuses on a scroll (or book); the second part focuses on the lamb, which has made of itself a sacrifice, but which is now standing. And this is a clear correspondence to the Liturgy of the Word and the Liturgy of the Eucharist, which comprise our Mass.

Therefore, Holy Mass for us is a kind of dress rehearsal for heaven.

That said, there will not be sacraments in heaven. For indeed, there our union with God is complete, and all the veils are lifted. The sacraments will have had their effect, and now the fuller experience to which they pointed and led will take hold. God's true presence will not be mediated through sacraments, for we shall behold him then, face to face.

Scripture says: "For now we see in a mirror dimly, but then face to face. Now I know in part; then I shall understand fully, even as I have been fully understood" (1 Cor 13:12). In heaven we will not receive Communion, for we shall already have it fully.

Sacraments are for wayfarers, those of us on a journey; something like the manna was for the Jewish people journeying across the desert. Of that manna Scripture says, "And the manna ceased on the next day, when they ate of the produce of the land; and the sons of Israel had manna no more, but ate of the fruit of the land of Canaan that year" (Jos 5:12). And so, too, for us who have been sustained by our Eucharistic manna. The day we enter the Promised Land of heaven, the Communion we received here will be eclipsed by the perfect communion of heaven to which it pointed and drew us.

Q. How can we be happy in heaven knowing that some of our loved ones did not make it there? — *Sandy Vignali*

The happiness of heaven cannot be equated with earthly categories and prerequisites. Exactly how we will be happy in heaven cannot be explained to us here. Scripture describes heavenly happiness as: "What no eye has seen, nor ear heard, / nor the heart of man conceived" (1 Cor 2:9) — these things God has prepared for those who love him.

Jesus also cautions the Sadducees, who tried to project the earthly realities of marriage and family into heaven. He said, "You are wrong because you know neither the Scriptures nor the power of God" (Mt 22:29). In other words, and for our purposes here, we have to admit that our grasp of what heaven is, and how it will be experienced, cannot be reduced to or explained merely in terms of how we are happy now.

That said, some have speculated that the happiness of heaven, even despite missing family members, will be possible in light of the deeper appreciation of God's justice that we will have there. Surely, we will concur in heaven with all God's judgments and in no way incur sorrow on account of them.

Hence we will see that those excluded from heaven are excluded rightly and have really chosen to dwell apart, preferring darkness to light (see Jn 3:19). And while it may currently be mysterious how this will not cause us sadness, God does in fact teach us that he will wipe every tear from our eyes (Rv 21:4).

Q.•Was heaven not available to the human race until Je-•sus died on the cross? — *Teresa Thompson*

You are correct that there was no access to heaven until the work of Jesus to reconcile us to the Father. Without this sanctifying grace from Jesus, we could not endure the holy presence of God. It would be like wax before fire.

Prior to Jesus, the dead were understood to go to Sheol, a shadowy place where the dead slept and were only vaguely aware, as they awaited the coming of the Messiah. After dying on the cross, Jesus went down to the dead and preached to them (see 1 Pt 3:19), gathering the righteous to him. And as he ascended to heaven, he led them there (Eph 4:8).

While there are stories of Enoch, Elijah, and possibly Moses being caught up to heaven, it is unlikely that the highest heaven of the Beatific Vision is meant in those passages.

Q.•The descriptions [of heaven] in the Bible seem to de-•scribe a vast amount of people, and the paintings I have seen from the Renaissance make it look rather crowded and busy. Frankly, I hate big cities and crowds. Are these descriptions accurate, or am I missing something? — *Doris Leben*

The danger to avoid when meditating on heaven is taking earthly realities and merely transferring them to heaven. Whatever similarities heavenly realities have to things on earth, they will be experienced there in a heavenly and perfected way, with joy unspeakable.

The more biblical and theological way to understand the multitudes in heaven is not as some physical crowding, but as a deep communion. In other words, the Communion of Saints is not just a lot of people standing around and perhaps talking or moving about.

Saint Paul teaches, "So we, though many, are one body in Christ, and individually members one of another" (Rom 12:5).

Though we experience this imperfectly here on earth, we will experience it perfectly in heaven. As members of one another we will have deep communion, knowing and being known in a deep and rich way. Your memories, gifts, and insights will be mine, and mine will be yours. There will be profound understanding and appreciation, a rich love and sense of how we all complete one another and really are one in Christ.

Imagine the glory of billions of new thoughts, stories, and insights that will come from being perfectly members of Christ and members of one another. Imagine the peace that will come from finally understanding and being understood, a deep, satisfying, and wonderful communion, not crowds of strangers.

Therefore, the biblical descriptions of heaven as multitudes should not be understood as mere numbers, but as the richness and glory of this communion. The paintings showing "crowds" should be understood as an allegory of this deep communion, of being close in a way we can only imagine now.

Saint Augustine had in mind the wonderful satisfaction of this deep communion when he described heaven as *Unus Christus amans seipsum* (One Christ loving himself). This is not some selfish Christ turned in on himself. This is Christ the head in deep communion with all the members of his body, and all the members in Christ experiencing deep mystical communion with him and one another, together swept up into the life of the Trinity. Again, as Saint Paul says, "and you are Christ's, and Christ is God's" (1 Cor 3:23).

Q. **Please tell me what happens to the souls of aborted babies. Are they in heaven?** — *Rosemary Easley*

In an absolute sense, we do not know if they are in heaven since the Lord has not revealed this to us, and the Church is not a in a position to set aside the Lord's teaching on the necessity of baptism for salvation (see Jn 3:3–5).

However, recent popes and theologians have taught that we are on good ground to hope and trust in God's mercy and justice toward these infants, and to confidently assume they are in his good care. Though in need of baptism to wash away original sin, these infants committed no personal sins that would merit hell. And though we are bound by sacraments, God is not, and he can lovingly save these infants in ways known to him.

Q. **Jesus says that heaven and earth will pass away, but his words remain forever. How can heaven pass away?** — *Ted Kochanski*

Ancient Jewish cosmology distinguished three levels to the heavens. The first level has the clouds. The second level contains the stars and planets. The third heaven is where God dwells.

It is the first and second heavens to which Jesus refers. Though the first and second heavens will vanish with a roar and give way to a newer and greater reality of new heavens and new earth (see Rv 21:1), the third heaven, where God lives, will endure and does not change.

Q: We were taught that no one could have the Beatific Vision here on earth. Yet a friend said this is not true and that many saints have seen Jesus here on earth. Please explain. — *Ora Mae Brigidi*

The term Beatific Vision refers to the immediate knowledge of God, which the angels and the souls of the just enjoy in heaven. Since, in beholding God one finds perfect happiness, the vision is termed "beatific," which means "blessed" or "joyful." The "vision" portion of this term means something richer than mere physical seeing, since, as pure spirit, God is not seen by us in the same way we might see a tree or some other physical object.

By definition, then, no one here on earth can see or experience God in this way. As for those who have had visions of the Lord Jesus here on earth, they were mediated visions, wherein they were permitted to see an aspect of the Lord (such as his physical appearance). But they did not, by that fact, grasp him in the fuller way the blessed do in heaven. Neither did visionaries here on earth necessarily grasp any aspect of the other members of the Blessed Trinity as do the saints in heaven.

Q: What exactly are we going to do for eternity in heaven? Eternity seems like a really long time. And I know that sounds like a joke, but that is how it was said to me! — *Marlene*

We are going to be caught up into the glorious love of God and the Communion of Saints. We will rejoice forever, experience the love, glory, wisdom, and beauty of God. Our union with God and with one another will be perfected and deepened in a way we cannot even imagine now. The heart of heaven is to be with God, who is the true answer to all our longings. We will be complete and lacking in nothing.

Although we will be "at rest," we ought not think of this as a lack of activity, but rather as a rest from the toils of this world. For indeed, within the Holy Trinity there is a great movement of love, a kind of procession or dance of love between the persons of the Trinity. The Greek Fathers termed this movement of love the *perichoresis.* It is reasonable to suppose that we who attain heaven will be caught up into this great experience and joy that is described as a movement of love, or a kind of dance.

As for the word eternity and the phrase eternal life, we ought not conceive of it merely as the length of life, but also as the fullness of life. To have eternal life means that we will be fully alive with God. For now, our life can seem wearisome or dull at times. Not so in heaven, where we will be fully alive with God as never before. There will be joy unspeakable, glories untold, and life that is full in unimaginable ways.

Can't wait. Get on your dancing shoes!

Q. **We hear about the Beatific Vision in heaven. But if God is pure spirit, how will we see him? Will our eyes have new powers?** — *Carl Minnick*

Though our eyes will likely have great powers in our resurrected bodies, a better approach to this question is to distinguish between physical seeing and spiritual seeing. Physical seeing is the experience of light particles or rays reaching our retina and neurologically informing our brain. Spiritual seeing is the capacity of our intellect to understand a thought. Thus when you express an idea to me, I might say, "Ah! I see." But I do not mean that light is reaching my retina. Rather, I mean my mind is illumined by what you have said.

It is in this spiritual way of seeing that we speak of the Beatific Vision. Our whole soul, mind, and heart will be illumined by God, and we will experience him in an unimaginably rich and satisfying way that brings stable, serene, and confident joy, which we call beatitude.

Q. •You said in a previous answer, "we need not pre-sume that we will see God with our physical eyes." This confuses me since Saint Paul says of heaven that we shall see [God] "face to face" (1 Cor 13:12). Can you elaborate? — *Scott*

My use of the word "presume" does not exclude physical seeing altogether, but rather seeks to avoid reducing the Beatific Vision to natural seeing — that is, light hitting our retina. But while not excluding it altogether, I remain dubious that such seeing will be necessary or even, to some extent, possible. Let's review and elaborate.

First, there are different ways of seeing, and we commonly use this in our language, as did the Scriptures. One way of seeing is the simple act of physical seeing, where light reaches our retina. But there is also an intellectual and spiritual way of seeing. If you are trying to explain something to me and I finally understand it, I will say, "Ah, I see." But I do not mean my physical eyes see, but that my inner vision comprehends the truth you have said and lights up my mind.

The passage that you quote does speak of seeing, but not physical seeing. The problem with seeing God's face with our physical eyes is that God does not have a physical face to see. Both "seeing" and "face" are used in passages like this as images or analogies of something deeper. Even now we know that the face is the most revelatory quality of a person. We might strain our neck to see a person's face because, somehow, we know that to see their face is to see them in the fullest sense. And thus, when Scripture speaks of seeing God's face, it means that we will see him the richest and most revelatory way possible.

It is true that in heaven our physical eyes will be able to see Jesus. But our physical eyes will see his human nature, not his divine nature per se. God as God is pure spirit and cannot be seen any more than a thought can be seen.

In the Old Testament, certain theophanies and visions of angels (who are also pure spirit) are seen with people's physical eyes. In this case we must conclude that God uses some aspects of physical creation to mediate his presence. Thus it is possible that God does this in heaven, too. But why would he? The inner vision of deep understanding and soulful connection is a far richer and more satisfying seeing of God, as anyone who experiences contemplative prayer will attest. All the great spiritual masters call for a dark night of the senses, pointing beyond the physical senses to the deeper "seeing" of contemplation beyond words or images. An ancient maxim says, "I close my eyes in order to see."

Q: Do the souls in heaven know our sins, or is that knowledge reserved to God alone? — *Peter Tate*

We are in the realm of speculative theology when it comes to answers like this. However, it does not seem to pertain to God's justice that he would reveal our sins to others (even the saints in heaven), especially our more hidden sins. We who are called to participate in God's justice are not to reveal to others the sins of people we might know, except in certain rare situations.

Only those who really need to know for a just reason should be informed. So, in justice, it seems unlikely that God would reveal the details of our sins, even to the saints in heaven, since they do not need to know such things.

Some will refer to Hebrews 12:1, which calls the saints in heaven a great cloud of witnesses. But the context there is that they are witnesses to us of *their* life and power of faith to transform, not that they are watching us like spectators.

There is another Scripture text that says, "For nothing is hidden that shall not be made manifest, nor anything secret that shall not be known and come to light" (Lk 8:7). But here the context is not our hidden deeds, but is the truth of the Gospel that comes out of the darkness to dawn on the minds of believers.

There are other verses that seek to console us in our oppression. For example, "So have no fear of them; for nothing is covered that will not be revealed, or hidden that will not be known" (Mt 10:26). But here the context is that unrepented sin will one day be revealed, not that a camera is running and the saints in heaven are seeing it as it happens now. Saints know our expressed needs and intercede for us (see Rv 5:8; 8:3–4), but that does not mean detailed knowledge of our immediate actions.

If there is to be a detailed revealing of sins committed, that would seem to wait for the Last Judgment. Saint Paul says, "Before the Lord comes, who will bring to light things now hidden in darkness and will disclose the purposes of the heart" (1 Cor 4:5). How detailed this revelation will be is not certain, but the distinction between the just and the unjust will be clear. The Lord implies that significant detail will be revealed at the Last Judgment: "Whatever you have said in the dark shall be heard in the light, and what you have whispered in private rooms shall be proclaimed on the housetops" (Lk 12:3).

INDEX